Rick Steves'®

ROME

Rick Steves & Gene Openshaw

2009

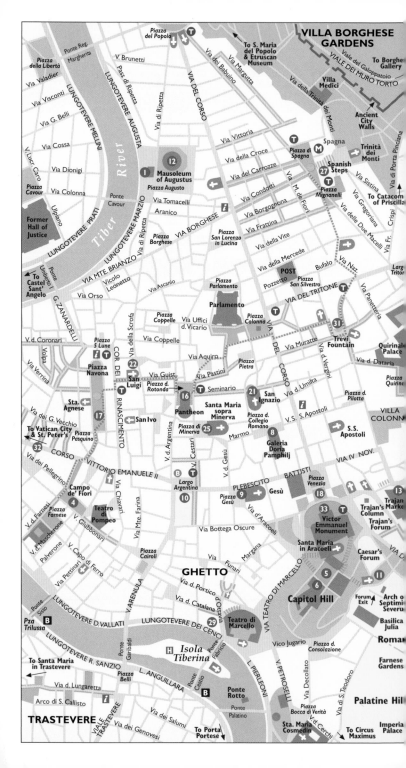

EAST ROME

1. Ara Pacis
2. Arch of Constantine
3. Baths of Diocletian
4. Campo de' Fiori
5. Capitol Hill
6. Capitoline Museums
7. Colosseum
8. Galleria Doria Pamphilj
9. Gesù Church
10. Largo Argentina
11. Mamertine Prison
12. Mausoleum of Augustus
13. Museum of the Imperial Forums
14. National Museum of Rome
15. Palatine Hill Entrance
16. Pantheon
17. Piazza Navona
18. Piazza Venezia
19. Roman Forum Entrance
20. San Clemente Church
21. San Ignazio Church
22. San Luigi dei Francesi Church
23. Santa Maria della Vittoria Church
24. Santa Maria Maggiore Church
25. Santa Maria sopra Minerva Church
26. Santa Susanna Church
27. Spanish Steps
28. St. Peter-in-Chains Church
29. Synagogue & Jewish Museum
30. Termini Train Station
31. Trevi Fountain
32. To Vatican City & St. Peter's
33. Victor Emmanuel Monument

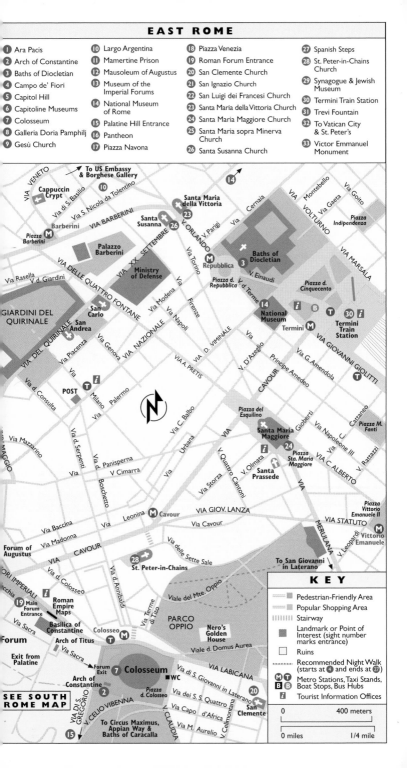

VIA VENETO
To US Embassy & Borghese Gallery
Cappuccin Crypt
VIA DI S. BASILIO
Via S. Nicola da Tolentino
Barberini
Piazza Barberini
VIA BARBERINI
Santa Susanna
Santa Maria della Vittoria
V. ORLANDO
V. Parigi
Cernaia
Via
VIA MONTEBELLO
Via Gaeta
Via Goito
Piazza Indipendenza
VOLTURNO
VIA MARSALA
Palazzo Barberini
VIA XX SETTEMBRE
Ministry of Defense
Via Modena
Via Torino
Republica
Piazza d. Repubblica
V. d. Terme
V. Einaudi
Baths of Diocletian
Piazza d. Cinquecento
Via Rasella
Via d. Giardini
VIA DELLE QUATTRO FONTANE
Via Firenze
GIARDINI DEL QUIRINALE
San Carlo
San Andrea
VIA DEL QUIRINALE
Via Piacenza
Via Genova
VIA NAZIONALE
Via Napoli
Via D. VIMINALE
Via
National Museum
Termini
Termini Train Station
VIA GIOVANNI GIOLITTI
Via d Consulta
Via
Via Milano
POST
Palermo
Via
Via C. Balbo
VIA A. PRETIS
V. D'Azeglio
Principe Amedeo
CAVOUR
Via G.Amendola
Cattaneo
Via Napoleone III
Piazza M. Fanti
Via Mazzarino
Via d. Serpenti
Via
Via d. Panisperna
V Cimarra
Urbana
Piazza del Esquilino
Santa Maria Maggiore
Gioberti
Piazza Vittorio Emanuele II
VIA STATUTO
MAGGIO
Boschetto
Via Storza
V. Quattro Cantoni
V. Olmata
Piazza Sta. Maria Maggiore
Santa Prassede
VIA C. ALBERTO
C.
Via L. Ratazzi
Via Baccina
Via
Leonina
Cavour
VIA GIOV. LANZA
Via Cavour
Vittorio Emanuele
Via Madonna
CAVOUR
Via delle Sette Sale
MERULANA
V. Leopardi
Forum of Augustus
VIA
Via d. Colosseo
St. Peter-in-Chains
To San Giovanni in Laterano
ORI IMPERIALI
cchia
Main Forum Entrance
Roman Empire Maps
Via Sacra
Basilica of Constantine
Arch of Titus
Forum
Exit from Palatine
Colosseo
Viale del Mte. Oppio
Via Terme di Tito
PARCO OPPIO
Nero's Golden House
Viale d. Domus Aurea
Forum Exit
Colosseum
WC
VIA LABICANA
Via di S. Giovanni in Laterano
SEE SOUTH ROME MAP
Arch of Constantine
Piazza d. Colosseo
VIA DI S. GREGORIO
V. CELIO VIBENNA
To Circus Maximus, Appian Way & Baths of Caracalla
Via dei S.S. Quattro
Via Capo d'Africa
V. Celimontana
V. M. Aurelio
V. CLAUDIA
San Clemente

KEY

Pedestrian-Friendly Area

Popular Shopping Area

Stairway

Landmark or Point of Interest (sight number marks entrance)

Ruins

Recommended Night Walk (starts at 4 and ends at 27)

Metro Stations, Taxi Stands, Boat Stops, Bus Hubs

Tourist Information Offices

0		400 meters

| 0 miles | | 1/4 mile |

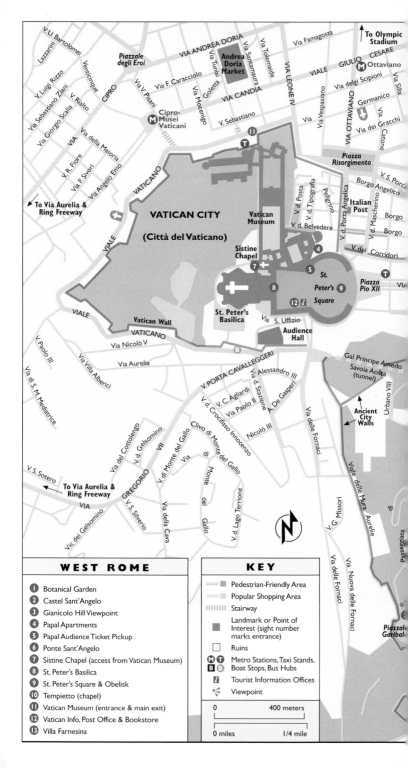

WEST ROME

1. Botanical Garden
2. Castel Sant'Angelo
3. Gianicolo Hill Viewpoint
4. Papal Apartments
5. Papal Audience Ticket Pickup
6. Ponte Sant'Angelo
7. Sistine Chapel (access from Vatican Museum)
8. St. Peter's Basilica
9. St. Peter's Square & Obelisk
10. Tempietto (chapel)
11. Vatican Museum (entrance & main exit)
12. Vatican Info, Post Office & Bookstore
13. Villa Farnesina

KEY

- Pedestrian-Friendly Area
- Popular Shopping Area
- Stairway
- Landmark or Point of Interest (sight number marks entrance)
- Ruins
- M T B B Metro Stations, Taxi Stands, Boat Stops, Bus Hubs
- i Tourist Information Offices
- Viewpoint

0 _____ 400 meters

0 miles _____ 1/4 mile

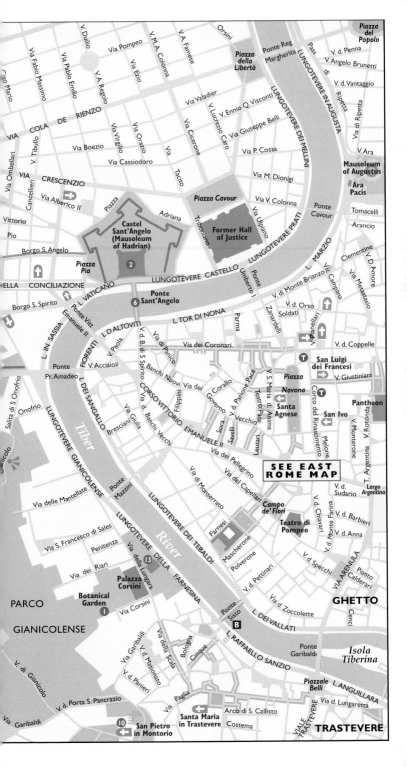

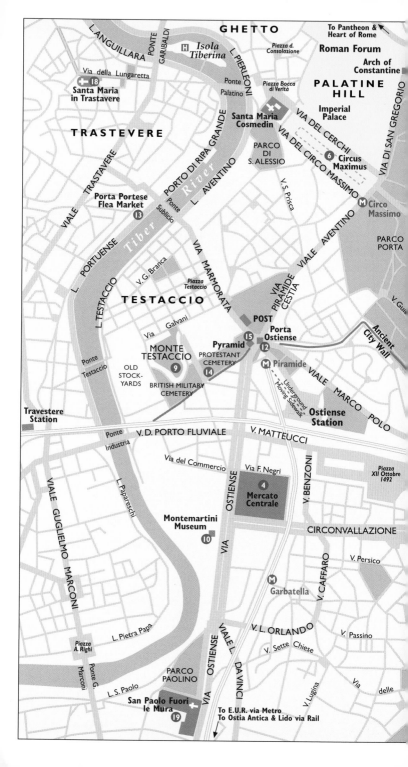

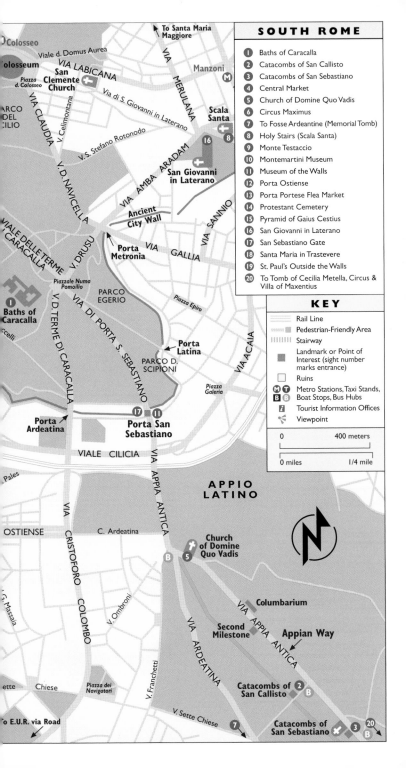

SOUTH ROME

1. Baths of Caracalla
2. Catacombs of San Callisto
3. Catacombs of San Sebastiano
4. Central Market
5. Church of Domine Quo Vadis
6. Circus Maximus
7. To Fosse Ardeatine (Memorial Tomb)
8. Holy Stairs (Scala Santa)
9. Monte Testaccio
10. Montemartini Museum
11. Museum of the Walls
12. Porta Ostiense
13. Porta Portese Flea Market
14. Protestant Cemetery
15. Pyramid of Gaius Cestius
16. San Giovanni in Laterano
17. San Sebastiano Gate
18. Santa Maria in Trastevere
19. St. Paul's Outside the Walls
20. To Tomb of Cecilia Metella, Circus & Villa of Maxentius

KEY

Rail Line
Pedestrian-Friendly Area
Stairway
Landmark or Point of Interest (sight number marks entrance)
Ruins
M T Metro Stations, Taxi Stands,
B B Boat Stops, Bus Hubs
Tourist Information Offices
Viewpoint

0   400 meters
0 miles   1/4 mile

Rick Steves'

ROME

2009

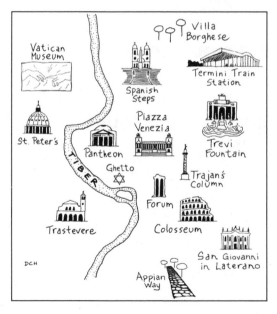

AVALON
TRAVEL

CONTENTS

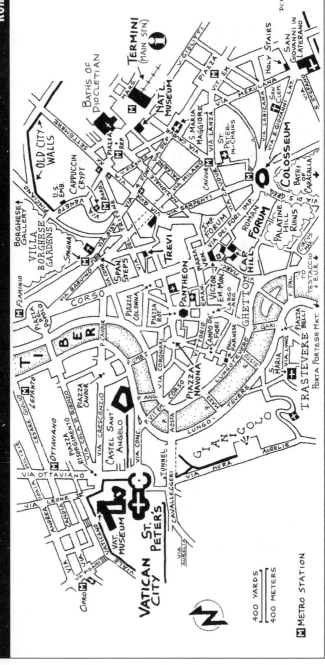

INTRODUCTION

Rome is magnificent and brutal at the same time. It's a showcase of Western civilization, with astonishingly ancient sights and a modern vibrancy. But if you're careless, you'll be run down or pickpocketed. And with the wrong attitude, you'll be frustrated by the kind of chaos that only an Italian can understand. On my last visit, a cabbie struggling with the traffic said, *"Roma chaos."* I responded, *"Bella chaos."* He agreed.

While Paris is an urban garden, Rome is a magnificent tangled forest. If your hotel provides a comfortable refuge; if you pace yourself; if you accept—and even partake in—the siesta plan; if you're well-organized for sightseeing; and if you protect yourself and your valuables with extra caution and discretion, you'll love it. (And Rome is much easier to live with if you avoid the mid-summer heat.)

For me, Rome is in a three-way tie with Paris and London as Europe's greatest city. Two thousand years ago, the word "Rome" meant civilization itself. Everything was either civilized (part of the Roman Empire, Latin- or Greek-speaking) or barbarian. Today, Rome is Italy's political capital, the capital of Catholicism, and the center of the ancient world, littered with evocative remains. As you peel through its fascinating and jumbled layers, you'll find Rome's buildings, cats, laundry, traffic, and 2.6 million people endlessly entertaining. And then, of course, there are its stupendous sights.

Tour St. Peter's, the greatest church on earth, and scale Michelangelo's 328-foot-tall dome, the world's largest. Learn something about eternity by touring the huge Vatican Museum. You'll find the story of creation—bright as the day it was painted—in the restored Sistine Chapel. Do the "Caesar Shuffle" through ancient Rome's Forum and Colosseum. Savor Europe's most sumptuous building, the Borghese Gallery, and take an early evening "Dolce Vita Stroll" down the Via del Corso with Rome's beautiful people. Enjoy an after dark walk from Campo de' Fiori to the Spanish Steps, lacing together Rome's Baroque and bubbly nightspots. Dine well at least once.

About This Book

Rick Steves' Rome 2009 is a personal tour guide in your pocket. Better yet, it's actually two tour guides in your pocket: The co-author of this book is Gene Openshaw. Since our first "Europe through the gutter" trip together as high school buddies in the 1970s, Gene and I have been exploring the wonders of the Old World. An inquisitive historian and lover of European culture, Gene wrote most of this book's self-guided museum tours and neighborhood walks. Together, Gene and I have kept this book up-to-date and accurate (though for simplicity, from this point "we" will shed our respective egos and become "I").

The book is organized this way:

Orientation includes tourist information, tips on public transportation, local tour options, and other helpful hints. The "Planning Your Time" section offers a suggested schedule for how to best use your limited time.

Sights provides a succinct overview of the most important sights, arranged by neighborhood, with ratings:

▲▲▲—Don't miss.

▲▲—Try hard to see.

▲—Worthwhile if you can make it.

No rating—Worth knowing about.

The **Self-Guided Walks** take you through Rome at night, connecting the great monuments and atmospheric squares; land you in Trastevere, the heart of the crusty, colorful neighborhood across the river; and give meaning to the Jewish Ghetto, the city's medieval Jewish quarter.

The **Self-Guided Tours** lead you through ancient Rome, with tours of the Colosseum, Roman Forum, Palatine Hill, Trajan's Column, Pantheon, and Baths of Diocletian. You'll also tour the pilgrimage churches, including the grandest of all—St. Peter's. You'll see the great museums: Vatican Museum, National Museum of Rome, Capitoline Museums, and the exciting Borghese Gallery. And you'll take a spin on the ancient Appian Way.

Sleeping is a guide to my favorite good-value hotels, mainly in several convenient (and for Rome, relatively quiet) neighborhoods near the sights.

Eating suggests restaurants ranging from inexpensive eateries to splurges, with an emphasis on good quality.

Rome with Children, Shopping, and **Nightlife** offer my best suggestions on those topics.

Transportation Connections covers connections by train and by plane (with information on Rome's airports), laying the groundwork for your smooth arrival and departure.

Day Trips cover nearby sights: Ostia Antica (includes self-guided tour), Tivoli, Naples, and Pompeii.

Roman History takes you on a whirlwind tour through the ages, covering three millennia from ancient Rome to the city today.

The **appendix** is a traveler's tool kit, with a handy packing checklist, recommended books and films, a climate chart, detailed instructions on how to use the telephone, useful Italian phone numbers, Italian survival phrases, and lots more.

Throughout this book, when you see a ✪ in a listing, it means that the sight is covered in much more detail in one of my tours (a page number will tell you where to look to find more information).

Browse through this book and choose your favorite sights. Then have a great trip! Traveling like a temporary local, you'll get the absolute most out of every mile, minute, and euro. As you visit places I know and love, I'm happy you'll be meeting my favorite Romans.

PLANNING

Trip Costs

Six components make up your trip costs: airfare, surface transportation, room and board, sightseeing/entertainment, shopping/miscellany, and gelato.

Airfare: A basic, round-trip United States-to-Rome (or even cheaper, to Milan) flight should cost $700–1,500, depending on where you fly from and when. Always consider saving time and money in Europe by flying "open jaw" (flying into one city and out of another).

Surface Transportation: For a typical one-week visit, allow $60 to $100 for taxis (which can be shared by up to four people); if you opt for buses and the Metro, figure about $25 per person. The cost of round-trip transportation to day-trip destinations ranges from minimal (a few dollars to get to Tivoli or Ostia Antica) to affordable ($50 for second-class train tickets for a day trip to Naples and Pompeii). For a one-way trip between Rome's main airport and the city center, allow $16 per person by train or about $60 by taxi (can be shared).

Room and Board: You can enjoy Rome on $140 a day per person for room and board. This allows $15 for lunch, $25 for dinner, and $100 for lodging (based on two people splitting the cost of a $200 double room that includes breakfast). If you've got more money, I've listed great ways to spend it. Students and tightwads can enjoy Rome for as little as $60 a day ($30 for a bed, $30 for meals and snacks).

Sightseeing and Entertainment: Figure about $10–17 per major sight (Colosseum, museums), $2 for minor ones (church treasuries), and $30 for splurge experiences (such as concerts). An overall average of $20 per day works for most. Don't skimp here. After all, this category is the driving force behind your trip—you came to sightsee, enjoy, and experience Rome.

INTRODUCTION

Major Holidays and Weekends

Popular places are even busier on weekends...and inundated on three-day weekends. Holidays bring many businesses to a grinding halt. Plan ahead and reserve your accommodations and transportation well in advance.

In Rome, hotels get booked up on Easter weekend (in 2009, that's Friday, April 10, through Monday, April 13), April 25 (Liberation Day), May 1 (Labor Day), June 29 (Saints Peter and Paul), November 1 (All Saints' Day), and on Fridays and Saturdays year-round. Religious holidays and train strikes can catch you by surprise anywhere in Italy.

Also check the list of festivals and holidays on page 393 of the appendix.

Shopping and Miscellany: Figure $3 per postcard, coffee, soft drink, and gelato. Shopping can vary in cost from nearly nothing to a small fortune. Good budget travelers find that this category has little to do with assembling a trip full of lifelong and wonderful memories.

When to Go

Rome's best travel months (also busiest and most expensive) are May, June, September, and October.

The most grueling thing about travel in Rome is the summer heat in July and August, when temperatures hit the high 80s and 90s. Most midrange hotels come with air-conditioning—a worthwhile splurge in summer. Air-conditioning, when available, usually only operates from June through September.

Between November and April, you can usually expect pleasant weather and you'll miss most of the sweat and stress of the tourist season. Spring and fall can be chilly, though, and many hotels do not turn on their heat. Rome is fine in winter—cold and crisp (in the 40s and 50s), with uncrowded sights. (For more information, see the climate chart in the appendix.)

Travel Smart

Many people visit Rome and think it's a chaotic mess. They feel any attempt at efficient travel is futile. This is dead wrong—and expensive. Rome, which seems as orderly as spilled spaghetti, actually functions well. Only those who understand this and travel smart can enjoy Rome on a budget.

This book can save you lots of time and money. But to have an "A" trip, you need to be an "A" student. Read it all before your trip; note the days when museums are closed and whether reservations are mandatory. For instance, to see the Borghese Gallery, you must reserve ahead. If you go to the Vatican Museum on a Sunday, you'll run smack

Know Before You Go

Plan ahead! Check this list of things to arrange while you're still at home.

Since **airline carry-on restrictions** are always changing, visit the Transportation Security Administration's website (www.tsa.gov/travelers) for an up-to-date list of what you can bring on the plane with you...and what you have to check.

Call your **debit and credit card companies** to let them know the countries you'll be visiting, so that they'll accept (and not deny) your international charges. Confirm what your daily withdrawal limit is; consider asking to have it raised so you can take out more cash at each ATM stop.

Be sure that your **passport** is valid at least six months after your ticketed date of return to the US. If you need to get or renew a passport, it can take up to two months.

Check to see if you'll be visiting Rome during any **holidays** (such as Holy Week), when rooms can cost more and get booked up quickly. (See "Major Holidays and Weekends" on page 4.)

If you're taking an **overnight train** (especially between Rome and Paris), and you need a *couchette* or sleeper—and you *must* leave on a certain day—book it in advance, even though it may cost more. Other Italian trains, like the high-speed ES trains, require a seat reservation, but it's usually possible to make arrangements in Italy just a few days ahead. (For more on train travel, see page 324.)

Renting a car to drive in traffic-crazy Rome is certifiably *pazzo* (crazy). But if you want a car for exploring the countryside, consider picking it up at the main airport. To drive in Italy, you'll need your driver's license and an International Driving Permit (IDP), available at your local AAA office ($15 plus the cost of two passport-type photos, www.aaa.com).

The **Borghese Gallery** requires advance reservations—book at least a week ahead in high season. (See page 190 for instructions.)

If you're bringing an iPod or other MP3 player, you can download our free audiotours of Rome's major sights at www.ricksteves.com (see page 382).

into closed doors, or—if it's the last Sunday of the month—huge crowds. You can wait an hour to buy a ticket at the Colosseum, or save time by buying it online, by phone, or at the nearby Palatine Hill. Day-tripping to Ostia Antica on Monday is bad news. A smart trip is a puzzle—a fun, doable, and worthwhile challenge.

Saturdays are virtually weekdays, with earlier closing hours. Sundays have the same pros and cons as they do in the US: Sightseeing attractions are generally open, while shops and banks are closed. City traffic is light. Rowdy evenings are rare on Sundays.

Rome vs. Milan: A Classic Squabble

In Italy, the North and South bicker about each other, hurling barbs, quips, and generalizations. All the classic North/South traits can be applied to Rome (the government capital) and Milan (the business capital). Although the differences have become less pronounced lately, the sniping continues.

The Milanese say the Romans are lazy. Roman government jobs come with short hours—cut even shorter by too many coffee breaks, three-hour lunches, chats with colleagues, and phone calls to friends and relatives. Milanese contend that *Roma ladrona* (Rome the big thief) is a parasite that lives off the taxes of people up North. Until recently, there was a strong Milan-based movement seriously promoting secession from the South.

Romans, meanwhile, dismiss the Milanese as uptight workaholics with nothing else to live for—gray like their foggy city. Romans do admit that in Milan, job opportunities are better and based on merit. And the Milanese grudgingly concede the Romans have a gift for enjoying life.

While Rome is more of a family city, Milan is the place for high-powered singles on the career fast track. Milanese yuppies mix with each other...not the city's long-time residents. Milan is seen as inward-looking and wary of foreigners, and Rome as fun-loving, tolerant, and friendly. In Milan, bureaucracy (like social services) works logically and efficiently, while in Rome, accomplishing even small chores can be exasperating. In Rome, everything—from finding a babysitter to buying a car—is done through friends. In Milan, while people are not as willing to discuss their personal matters, they are generous and active in charity work.

Milanese find Romans vulgar. The Roman dialect is considered one of the coarsest in the country. Much as they try, Milanese just can't say, "Damn your dead relatives" quite as effectively as the Romans. Still, they enjoy Roman comedians and love to imitate the accent.

The Milanese feel that Rome is dirty and Roman driving nerve-wracking. But despite the craziness, Rome maintains a genuine village feel. People share family news with their neighborhood grocer. Milan lacks people-friendly piazzas, and entertainment comes at a high price. But in Rome, *la dolce vita* is as close as the nearest square, and a full moon is enjoyed by all.

Be sure to mix intense and relaxed periods in your itinerary. Every trip (and every traveler) needs at least a few slack days. Pace yourself. Assume you will return.

Plan ahead for laundry, picnics, and Internet stops. Get online at Internet cafés or your hotel to research transportation connections, confirm events, check the weather, and get directions to your next hotel. Buy a phone card and use it for reservations, reconfirmations, and double-checking hours.

Enjoy the friendliness of the local people. Slow down and ask questions—most locals are eager to point you in their idea of the right direction. Keep a notepad in your pocket for organizing your thoughts. Wear your money belt, and learn the local currency and how to estimate prices in dollars. Those who expect to travel smart, do.

PRACTICALITIES

Red Tape: You need a passport—but no visa or shots—to travel in Italy. If traveling beyond Italy, you may be denied entry into certain countries if your passport is due to expire within six months of your ticketed date of return. Get it renewed if you'll be cutting it close. Pack a photocopy of your passport in your luggage in case the original is lost or stolen.

Time: In Italy—and in this book—you'll use the 24-hour clock. It's the same through 12:00 noon, then keep going: 13:00, 14:00, and so on. For anything over 12, subtract 12 and add p.m. (14:00 is 2:00 p.m.).

Italy, like most of continental Europe, is generally six/nine hours ahead of the East/West coasts of the US. The exceptions are the beginning and end of Daylight Saving Time: Europe "springs forward" the last Sunday in March (two weeks after most of North America), and "falls back" the last Sunday in October (one week before North America). For a handy online time converter, try www.timeanddate.com/worldclock.

Business Hours: Traditionally, Italy uses the siesta plan. People usually work from about 8:00 to 13:00 and from 15:30 to 19:00, Monday through Saturday. Nowadays, however, many businesses have adopted the government's recommended 8:00 to 14:00 workday. In tourist areas, shops are open longer. Banking hours are generally Monday through Friday 8:30 to 13:30 and 15:30 to 16:30, but they can vary wildly.

Watt's Up? Europe's electrical system is different from North America's in two different ways: the shape of the plug (two round prongs) and the voltage of the current (220 volts instead of 110 volts). For your North American plug to work in Europe, you'll need an adapter, sold inexpensively at travel stores in the US. As for the voltage, most newer electronics or travel appliances (such as hair dryers, laptops, and battery chargers) automatically convert the voltage—if

INTRODUCTION

Just the FAQs, Please

Who do I call in case of emergency?
Dial 113 for English-speaking police help. To summon an ambulance, call 118. For information on hospitals in Rome, see page 24, and for the American embassy, see page 387.

What if my credit card is stolen?
Act immediately. See "Damage Control for Lost Cards," page 10, for instructions.

How do I make a phone call to, from, and within Europe?
For detailed dialing instructions, refer to page 386.

How can I get tourist information about my destination?
See page 381 for a list of tourist information offices (abbreviated **TI** in this book) located in the US.

What's the best way to pack?
Light. For a recommended packing list, see page 396.

Does Rick have other materials that will help me?
For more on Rick's guidebooks, public television series, free audiotours, public radio show, guided tours, travel bags, accessories, and railpasses, see page 382.

Are there any updates to this guidebook?
Check www.ricksteves.com/update for changes to the most recent edition of this book.

Can you recommend any good books or movies for my trip?
For suggestions, see pages 384–385.

you see a range of voltages printed on the item or its plug (such as "110–220"), it'll work in Europe. Otherwise, you can buy a converter separately in the US (about $20).

News: Americans keep in touch via the *International Herald Tribune* (published almost daily via satellite throughout Europe). Every Tuesday, the European editions of *Time* and *Newsweek* hit the stands with articles of particular interest to European travelers. Sports addicts can get their daily fix online or from *USA Today*. Good websites include www.europeantimes.com and http://news.bbc.co.uk.

MONEY

Cash from ATMs

Throughout Europe, cash machines (ATMs) are the standard way for travelers to get local currency. Traveler's checks are a waste of time (long waits at slow banks) and a waste of money (in fees).

Bring plastic—credit and/or debit cards—along with several hundred dollars in hard cash as an emergency backup. It's smart to bring two cards, in case one gets demagnetized or eaten by a

Do I need to speak some Italian?
Many Italians—especially those in the tourist trade, and in big cities such as Rome—speak English. Still, you'll get better treatment if you learn and use Italian pleasantries. For a list of survival phrases, see page 397.

Do I need to carry my passport in Italy?
Yes. Because of anti-terrorism regulations, you may need to show your passport whenever you go online at an Internet café. Carry it in your money belt.

How much do I tip?
For tips on tipping, see page 11.

Will I get a student or senior discount?
Not likely. Discounts for sights are not listed in this book because they are generally limited to European residents and countries that offer reciprocal deals (the US does not).

How can I get a VAT refund on major purchases?
See the details on page 11.

How do I calculate metric amounts?
Europe uses the metric system. A liter is about a quart, four to a gallon. A kilometer is six-tenths of a mile. I figure kilometers to miles by cutting them in half and adding back 10 percent of the original (120 km: 60 + 12 = 72 miles, 300 km: 150 + 30 = 180 miles). For more metric conversions, see page 394.

temperamental machine. To use a bank machine (ATM) to withdraw money from your account, you'll need a debit card (ideally with a Visa or MasterCard logo for maximum usability), plus a PIN code. Know your PIN code in numbers; there are only numbers—no letters—on European keypads.

Before you go, verify with your bank that your card will work overseas, and alert them that you'll be making withdrawals in Europe; otherwise, the bank may not approve transactions if it perceives unusual spending patterns.

Try to take out large sums of money to reduce your per-transaction bank fees. If the machine refuses your request, try again and select a smaller amount or just try a different machine; some cash machines won't let you take out more than about €150 (don't take it personally). Also, be aware that some ATMs will tell you to take your cash within 30 seconds, and if you aren't fast enough, your cash may be sucked back into the machine...and you'll have a hassle trying to get it from the bank.

To keep your cash safe, use a money belt—a pouch with a strap that you buckle around your waist like a belt, and wear under your clothes. Thieves target tourists. A money belt provides peace of mind,

Exchange Rate

1 euro (€) = about $1.50

To convert prices in euros to dollars, add about 50 percent: €20 = about $30, €50 = about $75. Just like the dollar, one euro is broken down into 100 cents. You'll find coins ranging from €0.01 to €2, and bills ranging from €5 to €500.

Look carefully at any €2 coin you get in change. Some unscrupulous merchants are giving out similar-looking, gold-rimmed old 500-lire coins (worth $0) instead of €2 coins (worth $2.80). You are now warned!

allowing you to carry lots of cash safely. Don't waste time every few days tracking down a cash machine—withdraw a week's worth of money, stuff it in your money belt, and travel!

Credit and Debit Cards

For purchases, Visa and MasterCard are more commonly accepted than American Express. Just like at home, credit or debit cards work easily at larger hotels and stores, but smaller businesses prefer payment in local currency (in small bills—break large bills at a bank or larger store). Many restaurants accept only cash.

Credit and debit cards—whether used for purchases or ATM withdrawals—often come with additional, tacked-on "international transaction" fees of up to 3 percent plus up to $5 per transaction. To avoid unpleasant surprises, call your credit-card company before your trip to ask about these fees.

Damage Control for Lost Cards

If you lose your credit, debit, or ATM card, you can stop people from using your card by reporting the loss immediately to the respective global customer-assistance centers. Call these 24-hour US numbers collect: Visa (410/581-9994), MasterCard (636/722-7111), and American Express (623/492-8427).

At a minimum, you'll need to know the name of the financial institution that issued you the card, along with the type of card (classic, platinum, or whatever). Providing the following information will allow for a quicker cancellation of your missing card: full card number, whether you are the primary or secondary cardholder, the cardholder's name exactly as printed on the card, billing address, home phone number, circumstances of the loss or theft, and identification verification (your birth date, your mother's maiden name, or your Social Security number—memorize this, don't carry a copy). If you are the secondary cardholder, you'll also need to provide the primary cardholder's identification-verification details. You can generally receive a temporary card within two or three business days in Europe.

If you promptly report your card lost or stolen, you typically won't be responsible for any unauthorized transactions on your account, although many banks charge a liability fee of $50.

Tipping

Tipping in Italy isn't as automatic and generous as it is in the US, but for special service, tips are appreciated, if not expected. As in the US, the proper amount depends on your resources, tipping philosophy, and the circumstances, but some general guidelines apply.

Restaurants: Check the menu to see if the service is included (*servizio incluso*—generally 15 percent); if not, you could tip 5 to 10 percent for good service, though be advised that Italians rarely tip. For more information on tipping, see page 291.

Taxis: To tip the cabbie, round up. For a typical ride, round up to the next euro on the fare (to pay a €4.50 fare, give €5). If the cabbie hauls your bags and zips you to the airport to help you catch your flight, you might want to toss in a little more. But if you feel like you're being driven in circles or otherwise ripped off, skip the tip.

Special Services: It's thoughtful to tip a couple of euros to someone who shows you a special sight and who is paid in no other way. Tour guides at public sites sometimes hold out their hands for tips after they give their spiel; if I've already paid for the tour, I don't tip extra, though some tourists do give a euro or two, particularly for a job well done. I don't tip at hotels, but if you do, give the porter a euro for carrying bags and leave a couple of euros in your room at the end of your stay for the maid if the room was kept clean. In general, if someone in the service industry does a super job for you, a tip of a couple of euros is appropriate...but not required.

When in doubt, ask. If you're not sure whether (or how much) to tip for a service, ask your hotelier or the tourist information office; they'll fill you in on how it's done on their turf.

Getting a VAT Refund

Wrapped into the purchase price of your Italian souvenirs is a Value-Added Tax (VAT) of about 20 percent. If you purchase more than €155 (about $230) worth of goods at a store that participates in the VAT-refund scheme, you're entitled to get most of that tax back. Getting your refund is usually straightforward and, if you buy a substantial amount of souvenirs, well worth the hassle. If you're lucky, the merchant will subtract the tax when you make your purchase. (This is more likely to occur if the store ships the goods to your home.) Otherwise, you'll need to:

Get the paperwork. Have the merchant completely fill out the necessary refund document, called a "cheque." You'll have to present your passport.

Get your stamp at the border or airport. Process your cheque(s) at your last stop in the EU with the customs agent who deals with VAT refunds. It's best to keep your purchases in your carry-on for viewing, but if they're too large or dangerous (such as knives) to carry on, track down the proper customs agent to inspect them before you check your bag. You're not supposed to use your purchased goods before you leave. If you show up at customs wearing your new leather shoes, officials might look the other way—or deny you a refund.

Collect your refund. You'll need to return your stamped document to the retailer or its representative. Many merchants work with a service, such as Global Refund (www.globalrefund.com) or Premier Tax Free (www.premiertaxfree.com), which have offices at major airports, ports, or border crossings. These services, which extract a 4 percent fee, can refund your money immediately in your currency of choice or credit your card (within two billing cycles). If the retailer handles VAT refunds directly, it's up to you to contact the merchant for your refund. You can mail the documents from home, or quicker, from your point of departure (using a stamped, addressed envelope you've prepared or one that's been provided by the merchant)—and then wait. It could take months.

Customs for American Shoppers

You are allowed to take home $800 worth of items per person duty-free, once every 30 days. The next $1,000 is taxed at a flat 3 percent. After that, you pay the individual item's duty rate. You can also bring in duty-free a liter of alcohol or up to two bottles of wine (pack carefully in checked bag; you must be at least 21), 200 cigarettes, and up to 100 non-Cuban cigars. You may take home vacuum-packed cheeses; dried herbs, spices, or mushrooms; canned fruits or vegetables including jams, vegetable spreads, and pâtés; and olive oil (many producers pack their oil in stainless steel canisters for easier transport). Meats (even vacuum-packed or canned), and fresh fruits or vegetables are not permitted. Note that all liquids must be packed inside checked luggage. To check customs rules and duty rates before you go, visit www .cbp.gov, and click on "Travel," then "Know Before You Go."

SIGHTSEEING

Sightseeing can be hard work. Use these tips to make your visits to Rome's finest sights meaningful, fun, fast, and painless.

Plan Ahead

Set up an itinerary that allows you to fit in all your must-see sights. For a one-stop look at opening hours, see "Rome at a Glance" (page 44; also see "Daily Reminder" on page 21). Most sights keep stable hours, but you can easily confirm the latest by checking with the local TI.

Don't put off visiting a must-see sight—you never know when a place will close unexpectedly for a holiday, strike, or restoration. If you'll be visiting during a holiday, find out if a particular sight will be open by phoning ahead or visiting its website. If you want to see the Borghese Gallery, make reservations (see page 190).

When possible, visit key museums first thing (when your energy is best) and save other activities for the afternoon. Hit the highlights first, then go back to other things if you have the stamina and time.

Depending on the sight, there are ways to avoid crowds. This book offers tips on specific sights. Try visiting the sight very early, at lunch, or very late. Evening visits are usually peaceful with fewer crowds. Read ahead. To get the most out of the self-guided tours and sight descriptions in this book, read them before you visit.

At the Sight

All sights have rules, and if you know about these in advance, they're no big deal.

Some important sights such as the Colosseum have metal detectors or conduct bag searches that will slow your entry.

At churches—which generally offer interesting art (usually free) and a cool, welcome seat—a modest dress code (no bare shoulders or shorts) is encouraged and often required.

Most museums require you to check daypacks and coats. They'll be kept safely. If you have something you can't bear to part with, stash it in a pocket or purse. If you don't want to check a small backpack, carry it under your arm like a purse as you enter. From a guard's point of view, a backpack is generally a problem while a purse is not.

Cameras are normally allowed, but not flashes or tripods (without special permission). Flashes damage oil paintings and distract others in the room. Even without a flash, a handheld camera will take a decent picture (or buy postcards or posters at the museum bookstore). Video cameras are usually allowed.

Some museums have special exhibits in addition to their permanent collection. Some exhibits are included in the entry price, while others come at an extra cost (which you have to pay even if you don't want to see the exhibit).

Many sights rent audioguides, which generally offer excellent recorded descriptions of the art (about $4). If you bring along your own pair of headphones and a Y-jack, two people can share one audioguide and save. Or download free audiotours for the major sights at www.ricksteves.com (see page 382). Guided tours (usually $10) and widely ranging in quality) are most likely to occur during peak season.

Expect changes—paintings can be on tour, on loan, out sick, or shifted at the whim of the curator. To adapt, pick up any available free floor plans as you enter. If you can't find a particular painting, just

INTRODUCTION

How Was Your Trip?

Were your travels fun, smooth, and meaningful? If you'd like to share your tips, concerns, and discoveries, please fill out the survey at www.ricksteves.com/feedback. I value your feedback. Thanks in advance—it helps a lot.

ask the museum staff. Point to the photograph in this book and ask, *"Dov'è?"* (doh-VEH, meaning "Where?").

Some important sights have an on-site café or cafeteria (usually a good place to rest and have a snack or light meal). The WCs are free and generally clean.

Museums have bookstores selling postcards and souvenirs. Before you leave, scan the postcards and thumb through the biggest guide-book (or skim its index) to be sure you haven't overlooked something that you'd like to see.

Most sights stop admitting people 30–60 minutes before closing time, and some rooms close early (generally about 45 minutes before the actual closing time). Guards usher people out, so don't save the best for last.

Every sight or museum offers more than what is covered in this book. Use the self-guided tours in this book as an introduction—not the final word.

TRANSPORTATION

Transportation concerns within Rome are limited to the Metro, buses, and taxis, all covered in the Orientation chapter. If you have a car, stow it. You don't want to drive in Rome. For more information, see the various Day Trips chapters (for transportation pertinent to those sights) and the Transportation Connections chapter (for transportation into and out of Rome).

TRAVELING AS A TEMPORARY LOCAL

We travel all the way to Italy to enjoy differences—to become tem-porary locals. You'll experience frustrations. Certain truths that we find "God-given" or "self-evident," such as cold beer, ice in drinks, bottomless cups of coffee, hot showers, and bigger being better, are suddenly not so true. One of the benefits of travel is the eye-opening realization that there are logical, civil, and even better alternatives. A willingness to go local ensures that you'll enjoy a full dose of Italian hospitality.

If there is a negative aspect to Italians' image of Americans (apart from our foreign policy), it's that we are big, loud, aggressive, impolite, rich, and a bit naive. Think about the rationale behind "crazy" Italian decisions. For instance, hoteliers turn off the heat in early April and can't turn on air-conditioning until May. The point is to conserve energy, and it's mandated by the Italian government. You could complain about being cold or hot...or bring a sweater in winter, and in summer, be prepared to sweat a little like everyone else.

Europeans place a high value on speaking quietly in nice restaurants and on trains. Listen while on the bus or in a restaurant—the place can be packed, but the decibel level is low. Try to adjust your volume accordingly to show respect for their culture.

While Italians, flabbergasted by our Yankee excesses, say in disbelief, *"Mi sono cadute le braccia!"* ("I throw my arms down!"), they nearly always afford us individual travelers all the warmth we deserve.

Judging from all the happy feedback I receive from travelers who have used this book, it's safe to assume you'll enjoy a great, affordable vacation—with the finesse of an independent, experienced traveler.

Thanks, and *buon viaggio!*

BACK DOOR TRAVEL PHILOSOPHY
From *Rick Steves' Europe Through the Back Door*

Travel is intensified living—maximum thrills per minute and one of the last great sources of legal adventure. Travel is freedom. It's recess, and we need it.

Experiencing the real Europe requires catching it by surprise, going casual..."Through the Back Door."

Affording travel is a matter of priorities. (Make do with the old car.) You can travel—simply, safely, and comfortably—anywhere in Europe for $120 a day plus transportation costs (allow more for big cities such as Rome). In many ways, spending more money only builds a thicker wall between you and what you came to see. Europe is a cultural carnival, and, time after time, you'll find that its best acts are free and the best seats are the cheap ones.

A tight budget forces you to travel close to the ground, meeting and communicating with the people, not relying on service with a purchased smile. Never sacrifice sleep, nutrition, safety, or cleanliness in the name of budget. Simply enjoy the local-style alternatives to expensive hotels and restaurants.

Extroverts have more fun. If your trip is low on magic moments, kick yourself and make things happen. If you don't enjoy a place, maybe you don't know enough about it. Seek the truth. Recognize tourist traps. Give a culture the benefit of your open mind. See things as different but not better or worse. Any culture has much to share.

Of course, travel, like the world, is a series of hills and valleys. Be fanatically positive and militantly optimistic. If something's not to your liking, change your liking. Travel is addictive. It can make you a happier American as well as a citizen of the world. Our Earth is home to six and a half billion equally important people. It's humbling to travel and find that people don't envy Americans. Europeans like us, but, with all due respect, they wouldn't trade passports.

Globe-trotting destroys ethnocentricity. It helps you understand and appreciate different cultures. Regrettably, there are forces in our society that want you dumbed down for their convenience. Don't let it happen. Thoughtful travel engages you with the world—more important than ever these days. Travel changes people. It broadens perspectives and teaches new ways to measure quality of life. Rather than fear the diversity on this planet, travelers celebrate it. Many travelers toss aside their hometown blinders. Their prized souvenirs are the strands of different cultures they decide to knit into their own character. The world is a cultural yarn shop, and Back Door travelers are weaving the ultimate tapestry. Join in!

ORIENTATION

Sprawling Rome actually feels manageable once you get to know it. The old core, with most of the tourist sights, sits in a diamond formed by the Termini train station (in the east), the Vatican (west), Villa Borghese Gardens (north), and the Colosseum (south). The Tiber River runs through the diamond from north to south. In the center of the diamond sits Piazza Venezia, a busy square and traffic hub. It takes about an hour to walk from the Termini train station to the Vatican.

Think of Rome as a series of neighborhoods, huddling around major landmarks.

Ancient Rome: In ancient times, this was home for the grandest buildings of a city of a million people. Today, the best of the classical sights stand in a line from the Colosseum to the Forum to the Pantheon. (See "Ancient Rome" map, page 38.)

Pantheon Neighborhood (The Heart of Rome): The Pantheon anchors the neighborhood I like to call the "Heart of Rome." It stretches eastward from the Tiber River through Campo de' Fiori and Piazza Navona, past the Pantheon to the Trevi Fountain. (See "Pantheon Neighborhood" map, page 49.)

North Rome: With the Spanish Steps, Villa Borghese Gardens, and trendy shopping streets (Via Veneto and the "shopping triangle"), this is a more modern, classy area. (See "North Rome" map, page 57.)

Vatican City: Located west of the Tiber, it's a compact world of its own, with two great, huge sights: St. Peter's Basilica and the Vatican Museum. (See "Vatican City" map, page 63.)

Trastevere: This seedy, colorful, wrong-side-of-the-river neighborhood is village Rome. It's the city at its crustiest—and perhaps most "Roman." (See "Trastevere Walk" map, page 88.)

Termini: Though light on sightseeing highlights, the train

ORIENTATION

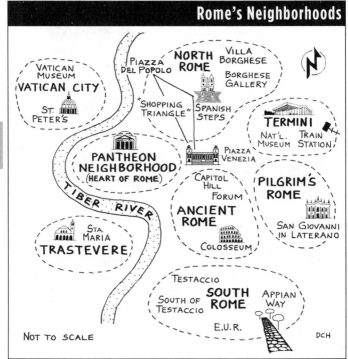

Rome's Neighborhoods

VATICAN MUSEUM
VATICAN CITY
ST. PETER'S

PIAZZA DEL POPOLO
NORTH ROME
VILLA BORGHESE
BORGHESE GALLERY

"SHOPPING TRIANGLE"
SPANISH STEPS

TERMINI
NAT'L. MUSEUM
TRAIN STATION

PANTHEON NEIGHBORHOOD
(HEART OF ROME)

PIAZZA VENEZIA

TIBER RIVER

STA. MARIA
TRASTEVERE

CAPITOL HILL
FORUM
ANCIENT ROME
COLOSSEUM

PILGRIM'S ROME
SAN GIOVANNI IN LATERANO

TESTACCIO
SOUTH OF TESTACCIO
SOUTH ROME
APPIAN WAY
E.U.R.

NOT TO SCALE   DCH

station neighborhood has many recommended hotels and public-transportation connections. (See "Hotels near Termini Train Station" map, page 280.)

Pilgrim's Rome: Several prominent churches dot the area south of the Termini train station. (See "Pilgrim's Rome" map, page 259.)

South Rome: South of the city center, you'll find the gritty/colorful Testaccio neighborhood, the 1930s suburb of E.U.R., and the Appian Way, home of the catacombs. (See "South Rome" color map at the beginning of this book.)

Within each of these neighborhoods, you'll find elements from the many layers of Rome's 2,000-year history: the marble ruins of ancient times; tangled streets of the medieval world; early Christian churches; grand Renaissance buildings and statues; Baroque fountains and church facades; 19th-century apartments; and 20th-century boulevards choked with traffic.

Since no one is allowed to build taller than St. Peter's dome, and virtually no buildings have been constructed in the city center since Mussolini got distracted in 1938, Rome has no modern skyline. The Tiber River is basically ignored—after the last floods (1870), the banks were built up very high, and Rome turned its back on its naughty river.

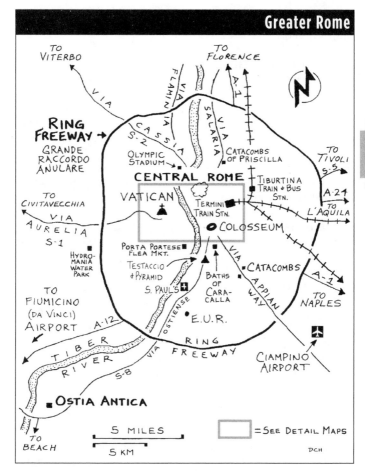

Planning Your Time

After considering Rome's major tourist sights, I've covered just my favorites. You won't be able to see all of these, so don't try—you'll keep coming back to Rome. After several dozen visits, I still have a healthy list of excuses to return.

Rome in a Day

Some people actually try to "do" Rome in a day. Crazy as that sounds, if all you have is a day, it's one of the most exciting days Europe has to offer. See Vatican City (two hours in the Vatican Museum and Sistine Chapel—if the line's not too long—then one hour in St. Peter's), taxi over the river to the Pantheon, enjoy a gelato, then hike over Capitol Hill, through the Forum, and to the Colosseum. Have dinner on Campo de' Fiori and dessert on Piazza Navona. (With typical crowds, you'll likely have to skip the Vatican Museum. But the rest is entirely doable.)

Rome in Two to Three Days

On the first day, do the "Caesar Shuffle" from the Colosseum to the Forum, then over Capitol Hill to the Pantheon. After a siesta, join the locals strolling from Piazza del Popolo to the Spanish Steps (see the "Dolce Vita Stroll," page 320). On the second day, see Vatican City (St. Peter's, climb the dome, tour the Vatican Museum). Have dinner on the atmospheric Campo de' Fiori, then walk to the Trevi Fountain and Spanish Steps (see the Night Walk Across Rome, page 78). With a third day, add the Borghese Gallery (reservations required) and the National Museum of Rome.

Rome in Seven Days

Rome is a great one-week getaway. Its sights can keep even the most fidgety traveler well-entertained for a week.

Day 1: Do the "Caesar Shuffle" from the Colosseum to the Forum, Mamertine Prison, Trajan's Column, Capitol Hill, and Pantheon.

Day 2: Morning—National Museum of Rome and the nearby Baths of Diocletian. Afternoon—"Dolce Vita Stroll" (page 320) and shopping.

Day 3: Vatican City—St. Peter's Basilica, dome climb, and Vatican Museum (pay careful attention to my "Avoiding Lines" tips for the Vatican Museum, on page 203).

Day 4: Side-trip to Ostia Antica (closed Mon, page 335). Take recommended Night Walk Across Rome (page 78) from Campo de' Fiori to the Spanish Steps.

Day 5: Borghese Gallery (reservation required) and Pilgrims' Rome (the churches of San Giovanni in Laterano, Santa Maria Maggiore, and San Clemente).

Day 6: Side-trip to Naples and Pompeii.

Day 7: You choose—Hadrian's Villa, Appian Way with Catacombs, E.U.R., Castel Sant'Angelo, Testaccio sights, Baths of Caracalla, Cappuccin Crypt, shopping, or more time at the Vatican.

OVERVIEW

Tourist Information

While Rome has several tourist information offices (abbreviated **TI** in this book), the dozen or so TI kiosks scattered around the town at major tourist centers are handy and just as helpful. If all you need is a map, get one at your hotel or at a newsstand kiosk.

Rome's single best source of up-to-date tourist information is its call center, answered by English-speakers. Dial 06-0608 (answered

Daily Reminder

Sunday: These sights are closed—the Vatican Museum (except for the last Sunday of the month, when it's free and even more crowded), Villa Farnesina, Nero's Golden House, Santa Susanna Church, Santa Maria della Vittoria, Protestant Cemetery in Testaccio, and the Catacombs of San Sebastiano. In the morning, the Porta Portese flea market hops, and the old center is delightfully quiet.

Monday: Many sights are closed, including the National Museum of Rome, Borghese Gallery, Capitoline Museums, Catacombs of Priscilla, Museum of the Bath (at the Baths of Diocletian), Museum of the Imperial Forums (includes Trajan's Market and Trajan's Forum), Castel Sant'Angelo, Ara Pacis, Montemartini Museum, E.U.R.'s Museum of Roman Civilization, Nero's Golden House, Etruscan Museum, Ostia Antica, and Villa d'Este (at Tivoli). All of the ancient sights (e.g., Colosseum and Forum) and the Vatican Museum, among others, are open. The Baths of Caracalla closes early in the afternoon.

Tuesday: All sights are open in Rome. This isn't a good day to side-trip to Naples because its Archaeological Museum is closed.

Wednesday: All sights are open, except for the Catacombs of San Callisto. St. Peter's Basilica may be closed in the morning for a papal audience.

Thursday: All sights are open, except for Galleria Doria Pamphilj.

Friday: All sights are open in Rome.

Saturday: Most sights are open in Rome, except for the Synagogue, Jewish Museum, Nero's Golden House, and Santa Susanna Church.

daily 9:00–22:30, press 2 for English). You can call to book museum tickets, sightseeing passes (see page 40), and theater tickets using your credit card. There's usually only a minimal €1.50 fee (and no fee for the Roma Pass), and you can generally order from several months in advance up until the day before your visit.

At Fiumicino Airport, the TIs are in Terminal C (daily 8:00–19:00) and Terminal B (daily 8:15–19:00, has brochures on walking itineraries but not much else).

Inside the Termini train station, there's a poorly marked TI (walk along track 24, go through the doors at the baggage-check sign, TI is just past the post office; if you get off the train far enough down the tracks you'll see the *sottopassaggio* shortcut—go down the stairs, walk toward track 24, then take the elevator up).

Smaller TIs (daily 9:00–18:00) include kiosks near the Forum (on Piazza del Tempio della Pace), in Trastevere (on Piazza Sonnino), on

Via Nazionale (at Palazzo delle Esposizioni), at Castel Sant'Angelo (at Piazza Pia), at Santa Maria Maggiore Church, at Piazza Navona (at Piazza delle Cinque Lune), and near the Trevi fountain (at Via del Corso and Via Minghetti).

At any TI, ask for a city map and a listing of sights and hours (in the free *Museums of Rome* booklet). The TIs don't offer room-booking services. If a commercial info-center offers to book you a room, just say no—you'll save money by booking direct.

The *Evento* booklet, given out free at TIs, has English-language pages that list the month's cultural events on art, museums, and music. *Roma c'è* is a cheap little weekly entertainment guide with a useful English section (in the back) on music, art, events, and nightclubs (€1.50, new edition every Wed, sold at newsstands, www.romace.it).

Arrival in Rome

For a rundown of Rome's train stations and airports, see "Transportation Connections," page 324.

Helpful Hints

Sightseeing Tips: Avid sightseers can save money by buying the Roma Pass (see page 40). To avoid lines at the Colosseum and Forum, buy a Roma Pass (online, by phone, or at a less crowded sight), or buy a combo-ticket online and print it out (see page 103). If you want to see the Borghese Gallery, remember to reserve ahead (see page 190). To bypass the long Vatican Museum line, consider reserving a tour (see page 204).

Internet Access: If your hotel doesn't offer free or cheap Internet access, your hotelier can point you to the nearest Internet café. Remember to bring your passport, which you may be asked to show before going online.

Bookstores: These stores (all open daily) sell travel guidebooks—**Borri Books** (at Termini train station), two handy locations of **Feltrinelli International** (one at Largo Argentina and the other just off Piazza della Repubblica at Via Vittorio Emanuele Orlando 84, tel. 06-482-7878), **Almost Corner Bookshop** in Trastevere (Via del Moro 45, tel. 06-583-6942), and the **Anglo American Bookshop** (a few blocks south of the Spanish Steps at Via della Vite 102, tel. 06-679-5222).

Laundry: Your hotelier can direct you to the nearest launderette. The **ondablu** launderette chain comes with Internet access (€2/hr, about €7 to wash and dry a 15-pound load, usually open daily 8:00–22:00, near Termini train station at Via Principe Amedeo 70b, tel. 06-474-4647).

Travel Agencies: You can get train tickets and railpass-related reservations and supplements at travel agencies, avoiding a trip to a train station. The cost is often the same, though sometimes there's a minimal charge. Your hotelier will know of a convenient agency nearby. The **American Express** office near the Spanish Steps sells train tickets and makes reservations for no extra fee (Mon–Fri 9:00–17:30, Sat 9:00–12:30, closed Sun, Piazza di Spagna 38, tel. 06-67641).

Dealing with (and Avoiding) Problems

Theft Alert: With sweet-talking con artists meeting you at the station, well-dressed pickpockets on buses, and thieving gangs of children at the ancient sites, Rome is a gauntlet of rip-offs. While it's nowhere near as bad as it was a few years ago, and pickpockets don't want to hurt you—they usually just want your money—green or sloppy tourists will be scammed. Thieves strike when you're distracted. Don't trust kind strangers. Keep nothing important in your pockets. Be most on guard while boarding and leaving buses and subways. Thieves crowd the door, then stop and turn while others crowd and push from behind. The sneakiest thieves are well-dressed businessmen (generally with something in their hands); lately many are posing as tourists with fanny packs, cameras, and even Rick Steves guidebooks. Scams abound: Don't give your wallet to self-proclaimed "police" who stop you on the street, warn you about counterfeit (or drug) money, and ask to see your cash. If a bank machine eats your ATM card, see if there's a thin plastic insert with a tongue hanging out that thieves use to extract it.

If you know what to look out for, the gangs of children picking the pockets and handbags of naive tourists are no threat, but an interesting, albeit sad, spectacle. Groups of city-stained children (just 8–10 years old—too young to be prosecuted, but old enough to rip you off) troll through the tourist crowds around the Colosseum, Forum, Piazza della Repubblica, and train and Metro stations. Watch them target tourists who are overloaded with bags or distracted with a video camera. The kids look like beggars and hold up newspapers or cardboard signs to confuse their victims. They scram like stray cats if you're on to them. A fast-fingered mother with a baby is often nearby. The terrace above the bus stop near the Colosseo Metro stop is a fine place to watch the action... and maybe even pick up a few moves of your own.

Reporting Losses: To report lost or stolen passports and documents, or to make an insurance claim, you must file a police report (at Termini train station, with Polizia at track 1 or with Carabinieri at track 20; offices are also at Piazza Venezia). To replace a passport, file the police report, then go to your embassy (see page 387). To report lost or stolen credit cards, see page 10.

Emergency Numbers: Police—tel. 113. Ambulance—tel. 118.

Pedestrian Safety: While petty crime is common in the city center, violent crime is very rare. Your main concern in Rome is crossing streets safely, using extreme caution. Scooters don't need to stop at red lights, and even cars exercise what drivers call the "logical option" of not stopping if they see no oncoming traffic. As noisy gasoline-powered scooters are replaced by electric ones, they'll be quieter (hooray) but more dangerous for pedestrians. Follow locals like a shadow when you cross a street (or spend a good part of your visit stranded on curbs). When you do cross alone, don't be a deer in the headlights. Find a gap in the traffic and walk with confidence while making eye contact with approaching drivers—they won't hit you if they can tell where you intend to go.

Staying/Getting Healthy: The siesta is a key to survival in summertime Rome. Lie down and contemplate the extraordinary power of gravity in the Eternal City. I drink lots of cold, refreshing water from Rome's many drinking fountains (the Forum has three).

There's a pharmacy (marked by a green cross) in every neighborhood. Pharmacies stay open late in the Termini train station (daily 7:30–22:00, downstairs below track 24) and at Piazza dei Cinquecento 51 (open 24 hours daily, next to Termini train station on the corner of Via Cavour, tel. 06-488-0019).

Embassies can recommend English-speaking doctors. Consider MEDline, a 24-hour home-medical service (tel. 06-808-0995, doctors speak English). Anyone is entitled to free emergency treatment at public hospitals. The hospital closest to the Termini train station is Policlinico Umberto 1 (entrance for emergency treatment on Via Lancisi, translators available, Metro: Policlinico). The American Hospital, a private hospital on the edge of town, is accustomed to helping Yankees (Via Emilio Longoni 69, tel. 06-22-551).

Getting Around Rome

Sightsee on foot, by city bus, by Metro, or by taxi. I've grouped your sightseeing into walkable neighborhoods. Make it a point to visit sights in a logical order. Needless backtracking wastes precious time.

The public transportation system, which is cheap and efficient, consists primarily of buses, a few trams, and the two underground metro lines. Consider it part of your Roman experience.

Buying Tickets

All public transportation uses the same ticket (€1, valid for one Metro ride—including transfers underground—plus unlimited city buses and *elettrico* buses during a 1.25-hour period); you can also buy an all-day bus/Metro pass (€4, good until midnight), a three-day pass (€11), or a one-week pass (€16—about the same cost of two taxi rides).

You can buy tickets and passes at some newsstands, tobacco shops (*tabacchi*, marked by a black-and-white *T* sign), and major Metro stations and bus stops, but not on board. It's smart to stock up on tickets early, or to buy an all-day pass or a Roma Pass (which includes a three-day transit pass—see page 40). That way, you don't have to run around searching for an open *tabacchi* when you spot your bus approaching. Metro stations rarely have human ticket-sellers, and the machines are often either broken or require exact change (it helps to insert your smallest coin first).

Validate your ticket by sticking it in the Metro turnstile (brown stripe facing toward you and angled down) or in the machine when you board the bus—watch others and imitate. If the validation machine won't work, you can ride with your ticket unstamped, but you must write the date, time, and bus number on it, or risk getting fined. For more information, visit www.atac.roma.it, or call 800-431-784.

Buses (especially the touristy #64) and the Metro are havens for thieves and pickpockets. Assume any commotion is a thief-created distraction. If one bus is packed, there's likely a second one on its tail with far fewer crowds and thieves. Once you know the bus system, it's easier than searching for a cab.

By Metro

The Roman subway system (Metropolitana, or "Metro") is simple, with two clean, cheap, fast lines—A and B—that intersect at the Termini train station (Line A runs Mon–Sat 5:30–22:00, Sun 6:30–22:00; Line B runs Sun–Thu 5:30–23:00, Fri–Sat 5:30–1:30 in the morning). The subway's first and last compartments are generally the least crowded.

You'll notice lots of big holes in the city as a new line is built. Line C, from the Colosseum to Largo Argentina, will likely be done in 2020.

While much of Rome is not served by its skimpy subway, the following stops are helpful.

Termini (intersection of lines A and B): Termini train station, National Museum of Rome, and recommended hotels

Repubblica (line A): Baths of Diocletian/Octagonal Hall, Via Nazionale, and recommended hotels

Barberini (line A): Cappuccin Crypt and Trevi Fountain

ORIENTATION

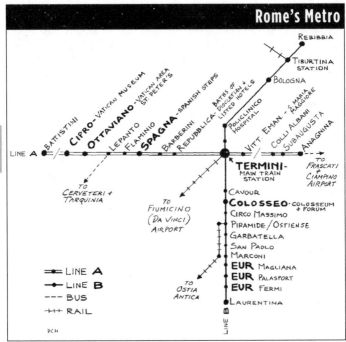

Spagna (line A): Spanish Steps, Villa Borghese, and classy shopping area

Flaminio (line A): Piazza del Popolo, start of recommended "Dolce Vita Stroll" down Via del Corso

Ottaviano (line A): St. Peter's and Vatican City

Cipro (line A): Vatican Museum and recommended hotels

Tiburtina (line B): Tiburtina train and bus station

Colosseo (line B): Colosseum, Roman Forum, bike rental, and recommended hotels

Piramide (line B): Protestant Cemetery and trains to Ostia Antica

E.U.R. (line B): Mussolini's futuristic suburb

By Bus

The Metro is handy, but it won't get you everywhere—take the bus. Bus routes are clearly listed at the stops. TIs usually don't have bus maps, but with some knowledge of major stops (see "Major Bus Routes" sidebar), you won't necessarily need one (though if you do want a route map, buy it from *tabacchi* shops; bus info: tel. 06-57-003, usually not in English).

Tickets have a barcode and must be stamped on the bus in the yellow box with the digital readout (be sure to retrieve your ticket).

Bus Bravado

Zip around Rome by bus like a local by using the following tips to read bus signs. Keep in mind that the major bus transfer points are at Largo Argentina, Piazza Venezia, and the Termini train station.

Where am I? Your current stop (or *fermata*) is listed at the top (see "Nazionale" in photo at right). It also appears on the list of bus stops, which are named after streets or piazzas.

Where am I going? First, check the list of bus stops to find your destination (or a major landmark where you can transfer). Next, figure out if you're standing on the right side of the street. See the arrow? The bus is heading in that direction—if your destination is listed *above* your current bus stop, you need to cross the street to catch the bus going in the right direction.

When will my bus come? If the bus number has an X or a U, the bus runs during normal waking hours. If it has an owl symbol and an N, it's a night bus. If the number is red within a rounded square, ignore it—that bus doesn't run often. To verify the bus schedule, check the bottom of the sign, which lists the first and last departure times from the top of the line.

Will pickpockets take my wallet? They probably will if you read this entire sidebar at the bus stop without paying attention to your surroundings.

Punch your ticket as you board (magnetic stripe down), or you are cheating. While relatively safe, riding without a stamped ticket on the bus is stressful. Inspectors fine even innocent-looking tourists €52. General bus etiquette (not always followed) is to board at the front or rear doors and exit out the middle.

Regular bus lines start running at about 5:30, and during the day, they run every 5–10 minutes. After 23:30, and sometimes earlier (such as on Sundays), buses are less frequent but dependable. Night buses are also reliable, and are marked N with an owl symbol on the bus-stop signs.

Rome's Public Transportation

¼ MILE

400 M.

TO M BATTISTINI

CIPRO M

VATICAN MUSEUM

M OTTAVIANO

492

LEPANTO M

TIBER

CASTEL SANT' ANGELO

40

492

23-280

64

ST. PETER'S

GIANICOLO TERMINAL

116

PIAZZA NAVONA

64 40

62

116

23-280

CAMPO DE FIORI

PORTA PORTESE

STA. MARIA TRASTEVERE

PIAZZA MASTAI

8

B

P.

BELLI

H

CIRCUS MAXIMUS

TO EUR + LAURENTINA

M FLAMINIO

117

PIAZZA DEL POPOLO

SPANISH STEPS

117

116

TREVI

PANTHEON

492

116

LARGO ARGENTINA

CAPITOL HILL

FORUM

PALATINE HILL

CIRCO MASSIMO M

M SPAGNA

116

BORGHESE MUSEUM

VIA VENETO

M BARBERINI

REPUB-BLICA M

40

H

64 40

VICTOR EMMANUEL MON.

H

492

BORGHESE MUSEUM

BATHS OF DIO.

64 40 H

714 H

NAT'L MUS.

M CAVOUR

COLOSSEO M

117

COLOSSEUM

CASTRO PRETORIO M

492

TO M TIBURTINA + REBIBBIA

TO TIBURTINA BUS + TRAIN STN.

TERMINI (TRAIN STATION)

TO FIUMICINO (DA VINCI) AIRPORT, FLORENCE, NAPLES, ETC.

S. MARIA MAGGIORE

VITTORIO EMANUELE M

M MANZONI

714

117

S. GIOVANNI M

TO M ANAGNINA

SAN GIOVANNI LAT.

492

M—M— METRO A

M—M— METRO B

64 — BUS ROUTES

ELETTRICO MINIBUS ROUTES

117
116

8 — TRAM

B •• BOATS

Major Bus Routes

The first two bus routes cut across the city, linking the Termini train station with the Vatican:

#64: Termini station, Piazza della Repubblica (sights), Via Nazionale (recommended hotels), Piazza Venezia (near Forum), Largo Argentina (near Pantheon), and St. Peter's Basilica (get off just past the tunnel). Ride it for a city over-view and to watch pickpockets in action (can get horribly crowded, awkward for female travelers uncomfortably close to male strangers).

#40: This express bus following the #64 route is espe-cially helpful—fewer stops, crowds, and pickpockets.

The following three routes conveniently connect Trastevere with other parts of Rome:

#H: This express bus connects Termini station and Trastevere, with a few stops on Via Nazionale (for Trastevere, get off at Piazza Belli, just after crossing the Tiber River).

#8: This tram connects Largo Argentina with Trastevere (get off at Piazza Belli).

#23 and #280: Links Vatican with Trastevere, stopping at Porta Portese (Sunday flea market), Trastevere (Piazza Belli), Castel Sant'Angelo, and Vatican Museum (nearest stop is Via Leone IV).

Here are other useful routes:

#62: Largo Argentina to St. Peter's Square.

#81: San Giovanni in Laterano, Largo Argentina, and Piazza Risorgimento (Vatican).

#85 and #87: Piazza Venezia, Colosseum, San Clemente, and San Giovanni in Laterano.

#492: Tiburtina (train and bus stations), Piazza Barberini, Piazza Venezia, Piazza Cavour (Castel Sant'Angelo), and Piazza Risorgimento (Vatican).

#714: Termini train station, Santa Maria Maggiore, San Giovanni in Laterano, Terme di Caracalla (Baths of Caracalla), and on to E.U.R.

These cute *elettrico* minibuses wind through the narrow streets of old and interesting neighborhoods, and are great for transport or simple joyriding:

***Elettrico* #116:** Through the medieval core of Rome: Ponte Vittorio Emanuele II (near Castel Sant'Angelo) to Campo de' Fiori, then to Piazza Barberini via the Pantheon, and finally through the scenic Villa Borghese Gardens.

***Elettrico* #117:** San Giovanni in Laterano, Colosseo, Via dei Serpenti, Trevi Fountain, Piazza di Spagna, and Piazza del Popolo.

ORIENTATION

By Taxi

I use taxis in Rome more often than in other cities. They're reasonable and useful for efficient sightseeing in this big, hot metropolis. Taxis start at about €2.50, then charge about €1 per kilometer (surcharges: €1 on Sun, €2.75 for nighttime hours of 22:00–7:00, €1 for luggage, tip by rounding up to the nearest euro). Sample fares: Termini train station to Vatican-€9; Termini train station to Colosseum-€6; Colosseum to Trastevere-€7. From the airport to anywhere in central Rome is a strictly fixed €40 rate (up to four people and their bags). Three or four companions with more money than time should taxi almost everywhere. It's tough to wave down a taxi in Rome. Find the nearest taxi stand by asking a passerby or a clerk in a shop, *"Dov'è una fermata dei taxi?"* (doh-VEH OO-nah fehr-MAH-tah DEHee TAHK-see). Some taxi stands are listed on my maps. To save time and energy, have your hotel or restaurant call a taxi for you; the meter starts when the call is received (generally adding a euro or two to the bill). To call a cab on your own, dial 06-4994 or 06-88177. It's routine for Romans to ask the waiter in a restaurant to call a taxi when they ask for the bill. The waiter will tell you how many minutes you have to enjoy your coffee.

Late at night, taxis are more expensive and hard to get. Don't try to hail one—go to a taxi stand. Beware of corrupt taxis. If hailing a cab on the street, be sure the meter is restarted when you get in (should be around €2.50, or around €5 if you or your hotelier phoned for the taxi). Many meters show both the fare and the time elapsed during the ride—and some tourists pay €10 for an eight-and-a-half-minute trip (more than the fair meter rate). When you arrive at the train station or airport, beware of hustlers conning naive visitors into unmarked rip-off "express taxis." Only use official taxis, with a *taxi* sign and phone number marked on the door. By law, they must display a multilingual official price chart. If you have any problems with a taxi, point to the chart and ask the cabbie to explain it to you. Making a show of writing down the taxi number (to file a complaint) can motivate a driver to quickly settle the matter. Tired travelers arriving at the airport might find it less stressful to take the airport shuttle to their hotel or catch the train to the Termini train station and take the Metro or a cheaper taxi from there (see page 328 for details on the shuttle and train).

By Bike

Biking in the big city of Rome can speed up sightseeing or simply be an enjoyable way to explore. Though Roman traffic can be stressful, Roman drivers are respectful of cyclists. The best rides are on small streets in the city center. A bike path along the banks of the Tiber River makes a good 20-minute ride (easily accessed from the ramps at Porta Portese and Ponte Regina Margherita near Piazza del Popolo). Get a bike with a well-padded seat—the little stones that pave Roman streets are unforgiving.

Top Bike Rental and Tours is professionally run by Roman bike enthusiasts who want to show off their city. Your rental comes with a handy map that suggests a route and indicates less-trafficked streets. Ciro and Riccardo also offer three- to four-hour-long guided tours around the city and the Ancient Appian Way; check their website for days and times (rental: €10/half-day, €15/day, more for mountain bikes, best to reserve in advance via email; bike tours: €15 plus bike rental fees, reservations required; leave ID for deposit, from Santa Maria Maggiore TI kiosk take Via Olmata and turn left one block down, Via dei Quattro Canti 40, tel. 06-488-2893, www.topbike rental.com, info@topbikerental.com).

Cool Rent, near the Colosseo Metro stop, is cheaper but less helpful (€3/hr, €10/day, 3-person bike cart €10/hr, daily 9:30–20:00, €100 cash or driver's license for deposit, 10 yards to the right as you exit the Metro). A second outlet is just off Via del Corso (on Largo di Lombardi, near corner of Via del Corso and Via della Croce). You can also rent a bike at the Appian Way (see page 161).

By Car with Driver

You can hire your own private car with driver through **Autoservizi Monti Concezio,** run by gentle, capable, and English-speaking Ezio (car-€35/hr, minibus-€40/hr, 3-hour minimum, mobile 335-636-5907 or 349-674-5643, www.montitours.com, concemon@tiscali.it).

TOURS

Rome has many highly competitive tour companies. I've listed some here, but without a lot of details on their offerings. Before your trip, spend some time on their websites; each company has a particular teaching and guiding personality. Some are highbrow, and others are less scholarly. It's sometimes required, and always smart, to book a spot in advance. The following companies all offer Vatican Museum tours—a convenient (if pricey) way to skirt that museum's exasperating lines if they use licensed guides (confirm before booking). While it may seem like a splurge to have a local or an American expat show you around, it's a treat that can suddenly turn brutal Rome into your friend.

Having said that, I must add that we get a lot of negative feedback on most of these tour companies. Readers report that their advertising can be misleading, and that scheduling mishaps are not uncommon. Especially considering the costliness of these guided tours, budget travelers should consider the alternative of simply using this book's self-guided tours or following my free Rome audiotours covering the Colosseum, the Roman Forum, the Pantheon, St. Peter's Basilica, and the Sistine Chapel (downloadable at www.ricksteves.com on your iPod or other MP3 player). If you don't mind me in your ear, they're hard to beat: nobody will stand you up, the quality is reliable (if not live), you can take the tour exactly when you like, and it's free.

Context Rome—Americans Paul Bennett and Lani Bevacqua offer informative walking tours for travelers with longer-than-average attention spans. Their orientation walks lace together lesser-known sights from antiquity to the present. Tours vary in length from two to four hours and range in price from €35 to €75. Try to book in advance, since their groups are limited to six and fill up fast (tel. 06-482-0911, US tel. 888-467-1986, www.contextrome.com). They also offer orientation chats in your hotel that can be well worth the price (€65/1 hour). Similar Context programs are offered in Venice, Florence, Naples, London, and Paris. See their website for other creative Context teaching initiatives.

Enjoy Rome—This English-speaking information service offers five different walking tours (€27 plus entry fees, 3 hours, groups limited to 25, reserve by phone or online). It also provides a free, useful city guide and an informative website (Mon–Fri 8:30–19:00, Sat 8:30–14:00, closed Sun, 3 blocks north of Termini train station, Via Marghera 8a, tel. 06-445-1843, fax 06-445-0734, www.enjoyrome.com, info @enjoyrome.com).

Rome Walks—The licensed guides give tours in fluent English to small groups (2–10 people). Sample tours include Colosseum/Forum/Palatine Walk (€51, includes admission to Colosseum, 3 hours), Scandal Tour (€40, 3 hours to dig up the dirt on Roman emperors, royalty, and popes), Vatican City Walk (€59, includes admission to Vatican Museum, 4 hours), Twilight Rome Evening Walk (€25, all the famous squares that offer lively people scenes, 2 hours), and a Jewish Ghetto and Trastevere Walk (€40, explore the back streets of Rome, 3 hours). They also do pricier, private tours to more far-flung places such as Orvieto (for wine and olives), Ostia Antica, the Appian Way, and the Catacombs (mobile 347-795-5175, www.romewalks.com, info @romewalks.com, Annie Frances Gray).

Roman Odyssey—This expat-led tour company offers various tours, led by native English speakers who are licensed guides. Tours have a maximum of 15 participants. Sample tours are their Ancient Rome walk (€25, Colosseum entrance extra, 3 hours) and Vatican Museum tour (€55, museum admission included, you get to skip the Vatican line, 4 hours; 15 percent discount for readers of this book in 2009, €60/hr for private guides, tel. 06-580-9902, mobile 328-912-3720, www.romanodyssey.com, Rahul).

Through Eternity—This company offers several walking tours, all led by native English speakers who strive to bring the history to life. The tours, which run nearly daily and are limited to groups of 15, do not include entry fees to museums or sights. Sample tours are St. Peter's and the Vatican Museum (€46, 5 hours); the Colosseum and Roman Forum (€30, 3 hours); and Rome at Twilight (€30, nightly). Their more unusual tours are "Underground Rome," which explores

Is the Pope Catholic?

Rome's tour guides, who introduce tourists to the city's great art and Christian history, field a lot of interesting questions and comments from their groups. Here are a few of their favorites:

- Oh, to be here in Rome...where our Lord Jesus walked.
- Is this where Christ fought the lions?
- Who's the guy on the cross?
- This guy who made so many nice things, Rene Sance, who is he? (Say it fast, and you'll get the gist.)
- Was John Paul II the son of John Paul I?
- What's the Sistine Chapel worth in US dollars?
- How did Michelangelo get Moses to pose for him?
- What's Michelangelo doing now?
- (Upon seeing the arrow-pierced St. Sebastian) Oh, you Italians had problems with the Indians, too.

the layers of ancient churches above and below ground, ending in Trastevere (€30, 3 hours); and "Secret Rome," which includes a visit to the National Museum of Rome, Santa Maria Maggiore, and other churches (€30, 3 hours). If you book by phone or online, the company offers a 10 percent Rick Steves discount for most of their tours and 20 percent for the Underground Rome and Secret Rome tours (tel. 06-700-9336, mobile 347-336-5298, www.througheternity.com, info @througheternity.com, Rob Allyn).

Angel Tours—This gang of hardworking Irish Italo-philes mix light narrative with their charming gift of gab. They generally do a free 19:00 Pantheon tour, hoping the charm and quality of the guide will encourage people to take the rest of that evening walk or book another tour. Note that these guides are not licensed or that knowledgeable about history—these tours are just for fun. Their website lists tours and departure times (€25 plus entry fees, €15 for students, 2–3 hours, English only, groups limited to 15, tel. 06-7720-3048, mobile 348-734-1850, www.angeltoursrome.com, Sean).

Artviva: The Original & Best Walking Tours—Their "Rome in One Glorious Day Package" consists of a four-hour walking introduction to Rome in the morning, and a Vatican Museum tour in the afternoon for €90 (March–Nov Mon, Wed, Fri, and Sat; ask for Rick Steves discount when you reserve). Check their website for all their tours, prices, and times. Groups are small (maximum of 14) and booking is necessary (tel. 055-264-5033 during day or mobile 329-613-2730 from 18:00–20:00, also private tours year-round, www.italy.artviva .com, staff@artviva.com).

Private Guides—Consider a personal tour. Any of the tour companies I list can provide a guide (about €60/hr). I work with Francesca

Caruso, a licensed Italian guide who speaks excellent English, loves to teach and share her appreciation of her city, and has contributed generously to this book. She has a broad range of expertise and can tailor a walk to your interests, and enjoys working with readers of this book (€45/hr, chris.fra@mclink.it).

The following licensed, independent local guides are also excellent and will tailor tours to your interests. Each guide charges a set fee for small groups: Carla Zaia (engaging Roman teacher, €180/half-day, mobile 349-759-0723, chrisecarla@tiscali.it); Sara Magister (a Roman with her doctorate in art history who wrote a book on Renaissance Rome (€50/hr, up to 10 people, tel. 06-583-6783, mobile 339-379-3813, a.magister@iol.it); and Jason Spiehler (Louisiana native with a Masters in Roman art history from Yale, €55/hr, mobile 340-798-0585, toursofrome@hotmail.com).

Hop-on, Hop-off Tours—Several different agencies, including the ATAC public bus company, run hop-on, hop-off tours around Rome. These tours are constantly evolving and offer varying combinations of sights. While you can grab one (and pay as you board) at any stop, the Termini train station and Piazza Venezia are handy hubs. Although the city is perfectly walkable and traffic jams can make the bus dreadfully slow, these open-top bus tours remain popular. Several tour companies offer essentially the same deal.

Trambus Open 110 seems to be the best. It's operated by the ATAC city bus lines, and offers an orientation tour on big red double-decker buses with an open-air upper deck. In less than two hours, you'll have 80 sights pointed out to you (with a next-to-worthless recorded narration). While you can hop on and off, the service can be erratic (mobbed midday, not ideal in bad weather) and it can be very slow in heavy traffic. It's best to think of this as a two-hour quickie orientation with scant information and lots of images. The 11 stops include Via Veneto, Via Tritone, Ara Pacis, Piazza Cavour, St. Peter's Square, Corso Vittorio Emanuele (for Piazza Navona), Piazza Venezia, Colosseum, and Via Nazionale. Bus #110 departs every 10 minutes (runs daily 8:00–20:00, tel. 06-684-0901, www.trambus open.com). Buy the €16 ticket as you board (or at platform E in front of Termini train station).

Archeobus is an open-top bus also operated by ATAC that runs hourly from the Termini train station out to the Appian Way (with stops at the Colosseum, Baths of Caracalla, San Callisto, San Sebastian, the Tomb of Cecilia Metella, and the Aqueduct Park). This is a handy way to see the sights down this ancient Roman road, but it can be frustrating for various reasons—sparse narration, sporadic service, and not ideal for hopping on and off (€13, €24 combo-ticket with Trambus, daily 9:00–16:00, hourly departures from Termini train station and Piazza Venezia, tel. 06-684-0901). A similar bus laces together all the Christian sights.

SIGHTS

I've clustered Rome's sights into walkable neighborhoods, some quite close together (see the "Rome's Neighborhoods" map on page 18). For example, the Colosseum and the Forum are a few minutes' walk from Capitol Hill; a 10-minute walk beyond that is the Pantheon. I like to group these sights into one great day, starting at the Colosseum and ending at the Pantheon.

Don't let the length of my descriptions determine your sight-seeing priorities. In this chapter, Rome's most important sights have the shortest listings and are marked with a ✪ (and page number). These sights are covered in much more detail in one of the tours included in this book.

To connect some of the sights by night, try my Night Walk Across Rome (page 78), which includes the Trevi Fountain and Spanish Steps. To join the parade of people strolling down Via del Corso every evening, take my "Dolce Vita Stroll" (page 320).

ANCIENT ROME

The core of the ancient city, where the grandest monuments were built, is between the Colosseum and Capitol Hill. To the north, this ancient area flows into the Renaissance at Capitol Hill, then into the modern era at Piazza Venezia.

The Colosseum and Nearby

▲▲▲Colosseum (Colosseo)—This 2,000-year-old building is the classic example of Roman engineering. Used as a venue for entertaining the masses, this colossal, functional stadium is one of Europe's most recognizable landmarks. Whether you're playing gladiator or simply marveling at the remarkable ancient design and construction, the Colosseum gets a unanimous thumbs-up (€11 combo-ticket includes Roman Forum and Palatine Hill, ticket valid two days—one entry per sight, buy ticket or Roma Pass—see page 40—at Palatine Hill to avoid long lines at Colosseum and Forum; daily 8:30 until one hour before sunset: April–Sept until 19:00, Oct until 18:15, Nov–Feb until 16:15, March until 16:30, last entry one hour before closing; Metro: Colosseo, tel. 06-3996-7700).

❂ See Colosseum Tour (includes tips on avoiding the long entry lines) on page 102.

▲**Arch of Constantine**—This well-preserved arch, which stands between the Colosseum and the Forum, commemorates a military

coup and, more importantly, the acceptance of Christianity by the Roman Empire. When the ambitious Emperor Constantine (who had a vision that he'd win under the sign of the cross) defeated his rival Maxentius in A.D. 312, Constantine became sole emperor of the Roman Empire and legalized Christianity. (Free, always open and viewable.)

❂ See Colosseum Tour on page 102.

▲**St. Peter-in-Chains Church (San Pietro in Vincoli)**—Built in the fifth century to house the chains that held St. Peter, this church is most famous for its Michelangelo statue. Check out the much-venerated chains under the high altar, then focus on mighty Moses (free, daily 8:00–12:30 & 15:00–19:00, until 18:00 in winter, modest dress required; the church is a 15-minute, uphill, zigzag walk from the Colosseum, or a shorter, simpler walk from the Cavour Metro stop—exiting the Metro stop, go up the steep flight of steps, take a right at the top, and walk a block to the church). Note that this isn't the famous St. Peter's Basilica, which is at Vatican City.

❂ See St. Peter-in-Chains Tour on page 254.

Nero's Golden House (Domus Aurea)—The sparse underground remains of Emperor Nero's "Golden House" are a faint shadow of their ancient grandeur. In its heyday, the gold-leaf-encrusted residence was huge, with its original entrance all the way over at the Arch of Titus in the Forum. Nero's massive estate once sprawled across the valley (where the Colosseum now stands) and up the hill—the part you tour today. Unfortunately, the Golden House is in a sad state of ruin, more historically significant than interesting—unless you're an archaeologist. Nero (ruled A.D. 54–68) was Rome's most notorious emperor. He killed his own mother, kicked his pregnant wife to death, and crucified St. Peter. When Rome burned in A.D. 64, Nero was accused of setting the fire to clear land for his domestic building needs. The Romans rebelled, the Senate declared him a public enemy, and his only noble option was suicide. With the help of a slave, Nero stabbed himself in the neck, crying, "What an artist dies in me!" (€4.50, Tue–Fri 10:00–16:00, closed Sat–Mon; 45-min English tour, advance booking required—reserve at www.pierreci.it or call 06-3996-7700.)

The Roman Forum and Nearby

▲▲▲Roman Forum (Foro Romano)—This is ancient Rome's birthplace and civic center, and the common ground between Rome's

famous seven hills. As just about anything important that happened in ancient Rome happened here, it's arguably the most important piece of real estate in Western civilization. While only a few fragments of that glorious past remain, history-seekers find plenty to ignite their imaginations amid the half-broken columns and arches (€11 combo-ticket includes Colosseum and Palatine Hill, daily 8:30 until one hour before sunset, Metro: Colosseo, tel. 06-3996-7700).

❂ See Roman Forum Tour on page 110.

▲▲▲Palatine Hill (Monte Palatino)—The hill overlooking the Forum was the home of the emperors and now contains a museum,

scant (but impressive when understood) remains of imperial palaces, and a view of the Circus Maximus (€11 combo-ticket covers Colosseum and Roman Forum, buy ticket or Roma Pass here to avoid long

lines, daily 8:30 until one hour before sunset, Metro: Colosseo).

❂ See Palatine Hill Tour on page 124.

▲Mamertine Prison—This 2,500-year-old, cistern-like prison, which once held the bodies of Saints Peter and Paul, is worth a look. When you step into the room, ignore the modern floor and look up at the hole in the ceiling, from which prisoners were lowered. Then take the stairs down to the level of the actual prison floor. Downstairs, you'll see the column to which Peter was chained. It's said that a

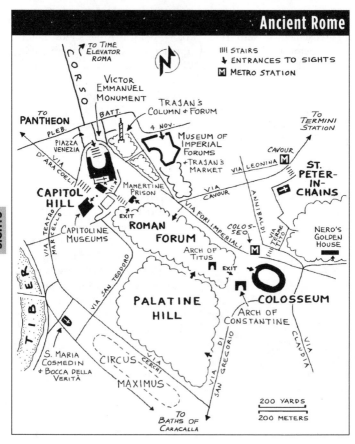

Ancient Rome

KEY:
IIII STAIRS
↓ ENTRANCES TO SIGHTS
Ⓜ METRO STATION

TO TIME ELEVATOR ROMA

TO PANTHEON

VICTOR EMMANUEL MONUMENT

TRAJAN'S COLUMN + FORUM

BATT. 4 NOV.

PLEB.

PIAZZA VENEZIA

MUSEUM OF IMPERIAL FORUMS
+ TRAJAN'S MARKET

CAVOUR Ⓜ

VIA LEONINA

TO TERMINI STATION

ST. PETER-IN-CHAINS

D'ARA COELI VIA

CAPITOL HILL

MAMERTINE PRISON

VIA CAVOUR

VIA FORI IMPERIALI

ANNIBALDI

COLOS-SEO Ⓜ

VIA TERME TITO

NERO'S GOLDEN HOUSE

VIA TEATRO MARCELLO

CAPITOLINE MUSEUMS

EXIT

ROMAN FORUM

ARCH OF TITUS

EXIT

TIBER

VIA SAN TEODORO

PALATINE HILL

ARCH OF CONSTANTINE

COLOSSEUM

VIA CLAUDIA

S. MARIA COSMEDIN + BOCCA DELLA VERITÀ

CIRCUS MAXIMUS

VIA DEI CERCHI

VIA DI SAN GREGORIO

200 YARDS
200 METERS

TO BATHS OF CARACALLA

miraculous fountain sprang up in this room so that Peter could convert and baptize his jailers, who were also subsequently martyred. The upside-down cross commemorates Peter's upside-down crucifixion (donation requested, daily 9:00–19:00, at the foot of Capitol Hill, near Forum's Arch of Septimius Severus).

Imagine humans, amid fat rats and rotting corpses, awaiting slow deaths. On the walls near the entry are lists of notable prisoners (Christian and non-Christian) and the ways they were executed: *strangolati, decapitato, morto per fame* (died of hunger). The sign by the Christian names reads, "Here suffered, victorious for the triumph of Christ, these martyr saints."

▲Trajan's Column, Forum, and Market (Colonna, Foro, e Mercati de Traiano)—This grand column is the best example of "continuous narration" that we have from antiquity (free, always open and viewable, on Piazza Venezia across street from Victor Emmanuel Monument). The market ruins are viewable for free from Via dei Fori

Imperiali. Paying the admission fee gets you inside Trajan's Market, Trajan's Forum, and the new Museum of the Imperial Forums. The museum features discoveries from the forums of several different emperors, as they remodeled and built over previous structures (€6.50, Tue–Sun 9:00–19:00, last entry one hour before closing, closed Mon, entrance is uphill from the column on Via IV Novembre 94, tel. 06-992-3521, www.mercatiditraiano.it).

❂ See Trajan's Column, Forum, and Market Tour on page 134.

Time Elevator Roma—This cheesy and overpriced show is really just for kids. The 45-minute, multi-screen show jolts you through the centuries. Equipped with headphones, you get nauseous in a comfortable, air-conditioned theater as the history of Rome unfolds before you—from the founding of the city, through its rise and fall, to its Renaissance rebound, and up to the present (€11, daily 10:30–19:30, shows at the bottom of each hour, no kids under 39 inches, just off Via del Corso, a 3-min walk from Piazza Venezia at Via dei S.S. Apostoli 20, tel. 06-9774-6243, www.time-elevator.it).

Capitol Hill

Of Rome's famous seven hills, this is the smallest, tallest, and most famous—home of the ancient Temple of Jupiter and the center of city government for 2,500 years. There are several ways to get to the top

of Capitol Hill. (While I call it "Capitol Hill" for simplicity, it's correctly called "Capitoline Hill," and the piazza on top is called the Campidoglio). If you're coming from the north (from Piazza Venezia), take Michelangelo's impressive stairway to the right of the big, white Victor Emmanuel Monument. Coming from the southeast (the Forum), take the steep staircase near the Arch of Septimius Severus. From near Trajan's Forum along Via dei Fori Imperiali, take the winding road. All three converge at the top, in the square called Campidoglio (kahm-pee-DOHL-yoh).

▲**Capitol Hill Square (Campidoglio)**—This square atop the hill, once the religious and political center of ancient Rome, is still the home of the city's government. In the 1530s, the pope called on Michelangelo to reestablish this square as a grand center. Michelangelo placed the ancient equestrian statue of Marcus Aurelius as the square's focal point. Effective. (The original statue is now in the adjacent museum.) The twin buildings on either side are the Capitoline Museums. Behind the replica of the statue is the mayoral palace (Palazzo Senatorio).

Michelangelo intended that people approach the square from his grand stairway off Piazza Venezia. From the top of the stairway, you

Tips on Sightseeing in Rome

Sightseeing Passes: Rome offers several passes to help you save money. For most visitors, the Roma Pass is the clear winner.

The **Roma Pass** costs €20 and is valid for three days, covering public transportation and free or discounted entry to Roman sights. You get free admission to your first two sights (where you also get to skip the ticket line), and then a discount on the rest within the three-day window. Sights covered (or discounted) by the pass include the following: Colosseum/Palatine Hill/Roman Forum, Borghese Gallery (though you still must make a reservation and pay the €2 booking fee), Capitoline Museums, Castel Sant'Angelo, Montemartini Museum, Ara Pacis, Museum of Roman Civilization, Etruscan Museum, Baths of Caracalla, Trajan's Market, some of the Appian Way sights. The pass also covers all four branches of the National Museum of Rome, considered as a single "sight": Palazzo Massimo (the main branch), Museum of the Bath at the Baths of Diocletian (Roman inscriptions), Crypta Balbi (medieval art), and Palazzo Altemps (so-so sculpture collection).

If you'll be visiting any two of the major sights in a three-day period, get the pass. It's sold at participating sights, online (www.romapass.it or www.pierreci.it), by phone (TI call-center tel. 06-0608), and at the TIs at the airport and Termini train station (includes map and brochure listing additional discounts). Sometimes the sights run out of passes, so if you see the pass for sale, buy it. The pass can also be purchased at *tabacchi* and newsstands inside Termini station.

Validate your Roma Pass by writing your name and validation date on the card. Then insert it directly into the turnstile at your first two (free) sights. At other sights, show it at the ticket office to get your reduced *(ridotto)* price—about 30 percent off.

To get the most of your pass, visit the two most expensive sights first—for example, the Colosseum (€11) and the National Museum (€10). Definitely use it to bypass the long ticket line at the Colosseum. For sights that normally sell a combined ticket (such as the Colosseum–Palatine–Roman Forum or the four National Museum branches), visiting the combined sight counts as a single entry.

The Roma Pass also includes a three-day transit pass. Write your name and birth date on the transit pass, validate it in the machine on your first bus or Metro ride, and you can take unlimited rides until midnight of the third day.

The more expensive (€25) **Roma and Più Pass** isn't useful for most visitors, as it includes sights and transportation in outlying areas of Rome.

Those visiting several ancient sights should also consider the **Archeologia Card.** It costs €22, is valid for seven days, and covers many of the biggies: the Colosseum, Palatine Hill, Roman Forum, Baths of Caracalla, Tomb of Cecilia Metella, Villa of the Quintilli, and all four branches of the National Museum. This combo-ticket saves you money if you plan to visit at least three of the major sights, such as the Colosseum, National Museum of Rome, and the Baths of Caracalla (sold at participating sights).

If buying both a Roma Pass and Archeologia Card, use your free Roma Pass entries for sights *not* covered by the Archeologia Card (such as the Borghese Gallery and Capitoline Museums).

Museums: Plan ahead. The Borghese Gallery requires **reservations** well in advance (see page 190). You can also reserve a tour through a tour company to avoid the long lines at the Vatican Museum (see page 204). Museum **hours** can vary. Get a current listing of opening times from one of Rome's TIs—ask for the free booklet *Museums of Rome*. On holidays, expect shorter hours or closures. For more tips on sightseeing, see page 12.

In museums, art is dated with A.C. (for *Avanti Cristo,* or B.C.) and D.C. (for *Dopo Cristo,* or A.D.). OK?

Churches: Churches offer amazing art (often free). They open early (around 7:00-7:30), close for lunch (roughly 12:00-15:00), and close late (about 19:00). Kamikaze tourists maximize their sightseeing hours by visiting churches before 9:00 and seeing the major sights that stay open during the siesta (St. Peter's, Colosseum, Forum, Capitoline Museums, and National Museum of Rome).

Many churches have "modest dress" requirements, which means no bare shoulders, miniskirts, or shorts—for men, women, or children. However, this dress code is only strictly enforced at St. Peter's and St. Paul's Outside the Walls. Elsewhere, you'll see many tourists in shorts (but not skimpy shorts) touring churches.

Spend money for light: A coin box near a piece of art in a church often illuminates the art for a coin. Some churches also have coin-operated audioboxes that describe the art and history. Consider these expenses a worthwhile donation.

Picnic Discreetly: There's a fine for public drinking and eating at major sights, though it will be difficult to enforce. Keep a low profile or choose an empty piazza for your picnic

Miscellaneous Tips: I carry a plastic water bottle and refill it at Rome's many public drinking spouts. Because public restrooms are scarce, use toilets at museums, restaurants, and bars.

SIGHTS

Capitol Hill and Piazza Venezia

S. APOST.

TIME ELEVATOR ROMA

VIA BATTISTI

(B) #64,40

VIA PLEBISCITO

■ CAPITOLINE MUSEUMS

→ ENTRY POINT TO SIGHTS

Ⓜ METRO STATION

Ⓣ TAXI STAND

Ⓑ BUS STOP

PALAZZO VENEZIA

❽

PIAZZA

Ⓣ

Ⓑ

VENEZIA

TRAJAN'S COLUMN

S. MARCO

TRAJAN'S

(B) #64

TO GESÙ & PANTHEON

VICTOR EMMANUEL MONUMENT

FORUM

VIA D'ARACOELI

#110

Ⓑ

CAFÉ

❶❶

STA. MARIA ARACOELI

❻

Ⓣ

VIA DEI FORI IMPERIALI

GRAND STAIRCASE

❾

❼

PALAZZO NUOVO

TO COLOSSEUM & Ⓜ

VIA MARCELLO

❶

❸

TO ❿

PIAZZA CAFFARELLI

STATUE

❷

❹

MAMERTINE PRISON

TEATRO

PUBLIC CAFÉ ENTRANCE

TABULARIUM

❺

EXIT

CAFÉ →

ARCH OF SEPTIMIUS SEVERUS

❺

PALAZZO SENATORIO

PALAZZO DEI CONSERVATORI

SAN TEODORO

ROMAN

FORUM

100 YARDS

100 METERS

DCH

❶ Campidoglio (Main Square)

❷ Capitoline Museums Entrance

❸ Copy of She-Wolf Statue

❹ "Il Nasone" Water Fountain

❺ Views of Forum

❻ Shortcut to Victor Emmanuel Monument

❼ Shortcut to Santa Maria in Aracoeli Church

❽ Mussolini's Balcony

❾ Michelangelo's Grand Staircase

❿ To Teatro Marcello Ruins

⓫ Rome from the Sky

see the new Renaissance face of Rome, with its back to the Forum. Michelangelo gave the buildings the "giant order"—huge pilasters make the existing two-story buildings feel one-storied and more harmonious with the new square. Notice how the statues atop these buildings welcome you and then draw you in.

The terraces just downhill (past either side of the mayor's palace) offer grand views of the Forum. To the left of the mayor's palace is a copy of the famous *She-Wolf* statue on a column. Farther down is *il nasone* ("the big nose"), a refreshing water fountain (see photo on the right). Block the spout with your fingers, and water spurts up for drinking. Romans joke that a cheap Roman boy takes his date out for a drink at *il nasone*. Near the *She-Wolf* statue is the staircase leading to a shortcut to the Victor Emmanuel Monument.

Shortcut to Victor Emmanuel Monument: A clever little "back door" gives you access from the top of Capitol Hill directly to the top of the Victor Emmanuel Monument, saving lots of uphill stair-climbing. Near the *She-Wolf* statue (to the left of the mayoral palace), climb the wide set of stairs (the highest set of stairs you see), pass through the iron gate at the top of the steps, and enter the small unmarked door at #13 on the right. You'll soon emerge on a café terrace at the top of the monument with vast views. The shortcut gives you easy access to several sights: the Rome from the Sky elevator, Museum of the Risorgimento (both listed under "Victor Emmanuel Monument," page 47), and Santa Maria in Aracoeli (described below).

▲▲Capitoline Museums (Musei Capitolini)—Some of ancient Rome's most famous statues and art are housed in the two palaces that flank the equestrian statue in the Campidoglio. You'll see the *Dying Gaul,* the original *She-Wolf,* and the original version of the equestrian statue of Marcus Aurelius. Admission includes access to the underground, vacant Tabularium, with its panoramic overlook of the Forum (€8, €10 combo-ticket with Montemartini Museum, Tue–Sun 9:00–20:00, closed Mon, last entry one hour before closing, good €5 audioguide, tel. 06-8205-9127, www.museicapitolini.org).

✪ See Capitoline Museums Tour on page 181.

Santa Maria in Aracoeli—This church is built on the site where Emperor Augustus (supposedly) had a premonition of the coming of Mary and Christ standing on an "altar in the sky" (Ara Coeli). The church is Rome in a nutshell, where you can time-travel across two thousand years by standing in one spot (daily 9:00–12:00 & 14:30–17:30). It's atop Capitol Hill, squeezed between the Victor Emmanuel

SIGHTS

Rome at a Glance

▲▲▲**Colosseum** Huge stadium where gladiators fought. **Hours:** Daily 8:30 until one hour before sunset: April–Sept until 19:00, Oct until 18:15, Nov–Feb until 16:15, March until 16:30. See page 102.

▲▲▲**Roman Forum** Ancient Rome's main square, with ruins and grand arches. **Hours:** Same hours as Colosseum. See page 110.

▲▲▲**Palatine Hill** Ruins of emperors' palaces, Circus Maximus view, and museum. **Hours:** Same hours as Colosseum. See page 124.

▲▲▲**Pantheon** The defining domed temple. **Hours:** Mon–Sat 8:30–19:30, Sun 9:00–18:00, holidays 9:00–13:00, closed for Mass Sat at 17:00 and Sun at 10:30. See page 139.

▲▲▲**National Museum of Rome** Greatest collection of Roman sculpture anywhere. **Hours:** Tue–Sun 9:00–19:45, closed Mon. See page 167.

▲▲▲**Borghese Gallery** Bernini sculptures and paintings by Caravaggio, Raphael, and Titian in a Baroque palazzo. Reservations mandatory. **Hours:** Tue–Sun 9:00–19:00, closed Mon. See page 190.

▲▲▲**Vatican Museum** Four miles of the finest art of Western Civilization, culminating in Michelangelo's glorious Sistine Chapel. **Hours:** Mon–Sat 8:30–17:30, last entry at 16:00 (official closing time is 18:00, but they start ushering you out at 17:30). Closed on religious holidays and Sun, except last Sun of the month (when it's open 8:30–14:00, last entry at 12:30). Hours are notoriously subject to constant change. See page 202.

▲▲▲**St. Peter's Basilica** Most impressive church on earth, with Michelangelo's *Pietà* and dome. **Hours:** Church—daily April–Sept 7:00–19:00, Oct–March 7:00–18:00, often closed Wed mornings; dome—daily April–Sept 8:00–17:45, Oct–March 8:00–16:45. See page 233.

▲▲**Capitoline Museums** Ancient statues, mosaics, and expansive view of Forum. **Hours:** Tue–Sun 9:00–20:00, closed Mon. See page 181.

▲▲**Ara Pacis** Shrine marking the beginning of Rome's Golden Age. **Hours:** Tue–Sun 9:00–19:00, closed Mon. See page 59.

▲▲**Catacombs** Layers of tunnels with tombs, mainly Christian, outside the city. **Hours:** Open 8:30–12:00 & 14:00–17:30, until

17:00 in winter (San Callisto opens at 9:00, closed Wed and Feb; San Sebastiano closed Sun and mid-Nov–mid-Dec; Priscilla closes on Mon and at 17:00 year-round). See pages 61, 76, and 77.

▲**Arch of Constantine** Honors the emperor who legalized Christianity. **Hours:** Always viewable. See page 36.

▲**St. Peter-in-Chains** Church with Michelangelo's *Moses.* **Hours:** Daily 8:00–12:30 & 15:00–19:00. See page 254.

▲**Trajan's Column** Tall column with narrative relief, on Piazza Venezia. **Hours:** Always viewable. See page 134.

▲**Museum of the Imperial Forums** Includes entry to Trajan's Market. **Hours:** Tue–Sun 9:00–19:00, closed Mon. See page 136.

▲**Capitol Hill Square** Hilltop piazza designed by Michelangelo, with a museum, grand stairway, and Forum overlooks. **Hours:** Always open. See page 39.

▲**Trevi Fountain** Baroque hotspot into which tourists throw coins to ensure a return trip to Rome. **Hours:** Always flowing. See page 84.

▲**Baths of Diocletian** Once ancient Rome's immense public baths, now a Michelangelo church—Santa Maria degli Angeli—and the skippable Museum of the Bath. **Hours:** Church—Mon–Sat 7:00–18:30, Sun 7:00–19:30; Octagonal Hall—Open sporadically Sun 9:00–13:00 only; Museum of the Bath—Tue–Sun 9:00–19:45, closed Mon. See page 50.

▲**Santa Maria della Vittoria** Church with Bernini's swooning *St. Teresa in Ecstasy.* **Hours:** Mon–Sat 8:30–12:00 & 15:30–18:00, closed Sun. See page 51.

▲**Rome from the Sky** Elevator to the top of the Victor Emmanuel Monument for a 360-degree city view. **Hours:** May–Sept Mon–Thu 9:30–19:30, Fri–Sat 9:30–23:30, Sun 9:30–20:30; Oct–April Mon–Thu 9:30–18:30, Fri–Sun 9:30–19:30. See page 47.

▲**Cappuccin Crypt** Decorated with the bones of 4,000 monks. **Hours:** Daily 9:00–12:00 & 15:00–18:00. See page 56.

▲**Castel Sant'Angelo** Hadrian's Tomb turned castle, prison, papal refuge, now museum. **Hours:** Tue–Sun 9:00–19:30, closed Mon. See page 63.

SIGHTS

Monument and the square called Campidoglio. While dedicated pilgrims climb up the long, steep staircase from street level (the right side of Victor Emmanuel Monument, as you face it), casual sightseers prefer to enter through the "back door," on the shortcut between the Capitoline Museums and Victor Emmanuel Monument (described above): As you climb the stairs from Campidoglio to the shortcut, look for an arrow pointing left to *Aracoeli*.

The building itself dates from Byzantine times (sixth century) and was expanded in the 1200s. Napoleon's occupying troops used the building as a horse stable. But like Rome itself, it survived and retained its splendor. Inside, the mismatched columns and marble floor are ancient, plundered from many different monuments. The early Renaissance is featured in beautiful frescoes by Pinturicchio (first chapel on the right if you entered through the main entrance and didn't take the shortcut). The coffered ceiling celebrates the Christian victory over the Turks (Battle of Lepanto, 1571), and the side chapels are a compressed history of architecture, from Gothic to Baroque. A famous wooden statue of the Baby Jesus (Santo Bambino) was stolen in 1994, but the copy is still venerated at Christmastime, a Roman tradition. The daunting, 125-step staircase up Capitol Hill to the entrance was once climbed—on their knees—by Roman women who wished for a child. Today, they don't...and Italy has Europe's lowest birthrate.

Piazza Venezia

This vast square, dominated by the big, white Victor Emmanuel Monument, is a major transportation hub and the focal point of modern Rome. (The square will be dug up for years—Metro line C is under construction, and when anything of archaeological importance is uncovered, progress is interrupted.) Stand with your back to the monument and look down the Via del Corso, the city's axis, surrounded by Rome's classiest shopping district. In the 1930s, Benito Mussolini whipped up Italy's nationalistic fervor from a balcony above the square (with your back to Victor Emmanuel Monument, it's the less-grand balcony on the left). Fascist masses filled the square screaming, "Four more years!"—or something like that. Mussolini created boulevard Via dei Fori Imperiali to open up views of the Colosseum in the distance to impress his visiting friend, Adolf Hitler. Mussolini lied to his people, mixing fear and patriotism to push his country to the right and embroil the Italians in expensive and regrettable wars. In 1945, they shot and hung Mussolini from a meat hook in Milan.

Circling around the right side of the Victor Emmanuel Monument, look down into the ditch on your left to see the ruins of an ancient apartment building from the first century A.D.; part of it was transformed into a tiny church (faded frescoes and bell tower). Rome was built in layers—almost everywhere you go, there's an earlier version beneath your feet. (The hop-on, hop-off Trambus Open 110 stops just across the busy intersection from here.)

Continuing on, you reach two staircases leading up Capitol Hill. One is Michelangelo's grand staircase up to the Campidoglio. The longer of the two leads to the Santa Maria in Aracoeli church, a good example of the earliest style of Christian churches (described above). The contrast between this climb-on-your-knees ramp to God's house and Michelangelo's elegant stairs illustrates the changes Renaissance humanism brought civilization.

From the bottom of Michelangelo's stairs, look right several blocks down the street to see a condominium actually built upon the surviving ancient pillars and arches of Teatro Marcello.

Victor Emmanuel Monument—This oversize monument to Italy's first king, built to celebrate the 50th anniversary of the country's uni-

fication in 1870, was part of Italy's push to overcome the new country's strong regionalism and to create a national identity. The scale of the monument is over-the-top. The 43-foot-long statue of the king on the horse is the biggest equestrian statue in the world. The king's moustache is over five feet wide, and a person could fit into the horse's hoof. Open to the public, the structure offers a grand view of the Eternal City.

Locals love to hate the "Altar of the Nation." Romans think of the 200-foot-high, 500-foot-wide monument not as an altar of the fatherland, but as "the wedding cake," "the typewriter," or "the dentures." It wouldn't be so bad if it weren't sitting on a priceless acre of ancient Rome and if they had chosen better marble (this is in-your-face white and picks up the pollution horribly). Soldiers guard Italy's Tomb of the Unknown Soldier as the eternal flame flickers.

The monument is filled with symbolism connecting the modern city and nation with its grand ancient past. The Tomb of the Unknown Soldier (flanked by Italian flags and armed guards) is overlooked by the goddess Roma (with the gold mosaic background). The eternal flames are reminiscent of the Vestal Virgins and the ancient flame of Rome. And it's crowned by glorious chariots like those that topped the ancient Arch of Constantine (free, 242 punishing steps to the top—unless you take the shortcut from Capitol Hill described on page 43).

The Victor Emmanuel Monument also houses a little-visited **Museum of the Risorgimento,** which explains the movement and war that led to the unification of Italy in 1870 (free, daily 9:30–18:00, café).

▲Rome from the Sky—This elevator, located near the top of the Victor Emmanuel Monument next to the outdoor café, zips you to the rooftop for the grandest, 360-degree view of the center of Rome (even better than from the top of St. Peter's dome). Helpful panoramic diagrams describe the skyline, with powerful binoculars available for zooming in on particular sights. Go in late afternoon, when it's beginning to cool off and Rome glows (€7; May–Sept Mon–Thu 9:30–19:30, Fri–Sat 9:30–23:30, Sun 9:30–20:30; Oct–April Mon–Thu 9:30–18:30, Fri–Sun

9:30–19:30; follow signs inside the Victor Emmanuel Monument to *ascensori panoramici* or take the shortcut from Capitol Hill).

PANTHEON NEIGHBORHOOD: THE HEART OF ROME

I like to call the area around the Pantheon the "Heart of Rome." This neighborhood stretches eastward from the Tiber River through Campo de' Fiori and Piazza Navona, past the Pantheon to the Trevi Fountain. Besides the neighborhood's ancient sights and historic churches, it's also the place that gives Rome its urban-village feel. Wander narrow streets, sample the many shops and eateries, and gather with the locals in squares marked by a bubbling fountain. Exploring is especially good in the evening, when the restaurants bustle and streets are jammed with foot-traffic. For more on nocturnal sightseeing, ✪ see the Night Walk Across Rome on page 78.

▲▲▲**Pantheon**—For the greatest look at the splendor of Rome, antiquity's best-preserved interior is a must. Built two millennia ago, this influential domed temple served as the model for Michelangelo's dome of St. Peter's and many others (free, Mon–Sat 8:30–19:30, Sun 9:00–18:00, holidays 9:00–13:00, closed for Mass Sat at 17:00 and Sun at 10:30, tel. 06-6830-0230).

✪ See Pantheon Tour on page 139.

▲▲**Churches near the Pantheon**—For more information on the following churches, see page 144. Modest dress is recommended at all churches.

The **Church of San Luigi dei Francesi** has a magnificent chapel painted by Caravaggio (free, Fri–Wed 7:30–12:30 & 15:30–19:00, Thu 8:00–12:30, sightseers should avoid Mass at 7:30 and 19:00). The only Gothic church in Rome is **Santa Maria sopra Minerva,** with a little-known Michelangelo statue, *Christ Bearing the Cross* (free, Mon–Sat 7:00–19:00, Sun 8:00–19:00, on a little square behind Pantheon, to the east). The **Church of San Ignazio,** several blocks east of the Pantheon, is a riot of Baroque illusions with a false dome (free, daily

Pantheon Neighborhood

TO PIAZZA
DEL POPOLO

TO
SPANISH
STEPS

TO M
BARB.

PONTE
UMBERTO

TIBER

PIAZZA
COLONNA

LUNGOTEVERE MARZIO

VIA

TRITONE

SAN LUIGI
(CARAVAGGIO)

PARL.

VIA

TREVI

ANCIENT
STADIUM
ENTRANCE

UFF. VICARIO

SABINA

CORONARI

COPPELLE

MURATTE

AQUIRO

PIAZZA DI
PIETRA

DATAR.

TRE
SCALINI

SALV.

GIUST.

PIAZZA
ROTUNDA

V. PASTINI

PIAZZA
NAVONA

SEMINARIO

SAN
IGNAZIO

PIAZZA
PASQUINO

CITY
MUSEUM

PANTHEON

STA. MARIA
SOPRA
MINERVA

GALLERIA
DORA
PAMPHILJ

IV NOV.

VIA

VITTORIO

ARG.

CESTARI

CAMPO
DE'
FIORI

E MANUELE

GESÙ

PIAZZA
VENEZIA

FORI IMP.

V. GIUBBO

VIA BOTT. OSC.

ARACOELI

VICTOR
EM. MON.

TO
COLOSSEUM

PALAZZO
FARNESE

LARGO
ARGENTINA RUINS
(+ CAT HOSPICE)

CAPITOL
HILL
& CAP.
MUSEUMS

M

LUNGOTEVERE

PONTE
SISTO

TO
TRASTEVERE

→ ENTRY POINT
TO SIGHTS

Ⓣ TAXI STAND

Ⓜ METRO STATION

Ⓑ BUS STOP

FORUM

200 YARDS

200 METERS

DCH

7:30–12:30 & 15:00–19:15). A few blocks away, across Corso Vittorio Emanuele, is the rich and Baroque **Gesù Church,** headquarters of the Jesuits in Rome (free, daily 6:30–12:45 & 16:00–19:15).

Walk out the Gesù Church and two blocks down Corso Vittorio Emmanuele to the Sacred Area (Largo Argentina), an excavated square facing the boulevard, about four blocks south of the Pantheon. Stroll around this square and look into the excavated pit at some of the oldest ruins in Rome. Julius Caesar was assassinated near here. The far (west) side of the square is a refuge for cats—volunteers care for some 250 of them.

▲**Galleria Doria Pamphilj**—This underappreciated gallery, tucked away in the heart of the old city, fills a palace on Piazza del Collegio Romano. It offers a rare chance to wander through a noble family's lavish rooms with the prince who calls this downtown mansion home. Well, almost. Through an audioguide, the prince lovingly narrates his family's story, including how the Doria Pamphilj (pahm-FEEL-yee) family's cozy relationship with the pope inspired the word "nepotism." Highlights include paintings by Caravaggio, Titian, and Raphael, and portraits of Pope Innocent X by Diego Velázquez (on canvas) and Gian Lorenzo Bernini (in marble). The fancy rooms of the palace are interesting, with a mini-Versailles-like hall of mirrors and paintings lining the walls to the ceiling in the style typical of 18th-century galleries (€8, includes worthwhile audioguide, Fri–Wed 10:00–17:00, closed Thu, from Piazza Venezia walk 2 blocks up Via del Corso and take a left, Piazza del Collegio Romano 2, tel. 06-679-7323, www .doriapamphilj.it).

Piazza di Pietra (Piazza of Stone)—This square was actually a quarry set up to chew away at the abandoned Roman building. You can still see the holes that hungry medieval scavengers chipped into the columns to steal the metal pins that held the slabs together (two blocks toward Via del Corso from Pantheon).

▲Trevi Fountain—This bubbly Baroque fountain, worth ▲▲ by night, is a minor sight to art scholars...but a major nighttime gathering spot for teens on the make and tourists tossing coins. The coins tourists deposit daily are collected to feed Rome's poor.

⚪ See Night Walk Across Rome on page 78.

NEAR TERMINI TRAIN STATION

These sights are within a 10-minute walk of the train station. By Metro, use the Termini stop for the National Museum and the Piazza Repubblica stop for the rest.

▲▲▲National Museum of Rome (Museo Nazionale Romano Palazzo Massimo alle Terme)—The National Museum's main branch, at Palazzo Massimo, houses the greatest collection of ancient Roman art anywhere, including busts of emperors and a Roman copy of the Greek *Discus Thrower* (€10 combo-ticket covers nearby Museum of the Bath and more—see page 167 for details, audioguide-€4.50, Tue–Sun 9:00–19:45, closed Mon, last entry 45 min before closing, Metro: Termini, tel. 06-3996-7700). The museum is about 100 yards from the Termini train station—as you leave the station, it's the sandstone-brick building on your left. Enter at the far end, at Largo di Villa Peretti.

⚪ See National Museum of Rome Tour on page 167.

▲Baths of Diocletian (Terme di Diocleziano)—Around A.D. 300, Emperor Diocletian built the largest baths in Rome. This sprawling meeting place—with baths and schmoozing spaces to accommodate 3,000 bathers at a time—was a big deal in ancient times. While much of it is still closed, three sections are open: the Church of Santa Maria degli Angeli, once the great central hall of the baths (free, Mon–Sat 7:00–18:30, Sun 7:00–19:30, closed to sightseers during Mass, faces Piazza Repubblica); the Octagonal Hall, once a gymna-

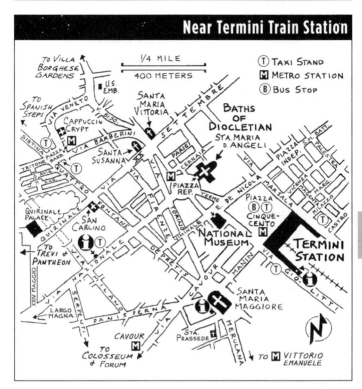

Near Termini Train Station

TO VILLA BORGHESE GARDENS

¼ MILE

400 METERS

Ⓣ TAXI STAND
Ⓜ METRO STATION
Ⓑ BUS STOP

U.S. EMB.

TO SPANISH STEPS

SANTA MARIA VITTORIA

BATHS OF DIOCLETIAN

VIA VENETO

CAPPUCCIN CRYPT

VIA BARBERINI

SANTA SUSANNA

STA. MARIA D. ANGELI

SETTEMBRE

PARIGI

CERNAIA

PIAZZA INDEP.

SM. BATT.

SISTINA

TRITONE PIAZZA BARB.

VIA AVIG.

QUATTRO

VIA

VIA

PIAZZA REP.

TERME DE NICOLA

E. DE NICOLA

PIAZZA CINQUE-CENTO

VIA MARSALA

VICENZA

VOLTURNO

MARG.

PIAZZO

CASTRO

QUIRINALE PALACE

SAN CARLINO

FONTANE

QUIRINALE

VIA

NAZIONALE

TORINO

VIMINALE

NATIONAL MUSEUM

VIA

TERMINI STATION

TO TREVI & PANTHEON

XXIV MAGGIO

SERPE

MILANO

DEPRETIS

VR

MANIN

VIA G.D. CITTI

SANTA MARIA MAGGIORE

LARGO MAGNA

PANISPERNA

SERPE

STA. PRASSEDE

MERULANA

CAVOUR

TO COLOSSEUM & FORUM

TO Ⓜ VITTORIO EMANUELE

Ⓝ

sium, now a gallery of Roman bronze and marble statues (free, open sporadically Sun 9:00–13:00 only, faces Piazza Repubblica); and the skippable Museum of the Bath, which displays ancient Roman inscriptions on tons of tombs and tablets—but, despite its name, has nothing on the baths themselves (€10 combo-ticket covers National Museum of Rome and more—see page 167 for details, Tue–Sun 9:00–19:45, closed Mon, last entry 45 min before closing, audioguide-€4, Viale E. de Nicola 79, entrance faces Termini train station, tel. 06-4782-6152).

✪ See Baths of Diocletian Tour on page 153.

▲**Santa Maria della Vittoria**—This church houses Bernini's statue, the swooning *St. Teresa in Ecstasy* (free, Mon–Sat 8:30–12:00 & 15:30–18:00, closed Sun, about 5 blocks northwest of Termini train station on Largo Susanna, Metro: Repubblica).

Once inside the church, you'll find St. Teresa to the left of the altar. Teresa has just been stabbed with God's arrow of fire. Now, the angel pulls it out and watches her reaction. Teresa swoons, her eyes roll up, her hand goes limp, she parts her lips...and moans. The smiling, cherubic angel understands just how she feels. Teresa, a 16th-century Spanish nun, later talked of the "sweetness" of "this intense pain," describing her oneness with God in ecstatic, even erotic, terms.

Soccer: The National Obsession

One of Rome's most local "sights" is a soccer match. Winston Churchill said that Italians lose wars like soccer matches and soccer matches like wars; soccer, or *calcio,* is the national obsession.

Everyone, regardless of age or social class, is an expert, quick with an opinion on a coach's lousy decision or a referee's unprofessional conduct. Fans love to insult officials: a favorite is *"arbitro cornuto!"*—the referee is a cuckold (i.e., his wife sleeps around). The country's obsession turned into jubilation on July 9, 2006, when Italy won the World Cup, and Rome— along with every other city, town, and village in Italy—went crazy with joy.

Rome has a special passion for soccer. It has two teams, Roma (representing the city) and Lazio (the region), and the rivalry is fanatic. When Romans are introduced, they ask each other, *"Laziale o romanista?"* The answer can compromise a relationship. Both Roma (jersey: yellow and red; symbol: she-wolf) and Lazio (jersey: light blue and white; symbol: imperial eagle) claim to be truly Roman. Lazio is older (founded in 1900), but Roma has more supporters. Lazio is supposed to be more upper-class, Roma more popular, but the social division is blurred. When Lazio was implicated in the match-fixing scandal that swept through Italy's professional soccer league in the summer

Bernini, the master of multimedia, pulls out all the stops to make this mystical vision real. Actual sunlight pours through the alabaster windows, bronze sunbeams shine on a marble angel holding a golden arrow. Teresa leans back on a cloud and her robe ripples from within, charged with her spiritual arousal. Bernini has created a little stage-setting of heaven. And watching from the "theater boxes" on either side are members of the family that commissioned the work.

Santa Susanna Church—The home of the American Catholic Church in Rome, Santa Susanna holds Mass in English daily at 18:00 and on Sunday at 9:00 and 10:30. They arrange papal audiences (see of 2006, Roma fans watched gleefully (Lazio escaped with a slap on the wrist).

The most eagerly awaited sporting event of the year is the derby, when the two teams fight it out at the Olympic Stadium. All of Italy acknowledges that team spirit is most fervent in Rome. Fans prepare months in advance, and on the day of the match they fill the entire stadium with team colors, flags, banners, and smoke candles.

Witty slogans on banners work like dialogues: A Roma ban-

ner proclaimed, "Roma: Only the sky is higher than you." The Lazio banner replied, "In fact, the sky is blue and white" (like its team colors). The exchange revealed that there had been a Lazio informer on the Roma side, which traumatized Roma fans for weeks. Tourists go to a match more for the action in the stands than the action on the field—it's one of the most Roman of all experiences.

Both teams call the Stadio Olimpico home, so you can catch a game most weekends from September to May (Metro line A to Flaminio, then catch tram #2 to the end of the line, Piazza Mancini, and cross the bridge to the stadium). If you're coming from the Termini train station, take bus #910; from the Vatican, take bus #32 from Piazza Risorgimento.

page 234), and their excellent website contains tips for travelers and a long list of convents that rent out rooms (Mon–Fri 9:00–12:00 & 16:00–18:00, closed Sat–Sun, Via XX Settembre 15, near recommended Via Firenze hotels, Metro: Repubblica, tel. 06-4201-4554, www.santa susanna.org).

PILGRIM'S ROME

East of the Colosseum (and south of Termini train station) are several venerable churches that Catholic pilgrims make a point of visiting. For more on the following sights, ✪ see the self-guided Pilgrim's Rome Tour on page 258.

Church of San Giovanni in Laterano—Built by Constantine, the first Christian emperor, this was Rome's most important church through medieval times. A building alongside the church houses the Holy Stairs said to have been walked up by Jesus, which today are

Pilgrim's Rome

ascended by pilgrims on their knees (free, church—daily 7:00–18:30, Holy Stairs—April–Sept 6:30–12:00 & 15:30–18:30, Oct–March 6:30–12:00 & 15:00–18:00, Piazza San Giovanni in Laterano, Metro: San Giovanni, or bus #85 or #87, tel. 06-6988-6392).

Church of Santa Maria Maggiore—Some of Rome's best-surviving mosaics line the nave of this church built as Rome was falling. The nearby Church of Santa Prassede has still more early mosaics (free, daily 8:00–18:30, Piazza Santa Maria Maggiore, Metro: Termini or Vittorio Emanuele, tel. 06-48-3058).

▲**Church of San Clemente**—Besides the church itself, with frescoes by Masolino, you can also descend into the ruins of an earlier church. Descend yet one more level and enter the eerie remains of a pagan temple to Mithras (upper church—free, lower church—€5, both open Mon–Sat 9:00–12:30 & 15:00–18:00, Sun 12:00–18:00, Via di San Giovanni in Laterano, Metro: Colosseo, or bus #85 or #87, tel. 06-7045-1018).

NORTH ROME

Borghese Gardens and Via Veneto

▲**Villa Borghese Gardens**—Rome's scruffy, three-square-mile "Central Park" is great for its shade and people-watching (plenty of modern-day Romeos and Juliets). The best entrance is at the head of Via Veneto (Metro: Barberini and 10-minute walk up Via Veneto). There you'll find a cluster of buildings with a café, a kiddie arcade, and bike rental (€6/4 hrs). Rent a bike and follow signs to discover the park's cafés, fountains, statues, museums (including the Borghese Gallery and Etruscan Museum—listed below), lake, and prime picnic spots. A park TI near the Borghese Gallery has info on the park and Rome sights (TI hours: April–Sept Mon–Thu 9:00–17:00, Fri–Sun 9:00–19:00; Oct–March daily 9:00–17:00; facing Borghese Gallery, turn left, walk 30 yards down, turn right toward the gate and find the poorly marked TI immediately on the left). For information on getting to the park, ✪ see the Borghese Gallery Tour on page 190.

▲▲▲**Borghese Gallery (Galleria Borghese)**—This plush museum, filling a cardinal's mansion in the park, was recently restored and offers one of Europe's most sumptuous art experiences. You'll enjoy a collection of world-class Baroque sculpture, including Bernini's *David* and his excited statue of Apollo chasing Daphne, as well as paintings by Caravaggio, Raphael, Titian, and Rubens. The museum's slick, mandatory reservation system keeps crowds to a manageable size.

Cost, Hours, Reservations: €8.50, €12.50 during special exhibits, prices include €2 reservation fee, credit cards accepted, Tue–Sun 9:00–19:00, closed Mon. No photos allowed. Reservations are mandatory and easy to get in English online (www.ticketeria.it) or by calling 06-32810 (if you get an Italian recording, press 2 for English; office hours Mon–Fri 9:00–18:00, Sat 9:00–13:00, office closed Sat in Aug and Sun year-round). Reserve a minimum of several days in advance for a weekday visit, at least a week ahead for weekends. For more on reservations, as well as a self-guided tour, ✪ see the Borghese Gallery Tour on page 190.

Etruscan Museum (Villa Giulia Museo Nazionale Etrusco)—

The fascinating Etruscan civilization thrived in this part of Italy around 600 B.C., when Rome was an Etruscan town. The Villa Giulia (a fine Renaissance palace) hosts a museum that tells the story. While I prefer the Vatican Museum's Etruscan section for a first look at this civilization, aficionados of all things Etruscan come here for the famous "husband and wife sarcophagus" (a dead couple seeming to enjoy an everlasting banquet from atop their tomb—sixth century B.C. from Cerveteri); the *Apollo from Veii* statue (of textbook fame); and an impressive room filled with gold sheets of Etruscan printing and temple statuary from the Sanctuary of Pyrgi (€4, Tue–Sun 9:00–19:30, closed Mon, closes earlier off-season, last entry one hour before closing, Piazzale di Villa Giulia 9, tel. 06-322-6571).

Via Veneto—In the 1960s, movie stars from around the world paraded down curvy Via Veneto, one of Rome's glitziest nightspots. Today it's still lined with the city's poshest hotels and the American Embassy, but any hint of local color has faded to bland.

▲**Cappuccin Crypt**—If you want to see artistically arranged bones, this is the place. The crypt is below the church of Santa Maria della Immacolata Concezione on  Via Veneto, just up from Piazza Barberini. The bones of more than 4,000 monks who died between 1528 and 1870 are in the basement, all lined up for the delight—or disgust—of the always-wide-eyed visitor. The soil in the crypt was brought from Jerusalem 400 years ago, and the monastic message on the wall explains that this is more than just a macabre exercise: "We were what you are...you will become what we are now. Buon giorno." Pick up a few of Rome's most interesting postcards (donation requested, daily 9:00–12:00 & 15:00–18:00, Metro: Barberini, tel. 06-487-1185). Just up the street, you'll find the American Embassy, Federal Express, Hard Rock Café, and fancy Via Veneto cafés filled with the poor and envious looking for the rich and famous.

Piazza del Popolo—This vast, oval square marks the traditional north entrance to Rome (its oval shape dates from the early 19th cen-  tury). Today the square, known for its symmetrical design and its art-filled churches, is the starting point for the city's evening *passeggiata* (see "Dolce Vita Stroll" on page 320). Since ancient times, visitors arriving along the main highway from Northern Europe have entered Rome at this point. In 1480, Pope Sixtus IV recognized that the ramshackle medieval city was making a miserable first impression on pilgrims who

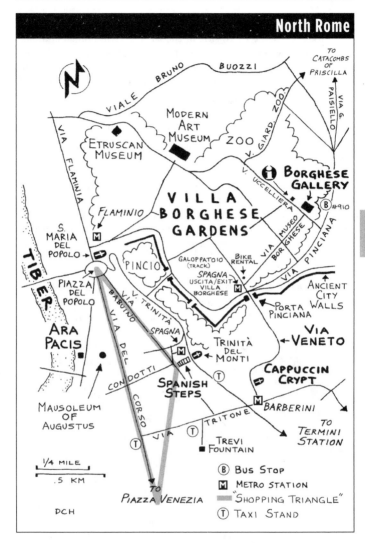

North Rome

TO CATACOMBS OF PRISCILLA

VIA G. PAISIELLO

BRUNO BUOZZI

VIALE

V. GIARD. ZOO

MODERN ART MUSEUM

ZOO

ETRUSCAN MUSEUM

V. UCCELLIERA

BORGHESE GALLERY

VIA FLAMINIA

FLAMINIO

V I L L A BORGHESE GARDENS

VIA MUSEO BORGHESE

B #910

SIGHTS

S. MARIA DEL POPOLO →

M

TIBER

PIAZZA DEL POPOLO

PINCIO

GALOPPATOIO (TRACK)

BIKE RENTAL

SPAGNA USCITA/EXIT VILLA BORGHESE

M

VIA PINCIANA

ANCIENT CITY WALLS

PORTA PINCIANA

VIA ← VENETO

ARA PACIS

VIA DEL BABUINO

V. TRINITÀ

SPAGNA

VIA TRINITÀ

TRINITÀ DEL MONTI

M

CAPPUCCIN CRYPT

CONDOTTI

CORSO

SPANISH STEPS

T

T

M

BARBERINI

MAUSOLEUM OF AUGUSTUS

VIA

TRITONE

T

TO TERMINI STATION

T

TREVI FOUNTAIN

1/4 MILE

.5 KM

DCH

TO PIAZZA VENEZIA

B BUS STOP

M METRO STATION

"SHOPPING TRIANGLE"

T TAXI STAND

walked here from all over Europe (similar to the Muslim pilgrimage to Mecca). He authorized city planners to appropriate property (establishing "eminent domain"), demolish old buildings, and create straight streets to accommodate traffic. This was the first of several papal campaigns to spruce up the square and make it a suitable entrance for the grand city.

From the Flaminio Metro stop, pass through the third-century Aurelian Wall via the Porta del Popolo gate, and look south. The 10-story obelisk in the center of the square once graced the temple of Ramses II in Egypt and the Roman Circus Maximus race track.

The obelisk was brought here in 1589 as one of the square's beautifica-
tion projects. At the south side of the square, twin domed churches
mark the spot where three main boulevards exit the square and form a
trident. The central boulevard (running between the churches) is Via
del Corso, which since ancient times has been the main north–south
drag through town, running to Capitol Hill (the governing center)
and the Forum. Along the north side of the square (flanking the Porta
del Popolo) are two more buildings, which give the square a pleasant
symmetry: the Carabinieri station and the church of Santa Maria del
Popolo.

From the square, the *Tridente* of roads takes people south to the
city center (along Via del Corso), to the Spanish Steps (via Babuino),
and to the Tiber River (via Ripetta). Two large fountains grace the
sides of the square—Neptune to the west and Roma to the east
(marking the base of Pincio Hill). Though the name Piazza del Popolo
means "Square of the People" (and it is a popular hangout), the word
was probably derived from the Latin *populus,* after the poplar trees
along the square's northeast side.

Santa Maria del Popolo—One of Rome's most overlooked
churches, this features two chapels with top-notch art and a facade

built of travertine scavenged
from the Colosseum. The
church is brought to you by
the Rovere family, which produced two popes, and you'll
see their symbol—the oak
tree and acorns—throughout
(free, Mon–Sat 7:00–12:00 &
16:00–19:00, Sun 8:00–13:30
& 16:30–19:30; on north side
of Piazza del Popolo; as you face gate in old wall from the square,
church entrance is to your right).

Go inside. The Chigi Chapel (second on the left) was designed
by Raphael and inspired (as Raphael was) by the Pantheon. Notice the
Pantheon-like dome, pilasters, and capitals. Above in the oculus, God
looks in, aided by angels who power the eight known planets. Raphael
built the chapel for his wealthy banker friend, Agostino Chigi, buried
in the pyramid-shaped tomb in the wall to the right of the altar. Later,
Chigi's great-grandson hired Bernini to make two of the four statues, and Bernini delivered a theatrical episode. In one corner, Daniel
straddles a lion and raises his praying hands to God for help. Kitty-
corner across the chapel, an angel grabs Habbakuk's hair and tells him
to go take some food to poor Daniel.

In the Cerasi Chapel (left of altar), Caravaggio's *The Conversion
on the Way to Damascus* shows Paul sprawled on his back beside his
horse while his servant looks on. The startled future saint is blinded

by the harsh light as Jesus' voice asks him, "Why do you persecute me?" In the style of the Counter-Reformation, Paul receives his new faith with open arms.

In the same chapel, Caravaggio's *Crucifixion of St. Peter* is shown as a banal chore; the workers toil like faceless animals. The light and dark are in high contrast. Caravaggio liked to say, "Where light falls, I will paint it."

Spanish Steps Area

▲**Spanish Steps**—The wide, curving staircase, culminating with an obelisk between two Baroque church towers, makes for one of Rome's iconic sights. Beyond that, it's a people-gathering place. By day, the area hosts shoppers looking for high-end fashions; on warm evenings, it attracts young people in love with the city. For more, ✪ see the Night Walk Across Rome on page 78.

"Shopping Triangle"—The triangular-shaped area between the Spanish Steps, Piazza Venezia, and Piazza del Popolo (along Via del Corso) contains Rome's highest concentration of upscale boutiques and fashion stores (see triangle at bottom of map on page 57).

▲▲**Ara Pacis (Altar of Peace)**—On January 30, 9 B.C., soon-to-be-emperor Augustus led a procession of priests up the steps and

into this newly built "Altar of Peace." They sacrificed an animal on the altar and poured an offering of wine, thanking the gods for helping Augustus pacify barbarians abroad and rivals at home. This marked the dawn of the Pax Romana (c. A.D. 1–200), a Golden Age of good living, stability, dominance, and peace (pax). The Ara Pacis (AH-rah PAH-chees) hosted annual sacrifices by the emperor until the area was flooded by the River Tiber. Buried under silt, it was abandoned and forgotten until the 16th century, when various parts were discovered and excavated. Mussolini gathered the altar's scattered parts and reconstructed them here in 1938. In 2006, the Altar of Peace reopened to the public in a striking modern building. As the first new building allowed to be built in the old center since 1938, it was controversial, but its quiet, air-conditioned interior may signal the dawn of another new age in Rome.

Cost, Hours, Location: €6.50, tightwads can look in through huge windows for free; Tue–Sun 9:00–19:00, closed Mon, last entry one hour before closing; audioguide (€3.50) also available as free podcast on the Web at www.arapacis.it, good WC downstairs. The Ara Pacis is a long block west of Via del Corso on Via di Ara Pacis, on the east bank of the Tiber near Ponte Cavour, Metro: Spagna; a 10-minute walk down Via dei Condotti. Tel. 06-32-111-1605.

⊃ Self-Guided Tour: Start with the model in the museum's lobby. The Altar of Peace was originally located east of here, along today's Via del Corso. The model shows where it stood in relation to the Mausoleum of Augustus (now next door) and the Pantheon. (The Ara Pacis originally faced west; now it faces east. The compass directions given below match the altar's current orientation, but be aware that some art history books and even the Ara Pacis website may describe it using the original—and opposite—orientation.)

SIGHTS

Entrance (East) Side: Approach the Ara Pacis and look through the doorway to see the raised altar. This simple structure has just the basics of a Roman temple: an altar for sacrifices surrounded by cubicle-like walls that enclose a consecrated space. Its well-preserved reliefs celebrate Rome's success. After a sacrifice, the altar was washed, and the blood flowed out drain holes still visible at the base of the walls. Flanking the doorway are (badly damaged) reliefs of Rome's legendary founders—Romulus and Remus—being suckled by the she-wolf (left), and bearded Aeneas (right), who's pouring a wine offering and preparing to sacrifice a sow.

North Side: This relief probably depicts the parade of dignitaries who consecrated the altar. Near the head is Augustus (his body sliced in two vertically by missing stone), honored with a crown of laurel leaves, having just conquered Spain and Gaul. Augustus is followed by a half-dozen bigwigs and priests (with spiked hats) and the man shouldering the sacrificial axe. Next comes Agrippa (wearing the hood of a priest), Augustus' right-hand man in battles against Mark Antony and Cleopatra. Agrippa married Augustus' daughter, Julia—their little son, Gaius, tugs on his dad's toga while turning to look at Livia, Augustus' wife. When Agrippa died, Gaius was adopted and named as successor by Augustus. Gaius also died young, making the next in line Tiberius, Livia's son by a first marriage, shown standing next to his mother. Confused? Find these names and other descendants of Julius Caesar on the genealogical chart in the museum lobby.

Before proceeding farther around the altar, look out the window to see the overgrown Mausoleum of Augustus and his family, once capped with a dome of earth, elegant spruces, and statues of the emperor. To the left is an example of Mussolini's fascist architecture—intended to remind Italians of their imperial Roman roots. Note the travertine, brick, low-relief propaganda, stony inscriptions, Roman numerals, and cold rationality. (Locals don't like it.) This area was the Field of Mars, Rome's only neighborhood continuously inhabited since ancient times.

West Side: The altar's back door is flanked with reliefs celebrating the two things Augustus brought to Rome: peace (goddess Roma as a conquering Amazon, right side) and prosperity (fertility goddess surrounded by children, plants, and animals). For a closer look at details from the various reliefs, see the model downstairs.

South Side: Leading the parade of senators is a *lictor*—a ceremonial bodyguard—carrying the *fasces*. This bundle of sticks symbolized how unity brings strength, and it gave us the modern word "fascism." The reliefs feature the first official portrayal of women and children in a public monument.

Beneath the parade, notice the elaborate floral relief that runs all the way around the Ara Pacis. Acanthus tendrils spiral out forming decorative garlands, intertwining with ivy, laurel, and more. Swans with outstretched wings hide among the patterns. Some 50 plants are blooming in this display of abundance. Imagine the altar as it once was, standing in an open field, painted in bright colors—a mingling of myth, man, and nature.

Catacombs of Priscilla (Catacombe di Priscilla)—For the most intimate catacombs experience—and a chance to see beyond the core of the historic center—many prefer this smaller, lesser-known option (operated by nuns) to the crowded catacombs on the Appian Way (San Sebastiano and San Callisto, described on pages 76 and 77). The Catacombs of Priscilla, once situated under the house of a Roman noble family, were used for some of the most important burials during antiquity. Best of all, because they're on the opposite side of town from the most popular catacombs, you'll have them mostly to yourself. The catacombs' evocative chambers supposedly show the first depiction of Mary nursing the baby Jesus (€6, Tue–Sun 8:30–12:00 & 14:30–17:00, last entry 30 min before closing, closed Mon, northeast of Termini station at Via Salaria 430, closed one random month a year—check website or call first, tel. 06-862-06272, http://web.tiscali.it/catacombe_priscilla). For more on catacombs, ✪ see the Ancient Appian Way Tour on page 158.

To get from the Termini train station to the Catacombs of Priscilla, take bus #92 or #310 from the north side of Piazza Cinquecento (6/hr, 15 min, tell the bus driver "kah-tah-KOHM-bay" and he'll tell you when to get off). From Piazza Venezia, take bus #63 or #630 from the stop on Via S. Veneziano (6/hr, 25 min; cross ahead at the crosswalk, backtrack up the hill, look for catacombs signs in the piazza, and after crossing the piazza, it's the first building on your left—easy to miss).

Make an excursion out of it—buy picnic supplies in advance, and after leaving the catacombs, turn left, and 50 yards down on the right is the entrance to the immense Villa Ada park. Or grab a quick, cheap, quality lunch at **Il Siciliano,** located near the catacombs. The Motta brothers make fresh Sicilian pasta dishes for lunch, as well as heavenly *arancini*—fried rice balls with cheese and ragu. Eat in their typical bar atmosphere or take it to go to the park (€4–5, daily 6:40–24:00, lunch 12:00–15:30, walk away from the Villa Ada park walls and go downhill 40 yards to Piazza Acilia 5, tel. 06-8632-3191).

VATICAN CITY

Vatican City, a tiny independent country, contains the Vatican Museum (with Michelangelo's Sistine Chapel) and St. Peter's Basilica (with Michelangelo's exquisite *Pietà*). A helpful **TI** is just to the left of St. Peter's Basilica as you're facing it (Mon–Sat 8:30–19:00, closed Sun, tel. 06-6988-1662, Vatican switchboard tel. 06-6982, www .vatican.va). The entrances to St. Peter's and to the Vatican Museum are a 15-minute walk apart (follow the outside of the Vatican wall, which links the two sights). The nearest Metro stops still involve a 10-minute walk to either sight: for St. Peter's, the closest stop is Ottaviano; for the Vatican Museum, it's Cipro. For information on Vatican tours, post offices, and the pope's schedule, see page 234.

▲▲▲**Vatican Museum (Musei Vaticani)**—The four miles of displays in this immense museum—from ancient statues to Christian frescoes to modern paintings—culminate in the Raphael Rooms and Michelangelo's glorious Sistine Chapel. Modest dress is required.

Cost and Hours: €14, Mon–Sat 8:30–17:30, last entry at 16:00 (the official closing time is 18:00, but the staff starts ushering you out at 17:30), closed on religious holidays and Sun except last Sun of the month (when it's free, more crowded, and open 8:30–14:00, last entry 12:30). Hours are notoriously subject to constant change and frequent holidays; check www.vatican.va for current times. Lines are extremely long, with no guarantee of entry—for information on strategies to avoid the wait, ✪ see the Vatican Museum Tour, page 202.

▲▲▲**St. Peter's Basilica (Basilica San Pietro)**—There is no doubt: This is the richest and grandest church on earth. To call it vast is like calling Einstein smart. The church strictly enforces its dress code. Dress modestly—a not-too-short dress or long pants, with shoulders covered (men, women, and children).

Hours: Daily April–Sept 7:00–19:00, Oct–March 7:00–18:00. The church often closes on Wednesday mornings during papal audiences. Masses occur throughout the day (see schedule on page 233); my favorite Mass—with compelling music—is in the late afternoon, when the church is less crowded (daily at 17:00). The view from the dome is worth the climb (€7 for elevator to roof, plus €5 to climb 323 steps to the very top, allow an hour to go up and down; daily April–Sept 8:00–17:45, Oct–March 8:00–16:45, www.saintpetersbasilica.org). Free 90-minute tours in English are offered weekdays; confirm schedule and meet at the TI next to the post office outside the basilica's entrance (tel. 06-6988-1662). The best time to visit the church is early or late.

✪ See St. Peter's Basilica Tour on page 233.

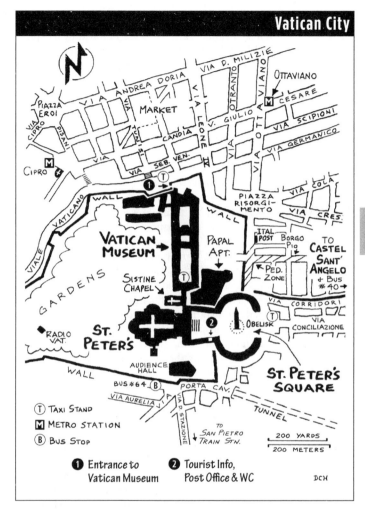

Vatican City

PIAZZA EROI

MARKET

VIA D. MILIZIE

OTTAVIANO

CESARE

VIA ANDREA DORIA

VIA CIPRO

VIA LEONE

VIA G. GIULIO

VIA OTRANTO

VIA OTTAVIANO

VIA SCIPIONI

VIA GERMANICO

CIPRO

CANDIA

VIA SEB. VEN.

T

VIA VATICANO

WALL

WALL

PIAZZA RISORGI-MENTO

VIA COLA

VIA CRES.

VATICAN MUSEUM

PAPAL APT.

ITAL. POST

Borgo Pio

TO CASTEL SANT' ANGELO

+ Bus #40 →

VIALE

GARDENS

SISTINE CHAPEL

T

PED. ZONE

VIA CORRIDORI

VIA CONCILIAZIONE

T

RADIO VAT.

ST. PETER'S

2

OBELISK

AUDIENCE HALL

ST. PETER'S SQUARE

WALL

BUS #64 B

PORTA CAV.

VIA AURELIA

VIA D. STAZIONE

TUNNEL

TO SAN PIETRO TRAIN STN.

200 YARDS

200 METERS

T TAXI STAND

M METRO STATION

B BUS STOP

1 Entrance to Vatican Museum

2 Tourist Info, Post Office & WC

DCH

SIGHTS

▲**Castel Sant'Angelo**—Built as a tomb for the emperor, used through the Middle Ages as a castle, prison, and place of last ref-

uge for popes under attack, and today a museum, this giant pile of ancient bricks is packed with history.

Ancient Rome allowed no tombs within its walls—not even the emperor's. So Emperor Hadrian grabbed the most commanding position just outside the walls and across the river and built a towering tomb (c. A.D. 139) well within view of the city. His mausoleum was a huge cylinder (210 by 70 feet) topped by a cypress grove and crowned by a huge statue of Hadrian himself riding a chariot. For nearly a hundred years, Roman emperors (from Hadrian to Caracalla, in A.D. 217) were buried here.

In the year 590, the Archangel Michael appeared above the mausoleum to Pope Gregory the Great. Sheathing his sword, the angel signaled the end of a plague. The fortress that was Hadrian's mausoleum eventually became a fortified palace, renamed for the "holy angel."

Castel Sant'Angelo spent centuries of the Dark Ages as a fortress and prison, but was eventually connected to the Vatican via an elevated corridor at the pope's request (1277). Since Rome was repeatedly plundered by invaders, Castel Sant'Angelo was a handy place of last refuge for threatened popes. In anticipation of long sieges, rooms were decorated with papal splendor (you'll see paintings by Carlo Crivelli, Luca Signorelli, and Andrea Mantegna). In 1527, during a sack of Rome by troops of Charles V of Spain, the pope lived inside the castle for months with his entourage of hundreds (an unimaginable ordeal, considering the food service at the top-floor bar).

Touring the place is a stair-stepping workout. After you walk around the entire base of the castle, take the small staircase down to the original Roman floor (following the route of Hadrian's funeral procession). In the atrium, study the model of the mausoleum as it was in Roman times. Imagine being surrounded by a veneer of marble, and the niche in the wall filled with a towering "welcome to my tomb" statue of Hadrian. From here, a ramp leads to the right, spiraling 400 feet. While some of the fine original brickwork and bits of mosaic survive, the marble veneer is long gone (notice the holes in the wall that held it in place). At the end of the ramp, a bridge crosses over the room where the ashes of the emperors were kept. From here, the stairs continue out of the ancient section and into the medieval structure (built atop the mausoleum) that housed the papal apartments. Don't miss the Sala del Tesoro (Treasury), where the wealth of the Vatican was locked up in a huge chest. (*Do* miss the 58 rooms of the military museum.) From the pope's piggy bank, a narrow flight of stairs leads to the rooftop and perhaps the finest view of Rome anywhere (pick out landmarks as you stroll around). From the safety of this dramatic vantage point, the pope surveyed the city in times of siege. Look down at the bend of the Tiber, which for 2,700 years has cradled the Eternal City.

Cost, Hours, Location: €5, Tue–Sun 9:00–19:30, last entry one hour before closing, closed Mon, audioguide—€4, near Vatican City, Metro: Lepanto or bus #64, tel. 06-3996-7600.

Ponte Sant'Angelo—The bridge leading to Castel Sant'Angelo was built by Hadrian for quick and regal access from downtown to his tomb. The three middle arches are actually Roman originals, and a fine example of the empire's engineering expertise. The statues of

angels (each bearing a symbol of the passion of Christ—nail, sponge, shroud, and so on) are Bernini-designed and textbook Baroque. In the Middle Ages, this was the only bridge in the area that connected St. Peter's and the Vatican with downtown Rome. Nearly all pilgrims passed this bridge to and from the church. Its shoulder-high banisters recall a tragedy: During a Jubilee Year festival in 1450, the crowd got so huge that the mob pushed out the original banisters, causing nearly 200 to fall to their deaths.

Today, as through the ages, pilgrims still cross the bridge, turn left, and set their sights on the Vatican dome. Around the year 1600, they would have also set their sights on a bunch of heads hanging from the crenellations of the castle. Ponte Sant'Angelo was infamous as a place for beheadings (banditry in the countryside was rife). Locals said, "There are more heads at Castel Sant'Angelo than there are melons in the market."

TRASTEVERE

Trastevere is the colorful neighborhood across *(tras)* the Tiber *(Tevere)* River. Trastevere (trahs-TAY-veh-ray) offers the best look at medieval-village Rome. The action unwinds to the chime of the church bells. Go there and wander. Wonder. Be a poet. This is Rome's Left Bank. For a self-guided tour, ✪ see the Trastevere Walk (page 86).

This proud neighborhood was long a working-class area. Now that it's becoming trendy, high rents are driving out the source of so much color. Still, it's a great people scene, especially at night. Stroll the back streets (for restaurant recommendations, see page 299).

To reach Trastevere by foot from Capitol Hill, cross the Tiber on Ponte Cestio (over Isola Tiberina). You can also take tram #8 from Largo Argentina, or bus #H from Termini train station and Via Nazionale (get off at Piazza Belli). From the Vatican (Piazza Risorgimento), it's bus #23 or #271.

Linking Trastevere with the Night Walk Across Rome: You can walk from Trastevere to Campo de' Fiori to link up with the beginning of the Night Walk Across Rome (page 78): From Trastevere's church square (Piazza di Santa Maria), take Via del Moro to the river and cross at Ponte Sisto, a pedestrian bridge that has a good view of St. Peter's dome. Continue straight ahead for one block. Take the first left, which leads down Via di Capo di Ferro through the scary and narrow darkness to Piazza Farnese, with the imposing Palazzo Farnese. Michelangelo contributed to the facade of this palace, now the French Embassy. The fountains on the square feature huge, one-piece granite hot tubs from the ancient Roman Baths of Caracalla. One block from there (opposite the palace) is the atmospheric square of Campo de' Fiori.

▲Santa Maria in Trastevere Church—One of Rome's oldest churches, this was made a basilica in the fourth century, when Christianity was legalized (free, daily 7:00–21:00). It was the first church dedicated to the Virgin Mary. The portico (covered area just outside the door) is decorated with fascinating ancient fragments filled with early Christian symbolism (for details, see page 165). The church is on Piazza di Santa Maria. While today's fountain is from the 17th century, there has been a fountain here since Roman times.

▲Villa Farnesina—Here's a unique opportunity to see a sumptuous Renaissance villa in Rome decorated with Raphael paintings. It was built in the early 1500s for the richest man in Renaissance Europe, Siennese banker Agostino Chigi. Architect Baldassare Peruzzi's design—a U-shaped building with wings enfolding what used to be a vast garden—successfully blended architecture and nature in a way that both ancient and Renaissance Romans loved. Orchards and flowerbeds flowed down in terraces from the palace to the riverbanks. Later construction of modern embankments and avenues robbed the garden of its grandeur, leaving it with a more melancholy charm.

Kings and popes of the day depended on generous loans from Agostino Chigi, whose bank had more than 100 branches in places as far-flung as London and Cairo. This villa was the meeting place of aristocrats, artists, beautiful women, and philosophers.

Cost, Hours, Location: €5; April–June and mid-Sept–Oct Mon–Sat 9:00–16:00, closed Sun; July–mid-Sept and Nov–March Mon–Sat 9:00–13:00, closed Sun; across the river from Campo de' Fiori, a short walk from Ponte Sisto on Via della Lungara, tel. 06-6802-7268.

❍ **Self-Guided Tour:** Enjoy the best bits of the villa with this commentary.

• *Begin in Room 1.*

Loggia of Galatea: Note the ceiling painted by Peruzzi, showing the position of the signs of the horoscope at the exact moment of Agostino's birth (21:30, November 29, 1466). The room's claim to fame is Raphael's painting of the nymph Galatea (on the wall by the entrance door). She shuns the doting attention of the ungainly, one-eyed giant Polyphemus (in the niche to the left, painted by another artist) and speeds away in the company of her rambunctious entourage on a chariot led by dolphins. She turns back and looks up, amused by the cyclops' crude love song (which, I believe, was "I Only Have Eye for You"). The trigger-happy cupids and lusty, entwined fauns and nymphs announce the pagan spirit revived in Renaissance Rome. All the painting's lines of sight (especially the cupids' arrows) point to the center of the work, Galatea's radiant face. Galatea is considered Raphael's vision of female perfection—not a portrait of an individual woman, but a composite of his many lovers in an idealized vision.

• *Continue into Room 2.*

Loggia of Psyche: This room was painted by Raphael and his assistants. Imagine it without the glass windows, as a continuation of the garden outside, where plays were performed to entertain Agostino's guests. Raphael's two ceiling frescoes were painted to

look like tapestries (complete with ruffled edges), suspended from the ceiling by garlands, making the room appear to be an open bower. View the frescoes from the top, with your back to the garden. The ceiling shows episodes in the myth of a lovely mortal woman, Psyche, who caught the eye of the winged boy-god Cupid (Eros). See the loving couple at the far left end, at the base of the ceiling. The big ceiling fresco on the left depicts the gods of Olympus gathered to plan a series of ordeals to test whether Psyche is worthy to marry a god. (Find Hercules with white beard and club, and Dionysius pouring the wine.) The other shows the happy ending, as Cupid (boy with wings) and Psyche (to his left, in topless robe) stand before Zeus to celebrate their wedding feast attended by the pantheon of gods.

The whole setting—the room by the gardens, the subject of the frescoes, the fleshy bodies—has an erotic subtext. At the time, Raphael was having a passionate affair with the celebrated Fornarina (the "baker's daughter," who lived down the street). Agostino, noticing that his painter was constantly interrupting his workday to be with her, had the girl kidnapped so that Raphael would finally concentrate. But production slowed even more, as Raphael was depressed. Agostino gave up and had the Fornarina move in with Raphael to keep him company as he happily resumed work in this cheery room. The room's imagery abounds with images both phallic and yonic (the female counterpart of phallic). Next to the ripe and split-open cantaloupe (right end, base of ceiling), find the gourd wearing a condom.

• *Upstairs, accessed from the stairway near the entrance, is the...*

Room of the Perspectives: Peruzzi, another trendsetter, painted this room. Walls seem to open onto views and perspectives that actually correspond with what lies outside. The insulting-to-Catholics graffiti (for example, on the wall at the far end) date from 1527, when Protestant mercenaries sent by Charles V sacked the city.

Agostino had his wedding banquet in this room. His parties were the talk of the town. On one occasion, he invited his guests in the (now lost) dining loggia overlooking the Tiber to toss the gold and silver dishes they had just used into the river. (The banker had nets conveniently placed just below the river's surface.)

The small chamber at the end of the Room of the Perspectives was the **bedroom.** The painting on the wall depicts the wedding of Alexander the Great and Roxanne. Roxanne has the features of Agostino's bride, and the bed is the jewel-encrusted ebony bed that received Agostino and his bride here in this room. On the entrance wall, find the three-arched ruins of the Basilica of Constantine in the Forum. The room was painted by Il Sodoma, a devoted fan of Michelangelo and one of the artists who was canned when Raphael took over the decoration of the papal apartments at the Vatican. Had that not happened, the Raphael Rooms at the Vatican might have looked like this.

Agostino had famous affairs with the most beautiful courtesans of his day. He eventually settled down, but his wild-living descendants didn't, and—in the space of a couple of generations—the Chigi family lost its fabulous fortune.

Gianicolo Hill Viewpoint—From this park atop a hill, the city views are superb, and the walk to the top holds a treat for architecture buffs. Start at Trastevere's Piazza di San Cosimato, and follow Via Luciano Manara to Via Garibaldi, at the base of the hill. Via Garibaldi winds its way up the side of the hill to the church of San Pietro in Montorio. To the right of the church, in a small courtyard, is the Tempietto by Donato Bramante. This tiny church, built to commemorate the martyrdom of St. Peter, is considered a jewel of Italian Renaissance architecture.

Continuing up the hill, Via Garibaldi connects to Passeggiata del Gianicolo. From here, you'll find a pleasant park with panoramic city views. Ponder the many Victorian-era statues, including that of baby-carrying, gun-wielding, horse-riding Anita Garibaldi. She was the Brazilian wife of the revolutionary General Giuseppe Garibaldi, who helped forge a united Italy in the late 19th century.

Near Trastevere: Jewish Quarter

From the 16th through the 19th centuries, Rome's Jewish population was forced to live in a cramped ghetto at an often-flooded bend of the Tiber River. While the medieval Jewish ghetto is long gone, this area—just across the river and toward Capitol Hill from Trastevere—is still home to Rome's synagogue and fragments of its Jewish heritage.

● See Jewish Ghetto Walk on page 94.

Synagogue (Sinagoga) and Jewish Museum (Museo Ebraico)—Rome's modern synagogue stands proudly on the spot where the medieval Jewish community lived in squalor for more than

300 years. The site of a historic visit by Pope John Paul II, this synagogue features a fine interior and a museum filled with artifacts of Rome's Jewish community. Modest dress is required. The only way to visit the synagogue—unless you're here for daily prayer service—is with a tour (€7.50 ticket includes museum and guided hourly tour of synagogue; June–Sept Sun–Thu 10:00–19:00, Fri 9:00–16:00, closed Sat; Oct–May Sun–Thu 10:00–17:00, Fri 9:00–14:00, closed Sat; English tours usually at :15 past the hour, 30 min, check schedule at ticket counter; on Lungotevere dei Cenci, tel. 06-6840-0661, www.museoebraico.roma.it). Walking tours of the Jewish Ghetto are conducted at least once a day (€8, daily except Sat, usually at 13:15, sign up at museum 30 min before departure, minimum of 3 required).

SOUTH ROME

The area south of the center contains some interesting but widely scattered areas. See the color map of South Rome at the beginning of this book.

Testaccio

In the gritty Testaccio neighborhood, four fascinating but lesser sights cluster at the Piramide Metro stop between the Colosseum and E.U.R. (This is a quick and easy stop as you return from E.U.R., or when changing trains en route to Ostia Antica.)

Working-class since ancient times, the Testaccio neighborhood has recently gone trendy-bohemian. Visitors wander through an awkward mix of yuppie and proletarian worlds, not noticing—but perhaps sensing—the "Keep Testaccio for the Testaccians" graffiti. This has long been the neighborhood of slaughterhouses, and its restaurants are renowned for their ability to cook up the least palatable part of the animals...the "fifth quarter." For a meal you won't forget, try **Trattoria "Da Oio" a Casa Mia** (at Via Galvani 43; see page 312 in Eating). High-end shoe and clothing boutiques are moving into the neighborhood, and this is now one of the best areas in Rome to have shoes custom-made. The Testaccio market in the center is hands-down the best, most authentic outdoor food market in Rome—this is where Romans shop while tourists flock to Campo de' Fiori. (It's on Piazza Testaccio, two blocks west of Via Marmorata.)

Pyramid of Gaius Cestius—The Mark Antony/Cleopatra scandal (c. 30 B.C.) brought exotic Egyptian styles into vogue. A rich Roman magistrate, Gaius Cestius, had this pyramid built as his tomb. Made

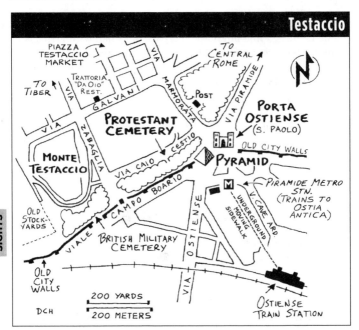

of brick covered in marble, it was completed in just 330 days (as stated in its Latin inscription). While much smaller than actual Egyptian pyramids, its proportions are correct. It was later incorporated into the Aurelian Wall, and it now stands as a marker to the entrance of Testaccio (next to the Piramide Metro stop).

Porta Ostiense and Museo della via Ostiense—This formidable gate (also next to the Piramide Metro stop; tiny museum free, Tue–Sun 9:00–13:30, closed Mon) is from the Aurelian Wall, begun in the third century under Emperor Aurelian. The wall, which encircled the city, was 12 miles long and averaged about 26 feet high, with 14 main gates and 380 72-foot-tall towers. Most of what you'll see today is circa A.D. 400, but the barbarians reconstructed the gate later, in the sixth century. If you climb up (enter nearest the pyramid), you can enjoy a free ramble along the ramparts and exhibits and models of Ostia Antica (Rome's ancient port; see page 335) and the Ostian Way. (For more on the wall, visit the San Sebastiano Gate and Museum of the Walls; see Ancient Appian Way Tour.)

Protestant Cemetery—The Cemetery for the Burial of Non-Catholic Foreigners (Cimitero Acattolico per gli Stranieri al Testaccio) is a tomb-filled park, running along the wall just beyond the pyramid. The cemetery is also the only English-style landscape (rolling hills, calculated vistas) in Rome, and a favorite spot for quiet picnics and strolls. From the Piramide Metro stop, walk between the pyramid and the Roman gate on Via Persichetti, then go left on Caio Cestio to the gate of the cemetery. Ring the bell to get inside (donation box, Mon–Sat 9:00–16:30, closed Sun, www.protestantcemetery.it).

Originally, none of the Protestant epitaphs were allowed to make any mention of heaven. Signs direct visitors to the graves of notable non-Catholics who died in Rome since 1738. Many of the buried were diplomats. And many, such as the poets Shelley and Keats, were from the Romantic Age. They came on the Grand Tour and—"captivated by the fatal charms of Rome," as Shelley wrote—never left. Head left toward the pyramid to find Keats' tomb, in the far corner. Keats died in his twenties, unrecognized. He wanted to be unnamed on a tomb that read, "Young English Poet, 1821. Here lies one whose name was writ in water." (To see Keats' tomb if the cemetery is closed, look through the tiny peephole on Via Caio Cestio, 10 yards off Via Marmarata.)

From inside the cemetery (nearest the pyramid), look down on Matilde Talli's cat hospice (flier at gate of cat zone, near pyramid). Volunteers use donations to care for these "Guardians of the Departed" who "provide loyal companionship to these dead."

Notice the beige travertine post office from 1932 (across the big street from the cemetery). This is textbook Mussolini-era fascist architecture. The huge X design on the stairwells celebrates the 10th anniversary of the dictator's reign.

Monte Testaccio—Just behind the Protestant Cemetery (as you leave, turn left and continue two blocks down Caio Cestio) is a 115-foot-tall ancient trash pile. It's made of broken *testae*—earthenware jars mostly used to haul oil 2,000 years ago, when this was a gritty port warehouse district. For 500 years, rancid oil vessels were discarded here. Slowly, Rome's lowly eighth hill was built. Because the caves dug into the hill stay cool, trendy bars, clubs, and restaurants compete with gritty car-repair places for a spot. The neighborhood was once known for a huge slaughterhouse and a Roma (Gypsy) camp that squatted inside an old military base. Now it's home to the Testaccio Village, a site for concerts and techno raves. To do the full monty, arrive after 21:00, when the restaurant-and-club scene is youthful and lively (Metro: Piramide).

South of Testaccio

▲**Montemartini Museum (Musei Capitolini Centrale Montemartini)**—This museum houses a dreamy collection of 400 ancient statues, set evocatively in a classic 1932 electric power plant, among generators and *Metropolis*-type cast-iron machinery. While the art is not as famous as the collections you'll see downtown, the effect is fun and memorable—and you'll encounter absolutely no tourists (€6.50, €10 combo-ticket with Capitoline Museums, Tue–Sun 9:00–19:00, closed Mon, last entry one hour before closing, Via Ostiense 106, a short walk from Metro: Garbatella, tel. 06-3996-7800, www.centrale montemartini.org). If tackling Rome with kids, this museum (cool, immersed in an old power plant, no crowds, art at kid level) is ideal.

South of Testaccio

TO CIRCUS MAXIMUS & BATHS OF CARACALLA

SEE TESTACCIO DETAIL

TIBER

PORTA OSTIENSE & MUSEUM

PYRAMID

PROT. CEM.

MONTE TESTACCIO

ANCIENT CITY WALL

M PIRAMIDE (TRAINS TO OSTIA ANTICA)

OSTIENSE STATION

TO TERMINI STATION

MERCATO CENTRALE

M GARBATELLA

MONTEMARTINI MUSEUM

VIA OSTIENSE

N

400 YARDS

400 METERS

ST. PAUL'S OUTSIDE THE WALLS

VIALE F. BALDELLI

M SAN PAOLO

M +++++ METRO

OTHER TRAIN LINES

TO OSTIA ANTICA BY ROAD

TO E.U.R. BY METRO

DCH

SIGHTS

▲**St. Paul's Outside the Walls (Basilica San Paolo Fuori le Mura)**—This was the last major construction project of Imperial Rome (c. A.D. 380) and the largest church in Christendom until St. Peter's. After a tragic 19th-century fire, St. Paul's was rebuilt in the same general style and size as the original. Step inside and feel as close as you'll get in the 21st century to experiencing a monumental Roman basilica. Marvel at the ceiling, and imagine building it with those massive wood beams in A.D. 380.

It feels sterile, but in a good way—like you're already in heaven. Along with St. Peter's Basilica, San Giovanni in Laterano, and Santa Maria Maggiore, this church is part of the Vatican rather than Italy. The church is built upon the supposed grave of St. Paul, whose body is buried under the altar. (Paul was decapitated two miles from this spot, and his head is at San Giovanni in Laterano.)

Alabaster windows light the vast interior, and fifth-century mosaics decorate the triumphal arch leading to the altar. Mosaic portraits

of 264 popes, from St. Peter to the present, ring the place—with blank spots ready to depict future popes. Pope #265—Benedict XVI—should show up here any day now; the portraits are put up near the start of a pope's reign. Find John Paul II (to the right of the high altar: *Jo Paulus II*) and John Paul I (to his right, with

a reign of only one month and three days). Wander the ornate yet peaceful cloister—decorated with fragments from early Christian tombs and sarcophagi of people who wanted to be buried close to Paul (cloister closed 13:00–15:00).

The courtyard leading up to the church is typical of early Christian churches—even the first St. Peter's had this kind of welcoming zone (free, daily 7:00–18:00, modest dress code enforced, Via Ostiense 186, Metro: San Paolo).

E.U.R.

In the late 1930s, Italy's dictator, Benito Mussolini, planned an international exhibition to show off the wonders of his fascist society. But these wonders brought us World War II, and Il Duce's celebration never happened. The unfinished mega-project was completed in the 1950s, and today it houses government offices and big, obscure museums filled with important, rarely visited relics.

If Hitler and Mussolini had won the war, our world might look like E.U.R. (AY-oor). Hike down E.U.R.'s wide, pedestrian-mean boulevards. Patriotic murals, aren't-you-proud-to-be-an-extreme-right-winger pillars, and stern squares decorate the soulless planned grid and stark office blocks. Boulevards named for Astronomy, Electronics, Social Security, and Beethoven are more exhausting than inspirational. Today, E.U.R. is worth a trip for its Museum of Roman Civilization (described later

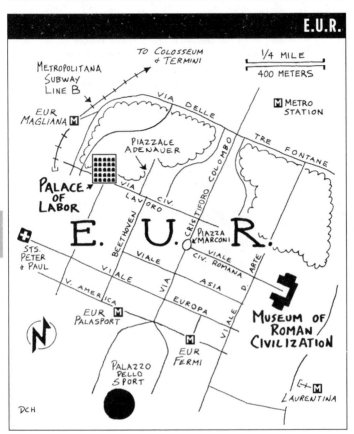

E.U.R.

TO COLOSSEUM & TERMINI

1/4 MILE

400 METERS

METROPOLITANA SUBWAY LINE B

M METRO STATION

EUR MAGLIANA M

VIA DELLE

TRE FONTANE

PIAZZALE ADENAUER

PALACE OF LABOR

VIA LAVORO

CIV.

CRISTIFORO COLOMBO

E. U. R.

BEETHOVEN

PIAZZA MARCONI

STS. PETER & PAUL

VIALE

VIALE CIV. ROMANA

VIALE D'ARTE

V. AMERICA

VIA

ASIA

EUR M PALASPORT

EUROPA

VIALE

MUSEUM OF ROMAN CIVILIZATION

N

M EUR FERMI

PALAZZO DELLO SPORT

M LAURENTINA

DCH

SIGHTS

in this section). And because a few landmark buildings of Italian modernism are located here and there, E.U.R. has become an important destination for architecture buffs.

The Metro skirts E.U.R. with three stops (10 minutes from the Colosseum). Use E.U.R. Magliana for the "Square Colosseum" and E.U.R. Fermi for the Museum of Roman Civilization (both described next). Consider walking 30 minutes from the palace to the museum through the center of E.U.R.

Palace of the Civilization of Labor (Palazzo della Civiltà del Lavoro)—From the Magliana Metro stop, stairs lead uphill to this epitome of fascist architecture. With its giant, no-questions-asked patriotic statues and its black-and-white simplicity, this is E.U.R.'s tallest building and key landmark. It's understandably nicknamed the "Square Colosseum." Around the corner, Café Palombini is still decorated in a 1930s style and is quite popular with young Romans (daily 7:00–22:00; good gelato, pastries, and snacks; Piazzale Adenauer 12, tel. 06-591-1700).

Mussolini and Imperial Rome

Benito Mussolini incorporated much from ancient Rome during his dictatorship. His military was organized according to Roman terminology (divided into legions and run by centurions and consuls). The salute with the right arm raised, flat palm down (later used by the Nazis), was also Roman. More hygienic and quicker than a handshake, it fit the dynamic character of fascism.

While the classical values of power and discipline were stressed in the rhythmic march of military parades, convincing the Italians of the need for order was a challenge even to Mussolini. He claimed it wasn't impossible to govern the Italian people...just useless.

Mussolini's title, Il Duce, was from the Latin *dux*—a generic term for leader. When chanted by crowds and carved onto monuments, it likely fueled Mussolini's belief that he was carrying out extraordinary historical missions like Caesar and Augustus before him.

For his fascist symbol, rather than the she-wolf or eagle, Mussolini used the *lictor's fasces*—an ax belonging to a Roman officer, with rods tied around the handle, carried in front of magistrates as a sign of authority. This was aimed at destroying the popular image of Italy as a joyous, carefree country and for promoting a new image of austerity and order. In ancient times, the ax stood for decapitation, the rods for flogging.

Fascist architecture, like ancient architecture, used a monumental scale, with arches, bold statues, and rhetorical inscriptions—resulting in an austere and impersonal feel that's generally disliked by Romans today.

In spite of his supposed passion for ancient Rome, Mussolini had a dreadful approach to archaeology. He would isolate a major monument and destroy everything around it. Sections of the Imperial Forums were sacrificed to build the wide street, Via dei Fori Imperiali, from Piazza Venezia to the Colosseum. A famous fountain by the Colosseum that had survived almost 2,000 years was torn down without another thought.

▲**Museum of Roman Civilization (Museo della Civiltà Romana)**—With 59 rooms of plaster casts and models illustrating the greatness of classical Rome, this vast and heavy museum gives a strangely lifeless, close-up look at Rome. Each room has a theme, from military tricks to musical instruments. One long hall is filled with casts of the reliefs of Trajan's Column. The highlight is the 1:250-scale model of Constantine's Rome, circa A.D. 300. The Planetarium and Astrological Museum are mostly of interest to children—so don't bother with the €8.50 combo-ticket unless you have kids (€6.50,

Tue–Sun 9:00–14:00, last entry one hour before closing, closed Mon, Piazza G. Agnelli; leave the E.U.R. Fermi Metro station on Via America, head towards McDonald's, and at T-intersection, turn left and go uphill three blocks to Via dell'Arte—you'll see its colonnade on the right; to return to the city center, access the Metro entrance across the street, tel. 06-592-6041).

The Ancient Appian Way and Southeast Rome

Most of these sights are covered in greater detail in the ✪ Ancient Appian Way Tour on page 158.

Baths of Caracalla (Terme di Caracalla)—Inaugurated by Emperor Caracalla in A.D. 216, this massive bath complex could accommodate 1,600 visitors at a time. Today it's just a shell—a huge shell—with all of its sculptures and most of its mosaics moved to museums. You'll see a two-story, roofless brick building surrounded by a garden, bordered by ruined walls. The two large rooms at either end of the building were used for exercise. In between the exercise rooms was a pool flanked by two small mosaic-floored dressing rooms. Niches in the walls once held statues.

In its day, this was a remarkable place to hang out. For ancient Romans, bathing was a social experience. The Baths of Caracalla functioned until Goths severed the aqueducts in the sixth century. In modern times, grand operas are performed here (€5, Mon 9:00–14:00, Tue–Sun 9:00–19:15—closing time is one hour before sunset, last entry one hour before closing, audioguide-€4, good €8 guidebook can be read in shaded garden while sitting on a chunk of column, Metro: Circus Maximus, plus a 5-minute walk south along Via delle Terme di Caracalla, tel. 06-3996-7700). The baths' statues are displayed else-where: several are in Rome's Octagonal Hall, and the immense *Toro Farnese* (a marble sculpture of a bull surrounded by people) snorts in Naples' Archaeological Museum (see page 352).

▲**The Appian Way**—For a taste of the countryside around Rome and more wonders of Roman engineering, take the four-mile trip from the Colosseum out past the wall to a stretch of the ancient Appian Way, where the original pavement stones are lined by several inter-esting sights. Ancient Rome's first and greatest highway, the Appian Way once ran from Rome to the Adriatic port of Brindisi, the gateway to Greece. Today you can walk (or bike) some stretches of the road, rattling over original paving stones, past crumbling monuments that once lined the sides. The Tomb of Cecilia Metella and the Circus of Maxentius are the two most impressive pagan sights. Just a few hun-dred yards away are the two best Christian Catacombs (see below).

✪ See Ancient Appian Way Tour on page 158.

▲▲**Catacombs of San Sebastiano**—A guide leads you under-ground through the tunnels where early Christians were buried. You'll see faded frescoes and graffiti by early-Christian tag artists. Besides the catacombs themselves, there's a historic fourth-century basilica with holy relics (€6, includes 25-min tour, 2/hr, Mon–Sat 8:30–12:00 & 14:00–17:30, last tour at 17:00, closed Sun and mid-Nov–mid-Dec, closes at 17:00 in winter, Via Appia Antica 136, tel. 06-785-0350).

✪ See Ancient Appian Way Tour on page 158.

▲▲**Catacombs of San Callisto**—The larger of the two sets of catacombs, San Callisto also is the more prestigious, having been the burial site for several early popes. Of the two main catacombs, which is the best to visit? All in all, they're both quite similar, and either one will fit the bill (€6, includes tour, Thu–Tue 9:00–12:00 & 14:00–17:30, closed Wed and Feb, closes at 17:00 in winter, Via Appia Antica 110, tel. 06-5130-1580).

✪ See Ancient Appian Way Tour on page 158.

Ostia Antica and Tivoli

For details on intriguing sights farther outside of Rome, see the chapters on day trips to Ostia Antica and Tivoli (Villa d'Este and Hadrian's Villa).

NIGHT WALK ACROSS ROME

*From Campo de' Fiori
to the Spanish Steps*

Rome can be grueling. But a fine way to mix romance into all the history, enjoy the cool of the evening, and enliven everything with some of Europe's best people-watching is to take an after-dark walk. My favorite nighttime stroll laces together Rome's floodlit nightspots and fine urban spaces with real-life theater vignettes.

Sitting so close to a Bernini fountain that traffic noises evaporate; jostling with local teenagers to see all the gelato flavors; observing lovers straddling more than the bench; jaywalking past *polizia* in flakproof vests; and marveling at the ramshackle elegance that softens this brutal city for those who were born here and can imagine living nowhere else—these are the flavors of Rome best tasted after dark.

THE WALK BEGINS

• *Start this mile-long walk at the Campo de' Fiori (Field of Flowers), my favorite outdoor dining room after dark (see the Eating chapter, page 300). To lengthen this walk, you can start in Trastevere; see directions on page 86. Alternatively, this walk is equally pleasant in reverse order: You can ride the Metro to the Spanish Steps if you'd rather finish at Campo de' Fiori, near many recommended restaurants.*

Campo de' Fiori
The center of the great, colorful square, Campo de' Fiori, is marked with the statue of Giordano Bruno (see sidebar), an intellectual heretic who was burned on this spot in 1600. Bruno overlooks a busy produce market in the morning and strollers after sundown. This neighborhood is still known for its free spirit and occasional demonstrations. When the statue of Bruno was erected in 1889, local riots overcame Vatican protests against honoring a heretic. Bruno faces his nemesis, the Vatican Chancellory (the big white building in the corner a bit to

Giordano Bruno
(1548–1600)

Lauded as a martyr to free thought and reviled as an intellectual con-man and heretic, the philosopher/priest Bruno has a legacy only a Roman could love. Details of his life are sketchy, and his writings range from the sublime to the ridiculous.

The young Dominican priest was nonconformist and outspoken from the start. He had to flee Italy to avoid a charge of heresy, and spent most of his adult life wandering Europe's capitals. In Geneva, he joined the Calvinists, until he was driven out for his unorthodox views. In London, he met with Queen Elizabeth, who found him subversive. In Germany, the Lutherans excommunicated him.

In his writings, Bruno claimed to have discovered the "Clavis Magna" (Great Key) to training the human memory. He published satirical plays tweaking Church morals. He advanced the still-heretical (Copernican) notion that the earth revolved around the sun, and speculated about other inhabited planets in the universe. All his works show a vast-ranging mind that was aware of the scientific trends of the day.

In 1593, Bruno was arrested by the Inquisition and sent to Rome, where he languished in prison for six years. (Tortured? Lost in bureaucracy? No one knows.) The exact charge against him remains debated by historians.

Bruno was sentenced to death by fire. He replied: "Perhaps you who pronounce this sentence are more fearful than I who receive it." On February 17, 1600, the civil authorities led him to the stake on Campo de' Fiori. As they lit the fire, he was offered a crucifix to hold. He pushed it away.

his right), while his pedestal reads, "And the flames rose up." Check out the reliefs on the pedestal for scenes from Bruno's trial and execution.

At the east end of the square (behind Bruno), the ramshackle apartments are built right into the old outer wall of ancient Rome's mammoth Theater of Pompey. This entertainment complex covered several city blocks, stretching from here to Largo Argentina. Julius Caesar was assassinated in the Theater of Pompey, where the Senate was renting space.

The square is lined with and surrounded by fun eateries. Bruno faces **Ristorante la Carbonara,** the only real restaurant on the square. The **Forno,** next door to the left (Mon–Sat 7:30–14:30 & 16:45–20:00, closed Sun), is a popular place for hot and tasty take-out *pizza bianco.* Step in at least to observe the frenzy as pizza is sold hot out of the oven. You can order an *etto* (100 grams) by pointing, then take your snack to the counter to pay. The many bars lining the square are fine for drinks and people-watching. Late at night on weekends, the place is packed with beer-drinking kids, turning what was once a charming medieval square into one vast Roman street party.

NIGHT WALK

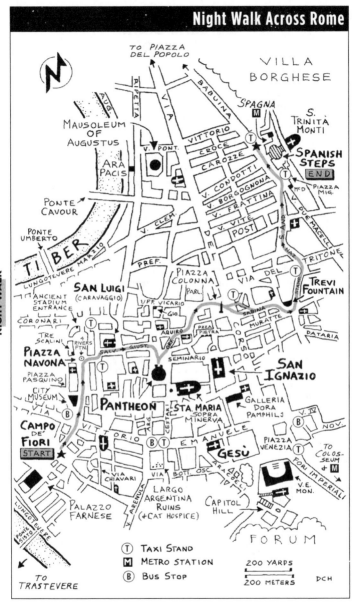

Night Walk Across Rome

TO PIAZZA
DEL POPOLO

VILLA
BORGHESE

SPAGNA
M

S.
TRINITÀ
MONTI

MAUSOLEUM
OF
AUGUSTUS

VITTORIO
CROCE
CAROZZE

SPANISH
STEPS
END

V. PONT.

ARA
PACIS

V. CONDOTTI

V. BORGOGNONA

MCD

PIAZZA
MIG.

PONTE
CAVOUR

V. FRATTINA

V. DUE MACELLI

V. VITE
POST

PONTE
UMBERTO

V. CLEM.

TIBER

PREF.

LUNGOTEVERE MARZIO

PIAZZA
COLONNA
PARL.

VIA DEL

TRITONE

TREVI
FOUNTAIN

SAN LUIGI
(CARAVAGGIO)

UFF. VICARIO

GIO

SABINA
MURATTE

DATARIA

ANCIENT
STADIUM
ENTRANCE

CORONARI

AQUIRO

PZEA
PIETRA

TRE
SCALINI

4
RIVERS
FTN.

SALV. GIUST.

SEMINARIO

CORSO

PIAZZA
NAVONA

SAN
IGNAZIO

PIAZZA
PASQUINO

CITY
MUSEUM

VIA

PANTHEON

STA MARIA
SOPRA
MINERVA

GALLERIA
DORA
PAMPHILJ

V. IV

NOV.

CAMPO
DE'
FIORI
START

VITTORIO

EMANUELE

GESÙ

PIAZZA
VENEZIA

TO
COLOS-
SEUM
+ M

VIA
CHIAVARI

BOTT. OSC.

ARENULA

LARGO
ARGENTINA
RUINS
(+CAT HOSPICE)

CAPITOL
HILL

FORI
IMPERIALI

V.E.
MON.

PALAZZO
FARNESE

LUNGOTEVERE

PONTE
SISTO

FORUM

TO
TRASTEVERE

T TAXI STAND
M METRO STATION
B BUS STOP

200 YARDS
200 METERS

DCH

• *If Bruno did a hop, step, and jump forward, then turned right on Via dei Baullari and marched 200 yards, he'd cross the busy Corso Vittorio Emanuele; then, continuing another 150 yards on Via Cuccagna, he'd find...*

Piazza Navona

Rome's most interesting night scene features street music, artists, fire-eaters, local Casanovas, ice cream, fountains by Bernini, and outdoor cafés (worthy of a splurge if you've got time to sit and enjoy Italy's human river).

This oblong square retains the shape of the original racetrack that was built by the emperor Domitian. (To see the ruins of the original entrance, exit the square at the far—or north—end, then take an immediate left, and look down to the left 25 feet below the current street level.) Since ancient times, the square has been a center of Roman life. In the 1800s, the city would flood the square to cool off the neighborhood.

The **Four Rivers Fountain** in the center is the most famous fountain by the man who remade Rome in Baroque style, Gian Lorenzo

Bernini. Four burly river gods (representing the four continents that were known in 1650) support an Egyptian obelisk that once stood on the ancient Appian Way. The water of the world gushes everywhere. The Nile has his head covered, since the headwaters were unknown then. The Ganges holds an oar. The Danube turns to admire the obelisk, which Bernini had moved here from a stadium on the Appian Way. And the Rio de la Plata from Uruguay tumbles backward in shock, wondering how he ever made the top four. Bernini enlivens the fountain with horses plunging through the rocks and exotic flora and fauna from these newly discovered lands. Homesick Texans may want to find the armadillo. (It's the big, weird armor-plated creature behind the Plata river statue.)

The Plata river god is gazing upward at the church of St. Agnes, worked on by Bernini's former-student-turned-rival, Francesco Borromini. Borromini's concave facade helps reveal the dome and epitomizes the curved symmetry of Baroque. Tour guides say that Bernini designed his river god to look horrified at Borromini's work.

Or maybe he's shielding his eyes from St. Agnes' nakedness, as she was stripped before being martyred. But either explanation is unlikely, since the fountain was completed two years before Borromini even started work on the church.

At the **Tre Scalini** bar (near the fountain), sample some *tartufo* "death by chocolate" ice cream, world-famous among connoisseurs of ice cream and chocolate alike (€5 to go, €10 at a table, open daily). Or

get it cheaper next door (to the south) at Ai Tre Tartufi and choose from white chocolate or dark chocolate. Admire a painting by a struggling artist, and listen to the white noise of gushing water and exuberant café-goers.

• *Leave Piazza Navona directly across from the Tre Scalini bar, go east past rose peddlers and palm readers, jog left around the guarded building, and follow the brown sign to the Pantheon. The Pantheon is straight down Via del Salvatore. (There's a cheap pizza place on the left a few yards before you reach the piazza, and a WC at the McDonald's.)*

The Pantheon

Sit for a while under the floodlit and moonlit Pantheon's portico.

The 40-foot, single-piece granite columns of the Pantheon's entrance show the scale the ancient Romans built on. The columns support a triangular, Greek-style roof with an inscription that says "M. Agrippa" built it. In fact, it was built *(fecit)* by Emperor Hadrian (A.D. 120), who gave credit to the builder of an earlier structure. This impressive entranceway gives no clue that the greatest wonder of the building is inside—a domed room that inspired later domes, includ-

ing Michelangelo's St. Peter's and Brunelleschi's Duomo (in Florence).

❂ For more information, see the Pantheon Tour on page 139.

• *With your back to the Pantheon, veer to the right down Via Orfani, toward the Albergo Abruzzi.*

NIGHT WALK

Egyptian Obelisks

Rome has 13 obelisks, more than any other city in the world. In Egypt, they were connected with the sun god Ra (like stone sunrays) and the power of the pha-raohs. The ancient Romans, keen on exotic novelty and sheer size, brought the obelisks here and set them up in key public places as evidence and celebration of their occupation of Egypt. Starting from the 1580s, Rome's new rulers—the popes—relocated the obelisks, often topping them with Christian crosses so they came to acquire yet another significance that guaran-teed their survival: the triumph of Christianity over all other religions.

The tallest (105 feet) and the most ancient (16th century B.C.) is the one by San Giovanni in Laterano. It once stood in the Circus Maximus next to its sister, which now marks the center of Piazza del Popolo.

The obelisks were carved out of single blocks of granite. Imagine the work, with only man- and horsepower, to first

quarry them and set them up in Egypt, then—after the Romans came along—to roll them on logs to the river or the coast, sail (or row) them in special barges across the Mediterranean and up the Tiber, and finally hoist them up.

Rome wasn't above cheap imitations. A couple of the obelisks are ancient Roman copies. The one at the top of the Spanish Steps has spelling mistakes in the hieroglyphics.

From the Pantheon to Piazza Colonna

• *On the right, you'll immediately see a sign for La Casa del Caffè.*

Tazza d'Oro Casa del Caffè, one of Rome's top coffee shops, dates back to the days when this area was licensed to roast coffee beans. Locals come here for its fine *granita di caffè con panna* (coffee slush with cream).

• *Look back at the fine view of the Pantheon from here. Then take Via Orfani uphill to Piazza Capranica.*

Piazza Capranica is home to the big, plain, Florentine

Renaissance–style Palazzo Capranica (directly opposite as you enter the square). Big shots, like the Capranica family, built towers on their palaces—not for any military use, but just to show off. Leave the piazza to the right of the palace, between the palace and the church. The street Via Aquiro leads to a sixth-century B.C. **Egyptian obelisk** (taken as a trophy by Augustus after his victory in Egypt over Mark Antony and Cleopatra). The obelisk was set up as a sundial. Walk the zodiac markings to the front door of the guarded parliament building.

• *To your right is Piazza Colonna, where we're heading next—unless you like gelato...*

A short detour to the left (past Albergo National) brings you to Rome's most famous *gelateria*. **Giolitti's** is cheap for take-out or elegant and splurge-worthy for a sit among classy locals (open daily until past midnight, Via Uffici del Vicario 40); get your gelato in a cone *(cono)* or cup *(coppetta)*.

Piazza Colonna features a huge second-century column. Its reliefs depict the victories of Emperor Marcus Aurelius over the barbarians. When Marcus died in A.D. 180, the barbarians began to get the upper hand, beginning Rome's long three-century fall. The big, important-looking palace houses the headquarters for the deputies (or cabinet) of the prime minister. The **Via del Corso** is named for the Berber horse races—without riders—that took place here during Carnevale until the 1800s when a horse trampled a man to death in front of a horrified queen. Historically the street was filled with meat shops. When it became Rome's first gas-lit street in the 1800s, these butcher shops were banned and replaced by classier boutiques, jewelers, and antiques dealers. Nowadays most of Via del Corso is closed to traffic every evening and becomes a wonderful parade of Romans out for a stroll (see "Dolce Vita Stroll" on page 320 in the Nightlife chapter).

• *Cross Via del Corso, Rome's noisy main drag. Turn left under the portico to enter the Y-shaped Galleria del Sordi shopping gallery, forking to the right and exiting onto Via Sabini. (But if you're here past 20:00, the shops are closed; instead, cross Via del Corso at the crosswalk and then head straight on Via dei Sabini). Head down Via dei Sabini to the roar of the water, light, and people of...*

The Trevi Fountain

The Trevi Fountain shows how Rome took full advantage of the abundance of water brought into the city by its great aqueducts. This watery Baroque avalanche was completed in 1762 by Nicola Salvi, hired by a pope who was celebrating the reopening of the ancient aqueduct that powers it. Salvi used the palace behind the fountain as a theatrical backdrop for the figure of "Ocean," who represents water in every form. The statue surfs through his wet kingdom—with water gushing from 24 spouts and tumbling over 30 different kinds of plants—while Triton blows his conch shell.

The magic of the square is enhanced by the fact that no streets directly approach it. You can hear the excitement as you approach, and then—*bam!*—you're there. The scene is always lively, with lucky Romeos clutching dates while unlucky ones clutch beers. Romantics toss a coin over their shoulder, thinking it will give them a wish and assure their return to Rome. That may sound silly, but every year I go through this tourist ritual...and it actually seems to work.

Take some time to people-watch (whisper a few breathy *bellos* or *bellas*) before leaving. There's a peaceful zone at water level on the far right.

• *Facing the fountain, take the street on the right (Via della Stamperia) and cross the busy Via del Tritone. Continue 100 yards and veer right at Via S. Andrea, a street that changes its name to Via Propaganda before ending at...*

The Spanish Steps

The Piazza di Spagna, with the very popular Spanish Steps, is named for the Spanish Embassy to the Vatican, which has been here for 300 years. It's been the hangout of many Romantics over the years (Keats,

Wagner, Openshaw, Goethe, and others). In the 1700s, British aristocrats on the "Grand Tour" of Europe came here to ponder Rome's decay. The British poet John Keats pondered his mortality, then died in the pink building on the right side of the steps. Fellow Romantic Lord Byron lived across the square at #66.

The Sinking Boat Fountain at the foot of the steps, built by Bernini or his father, Pietro, is powered by an aqueduct. All of Rome's fountains are aqueduct-powered; their spurts are determined by the water pressure provided by the various aqueducts. This one, for instance, is much weaker than Trevi's gush.

The piazza is a thriving night scene. Window-shop along Via Condotti, which stretches away from the steps. This is where Gucci and other big names cater to the trendsetting jet set. Facing the Spanish Steps, you can walk right, about a block, to tour one of the world's biggest and most lavish McDonald's (salad bar, WC).

• *Our walk is finished. If you'd like to head up to the top of the steps sweat-free, there's a free elevator just outside the Spagna Metro stop (elevator closes at 21:00; Metro stop is to the left of the Spanish Steps). Afterward, you can zip home on the Metro (usually open until 22:00); or, if you'd prefer, grab a taxi at the north or south side of the piazza.*

NIGHT WALK

TRASTEVERE WALK

From the Tiber to the Church of Santa Maria in Trastevere

Trastevere—the colorful neighborhood across the river from downtown—is *the* place to immerse yourself in the crustier side of Rome. This half-mile walk, which at a slow stroll takes 30 minutes, is designed to train your eye to see Rome more intimately. You'll discover a secret, hidden city of heroic young martyrs, lovers kissing on Vespas, party-loving Renaissance bankers, and feisty "Trasteverini"—old-timers who pride themselves on never setting foot on the opposite bank of the Tiber River.

ORIENTATION

Getting There: Trastevere (trahs-TAY-veh-ray) is on the west side of the Tiber River, south of Vatican City and across the river from the Forum and Capitol Hill area. To get there by foot from Capitol Hill, cross the Tiber on Ponte Cestio (which goes over Isola Tiberina). You can also reach it on tram #8 from Largo Argentina or express bus #H from the Termini train station and Via Nazionale; if taking either of these, get off at Piazza Belli, just after crossing the Tiber. From the Vatican (Piazza Risorgimento), take bus #23 or #271.

Church of Saint Cecilia: Free, daily 9:30–12:30 & 16:00–18:30; crypt-€2.50; loft with frescoes-€2.50, Mon–Fri 10:15–12:15, Sat–Sun 11:15–12:15, ask the nuns to open the door.

Church of Santa Maria in Trastevere: Free, daily 7:00–21:00.

THE WALK BEGINS

• *Start halfway across the Ponte Cestio (Cestius Bridge)—called the "Ponte Fabricio" on the east side of the river—which connects Isola Tiberina (Island in the Tiber) to Trastevere.*

Isola Tiberina and the Tiber River

Rome got its start 3,000 years ago along the Tiber River at this point. This was as far upstream as big boats could sail and the first place the river could be crossed by bridge. As a center of river trade, Rome connected the interior of the Italian peninsula with the Mediterranean. The area below you would have been bustling in ancient times. Look down and imagine small ports, water mills, ramshackle boats, and platforms for fishing.

The island itself was once the site of a temple dedicated to Aesclepius, the god of medicine. Ancient Romans who were ill spent the night here and left little statues of their healed body parts (feet, livers, hearts...) as thank-you notes. This tradition survives: Today, throughout Italy, Catholic altars are often encrusted with votive offerings, symbolizing gratitude for answered prayers. During plagues and epidemics, the sick were isolated on the island. These days, the island's largest building is the Fatebenefratelli, the public hospital favored by Roman women for childbirth. The island's reputation for medical care lives on.

The high point of the bridge (upon which you're probably leaning) is an ancient stone with a faded inscription dating from about A.D. 370, when this then-400-year-old bridge was rebuilt. The eroding plaque is stapled into the balustrade like a piece of recycled scrap. Run your fingers over the word "Caesar" (top line, just right of center). This part of the Tiber River flooded frequently, which unfortunately made the land on the north bank the ideal location for the medieval Jewish ghetto (now long gone, but Rome's synagogue remains—see Jewish Ghetto Walk, next chapter).

In the 1870s, the Romans removed the threat of flooding by practically walling off the Tiber, building the tall, anonymous embankments that continue to isolate the river from the city today.

• *Head south to leave the bridge. If the green riverside Sora Mirella kiosk on the right is open, refresh yourself with the city's most famous* grattachecca, *crushed ice with fruit-flavored syrup and chopped fruit. Then cross the street and go down the steps into the car-filled piazza.*

Piazza in Piscinula

This square is famous for its church bell tower (the cute little thing directly across from the bridge); dating from 1069, it's the oldest working one in the city. Study the brown building on the riverside and spot faint traces of Renaissance decoration. Today's earth-tone shades of the city echo this original Roman brown. (If you want to get wired, you'll find an easyInternetcafé on this square.)

• *Facing the tower, exit the square from the far right corner, opposite where you entered, going uphill on Via dell'Arco de' Tolomei.*

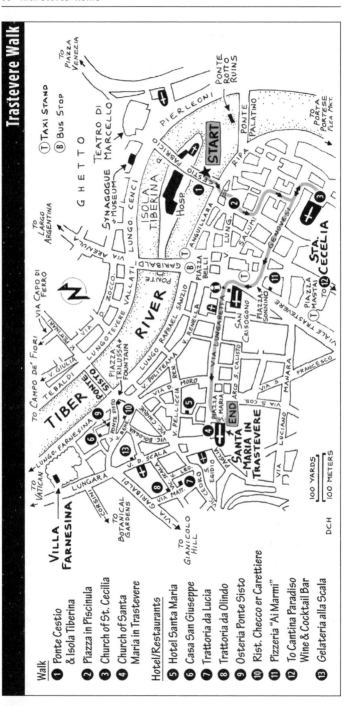

TRASTEVERE WALK

Trastevere Walk

Ⓣ TAXI STAND
Ⓑ BUS STOP

Walk

1. Ponte Cestio & Isola Tiberina
2. Piazza in Piscinula
3. Church of St. Cecilia
4. Church of Santa Maria in Trastevere

Hotel/Restaurants

5. Hotel Santa Maria
6. Casa San Giuseppe
7. Trattoria da Lucia
8. Trattoria da Olindo
9. Osteria Ponte Sisto
10. Rist. Checco er Carettiere
11. Pizzeria "Ai Marmi"
12. To Cantina Paradiso Wine & Cocktail Bar
13. Gelateria alla Scala

Trastevere Back Lanes

Look up and directly ahead to see the elegantly restored remains of a tower sandwiched between apartments. In medieval times, the city skyline had 300 of these towers (about 50 survive). Each noble family competed for the tallest one until, in about 1250, city authorities got fed up and had them all lopped off. Later—mainly Baroque—construction incorporated most of the remaining "stumps," and you can still see these remnants of medieval Rome all over the old center. Incorporating old structures into new ones was always considered more economical and practical than demolishing and starting again from scratch. In the Middle Ages, Rome had regressed to being a big village; any idea of town planning was lost until the Renaissance.

Notice the many rooftop terraces—the Roman equivalent of a leafy backyard. An *attico con terrazzo* (penthouse with a terrace) is every Roman's dream.

Continue on, walking under the low arch. Lots of aristocratic buildings were connected by these elevated passages. Imagine herds of sheep shuffling through here in medieval times while smoke billowed from the windows and doors of homes that lacked chimneys.

Turn left and walk along Via dei Salumi ("Cold Cuts Street"). Because of its vicinity to the river, Trastevere was always a commercial neighborhood, and many of its alleys were named after businesses based here. The streets—rarely paved—were clogged by shop stalls.

The red-brown building on your right (pretty ugly unless you're a fascist) is a school from the Mussolini era. The fascist leader believed in the classical motto *"mens sana in corpore sano"* ("a healthy mind in a healthy body"), and loved being seen fencing, boxing, swimming, and riding. He endowed school buildings with lots of gyms.

After passing the school, turn right again, heading up Vicolo dell'Atleta ("Alley of the Athlete"). Check out the latest fashions in underwear hanging out to dry. Apartments in Rome tend to be quite small, and electricity is more expensive than in the US, so few have clothes dryers.

Strolling here, you'll understand why the Italian language has no word for "privacy" (they use our word and roll the *r*). Reading a letter on the Metro attracts a crowd. Young lovers with no place to go are adept at riding *motorini*...while parked.

All around, ancient fragments are recycled ingloriously into medieval buildings. Halfway down the alley on the right is a restaurant that, a thousand years ago, was a synagogue. Find the Hebrew faintly inscribed on the base of the columns of the exposed brick structure. A large part of Rome's Jewish community, the most ancient outside Palestine, lived in Trastevere until the popes moved them into the ghetto on the other side of the river in the 1500s.

• *Continue, turning left on Via dei Genovesi, then right on Via di Santa Cecilia to reach Piazza di Santa Cecilia. Enter the convent courtyard of the church, sit by the fountain, and take a moment to enjoy the peace and quiet.*

Church of St. Cecilia

Trastevere has many early Christian churches like St. Cecilia (daily 9:30–12:30 & 16:00–18:30). This is because, in the second and third centuries, a large community of foreigners lived here, including early Christians from Greece and Judaea, who introduced their cultures and religions to the neighborhood.

Notice the church's eclectic exterior. Its mismatched columns were recycled from pagan temples. The typical medieval bell tower sports an 18th-century facade. This church, dedicated to Cecilia, patron saint of musicians and singers, is popular for weddings. Of Rome's 40 medieval churches, many have two-year waiting lists for weekend weddings. While most young Roman couples favor the more sober elegance of medieval churches over Baroque (usually dismissed as *troppo pesante*—"too heavy"), the typical Italian wedding gowns are far from understated.

Inside the church, find the statue of St. Cecilia by Stefano Maderno (in the case below the altar). A Christian convert from a wealthy family in a time of persecution, Cecilia revealed her faith to her pagan husband on their wedding night and told him of her aspiration to remain chaste (uh-oh...). An angel appeared to reason with the frustrated groom. Once converted, he devoted himself to carrying out Christian burials in the catacombs, until he himself was killed. Cecilia was soon condemned as well. The Romans, who tried unsuccessfully for three days to suffocate her with steam in her bath to make it appear accidental, finally lost patience and beheaded her. Cecilia bequeathed her house to the neighborhood community, and this spot has been a place of worship ever since.

In the days when Christianity was illegal, wealthy converts hosted Mass for the local community in their homes. When Christians were finally allowed to build churches, they often did so on the sites of these homes for the sake of continuity. While the Church of St. Cecilia originated in the third century, what we see today was built in the ninth century and extensively restored in the 18th century.

Viewing Maderno's statue of Cecilia, remember that during the Catholic Counter-Reformation, art charged with great emotional impact was used to enhance faith. The new appetite for relics led to a search for Cecilia's remains. When her tomb was opened, Maderno was present and claimed, along with other bystanders, to have seen her body perfectly preserved for an unforgettable instant before it turned to dust. He created this touching statue from his memory of that scene. Cecilia lies with her face turned and hidden, the violence of her death suggested only by the gash in her neck, the position of her fingers indicating the oneness of the Trinity. (Like Italians today, she counted starting with her thumb.)

The canopy above the altar, dating from the 1200s, represents an innovative fusion of Roman and French Gothic architecture and sculpture, showing that the artist (Arnolfo di Cambio) knew his classics and had also been to Paris.

The mosaic in the apse dates from the ninth century. Pope Paschal (on the left), who built the church, holds a little model of it in his hands. His square halo signifies that he was alive when the mosaic was made. His small head suggests he was less important than the others in the scene.

If you visit mid-morning (Mon–Fri 10:15–12:15, Sat–Sun 11:15–12:15), you have two options before leaving: Go downstairs to see the crypt, which contains the ancient remains of Cecilia's house, or go upstairs to the loft to view fancy frescoes. Cecilia's house is pretty bare, but it does have some early Christian iconography, original mosaic floors, and grain storage bins (follow sign to *crypt*, €2.50).

In the loft, where cloistered nuns would view the Mass while hidden behind a screen, are some extraordinary frescoes of angels painted by Pietro Cavallini, a contemporary of Giotto (c. 1300). Scholars debate who influenced whom: Giotto or Cavallini. But there's no debate that the art here shows cutting-edge realism in the expressive faces of angels who sit believably in their chairs (loft—€2.50; you'll need to ask the nuns to open the door on the left side of the facade). If you're here at 18:00 on a Saturday, you're welcome to read the Lectio Divina with the nuns.

• *Leaving the church, backtrack left, take the first left onto Via de Genovesi, and hike straight ahead to where it meets a busy street.*

Viale Trastevere to Piazza Santa Maria

The wide, modern boulevard called Viale Trastevere bisects Trastevere, which was otherwise spared most of the demolishing and rebuilding suffered by other traditional neighborhoods when Rome become the capital of united Italy in 1870. Cross to the other side of Viale Trastevere and turn right, then left into Largo San Giovanni de Matha. Pass by the TI and the textbook Baroque facade of the yellow church and continue to Via Lungaretta. You'll notice a change in atmosphere—the quiet, mystical charm of the first part of your walk has given way to livelier, more colorful, more touristy (and higher-rent) surroundings. Look up. Now, along with underwear...you see art. Walk to the big square and sit down on the fountain steps.

Piazza Santa Maria in Trastevere

You're in the heart of the neighborhood—Piazza Santa Maria in Trastevere, the thumbhole in this urban palette. Here you can easily imagine the Trasteverini of the past preparing for their legendary fights against the inhabitants of other districts.

Piazza Santa Maria is the neighborhood's most important meeting place. During major soccer games, a large screen is set up here so that everybody can share in the tension and excitement. At other times, children gather here with a ball and improvise matches of their own.

• *Dominating the square is the...*

Church of Santa Maria in Trastevere

One of Rome's oldest churches, this was built on the site where early Christians worshipped illegally. It was made a basilica—the first church dedicated to the Virgin Mary—in the fourth century, when Christianity was legalized (free, daily 7:00–21:00). The portico (covered area just outside the door) is decorated with fascinating ancient fragments filled with early Christian symbolism.

Step inside and grab a pew. Most of what you see dates from around the 12th century, but the granite columns are from ancient Roman buildings (notice the mismatched capitals, some with tiny pagan heads of Egyptian gods), and the ancient basilica floor plan (and ambience) survives. The intricate coffered ceiling has an unusual image of Mary painted on copper at the center. The striking 12th-century mosaics behind the altar are notable for their portrayal of Mary—which local tour guides claim is the first to show her at the throne with Jesus in Heaven. He has his arm around his mother, as if introducing her to us.

Below, the scenes from the life of Mary (mosaics by Cavallini, 1300s) predate the Renaissance by a hundred years. (Pop a coin in the box for light.) The first of six panels (to the left of the curved apse) shows the birth of Mary. A servant in the corner checks the temperature of the water with her hand before she bathes the baby, introducing an element of tenderness that breaks the abstract rigidity of medieval art. Next comes the angel announcing Jesus' coming to Mary, Jesus' birth, the adoration of the Magi, the presentation of Jesus in the Temple, and Mary's death. The gold mosaic backgrounds show buildings that are unrealistic, but a good step toward accurate 3-D representation.

The incredibly expensive 13th-century floor is a fine example of Cosmati mosaic work—a style of mosaic featuring intricate geometric shapes (in this case, made with marble scavenged from Roman ruins).

Tour Over

From here, enjoy simply exploring Rome's most colorful district. Saunter around the streets to the left of the church as you leave. The farther you venture from the square, the less touristy and more rustic the neighborhood becomes. Wandering the back lanes and pondering the earthy enthusiasm people seem to have for life here, I can imagine that bygone day when proud Trastevere locals would brag that they never crossed the river.

To cap off your Trastevere stroll with one more sight, consider visiting **Villa Farnesina,** a Renaissance villa decorated by Raphael (closes by 13:00 in summer and winter; see the description and self-guided tour on page 66). To get there, face the Church of Santa Maria in Trastevere and leave the piazza by walking along the right side of the church, following Via della Paglia to Piazza di S. Egidio. Exit the piazza near the church and you'll be on Via della Scala. Follow through the Porta Settimiana, where it changes names to Via della Lungara. On your right, you'll pass John Cabot University. Look for a white arch that reads Accademia dei Lincei. The villa is through this gate.

JEWISH GHETTO WALK

North Bank of the Tiber

For centuries, Rome's Jewish ghetto has been the site of both relentless persecution and the undying pride and solidarity of a tight-knit community. Built in 1555 on the banks of a frequently flooded bend of the Tiber River, the ghetto was the forced home of the Roman Jewish population for more than 300 years, between the Counter-Reformation (16th century) and Italian unification (19th century). Though most of the old ghetto has been torn down, you can still find a few reminders of the Roman Jews' storied past and lively present. If you want to visit the synagogue and museum, avoid this walk on a Saturday, when they're closed.

ORIENTATION

Getting There: The Jewish ghetto was—and Rome's main synagogue still is—on the east bank of the Tiber, near the Isola Tiberina (Island in the Tiber) and the ancient ruins of the Theater of Marcellus (Teatro di Marcello). It's a 10-minute walk southwest from Piazza Venezia.

Synagogue and Jewish Museum: €7.50 ticket includes both; June–Sept Sun–Thu 10:00–19:00, Fri 9:00–16:00, closed Sat; Oct–May Sun–Thu 10:00–17:00, Fri 9:00–14:00, closed Sat; on Lungotevere dei Cenci, tel. 06-6840-0661, www.museoebraico .roma.it. Modest dress is required. If you're not there for a prayer service, the only way to visit the synagogue is with an hourly tour (included in admission, English tours usually at :15 past the hour, 30 min, check schedule at ticket counter).

Walking Tour: Walking tours of the Jewish Ghetto are conducted at least once a day Sun–Fri (€8, usually at 13:15, no Sat tours). Ask for the schedule at the museum entry and sign up at least 30 minutes prior to the tour departure time (a minimum of three participants is required).

Local Guide: Micaela Pavoncello is uniquely equipped to guide visitors through the neighborhood that her family has lived in since ancient Roman times (€130/2 hrs, ask for Ghetto Tour, tel. 328-863-8128, www.jewishroma.com, info@jewishroma.com).

Cuisine Art: One of the stops near the end of this tour is at a Jewish bakery. There are also two eateries: **Sora Margherita Associazione Culturale,** offering traditional Roman and Jewish fare, hides without a sign on a square a block from the end of this tour (closed Mon except in winter when it's closed Sat–Sun instead, Piazza delle Cinque Scole 30; see listing on page 300). **Alberto Pica Gelateria** serves up gelato and light meals in a fine shaded setting on a small street off Via Arenula just beyond the tour's end (closed Sun, Via della Seggiola 12).

History

Today, of Italy's 35,000 Jews, nearly half call Rome home. Jews here have a uniquely Roman style of worship, and even preserve remnants of their own Judaic-Roman dialect. That's because, unlike most of the world's Jewish people, Roman Jews are neither Sephardic (descended from Spain) nor Ashkenazi (descended from Eastern Europe). Italy's Jews came directly from the Holy Land before the Diaspora, first arriving in Rome in the second century B.C. as esteemed envoys (hoping to establish business ties), and then, after Rome invaded Judaea in the first century A.D., as POWs sold into slavery.

Julius Caesar favored the Jews because they were well-networked throughout the empire, and they didn't push their religion on others. As Christianity enveloped Rome and the pope became literally the king of Rome's Jews, the Jews experienced discrimination, with laws intended to limit the spread of Judaism (e.g., no proselytizing, new synagogues, or intermarriage). The severity of these laws varied from pope to pope. Through most of the Middle Ages, Rome's Jews prospered and were often held in high regard as physicians, businessmen, and confidants of popes. The community in Trastevere was even allowed to spill across to the opposite bank of the Tiber.

Starting in the eighth century, anti-Semitism began increasing throughout Europe. Then, in 1492, all of Spain's Jews were either baptized or expelled, with similar decrees following in other European countries. Rome's Jewish population doubled, swelling with refugees. By the 1500s, the Catholic Counter-Reformation—begun to combat rising Protestantism—turned its attention to anything deemed a "heresy" or simply not Catholic, including Judaism. In 1555, Pope Paul IV forcibly moved all of Rome's Jews into a ghetto (across the river from Trastevere), enclosing some 4,000 Jews inside, on a mere seven acres of land. There they lived—in cramped conditions, behind a wall, with a curfew—for three centuries. They could go out by day, but

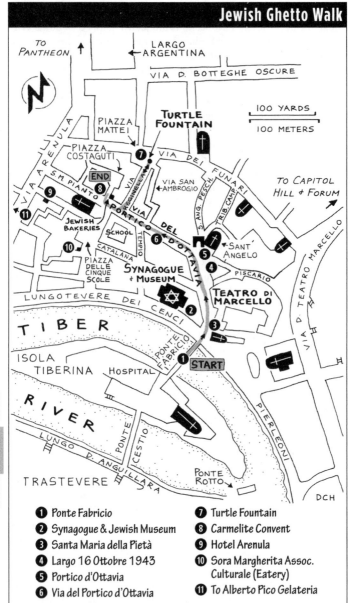

Jewish Ghetto Walk

1 Ponte Fabricio

2 Synagogue & Jewish Museum

3 Santa Maria della Pietà

4 Largo 16 Ottobre 1943

5 Portico d'Ottavia

6 Via del Portico d'Ottavia

7 Turtle Fountain

8 Carmelite Convent

9 Hotel Arenula

10 Sora Margherita Assoc. Culturale (Eatery)

11 To Alberto Pico Gelateria

JEWISH GHETTO WALK

had to return before the gates were locked at night. Jews were forced to wear yellow scarves and caps, and were prohibited from owning property or holding good jobs. During Carnevale (Mardi Gras), they were forced to parade down Via del Corso while Christians lined the streets and shouted insults. Through this long stretch of oppression, the synagogue was the only place Jews could feel respected and dignified. It's no wonder such loving attention was given to the Jewish tools of worship.

Rome's Jews enjoyed a little boost in freedom when Napoleon occupied the city (1805–1814) and after the ghetto walls were torn down in 1848. But it was only after Italian unification in 1870 that the ghetto's inhabitants were granted full rights and citizenship. When Rome became the country's capital, the city—ashamed of its shoddy Jewish quarter—destroyed the old ghetto and modernized the district, giving it the street plan we see today.

Then came the rise of fascism. Even though Mussolini wasn't rabidly anti-Semitic, he instituted a slew of anti-Jewish laws as he allied himself more strongly with Hitler. When Mussolini was deposed and the Nazis occupied Rome late in the war, the ghetto community was in even greater danger. Of the 13,000 ghetto-dwellers, 2,000 were sent off to concentration camps.

A measure of healing and reconciliation came with Pope John Paul II, who took a special interest in fostering relations with the Jewish community. It was the late pope who finally acknowledged that the Church should have intervened more forcefully to defend the Jews during the Holocaust. He was also the first pope in history to enter a synagogue (in this very neighborhood—described on this walk). In his last letter, John Paul II thanked Rome's emeritus rabbi for allowing him to initiate this Catholic-Jewish rapprochement he felt was so long overdue.

THE WALK BEGINS

• *Start at the north end of Ponte Fabricio, which connects central Rome with the Isola Tiberina and the neighborhood of Trastevere. You'll see the big synagogue with its square dome. The former ghetto consists of the synagogue and the several blocks behind it.*

Ponte Fabricio

Ponte Fabricio is nicknamed Ponte Quattro Capi ("Bridge of the Four Heads") for its statues of the four-faced pagan god Janus. In ancient times, it was called Pons Judaeocum ("Jews' Bridge") because foreigners, immigrants, and Jews—who weren't allowed to live in central Rome—would commute across this bridge to get into town. Some 30,000 Jews lived in a thriving community in Trastevere. Look down at the river. The embankment was only built in the late 19th century.

In the Ghetto

The word "ghetto" is Italian, first used in Venice in the 1600s to describe the part of town where Jews lived—near the copper foundry ("ghetto" came from *gettare*, "to cast"). Initially the term meant only Jewish neighborhoods, but as the word spread through Europe and beyond, it was used generically to mean any neighborhood where a single ethnic group is segregated.

Before then, this was the worst flood zone of the Roman riverbank—just right for a ghetto for the politically powerless.

• *With your back to the river, at your left is the...*

Synagogue (Sinagoga) and Jewish Museum (Museo Ebraico)

In the 16th century, when Pope Paul IV forced the Jews to reside within a walled ghetto, the center of its four-square-block area was this synagogue. When Italy became unified in 1870, the ghetto was essentially demolished, replaced with the modern blocks you see today.

The Jews were initially offered better real estate for their synagogue, but chose instead to rebuild here, on the original site. This new "Synagogue of Emancipation" was built in a remarkable three years (completed 1904) with the enthusiastic support of the entire Roman community. This is where Pope John Paul II made his historic visit in 1986.

Follow his Holiness' footsteps and enter the synagogue via the main door on the riverside. The €7.50 admission, which includes museum entrance and a guided synagogue visit, is the only way to access the interior, unless you're here for daily prayer service. (For details on the synagogue tour, see "Orientation," on page 94.)

Inside the synagogue, take in the impressive dome, which is square to distinguish it from a Christian church. Ponder the inside of the dome, painted with the colors of the rainbow—symbolic of God's promise to Noah that there would be no more floods. The stars on the ceiling recall God's pledge that Abraham's descendants would flourish and be as many as the stars in the sky. As there were no Jewish architects and no models to study when it was built, this churchlike synagogue is Art Nouveau with a dash of Tiffany. The sandy color tones are a reminder of the community's desert heritage.

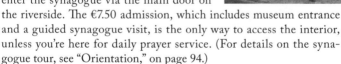

JEWISH GHETTO WALK

The museum shows off historically significant artifacts described in English. You'll see second-century B.C. reliefs with Jewish symbols, finely worked Judaica (religious items), and other relics of the Jewish past. As the Jews were not allowed to be craftsmen during the ghetto period, they had to commission many of the pieces you'll see from some of the finest Christian artists of that time—the same artists working for the kings and aristocracy of Europe—making these items historically and artistically significant. Note that Jewish historians don't use "B.C." (Before Christ) or "A.D." (Anno Domini), but rather "B.C.E." (Before the Common Era) and "C.E." (Common Era). The museum also shows a film in English of the Nazi occupation of Rome.

Back outside, you may notice security measures around the synagogue: heavy concrete planter boxes (that double as car-bomb barriers), policemen in kiosks, and video cameras on the fences.

• *Look for the yellow church across from the Ponte Fabricio...*

Santa Maria della Pietà (a.k.a. San Gregorio)

When the ghetto was a walled-in town, Catholics built churches at each gate to try and spread their faith to the Jews. Notice the Hebrew script under the crucifix. It quotes the Jewish prophet Isaiah—"All day long, I have stretched out my hands to a disobedient and faithless nation that has lost its way" (Isaiah 65:2)—but misuses the quote to give it an anti-Semitic twist.

• *Walk behind the synagogue toward the ancient Roman ruins. The small square in front of the ruins is called...*

Largo 16 Ottobre 1943

This square is named for the day when Nazi trucks parked here and threatened to take the Jews to concentration camps unless the community came up with 110 pounds of gold in 24 hours. Everyone, including non-Jewish Romans, tossed in their precious gold, and the demand was met. The Nazis took the gold—and later, they took the Jews as well.

• *The big ancient ruin is the...*

Portico d'Ottavia

This monumental gateway—with columns supporting a triangular pediment—was built by soon-to-be emperor Augustus. Once flanked by temples and libraries, the passageway served as a kind of cultural center. After Rome's fall, the portico housed a thriving fish market. In the eighth century, the Portico became incorporated into the Church of Sant'Angelo in Pescheria. For centuries, this Christian church was packed every Saturday with Jews—forced by decree to listen to Christian sermons.

Locals love to tell of the poor old woman who refused to sell her land and now owns a priceless bit of real estate that includes an ancient arch (at #25 under the arch).

Facing the Portico d'Ottavia, look to the right to see the huge Roman ruins of the Teatro di Marcello. (You may need to back up or move forward to get a glimpse of the theater.) The ancient stone arches are now topped with more modern structures. Sophia Loren bought a flat on its top floor.

• *Now walk to the left along the street called...*

Via del Portico d'Ottavia

This main drag—the best-preserved of the old streets—is a fine place to get a taste of yesterday's ghetto and today's Rome. From the start

(near the Roman arch), look down the street. On the left is the new building from 1911. On the right, in the distance, is the only surviving line of old ghetto building fronts. Imagine today's street as it was then: much narrower. Walking down the street, notice kosher restaurants proudly serving *carciofi* (artichokes, which only Jewish grandmothers can cook properly) and shops of fine, locally produced Judaica. You might see posters for community events, a few men wearing yarmulkes, and political graffiti, both pro- and anti-Israel. The Palestine Liberation Organization attacked this area in 1982, and a police presence still lingers.

After a block, you reach the center of the district. Look right, down Via San Ambrogio, to see an old surviving street. The square ahead is newly pedestrianized. This is where older folks hang out together and shoot the breeze, sometimes even bringing their favorite chairs from home. Though the Jewish community has long since dispersed all over Rome, most Roman Jews continue to spend time in this neighborhood to enjoy the strong feeling of community that survives. The big yellow building (on the left) houses the Jewish school.

This neighborhood has become trendy recently, and apartment prices are now beyond the means of most members of the Jewish community. Ironically, only the richest Jews could afford to relocate after 1870—and because the poor had to stay, their descendants have enjoyed healthy real-estate appreciation.

Opposite the big school, take a one-block detour down Via della Reginella. At #28, notice where the six-floor buildings end and more elegant and spacious (but no taller) three-floor buildings begin...marking the end of the ghetto. In the square (Piazza Mattei) at the end of the lane is a fun fountain—an old Mannerist work, later embellished with turtles by Bernini. It's said that Bernini cared about the Jews and honored them with the symbol of a turtle—an ancient creature that carries all its belongings on its back.

Back on the main drag (Via del Portico Ottavia), continue to Bar Toto, where you'll see a slot in the wall—a ghetto-era charity box for orphans that still accepts donations for worthy causes. The ancient relief above the box marks the home of a big shot who, at the start of the Renaissance age (before the ghetto's establishment in 1555), plugged this chunk of ancient Rome into his facade for prestige.

At the next intersection (Piazza Costaguti), stand in the white decorative square in the cobbles. The Sora Margherita Associazione Culturale, a restaurant with no sign, is located on the car-filled square—Piazza delle Cinque Scole—30 yards to the left, at #30 (see listing on page 300). On your right is a

traditional Jewish bakery. Go inside to check out the braided challah bread, cheesecakes, almond-paste-filled macaroons, and "Jewish Pizzas"—like little €2 fruitcakes. Just beyond that, the curving, white-columned structure is part of a former Carmelite convent. Imagine the outrage of the Jewish community when the Church built a convent and a Catholic school here in the ghetto to preach to their children.

Pop into the tunnel-like alleyway next to it, and—in the evocative little courtyard—imagine the tight conditions of thousands of Jews living in this small seven-acre area. Then head back to the main square and consider how times are much better today.

JEWISH GHETTO WALK

COLOSSEUM TOUR

Colosseo

Rome has many layers—modern, Baroque, Renaissance, Christian. But let's face it: "Rome" is Caesars, gladiators, chariots, centurions, *Et tu, Brute,*" trumpet fanfares, and thumbs-up or thumbs-down. That's the Rome we'll look at. Our "Caesar Shuffle" begins with the downtown core of ancient Rome, the Colosseum. A logical next stop is the Roman Forum, just next door (and the next chapter).

ORIENTATION

Cost: €11 combo-ticket includes Palatine Hill and Roman Forum, ticket valid two days—one entry per sight.

Hours: Daily 8:30 until one hour before sunset (April–Sept until 19:00, Oct until 18:15, Nov–Feb until 16:15, March until 16:30), last entry one hour before closing.

Getting There: The Colosseo Metro line B stop is just across the street from the monument. Bus #60 is handy for hotels near Via Firenze and Via Nazionale. Bus #87 links Largo Argentina with the Colosseum.

Avoiding Lines: The lines in front of the Colosseum are for buying tickets and for security checks, not for actually entering the sight. While everyone has to wait in the security line to go through the metal detectors, once you're through that—if you have your ticket already—stay to the left and muscle your way past the ticket-buying crowd to go directly to the turnstile, which never has a line. You'll likely save lots of time if you get your ticket in advance using one of these alternatives:

1. Consider buying the €20 Roma Pass or €22 Archeologia Card at a less-crowded sight, and then use it to bypass the ticket-buying line at the Colosseum; you can insert your pass directly into the turnstile. Note: You can buy a Roma Pass at the *tabacchi*

shop in the Colosseo Metro station, at the entrance to Palatine Hill, or at the entrance to the Forum (as well as online or by phone). For details on these passes, see page 40.

2. Buy and print your ticket online, choosing the day you'll visit and paying a €1.50 booking fee (www.ticketclic.it). Note that "free tickets" are valid only for EU citizens with ID.

3. Buy your ticket at the less-crowded Palatine Hill entrance on Via di San Gregorio (facing the Forum, with Colosseum at your back, go left down the street). Technically, the Palatine Hill entry is "entrance-only," but this rule is not strictly enforced, meaning you could buy the ticket, exit, and head straight back to the Colosseum.

4. Purchase a €4 guided tour. Tickets for official tours, offered hourly by the Colosseum's guides, are available inside the

Colosseum near the ticket counter (see "Tours," below). Tell the guard that you want to purchase a guided tour and he will usher you toward the ticket booth.

Private walking-tour guides (or their American assistants) linger outside the Colosseum, offering tours that include the admission fee and allow you to skip the line. This will cost you a few extra euros (€21 for two-hour tours of the Colosseum, Palatine Hill, and Forum, including the €11 ticket), but can save time; however, see the warning below.

Warnings: It can be hard to judge the length of the ticket line, because it's tucked into the Colosseum arcade—and besides, there's often a line just to get through security. **Unscrupulous private guides** might tell you that there's a long line, when really there's no line at all. They might say the Palatine Hill and Forum are included in their tour, only to give just a few minutes of commentary. (They purchase a group Colosseum ticket, but say "ciao" after the Colosseum tour, leaving you to buy a new ticket for Palatine Hill and the Forum.) Also note that you may buy a tour ticket to save time, only to get stuck waiting for the guide to sell enough tickets to assemble a group.

Also beware of the **goofy gladiators.** For a fee, the incredibly crude modern-day gladiators snuff out their cigarettes and pose for photos. They take easy-to-swindle tourists for too much money. Watch out if you tangle with these guys (they're armed... and accustomed to getting as much as €100 from naive tourists). If you go for it, €4–5 for one photo usually keeps them appeased.

And finally, look out for **pickpockets.** The Colosseum's exterior is traditionally a happy hunting ground for gangs of children pickpockets who distract you by shoving sheets of card-board (or newspapers or magazines) close to you as they steal your things.

Information: Outside the entrance of the Colosseum, vendors sell handy little *Rome: Past and Present* books with plastic overlays to un-ruin the ruins (marked €25 with DVD, €20 for smaller book, price soft so offer less). For an in-depth guidebook, pick up the green, lightweight *Roman Forum, Palatine, Colosseum Guide* by Electa (€8, buy at bookstore next to Colosseum ticket office). Information tel. 06-3996-7700.

Tours: A dry but fact-filled **audioguide** is available just past the turnstiles (€4.50 for 2 hours of use; or download our free audio-tour at www.ricksteves.com—see page 382). A handheld **video-guide** senses where you are in the site and plays related video clips (available in 2009, €5.50, pick up after turnstiles). Guided 45-minute to one-hour **tours** in English depart nearly hourly between 9:45 and 17:15 (€4, purchase inside the Colosseum near the ticket counter at windows marked *Visite Guidate*). Taking the official Colosseum tour allows you to skip the ticket line.

Length of This Tour: Allow 45 minutes.

Services: Tiny, crowded WCs are inside; the better, bigger, and cleaner WC is behind the Colosseum (facing ticket entrance, go right; WC is under stairway). The Palatine Museum has good public WCs—worth noting if you're headed there next (see ❷ Palatine Hill Tour on page 124).

Cuisine Art: For a quick lunch, climb the steps above the WC and cross the busy street to the cafés with expansive views of the Colosseum. However, for a better value (but no views at all), see the recommended restaurants on page 308. Generally, the Colosseum-Forum area has limited food options. Consider pack-ing a light picnic.

Bike Rental: At Cool Rent—10 yards to the right as you exit the Colosseo Metro stop—you can get a bike and pedal from the Colosseum out to the Appian Way. Be prepared for some heavy traffic (€3/hr, €10/day, daily 9:30–20:00, leave your driver's license or €100 cash for deposit).

THE TOUR BEGINS

Exterior

• *View the Colosseum from the Forum fence, across the street from the Colosseo Metro station.*

Built when the Roman Empire was at its peak in A.D. 80, the Colosseum represents Rome at its grandest. The Flavian Amphi-theater (Anfiteatro Flavio, its real name) was an arena for gladia-tor contests and public spectacles. When killing became a spectator sport, the Romans wanted to share the fun with as many people as possible, so they stuck two semicircular theaters together to create

a freestanding amphitheater. The outside (where slender cypress trees stand today) was decorated with a 100-foot-tall bronze statue of Nero that gleamed in the sunlight. In a later age, the colossal structure was nicknamed a "coloss-eum," the wonder of its age. It could accommodate 50,000 roaring fans (100,000 thumbs).

The Romans pioneered the use of concrete and the rounded arch, which enabled them to build on this tremendous scale. The exterior is a skeleton of 3.5 million cubic feet of travertine stone. (Each of the pillars flanking the ground-level arches weighs five tons.) It took 200 ox-drawn wagons shuttling back and forth every day for four years just to bring the stone here from Tivoli. They stacked stone blocks (without mortar) into the shape of an arch, supported temporarily by wooden scaffolding. Finally, they wedged a keystone into the top of the arch—it not only kept the arch from falling, it could bear even more weight above. Iron pegs held the larger stones together—notice the small holes that pockmark the sides.

The exterior says a lot about the Romans. They were great engineers, not artists, and the building is more functional than beautiful. While the essential structure is Roman, the four-story facade is decorated with mostly Greek columns—Doric-like Tuscan columns on the ground level, Ionic on the second story, Corinthian on the next level, and at the top, half-columns with a mix of all three. Originally, copies of Greek statues stood in the arches of the middle two stories, giving a veneer of sophistication to this arena of death. If ancient Romans visited the United States today as tourists, they might send home postcards of our greatest works of "art"—freeways.

Only a third of the original Colosseum remains. Earthquakes destroyed some of it, but most was carted off as easy pre-cut stones for other buildings during the Middle Ages and Renaissance.

• *To enter, first go through the security line. Then join the ticket line or—if you've already purchased a ticket or pass elsewhere—walk past the line of people waiting to buy tickets on your right, and go directly to the turnstile. To pay for an official tour, bypass the ticket line and go instead to the windows marked* Visite Guidate.

Once past the turnstiles, turn right and belly up to the railing near the large cross. You're on the north side of the arena, at the Emperor's Box (see map on next page).

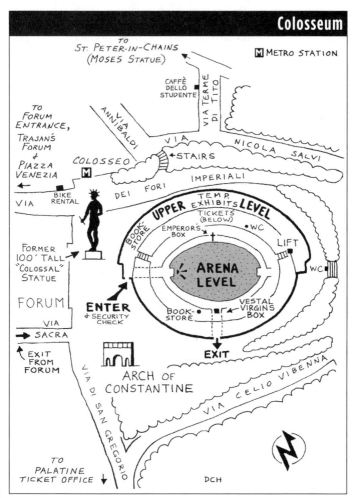

Colosseum

TO
ST. PETER-IN-CHAINS
(MOSES STATUE)

Ⓜ METRO STATION

CAFFÈ
DELLO
STUDENTE

VIA TERME DI TITO

TO
FORUM
ENTRANCE,
TRAJAN'S
FORUM
&
PIAZZA
VENEZIA

VIA ANNIBALDI

VIA

NICOLA SALVI

COLOSSEO
Ⓜ

←STAIRS

IMPERIALI

VIA

BIKE
RENTAL

DEI FORI

TEMP.
EXHIBITS
UPPER   LEVEL

TICKETS
(BELOW)

BOOK-STORE

EMPEROR'S
BOX

• WC

LIFT

FORMER
100' TALL
"COLOSSAL"
STATUE

ARENA
LEVEL

WC •

FORUM

ENTER
& SECURITY
CHECK

BOOK-
STORE •

VESTAL
VIRGINS
BOX

VIA

SACRA

EXIT
FROM
FORUM

EXIT

VIA DI SAN GREGORIO

ARCH OF
CONSTANTINE

VIA CELIO VIBENNA

N

TO
PALATINE
TICKET OFFICE ↓

DCH

Interior

You're at the "50-yard line" on arena level. What you see now are the underground passages beneath the playing surface. The oval-shaped arena (280 by 165 feet) was originally covered with a wooden floor, then sprinkled with sand (*arena* in Latin). The new bit of reconstructed Colosseum floor gives you an accurate sense of the original floor and the subterranean warren where animals and prisoners were held. As in modern stadiums, the spectators

ringed the playing area in bleacher seats that slant up from the arena floor. The brick masses around you supported the first small tier of seats, and you can see two larger, slanted supports higher up.

A variety of materials were used to build the stadium. Look around. Big white travertine blocks stacked on top of each other

formed the skeleton. The brick pillars for the bleachers were made with a shell of brick, filled in with concrete. Marble columns or ornamental facing covered the bare brick. (For the upper-floor cheap seats, they used plaster.) A few marble seats have been restored (at the left, or east end). The whole thing was topped with an enormous canvas awning that could be hoisted across by armies of sailors to provide shade for the spectators—the first domed stadium.

• *Stroll counterclockwise to the west end.*

"Hail, Caesar! *(Ave, Cesare!)* We who are about to die salute you!" The gladiators would enter the arena from the west end, parade around to the sound of trumpets, acknowledge the Vestal Virgins (on the south side), stop at the emperor's box (supposedly marked today by the cross—although no one knows for sure where it was), raise their weapons, shout, and salute—and then begin fighting. The fights pitted men against men, men against beasts, and beasts against beasts.

Picture 50,000 screaming people around you (did gladiators get stage fright?), and imagine that they hate you and want to see you die. Find the shafts of little elevators near the center that brought you unpleasant surprises like wild animals.

The games began with a few warm-up acts—watching dogs bloody themselves attacking porcupines, female gladiators fighting each other, or a little person battling a one-legged man. Then came the main event—the gladiators.

Some wielded swords, protected only with a shield and a heavy helmet. Others represented fighting fishermen, with a net to snare opponents and a trident to spear them. The gladiators were usually slaves, criminals, or poor people who got their chance for freedom, wealth, and fame in the ring. They learned to fight in training schools, then battled their way up the ranks. The best were rewarded like our modern sports stars, with fan clubs, great wealth, and, yes, product endorsements.

The animals came from all over the world: lions, tigers, and bears (oh my!), crocodiles, elephants, and hippos (not to mention exotic human "animals" from the "barbarian" lands). They were kept in cages beneath the arena floor, then lifted up in elevators. Released at floor level, the animals would pop out from behind blinds into the arena—the gladiator didn't know where, when, or by what he'd be attacked. (This brought howls of laughter from the hardened fans in the cheap seats who had a better view of the action.) Nets ringed the arena to protect the crowd. The stadium was inaugurated with a 100-day festival in which 2,000 men and 9,000 animals were killed. Colosseum employees squirted perfumes around the stadium to mask the stench of blood.

If a gladiator fell helpless to the ground, his opponent would approach the emperor's box and ask: Should he live or die? Sometimes the emperor left the decision to the crowd, who would judge based on how valiantly the man had fought. They would make their decision—thumbs-up or thumbs-down. Consider the value of these games in placating and controlling the huge Roman populace. Seeing the king of beasts—a lion—slain by a gladiator reminded the masses of man's triumph of nature. Seeing exotic animals from Africa heralded their conquest of distant lands. And having the thumbs-up or thumbs-down authority over another person's life gave them a real sense of power. Imagine the psychological boost the otherwise downtrodden masses felt when the emperor granted them this thrilling decision.

Did they throw Christians to the lions like in the movies? Christians were definitely thrown to the lions, made to fight gladiators, crucified, and burned alive...but probably not here in this particular stadium. Maybe, but probably not.

Rome was a nation of warriors that built an empire by conquest. The battles fought against Germans and other barbarians, Egyptians, and strange animals were played out daily here in the Colosseum for the benefit of city-slicker bureaucrats, who got vicarious thrills by watching brutes battle to the death. The contests were always free, sponsored by the government to bribe the people's favor or to keep Rome's growing masses of unemployed rabble off the streets.

• *With these scenes in mind, wander around. Climb to the upper deck, where you'll find a more colossal view of the arena and a nice look at the Arch of Constantine, plus a bookstore and temporary exhibits. There are stairs near either long end (east or west), as well as an elevator at the east end (circle clockwise to get there).*

After you exit, head to the Arch of Constantine (between the Colosseum and Forum, at the west corner of the Colosseum).

Arch of Constantine

If you are a Christian, were raised a Christian, or simply belong to a so-called "Christian nation," ponder this arch. It marks one of the great turning points in history—the military coup that made

Christianity mainstream. In A.D. 312, Emperor Constantine defeated his rival Maxentius in the crucial Battle of the Milvian Bridge. The night before, he had seen a vision of a cross in the sky. Constantine—whose mother and sister were Christians—became sole emperor and legalized Christianity. With this one battle, a once-obscure Jewish sect with a handful of followers was now the state religion of the entire Western world. In A.D. 300, you could be killed for being a Christian; later, you could be killed for not being one. Church enrollment boomed.

This newly restored arch is like an ancient museum. It's decorated entirely with recycled carvings originally made for other buildings. By covering it with exquisite carvings of high Roman art—works that glorified previous emperors—Constantine put himself in their league. Hadrian is featured in the round reliefs, with Marcus Aurelius in the square reliefs higher up. The big statues on top are of Trajan and Augustus. Originally, Augustus drove a chariot similar to the one topping the modern Victor Emanuel II monument. Fourth-century Rome may have been in decline, but Constantine clung to its glorious past.

• *The Roman Forum (Foro Romano) is to the right of the arch, 100 yards away; you can enter it through the Forum entrance on Via dei Fori Imperiali (or you can enter it when you leave Palatine Hill, exiting into the Forum—see map on page 112). If you're ready for a visit, turn to the next chapter.*

ROMAN FORUM TOUR

Foro Romano

The Forum was the political, religious, and commercial center of the city. Rome's most important temples and halls of justice were here. This was the place for religious processions, political demonstrations, elections, important speeches, and parades by conquering generals. As Rome's empire expanded, these few acres of land became the center of the civilized world.

ORIENTATION

Cost: €11 combo-ticket includes Colosseum and Palatine Hill, ticket valid two days—one entry per site. To avoid standing in a long ticket-buying line, see the information on "Avoiding Lines" on page 102 of the Colosseum Tour.

Hours: Daily 8:30 until one hour before sunset (April–Sept until 19:00, Oct until 18:15, Nov–Feb until 16:15, March until 16:30), last entry one hour before closing.

Tips: The ancient paving at the Forum is uneven; wear sturdy shoes. I carry a water bottle and refill it at the Forum's public drinking fountains.

Getting There: The closest Metro stop is Colosseo. The Forum's only entrance—where this tour begins—is on Via dei Fori Imperiali ("Road of the Imperial Forums"). From the Colosseum Metro stop, walk away from the Colosseum on Via dei Fori Imperiali to find the ticket office near the intersection with Via Cavour.

You can also enter the Forum (although this isn't an official entrance, it's allowable) through the Palatine Hill ticket office on Via di San Gregorio—after buying your ticket, take the path on the right to avoid climbing the hill, and wind around to enter the Forum at the Arch of Titus.

Information: There's a TI near the Via dei Fori Imperiali entrance (near Basilica Aemilia). Just like at the Colosseum, vendors at the Forum sell small *Rome: Past and Present* books with plastic overlays that restore the ruins (includes DVD, marked €25, sometimes you'll find the smaller book for €20). The green, light-weight *Roman Forum, Palatine, Colosseum Guide* by Electa is good (€8, buy at bookstore next to ticket office). Information office tel. 06-3996-7700.

Tour: A €4 unexciting yet informative audioguide helps decipher the rubble, but you'll have to return it to the Forum entrance on Via dei Fori Imperiali instead of being able to exit directly to Capitol Hill or the Colosseum. Remember you can download a free audiotour at www.ricksteves.com (see page 382). Official guided tours in English run once a day at around 13:00 (€4, 45 min, confirm time at ticket office).

Services: There's a WC at the ticket office.

Length of This Tour: Allow 90 minutes.

THE TOUR BEGINS

• *Walk through the entrance, located on Via dei Fori Imperiali, and stroll down the hill to the main road: the Via Sacra.*

Overview

With your back to the entrance, the hill on the right with the bell tower is Capitol Hill. Using an imaginary clock for a compass, you'll see Palatine Hill at 10 o'clock; it's the hill with all the trees. The valley in between is rectangular, running roughly east (the Colosseum end) to west (Capitol Hill end). The rocky path at your feet is the Via Sacra, leading past the large brick Senate building and up Capitol Hill to your right. To the left, it passes trees, temples, and basilicas to the Arch of Titus.

Picture being here when a conquering general returned to Rome with crates of booty. The valley was full of gleaming white buildings  topped with bronze roofs. The Via Sacra—Main Street of the Forum—would be lined with citizens waving branches and carrying torches. The trumpets would sound as the parade began. First came porters, carrying chests full of gold and jewels. Then a parade of exotic animals from the conquered lands—elephants, giraffes, hippopotamuses—for the crowd to "ooh" and "ahh" at. Next came the prisoners in chains, with the captive king on a wheeled platform so the people could jeer and

ROMAN FORUM TOUR

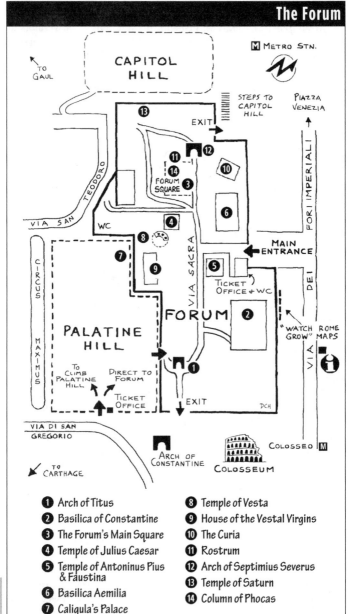

The Forum

1. Arch of Titus
2. Basilica of Constantine
3. The Forum's Main Square
4. Temple of Julius Caesar
5. Temple of Antoninus Pius & Faustina
6. Basilica Aemilia
7. Caligula's Palace
8. Temple of Vesta
9. House of the Vestal Virgins
10. The Curia
11. Rostrum
12. Arch of Septimius Severus
13. Temple of Saturn
14. Column of Phocas

ROMAN FORUM TOUR

spit at him. Finally, the conquering hero himself would drive down in his four-horse chariot, with rose petals strewn in his path. The whole procession would run the length of the Forum and up the face of Capitol Hill to the Temple of Saturn (the eight big columns midway up the hill—#13 on map on page 112), where they'd place the booty in Rome's coffers. Then they'd continue up to the summit to the Temple of Jupiter (only ruins of its foundation remain today) to dedicate the victory to the King of the Gods.

• *Take a left down the Via Sacra and amble all the way to the...*

❶ Arch of Titus (Arco di Tito)

The Arch of Titus commemorated the Roman victory over the province of Judaea (Israel) in A.D. 70. The Romans had a reputation as

benevolent conquerors who tolerated the local customs and rulers. All they required was allegiance to the empire, shown by worshipping the emperor as a god. No problem for most conquered people, who already had half a dozen gods on their prayer lists anyway. But Israelites believed in only one god, and it wasn't the emperor. Israel revolted. After a short but bitter war, the Romans defeated the rebels, took Jerusalem, destroyed their temple (leaving only the foundation wall—today's revered "Wailing Wall"), and brought home 50,000 Jewish slaves...who were forced to build this arch (and the Colosseum).

Roman propaganda decorates the inside of the arch, where a relief shows the emperor Titus in a chariot being crowned by the

goddess Victory. (Thanks to modern pollution, they both look like they've been through the wars.) The other side shows booty from the sacking of the temple in Jerusalem—soldiers carrying a Jewish menorah and other plunder. The two (unfinished) plaques on poles were to have listed the conquered cities. Look at the top of the ceiling. Constructed after his death, the relief shows Titus riding an eagle to heaven, where he'll become one of the gods.

The brutal crushing of the A.D. 70 rebellion (and another one 60 years later) devastated the nation of Israel. With no temple as a center for their faith, the Jews scattered throughout the world (the Diaspora). There would be no Jewish political entity again for almost two thousand years, until modern Israel was created after World War II.

• Backtrack down the Via Sacra into the Forum. After about 50 yards, turn right and follow a path uphill to the three huge arches of the...

❷ Basilica of Constantine (a.k.a. Basilica Maxentius)

Yes, these are big arches. But they represent only one-third of the original Basilica of Constantine, a mammoth hall of justice. The arches were matched by a similar set along the Via Sacra side (only a few squat brick piers remain). Between them ran the central hall, which was spanned by a roof 130 feet high—about 55 feet higher than the side arches you see. (The stub of brick you see sticking up began an arch that once spanned the central hall.) The hall itself was as long as a football field, lavishly furnished with colorful inlaid marble, a gilded bronze ceiling, and statues, and filled with strolling Romans. At the far (west) end was an enormous marble statue of Emperor Constantine on a throne. (Pieces of this statue, including a hand the size of a man, are on display in Rome's Capitoline Museums.)

The basilica was begun by the emperor Maxentius, but after he was trounced in battle (see page 36), the victor—Constantine—completed the massive building. No doubt about it, the Romans built monuments on a more epic scale than any previous Europeans, wowing their "barbarian" neighbors.

• Now stroll deeper into the Forum, downhill along the Via Sacra, through the trees. Many of the large basalt stones under your feet were walked on by Caesar Augustus 2,000 years ago. Pass by the only original bronze door still swinging on its ancient hinges (green, on right) and continue between ruined buildings until the Via Sacra opens up to a flat, grassy area.

❸ The Forum's Main Square

The original Forum, or main square, was this flat patch about the size of a football field, stretching to the foot of Capitol Hill. Surrounding it were temples, law courts, government buildings, and triumphal arches.

Rome was born right here. According to legend, twin brothers Romulus (Rome) and Remus were orphaned in infancy and raised by

---

Rome—Republic and Empire
(500 B.C.–A.D. 500)

Ancient Rome spanned about a thousand years, from 500 B.C. to A.D. 500. During that time, Rome expanded from a small tribe of barbarians to a vast empire, then dwindled slowly to city size again. For the first 500 years, when Rome's armies made her ruler of the Italian peninsula and beyond, Rome was a republic governed by elected senators. Over the next 500 years, a time of world conquest and eventual decline, Rome was an empire ruled by a military-backed dictator.

Julius Caesar bridged the gap between republic and empire. This ambitious general and politician, popular with the people because of his military victories and charisma, suspended the Roman constitution and assumed dictatorial powers in about 50 B.C., and in a few years was assassinated by a conspiracy of senators. His adopted son, Augustus, succeeded him, and soon "Caesar" was not just a name but a title.

Emperor Augustus ushered in the Pax Romana, or Roman peace (from A.D. 1–200), a time when Rome reached her peak and controlled an empire that stretched even beyond Eurail—from Scotland to Egypt, from Turkey to Morocco.

---

a she-wolf on top of Palatine Hill. Growing up, they found it hard to get dates. So they and their cohorts attacked the nearby Sabine tribe and kidnapped their women. After they made peace, this marshy valley became the meeting place and then the trading center for the scattered tribes on the surrounding hillsides.

The square was the busiest and most crowded—and often the seediest—section of town. Besides the senators, politicians, and currency exchangers, there were even sleazier types—souvenir hawkers, pickpockets, fortune-tellers, gamblers, slave marketers, drunks, hookers, lawyers, and tour guides.

The Forum is now rubble, but imagine it in its prime: blinding white marble buildings with 40-foot-high columns and shining bronze roofs; rows of statues painted in realistic colors; processional chariots rattling down the Via Sacra. Mentally replace tourists in T-shirts with tribunes in togas. Imagine the buildings towering and the people buzzing around you while an orator gives a rabble-rousing

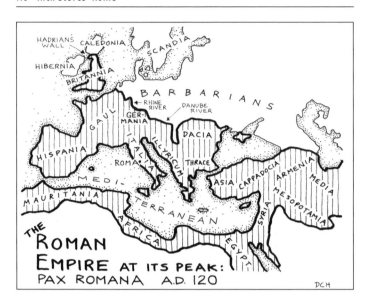

THE **ROMAN EMPIRE** AT ITS PEAK: PAX ROMANA A.D. 120

speech from the Rostrum. If things still look like just a pile of rocks, at least tell yourself, "But Julius Caesar once leaned against these rocks."

• *At the near (east) end of the main square (the Colosseum is to the east) are the foundations of a temple now capped with a peaked wood-and-metal roof.*

❹ Temple of Julius Caesar (Tempio del Divo Giulio, or Ara di Cesare)

Julius Caesar's body was burned on this spot (under the metal roof) after his assassination. Peek behind the wall into the small apse area, where a mound of dirt usually has fresh flowers—given to remember the man who, more than any other, personified the greatness of Rome.

Caesar (100–44 b.c.) changed Rome—and the Forum—dramatically. He cleared out many of the wooden market stalls and began to ring the square with even grander buildings. Caesar's house was located behind the temple, near that clump of trees. He walked right by here on the day he was assassinated ("Beware the Ides of March!" warned a street-corner Etruscan preacher).

Though he was popular with the masses, not everyone liked Caesar's urban design or his politics. When he assumed dictatorial powers, he was ambushed and stabbed to death by a conspiracy of senators, including his adopted son, Brutus (*"Et tu, Brute?"*).

The funeral was held here, facing the main square. The citizens gathered, and speeches were made. Mark Antony stood up to say (in Shakespeare's words), "Friends, Romans, countrymen, lend me your ears. I come to bury Caesar, not to praise him." When Caesar's body was burned, the citizens who still loved him threw anything at hand on the fire, requiring the fire department to come put it out. Later, Emperor Augustus dedicated this temple in his name, making Caesar the first Roman to become a god.

• *Behind and to the left of the Temple of Julius Caesar are the 10 tall columns of the...*

❺ Temple of Antoninus Pius and Faustina

The Senate built this temple to honor Emperor Antoninus Pius (A.D. 138–161) and his deified wife, Faustina. The 50-foot-tall Corinthian (leafy) columns must have been awe-inspiring to out-of-towners who grew up in thatched huts. Although the temple has been inhabited by a church, you can still see the basic layout—a staircase led to a shaded porch (the columns), which admitted you to the main building (now a church), where the statue of the god sat. Originally, these columns supported a triangular pediment decorated with sculptures.

Picture these columns, with gilded capitals, supporting brightly painted statues in the pediment, and the whole building capped with a gleaming bronze roof. The stately gray rubble of today's Forum is a faded black-and-white photograph of a 3-D Technicolor era.

The building is a microcosm of many of the changes that occurred after Rome fell. In medieval times, the temple was pillaged. Note the diagonal cuts high on the marble columns—a failed attempt by scavengers to cut through the pillars to pull them down for their precious

stone. (Vinegar and rope cut marble...but because vinegar also eats through rope, they abandoned the attempt.) In 1550, a church was housed inside the ancient temple. The door shows the street level at the time of Michelangelo. The long staircase was underground until excavated in the 1800s.

• *There's a ramp next to the Temple of A. and F. Walk halfway up it and look to the left to view the...*

Religion in Ancient Rome

Religion in ancient Rome was all about the *pax deorum* (peace, or pact, with the gods) that guaranteed the prosperity of the incredibly superstitious Romans. To appease the fickle gods, they performed elaborate rituals at lavish temples and shrines. Romans had a god for every moment of their days and each important event in their lives. While the Romans adopted the Greek pantheon, they also embraced the gods from many of the people they came into contact with, sometimes using elaborate ceremonies to persuade these new gods to "move" to Rome. Scholars estimate Romans had about 30,000 gods to keep happy. In this high-maintenance religion, there was Cunina, the goddess who protected cradles; Statulinus, to help children stand up; and Fabulina, for their first words. Fornax was the oven god, Pomona the fruit tree goddess, Sterculinus the manure god, and Venus Cloacina the sewer goddess.

Priests interpreted the will of the gods by studying the internal organs of sacrificed animals, the flight of birds, and prophetic books. A clap of thunder was enough to postpone a battle.

Astrology, magic rites, the cult of deified emperors, house gods, and the near-deification of ancestors permeated Roman life. But all these gods didn't quite do it for the Romans—the gods were gradually replaced by the rise of monotheistic religions from the East. In A.D. 312, Emperor Constantine legalized and embraced Christianity. By 390, the Christian God was the only legal god in Rome.

❻ Basilica Aemilia

A basilica was a covered public forum, often serving as a Roman hall of justice. In a society that was as legal-minded as America is today, you needed a lot of lawyers—and a big place to put them. Citizens came here to work out matters such as inheritances and building permits, or to sue somebody.

Notice the layout. It was a long, rectangular building. The stubby columns all in a row form one long, central hall flanked by two side aisles. Medieval Christians required a larger meeting hall for their worship services than Roman temples provided, so they used the spacious Roman basilica as the model for their churches. Cathedrals from France to Spain to England, from Romanesque to  Gothic to Renaissance, all have the same basic floor plan as a Roman basilica.

• *Return again to the Temple of Julius Caesar. To the right of the temple are the three tall Corinthian columns of the Temple of Castor and Pollux. Beyond that is Palatine Hill—the corner of which may have been...*

❼ Caligula's Palace (a.k.a. the Palace of Tiberius)

Emperor Caligula (ruled A.D. 37–41) had a huge palace on Palatine Hill overlooking the Forum. It actually sprawled down the hill into the Forum (some supporting arches remain in the hillside).

Caligula was not a nice person. He tortured enemies, stole senators' wives, and parked his chariot in handicap spaces. But Rome's luxury-loving emperors only added to the glory of the Forum, with each one trying to make his mark on history.

• *To the left of the Temple of Castor and Pollux, find the remains of a small, white, circular temple.*

❽ Temple of Vesta

This is perhaps Rome's most sacred spot. Rome considered itself one big family, and this temple represented a circular hut, like the kind that Rome's first families lived in. Inside, a fire burned, just as in a Roman home. And back in the days before lighters and butane, you never wanted your fire to go out. As long as the sacred flame burned, Rome would stand. The flame was tended by priestesses known as Vestal Virgins.

• *Around the back of the Temple of Vesta, you'll find two rectangular brick pools. These stood in the courtyard of the...*

❾ House of the Vestal Virgins

The Vestal Virgins lived in a two-story building surrounding a long central courtyard with these two pools at one end. Rows of statues depicting leading Vestal Virgins flanked the courtyard. This place was the model—both architecturally and sexually—for medieval convents and monasteries.

Chosen from noble families before they reached the age of 10, the six Vestal Virgins served a 30-year term. Honored and revered by the Romans, the Vestals even had their own box opposite the emperor in the Colosseum.

As the name implies, a Vestal took a vow of chastity. If she served her term faithfully—abstaining for 30 years—she was given a huge dowry, and allowed to marry. But if they found any Virgin who wasn't, she was strapped to a funeral car, paraded through the streets of the Forum, taken to a crypt, given a loaf of bread and a lamp...and buried alive. Many women suffered the latter fate.

• *Return to the Temple of Julius Caesar and head to the Forum's west end (opposite the Colosseum). As you pass alongside the big open space of the Forum's main square, consider how the piazza is still a standard part of any Italian town. It has reflected and accommodated the gregarious and outgoing nature of the Italian people since Roman times.*

Stop at the big, well-preserved brick building (on right) with the triangular roof and look in.

⓾ The Curia (Senate House)

The Curia was the most important political building in the Forum. While the present building dates from A.D. 283, this was the site of Rome's official center of government since the birth of the republic. Three hundred senators, elected by the citizens of Rome, met here to debate and create the laws of the land. Their wooden seats once circled the building in three tiers; the Senate president's podium sat at the far end. The marble floor is from ancient times. Listen to the echoes in this vast room—the acoustics are great.

Rome prided itself on being a republic. Early in the city's history, its people threw out the king and established rule by elected representa-

tives. Each Roman citizen was free to speak his mind and have a say in public policy. Even when emperors became the supreme authority, the Senate was a power to be reckoned with. The Curia building (A.D. 280) is well-preserved, having been used as a church since early Christian times. In the 1930s, it was restored and opened to the public as a historic site. (Note: Although Julius Caesar was assassinated in "the Senate," it wasn't here—the Senate was temporarily meeting across town.)

A statue and two reliefs inside the Curia help build our mental image of the Forum. The statue, made of porphyry marble in about

A.D. 100 (with its head, arms, and feet now missing), was a tribute to an emperor, probably Hadrian or Trajan. The two relief panels may have decorated the Rostrum. Those on the left show people (with big stone tablets) standing in line to burn their debt records following a government amnesty. The other shows the distribution of grain (Rome's welfare system), some buildings in the background, and the latest fashion in togas.

• *Go back down the Senate steps and find the 10-foot-high wall just to the left of the big arch, marked...*

⓫ Rostrum (Rostri)

Nowhere was Roman freedom more apparent than at this "Speaker's Corner." The Rostrum was a raised platform, 10 feet high and 80 feet long, decorated with statues, columns, and the prows of ships (rostra).

On a stage like this, Rome's orators, great and small, tried to draw a crowd and sway public opinion. Mark Antony rose to offer Caesar the laurel-leaf crown of kingship, which Caesar publicly (and hypocritically) refused while privately becoming a dictator. Men such as Cicero railed against the corruption and decadence that came with the city's newfound wealth. In later years, daring citizens even spoke out against the emperors, reminding them that Rome was once free. Picture the backdrop these speakers would have had—a mountain of marble buildings piling up on Capitol Hill.

In front of the Rostrum are trees bearing fruits that were sacred to the ancient Romans: olives (provided food, light, and preservatives), figs (tasty), and wine grapes (made a popular export product).

• *The big arch to the right of the Rostrum is the...*

⓬ Arch of Septimius Severus

In imperial times, the Rostrum's voices of democracy would have been dwarfed by images of empire such as the huge, six-story-high

Arch of Septimius Severus (A.D. 203). The reliefs commemorate the African-born emperor's battles in Mesopotamia. Near ground level, see soldiers marching captured barbarians back to Rome for the victory parade. Despite Severus' efficient rule, Rome's empire was crumbling under the weight of its own corruption, disease, decaying infrastructure, and the constant attacks by foreign "barbarians."

• *Pass underneath the Arch of Septimius Severus and turn left. On the slope of Capitol Hill are the eight remaining columns of the...*

Rome Falls

Remember that Rome lasted 1,000 years—500 years of growth, 200 years of peak power, and 300 years of gradual decay. The fall had many causes, among them the barbarians who pecked away at Rome's borders. Christians blamed the fall on moral decay. Pagans blamed it on Christians. Socialists blamed it on a shallow economy based on the spoils of war. (Republicans blamed it on Democrats.) Whatever the reasons, the far-flung empire could no longer keep its grip on conquered lands, and it pulled back. Barbarian tribes from Germany and Asia attacked the Italian peninsula and even looted Rome itself in A.D. 410, leveling many of the buildings in the Forum. In 476, when the last emperor checked out and switched off the lights, Europe plunged into centuries of ignorance, poverty, and weak government—the Dark Ages.

But Rome lived on in the Catholic Church. Christianity was the state religion of Rome's last generations. Emperors became popes (both called themselves "Pontifex Maximus"), senators became bishops, orators became priests, and basilicas became churches. The glory of Rome remains eternal.

⓭ Temple of Saturn

These columns framed the entrance to the Forum's oldest temple (497 B.C.). Inside was a humble, very old wooden statue of the god Saturn. But the statue's pedestal held the gold bars, coins, and jewels of Rome's state treasury, the booty collected by conquering generals.

• *Standing here, at one of the Forum's first buildings, look east at the lone, tall...*

⓮ Column of Phocas

This is the Forum's last monument (A.D. 608), a gift from the powerful Byzantine Empire to a fallen empire—Rome. Given to commemorate the pagan Pantheon's becoming a Christian church, it's like a symbolic last nail in ancient Rome's coffin. After Rome's 1,000-year reign, the city was looted by Vandals, the population of a million-plus shrank to about 10,000, and the once-grand city center—the Forum—was abandoned, slowly covered up by centuries of silt and dirt. In the 1700s, an English historian named Edward Gibbon overlooked this spot from Capitol Hill. Hearing Christian monks singing at these pagan ruins, he looked out at the few columns poking up from the ground, pondered the "Decline and Fall of the Roman Empire," and thought, "Hmm, that's a catchy title...."

• *There are several ways to exit the Forum:*

1. Exiting past the Arch of Titus lands you at the Arch of Constantine and Colosseum.

2. Exiting near the Arch of Septimius Severus and Mamertine Prison gets you to the stairs up to Capitol Hill.

3. Though the Forum entrance on Via dei Fori Imperiali is not officially an exit, guards will usually let you exit here.

PALATINE HILL TOUR

Monte Palatino

While many tourists consider the Palatine Hill just extra credit after the Forum, it offers an insight into the greatness of Rome that's well worth the effort. (And, if you're visiting the Colosseum or Forum, you've got a ticket whether you like it or not.) Palatine Hill is jam-packed with history—"the huts of Romulus and Remus," the huge Imperial Palace, a view of the Circus Maximus—but there's only the barest skeleton of rubble left to tell the story. This tour will enable the thoughtful sightseer to bring those remains to life. Palatine Hill is ideal for those who want to get away from the crowds and discover the romantic, melancholy essence of ruins. Become a 19th-century poet or a painter on the Grand Tour meditating on the destiny of once-great civilizations, and wander through the remains of the palaces that Nature seems to have reclaimed for herself.

ORIENTATION

Cost: €11 combo-ticket includes Roman Forum and Colosseum, ticket valid two days—one entry per site. It makes sense to buy a ticket or pass here to avoid lines at the Colosseum (see tips on "Avoiding Lines" on page 102).

Hours: Daily 8:30 until one hour before sunset (April–Sept until 19:00, Oct until 18:15, Nov–Feb until 16:15, March until 16:30), last entry one hour before closing.

Getting There: The closest Metro stop is Colosseo. The entrance is on Via di San Gregorio (facing the Forum with the Colosseum at your back, it's down the street to your left).

Tours: Audioguides cost €4 (must leave ID). Guided tours in English are offered once daily at 11:30 (€4, 45 min); ask for information at the ticket booth.

Length of This Tour: Allow 90 minutes.

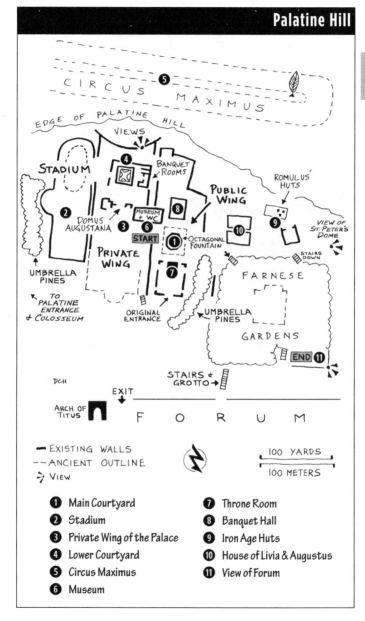

Palatine Hill

CIRCUS MAXIMUS ❺

EDGE OF PALATINE HILL

VIEWS

STADIUM

BANQUET ROOMS

PUBLIC WING

ROMULUS HUTS

❹

❷

DOMUS AUGUSTANA

MUSEUM & WC

❽

❸ ❻

START

❶ OCTAGONAL FOUNTAIN

❿

❾

VIEW OF ST. PETER'S DOME

PRIVATE WING

❼

STAIRS DOWN

UMBRELLA PINES

FARNESE

TO PALATINE ENTRANCE & COLOSSEUM

ORIGINAL ENTRANCE

UMBRELLA PINES

GARDENS

END ⓫

STAIRS & GROTTO →

DCH

EXIT

ARCH OF TITUS

F   O   R   U   M

— EXISTING WALLS
-- ANCIENT OUTLINE
↷ VIEW

100 YARDS

100 METERS

❶ Main Courtyard
❷ Stadium
❸ Private Wing of the Palace
❹ Lower Courtyard
❺ Circus Maximus
❻ Museum

❼ Throne Room
❽ Banquet Hall
❾ Iron Age Huts
❿ House of Livia & Augustus
⓫ View of Forum

Services: You'll find some WCs at the ground level of the museum in the center of the site. These are usually the least-crowded WCs in the whole Colosseum-Forum-Palatine area—use them. Another is at the ticket office when you enter, and one is hiding among the orange trees in the Renaissance Gardens.

THE TOUR BEGINS

• *We'll start our tour on top of the hill at the Palatine Museum (Antiquario Palatino, see photo; the museum is #6 on the map). From the entrance,*

take the stairs on the left and follow the path up. Walk past the stadium and some more ruins to the one modern building on the crest of the hill. It's the big, gray 1930s-style building that houses the museum. We'll visit the museum later. For now, grab a stone and sit with your back to the museum to orient yourself, facing in the direction of the Forum (roughly north).

THE IMPERIAL PALACE

You're sitting at the center of what was once a huge palace, the residence of emperors for three centuries. Orgies, royal weddings, assassinations, concerts, intrigues, births, funerals, banquets, and the occasional Tupperware party took place within these walls. What walls? The row of umbrella pines about 200 yards to the east (to your right) now marks one edge of the palace. The reconstructed brick tower (at about 11 o'clock) was the northwest corner. The palace also stretched behind you (the area behind the museum) and beneath you, since some of the palace had a lower floor. (Right now, you're standing not on the original palace's ground level, but several floors up.)

The area in front was the official wing of the palace; behind were the private quarters. All in all, it made for a cozy little 150,000-square-foot pad.

The palace was built by Emperor Domitian in about A.D. 81. A poet of the day described it as so grand that it "made Jupiter jealous."

• *Now proceed, following the map for this 11-stop tour. To your left (with your back to the museum) is a big rectangular field with an octagonal brick design in the center—the Main Courtyard of the palace.*

❶ Main Courtyard (Peristilio)

The brick octagon was a sunken fountain in the middle of an open-air courtyard. Like many fine Roman homes, this palace was built around

an oasis of peace where you could enjoy the sun, catch the precious rain, and listen to the babble of moving water. The courtyard was lined with columns (notice the fragments) supporting an arcade for shade. Originally, the floor and walls of the courtyard were faced with colorful marble.

• The palace's stadium is 100 yards behind you (to the east), near the long row of pine trees. Belly up to the railing and look down on the elliptical track.

❷ Stadium (Stadio)

This cigar-shaped, sunken stadium (500 feet long) was the palace's rec room. It looks like a racetrack, but it just held gardens with strolling paths. The oval running track at the south end was added later. The emperor had a raised box on the 50-yard line, in the curved apse across from you. At the north end were changing rooms, and the marble fragments that litter the ground once held up an arcade.

• Now, walk through the arch in the wall and imagine the…

❸ Private Wing of the Palace (Domus Augustana)

The area between the stadium and the museum held the private rooms of the emperor and his extended family. Today, a lone umbrella pine on a mound marks the courtyard of this wing. To the left are the brick ruins of the Domus.

- Wander southward under the arches and through the maze of brick rooms (many of them reconstructed), noticing…
- The typical Roman building method: Build a rectangular shell of brick, fill it with concrete, then finish it with either plaster (you'll see an occasional faded fresco) or slabs of marble. The small, round pockmarks on many walls show where the marble was fastened.
- The square holes in the walls held wooden beams, used for scaffolding during construction and maintenance, for shelves, and for wooden floors.
- Over the doorways, the bricks in the walls form the pattern of an arch. These "blind arches" were structural elements that allowed

the walls to be built higher. The iron bar clamps are recent additions and hold the crumbling walls together.

- Niches and apses once held statues. Every family had their own household gods and displayed small images of these guardian spirits, as well as busts of honored ancestors.
- The fragments of columns, reliefs, and sculpture scattered about suggest the wealth of this great palace.
- Finally, notice the floor plan—a complex, fantasyland maze of small, private, sometimes even curved rooms.

• In the south part of the Domus Augustana, you can look down on the ruins of the lower story.

❹ Lower Courtyard (Peristilio)

This open-air courtyard has the concave-convex remains of a large fountain that must have been a marvel. Try to mentally reconstruct

the palace that surrounded this fountain. The emperors could look down on it from the upper story (where you're standing) or view it from the rooms around it on the lower story, where the emperor and his family ate their meals in private.

The lower story was built into the slope of the hill. The southern part of the palace was an extension of the hillside, supported beneath your feet by big arches.

• Continue to the southern edge of the hill (directly behind the museum), overlooking a long, wide, grassy field—what once was the Circus Maximus. Lean over the railing and you might be able to make out the concave shape of the palace's southern facade.

❺ Circus Maximus

If the gladiator show at the Colosseum was sold out, you could always get a seat at the Circus Max. In an early version of today's demolition derby, Ben-Hur and his fellow charioteers once raced recklessly around this oblong course.

The chariots circled around the cigar-shaped mound in the center (notice the lone cypress tree that now marks one end of the mound). Bleachers (now grassy banks) originally surrounded the track (see artist's reconstruction, on next page).

The track was 1,300 feet long, while the whole stadium measured 2,130 feet by 720 feet and seated—get this—250,000 people. The wooden bleachers once collapsed during a race, killing thousands.

The horses began at a starting gate at the west end (to your right), while the public entered at the other end. Races consisted of seven laps (about 3.5 miles total). In such a small space, collisions and overturned

chariots were common. The charioteers were usually poor lowborn people who used this dangerous sport to get rich and famous. Some succeeded. Most died.

The public was crazy about the races. There were 12 per day, 240 days a year. Four teams dominated the competition—Reds, Whites, Blues, and Greens—and every citizen was fanatically devoted to one of them. Obviously, the emperors had the best seats in the house; built into the palace's curved facade was a box overlooking the track. For their pleasure, emperors occasionally had the circus floor carpeted with designs in colored powders.

Picture the scene: intact palace; emperor watching; a quarter of a million Romans cheering, jeering, and furiously betting. Horses raced here for more than a thousand years. The track dates from 300 B.C., and the spectacles continued into the Christian era, until A.D. 549, despite Church disapproval.

From this viewpoint, looking to the left, you can see the ruins of the Baths of Caracalla (not worth touring if you've seen the Palatine) rising above the trees a half-mile away. About a mile beyond that, the Appian Way led from a grand gate in the ancient wall, past the catacombs, to Brindisi.

• *Turn around and head back toward the museum—the shortest route is to the right.*

❻ Museum (Antiquario Palatino)

The museum contains statues and frescoes that help you imagine the luxury of the imperial Palatine. To the left after you enter, pause at

the statue of "Magna Mater" on her throne. This Great Mother brought life and fertility to the Roman people, who worshipped her at the nearby Temple of Cybele. Her arms and foot were destroyed by time, but there was always a cavity where her head should be—this was a standard Roman device in which interchangeable heads could be inserted. In this case, the Magna Mater's "head" was actually a sacred, black, cone-shaped meteorite that caused astonishment when it fell from the sky.

Also on this floor, Room V holds frescoes and statues from the time of Augustus and fine decorative terra-cotta panels. Room VII has busts of the notorious Emperor Nero ("Nerone") and exquisite marble-inlay work. In Room

VIII is a statue fragment of a river god's stomach. And finally, back near the entrance is a large, headless statue of a Muse that once decorated the Hippodrome.

Go back outside, down the stairs, and into the doorway directly below the staircase. In Room II, there's a (well-described in English) model of the eighth-century B.C. Iron Age huts of Romulus (and a modern WC).

Back outside, you'll see marble scraps nearby (and strewn all across Palatine Hill). Flashy building stone was used to boast of the power and vastness of the empire. Citizens knew that the Numidian yellow marble was from Tunisia, the veined Cipollino marble (with swirling designs like an onion) was from the island of Euboea in Greece, and the pink granite was from Aswan in Egypt. This was all sliced and laid out in fine pavement and wall designs, enjoyed by those who could only be thankful they were on the winning team. In later centuries, the Christian Church used marble as well—to symbolize its conquest over the pagan world.

• *From the museum, begin circling the Main Courtyard (with its octagonal fountain) counterclockwise. When the path turns left, keep walking another 40 feet or so to the squat brick pillar with a stubby column on top. Step into the...*

❼ Throne Room

The nerve center of an empire that controlled some 50 million people from Scotland to Africa, this was the official seat of power. The curved apse of the largest brick stump (there's now a plaque on it) marks the spot where the emperor sat on his throne for official business.

Imagine being a Roman citizen summoned by the emperor. You'd enter the palace through the main doorway (now a gap) at the far (Forum) end of the room, having climbed up three flights of a monumental staircase. The floor and walls dazzled with green, purple, red, white, and yellow marble. Along the walls were 12 colossal statues of Roman gods. The ceiling towered seven stories overhead. On either side were doorways leading to a basilica and the emperor's private temple.

You'd approach the emperor, who sat on a raised throne in the apse, dressed in royal purple, with a crown of laurel leaves on his head and a scepter cradled in his arm. Big braziers burned on either side, throwing off a flickering light. As you approached, you'd raise your arm to greet him, saying, *"Ave, Cesare!"* The words would echo through the great hall.

Now imagine yourself as emperor. Stand on the small white stone marking the location of the throne (a few feet in front of the plaque) and look out over your palace. (The ceiling was a barrel vault sitting upon towers as high as the brick tower in the distance to the left.)
• *Continue circling the Main Courtyard counterclockwise until it dead-ends at the...*

❽ Banquet Hall (Triclinium)

The floor of the banquet room had a hollow space beneath it (you can see the two-foot gap between the two original floors). Slaves stoked fires from underground stoves to heat the floor with forced air. At

the far end of the room, the platform and curved apse mark the spot where the emperor ate while looking down on his subjects. Guests could look into the adjoining room, where an elliptical-shaped fountain (see the brick remains) spurted for their amusement.

Here, the wealthiest Romans enjoyed the spoils that poured into Rome from its vast empire. Reclining on a couch, waited on by slaves, you'd order bowls of larks' tongues or a roast pig stuffed with live birds, then wash it down with wine. If you were full but tempted by yet another delicacy, you could call for a feather, vomit, and start all over. Dancing, dark-skinned slave girls from Egypt or flute players from Greece entertained. If you fancied one, he or she was yours—the bedrooms were just down the hall.

Or so went the stories. In fact, many emperors were just and simple men, continuing the old Roman traditions of hard work and moderate tastes. But just as many were power-mad scoundrels who used their authority to indulge their every desire.
• *From the Banquet Hall, work your way west through openings in the low brick wall by following the signs to the* Casa di Augusto *(described below). You'll run into a railing and a guarded gate. You'll be funneled through a few waiting points. Only five visitors at a time are allowed to enter the actual dwelling of Augustus—and then for just five minutes. After the first guarded gate, you'll pass by a little bit of pre-history...*

❾ Iron Age Huts ("The Huts of Romulus and Remus")

Looking down into the pit from the railing (stand at the far right), you can make out some elliptical and rectangular shapes carved into the stony ground (under the metal roof)—the partial outlines of huts from about 850 B.C. Some have holes that once held the wooden posts of round, thatched huts.

According to legend, Romulus and Remus (see photo of statue on page 184) were children of the first Vestal Virgin. For complicated family reasons, she was executed and her babies set adrift on the flooding Tiber, eventually to be washed ashore at the foot of Palatine Hill. In a cave just downhill from here, a shepherd discovered them being suckled by a mother wolf. He took them home—maybe right here—and raised them as his own. When Romulus grew up, he killed his brother and built a square wall (Roma Quadrata) on the hilltop, thus founding the city of Rome.

For centuries, the Romans believed this myth. They honored the wolf's cave (called the "Lupercale," where every February 15, men dressed up in animal skins and whipped women), as well as the spot where Romulus was said to have lived. Lo and behold, in the 1940s, these huts were unearthed, and the legend became history. The more they dig, the more they find to confirm the legends. A nearby cave discovered in 2007—ornamented with seashells, colored marble, and a wolf mosaic—may be that original Lupercale. (It's not open to the public, and dissenting archaeologists believe it's a temple to water nymphs).

❿ House of Livia and Augustus (Casa di Augustus)

Augustus, a.k.a. Octavian, the first emperor, lived in this house (and the neighboring house to the left) with his wife, Livia. Peer down the

hallways at the small rooms with honeycomb brick walls that surrounded a small courtyard. This relatively humble dwelling, dating from before Octavian became emperor, is a far cry from the later Imperial Palace which was built on top. The three humble rooms with their finely restored frescoes (opened in 2008) are well worth the 15–30 minute wait to see their vibrantly colored, domestic art (climb the steps outside to see a fourth room). You'll see that Livia and Augustus had little of the lavish marble found in most homes of the wealthy.

Augustus was a modest man who believed in traditional Roman values. His wife and daughter wove the clothes he wore. He slept in the same small bedroom for 40 years. He burned the midnight oil in his study, where he read and wrote his memoirs. Augustus set a standard for emperors' conduct that would last...until his death.

Augustus wanted to be the new Romulus, building his house adjacent to the home of the mythological founder of Rome.

Here at Rome's birthplace, reflect on the rise of this great culture—from thatched huts to the modest house of Augustus to the massive Imperial Palace of Domitian, with its stadium and view over the Circus Maximus. It's no wonder that the hill's name gave us our English word "palace."

• *Continue down the stairs to the...*

⓫ View of Forum Fit for an Emperor

Finish your tour with a stroll through the Renaissance gardens of the Farnese family. Admire the exotic plants, fountains, underground grotto, and pavilions. When you see the incredible view of the Forum from the end of the gardens, you'll know why the Palatine Hill was Rome's best address.

• *To exit, wind down Palatine Hill to the Forum, ending up at the Arch of Titus.*

TRAJAN'S COLUMN, FORUM, AND MARKET TOUR

*Colonna, Foro,
e Mercati de Traiano*

Rome peaked under Emperor Trajan (ruled A.D. 98–117)—the empire stretched from Scotland to the Sahara, from Spain to the Fertile Crescent. A triumphant Trajan returned to Rome with his booty and shook it all over the city. He extended the Forum by building his own commercial, political, and religious center nearby, complete with temples, law courts, squares lined with shops, and a monumental column covered with detailed carvings that tell the story of one of his most famous conquests. This column, Trajan's Market, and the new Museum of the Imperial Forums are the highlights of this tour. Much of Trajan's Forum can be seen quickly between other nearby sights.

ORIENTATION

Trajan's Column: It's free and viewable at all times.

Trajan's Market: You can view it for free from Via dei Fori Imperiali, but wandering through the market is possible only with paid admission to the Museum of the Imperial Forums, below.

Museum of the Imperial Forums: €6.50, includes entry to the market ruins, open Tue–Sun 9:00–19:00, last entry one hour before closing, closed Mon, Via IV Novembre 94, tel. 06-992-3521, www .mercatiditraiano.it. Skip the museum's slow, dry €3.50 audioguide—instead pick up the €4 "Brief Guide" for sale at the ticket counter.

Getting There: Trajan's Column is just a few steps off Piazza Venezia (a hub for major bus routes #40, #64, and #87), on Via dei Fori Imperiali, across the street from the Victor Emmanuel Monument. Trajan's Market can be entered only through the Museum of the Imperial Forums at Via IV Novembre 94. Trajan's Forum stretches southeast of the column toward the Colosseo Metro stop and the Colosseum itself.

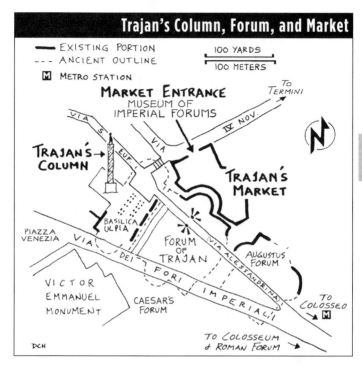

Length of This Tour: Allow 30 minutes if you're viewing the column and market from the street, or an hour and a half if you pay admission to enter the museum and market ruins.

THE TOUR BEGINS

Trajan's Column

Rising 140 feet and decorated with a spiral relief of 2,500 figures trumpeting Trajan's exploits, this is the world's grandest column from antiquity. The ashes of Trajan and his wife were once held in the base,

and the sun once glinted off a polished bronze statue of Trajan at the top. (Today, St. Peter is on top.) Built as a stack of 17 marble doughnuts, the column is hollow (note the small window slots) with a spiral staircase inside, leading up to the balcony.

The relief unfolds like a scroll, telling the story of Trajan's conquest of Dacia (modern-day Romania). It starts at the bottom with a trickle of water that becomes a river and soon picks up boats full of supplies. Then come the soldiers themselves, who spill out from the gates of the city. A river god (bottom band, south side) surfaces to bless the journey. Along the way (second band), they build roads and forts to sustain the vast enterprise, including (third band, south side) Trajan's half-mile-long bridge over the Danube, the longest for a thousand years. (Find the three tiny, crisscross rectangles representing the wooden span.) Trajan himself (fourth band, in military skirt with toga over his arm) mounts a podium to fire up the troops. They hop into a Roman galley ship (fifth band) and head off to fight the valiant Dacians in the middle of a forest (eighth band). Finally, at the very top, the Romans hold a sacrifice to give thanks for the victory, while the captured armor is displayed on the pedestal.

Originally, the entire story was painted in bright colors—and plans are afoot to recreate the column's colors with bright lights on weekend nights beginning in 2009. If you unwound the scroll, it would stretch over two football fields—it's far longer than the frieze around the Greek Parthenon. (An unscrolled copy is in E.U.R.'s Museum of Roman Civilization; see page 75.)

• *You can view Trajan's Market for free from Via dei Fori Imperiali. To walk around inside the market you must pay admission and enter through the...*

Museum of the Imperial Forums

This new museum features discoveries from the forums of several different emperors who built over the works of their predecessors. Start with the room across from the ticket office for an introduction, then delve deeper into the forums of Trajan, Caesar, Augustus, and Nerva. Highlights include a marble re-creation of Aeneas, father of Romulus; a bronze foot from a Winged Victory; a hand fragment from a colossal Augustus; and a central architectural reconstruction with caryatid pillar-statues.

• *Descend the stairs to the lowest level for an up-close view and access to the so-called "market."*

Trajan's Market

Nestled into the cutaway curve of Quirinal Hill is the semicircular brick complex of Trajan's Market. It was likely part shopping mall, part warehouse, and part administration building. Or, as some archaeologists have recently suggested, it may have contained mostly government offices.

For now the conventional wisdom holds that at ground level, the 13 tall (shallow) arches housed shops selling fresh fruit, vegetables, and flowers to shoppers who passed by on the street. The 26 arched windows (above) lit a covered walkway

lined with shops that sold wine and olive oil. On the roof (now lined with a metal railing) ran a street that likely held still more shops, making about 150 in all. Shoppers could browse through goods from every corner of Rome's vast empire—exotic fruits from Africa, spices from Asia, and fish and chips from Londinium.

Above the semicircle, the upper floors of the complex housed bureaucrats in charge of a crucial element of city life: doling out free grain to unemployed citizens, who lived off the wealth plundered from distant lands. Better to pacify them than risk a riot. Above the offices, at the very top, rises a tower added in the Middle Ages.

A walk around the market (which costs €6.50, entry via Museum of the Imperial Forums) is worth it only for those with a good imagination, stamina for stairs, or a Masters in Food Distribution. As you walk by the shops in the welcome shade of the arcade, you'll get a better sense of how inviting the market must have been in its heyday. Today, only one shop is "furnished"—crammed with the clay jugs used to store olive oil (upstairs from ticket booth). Throughout the market, you'll get expansive views of the ancient Trajan's Forum and modern Victor Emmanuel Monument.

The market was beautiful and functional, filling the space of the curved hill perfectly and echoing the curved side of the Forum's main courtyard. (The wall of rough volcanic stones on the ground once extended into a semicircle.) Unlike most Roman buildings, the brick facade wasn't covered with plaster or marble. The architect liked the simple contrast between the warm brick and the white stone lining the arches and windows.

Trajan's conquest of the Dacians was Rome's last and greatest foreign conquest. It produced this Forum, which stood for centuries as a symbol of a truly cosmopolitan civilization.

• *Turn around and look down at the ruins of...*

The Rest of Trajan's Forum (Foro di Traiano)

Trajan's Forum starts at Trajan's Column and runs about 120 yards southeast toward the Colosseum. It's mostly rubble today, except for the crescent-shaped Trajan's Market, rising up the flank of Quirinal Hill.

In Roman times, you would have entered at the Colosseum end through a triumphal arch and been greeted in the main square by a large statue of the soldier-king on a horse. Continuing on, you'd enter the Basilica Ulpia (the gray granite columns near Trajan's Column), the largest law court of its day. Finally, at the far end, you would have found Trajan's Column, flanked by two libraries that contained the world's knowledge in Greek and Latin. Balconies on the libraries gave close-up looks at the upper reliefs of the column, in case anyone doubted the outcome of Trajan's war.

Trajan's Forum was a crucial expansion of the old Roman Forum, which was too small and ceremonial to fill the commercial needs of a booming city of more than a million people. It trumped the forums of previous Romans (the adjacent forums of Julius Caesar, Augustus, and Vespasian). Built with the staggering haul of gold plundered from Dacia (Romania), this was the largest forum ever—its opulence astounded even the jaded Romans.

To build his Forum, Trajan literally moved mountains. He cut away a ridge that once connected the Quirinal and Capitol hills, creating this valley. Trajan's Column marks the hill's original height—140 feet.

• *The tour is over. If you walked down into the market, exit the way you came, into the museum. You are just a toga's toss from many other sights of ancient Rome. From here, you can cross over to the other side of the busy Via dei Fori Imperiali and visit the Capitol Hill sights, the Roman Forum, or the Colosseum that looms in the distance.*

PANTHEON TOUR

The Roman Temple and Nearby Churches

If your imagination is fried from trying to reconstruct ancient buildings out of today's rubble, visit the Pantheon, Rome's best-preserved monument. Engineers still admire how the Romans built such a mathematically precise structure without computers, fossil fuel–run machinery, or electricity. (Having unlimited slave power didn't hurt.) Stand under the Pantheon's solemn dome to gain a new appreciation for the enlightenment of these ancient people.

Several interesting churches are clustered nearby, easy to visit after you tour the Pantheon.

ORIENTATION

Pantheon: Free, Mon–Sat 8:30–19:30, Sun 9:00–18:00, holidays 9:00–13:00, closed for Mass Sat at 17:00 and Sun at 10:30. The audioguide is cheap but still probably not worth it (€3, 25 min). You can download a free audiotour at www.ricksteves.com (see page 382). Tel. 06-6830-0230.

Church of San Luigi dei Francesi: Free but bring coins to buy light, Fri–Wed 7:30–12:30 & 15:30–19:00, Thu 8:00–12:30, sightseers should avoid Mass at 7:30 and 19:00.

Gesù Church: Free, daily 6:30–12:45 & 16:00–19:15.

Church of Santa Maria sopra Minerva: Free, Mon–Sat 7:00–19:00, Sun 8:00–19:00.

Church of San Ignazio: Free, daily 7:30–12:30 & 15:00–19:15.

Dress Code: Modest dress is recommended for the churches near the Pantheon.

Getting There: To reach the Pantheon neighborhood, you can walk (it's a 20-minute walk from Capitol Hill), take a taxi, or catch a bus. Buses #64 and #40 carry tourists and pickpockets frequently between the Termini train station and Vatican City, stopping at a chaotic square called Largo Argentina located a few blocks south of the Pantheon. (Take either Via dei Cestari or Via Torre Argentina north to the Pantheon.) The *elettrico* minibus #116 runs between Campo de' Fiori and Piazza Barberini via the Pantheon. The most dramatic approach is on foot coming from Piazza Navona along Via Giustiniani, which spills directly into Piazza della Rotunda, offering the classic Pantheon view. See the ✪ Night Walk Across Rome on page 78.

Length of This Tour: Allow a half-hour to see the Pantheon, and at least another hour to visit all the churches.

Photography: It's allowed—even with flash—in the Pantheon. No flash in churches.

Services: The nearest WCs are at bars and downstairs in the McDonald's on the square.

Cuisine Art: Restaurants abound. Several reasonable eateries are a block or two north up Via del Pantheon. Some of Rome's best gelato and coffee are nearby. For recommendations, see page 307.

Overview

The Pantheon is the centerpiece of this tour, and is a must-see on any visit to Rome. The second part of this tour features several nearby churches with art by Michelangelo and Caravaggio, and connections with Galileo, St. Ignatius, and the Jesuit Order.

THE TOUR BEGINS

• *Start the tour at the top of the square called Piazza della Rotunda, which is surrounded by cafés and restaurants with an obelisk-topped fountain in the center. You're looking at...*

THE PANTHEON

Exterior

The Pantheon was a Roman temple dedicated to all *(pan)* of the gods *(theos)*. The original temple was built in 27 B.C. by Augustus' son-in-law, Marcus Agrippa. In fact, the inscription below the triangular pediment proclaims in Latin, "Marcus Agrippa, son of Lucio, three times consul made this." But after a couple of fires, the structure we see today was completely rebuilt by the emperor Hadrian around A.D. 120. Some say that Hadrian, an amateur architect (and voracious traveler), helped design it.

The Pantheon looks like a

pretty typical temple from the outside, but this is perhaps the most influential building in art history. Its dome was the model for the Florence cathedral dome, which launched the Renaissance, and for Michelangelo's dome of St. Peter's, which capped it all off. Even Washington, D.C.'s Capitol Building was inspired by this dome.

The 40-foot-high columns of the portico (entrance porch) are made from single pieces of red-gray granite (not the standard stacks of cylindrical pieces). They were taken from an Egyptian temple. The holes in the triangular pediment once held a huge bronze Roman eagle. Back up or step to one side to look above the pediment to the building itself. You'll see a roofline that was abandoned mid-construction. The pediment was originally intended to be higher, but when the support columns arrived, they were shorter than expected. Even the most enlightened can forget to "measure twice, cut once."

• *Pass through the portico, with its forest of enormous columns. Look up at the porch roof, and imagine the ceiling covered in its original bronze plating. It was removed in the 17th century by a scavenging pope from the Barberini family, inspiring the well-known quip, "What the barbarians didn't do, the Barberini did." Melted down, some of the bronze was used to build the huge bronze canopy over the altar at St. Peter's. Now pass through the giant bronze door—a copy of the original. Take a seat and take it all in.*

Interior

The dome, which was the largest made until the Renaissance, is set on a circular base. The mathematical perfection of this dome-on-a-base design is a testament to Roman engineering. The dome is as high as it is wide—142 feet from floor to rooftop and from side to side. To picture it, imagine a basketball set inside a wastebasket so that it just touches bottom.

The dome—newly cleaned and feeling loftier than ever—is made from concrete (a Roman invention) that gets lighter and thinner as it reaches the top. The base of the dome is 23 feet thick and made from heavy concrete mixed with travertine, while near the top, it's less

than five feet thick and made with a lighter volcanic rock (pumice) mixed in. Note the square indentations in the surface of the dome. This coffered ceiling reduces the weight of the dome without compromising strength. The walls are strengthened by blind arches built into the wall (visible outside—see photo).

Both Brunelleschi and Michelangelo studied this dome before building their own (in Florence and the Vatican, respectively). Remember, St. Peter's Basilica is really only the dome of the Pantheon atop the Forum's Basilica of Constantine.

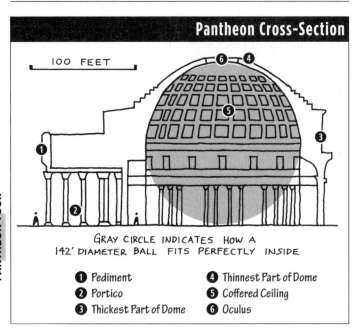

Pantheon Cross-Section

100 FEET

GRAY CIRCLE INDICATES HOW A
142' DIAMETER BALL FITS PERFECTLY INSIDE

1 Pediment
2 Portico
3 Thickest Part of Dome
4 Thinnest Part of Dome
5 Coffered Ceiling
6 Oculus

At the top, the oculus, or eye-in-the-sky, is the building's only light source and is almost 30 feet across. The 1,800-year-old floor has holes in it and slants toward the edges to let the rainwater drain. Though some of the floor's marble has been replaced over the years, the design—alternating circles and squares—is original.

In ancient times, this was a one-stop-shopping temple where you could worship any of the gods whose statues decorated the niches. Entering the temple, Romans came face-to-face with a larger-than-life statue of Jupiter, the King of the Gods, where the altar stands today. Early in the Middle Ages, the Pantheon became a Christian church (from "all the gods" to "all the martyrs"), which saved it from architectural cannibalism and ensured its upkeep through the Dark Ages. (The year 2009 will be the building's 1,400th anniversary as a church.) In the seventh century, a Byzantine emperor stripped the dome's interior of its original golden-tile ceiling. The twin grilled windows just right of the altar (at 2:00) are original and, along with the inlaid marble floor, give you a sense of the ancient decor.

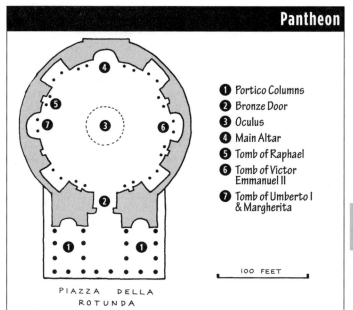

Pantheon

1 Portico Columns
2 Bronze Door
3 Oculus
4 Main Altar
5 Tomb of Raphael
6 Tomb of Victor Emmanuel II
7 Tomb of Umberto I & Margherita

100 FEET

PIAZZA DELLA ROTUNDA

PANTHEON TOUR

Tombs

The only new things in the interior are the decorative statues and the tombs of famous people.

The artist Raphael lies to the left of the main altar, which is in the lighted glass niche (pictured here). Above him is a statue of the Madonna and Child that Raphael himself commissioned for his tomb. The Latin inscription on his tomb reads, "In life, Nature feared to be outdone by him. In death, she feared she too would die."

You'll also see the tombs of modern Italy's first two kings. To the right is Victor Emmanuel II (*"Padre della Patria,"* father of his country). To the left is Umberto I (son of the father). These tombs are a hit with royalists. In fact, there is often a guard standing by a guest-book, where visitors can register their support for these two kings' now-controversial family, the Savoys (see sidebar). And finally, under Umberto, lies his queen, Margherita...for whom the classic pizza Margherita (mozzarella, tomato sauce, and basil) was named in 1889.

The Pantheon is the only ancient building in Rome continuously

The Italian Royal Family... in Switzerland

From Italy's unification in 1870 to the end of World War II, the country had four kings, all members of the Savoy family. One of Europe's oldest royal families (from the 10th century), the Savoia had long ruled the kingdom of Piedmont (in present-day northern Italy).

In 1946, the Italians voted for a republic and sent the Savoia into exile. Until 2002, a law proclaimed that no male Savoia could set foot on Italian soil. That's why only the first two kings are buried in the Pantheon (the last two died in exile).

The Savoia lost favor with their Italian subjects for several good reasons: When Mussolini marched on Rome in 1922, King Victor Emmanuel III actually asked him to form a government. When the Mussolini government issued anti-Semitic laws, the king signed them. And in 1943, instead of standing by his people, the king abandoned Rome to the Germans and fled south to Allied protection.

Even today, the Savoia heir to Italy's throne is considered a jerk with a knack for saying stupid things. When asked to comment on the racist laws signed by his grandfather, he candidly answered that he was too young at the time so he did not need to apologize, and, he said, the laws were not really all that bad. When the Savoia were allowed back into Italy in 2002, their first mistake was to visit the pope rather than the president of the Republic. And while they live in stunning wealth in Switzerland, they still complain that Italy owes them more of the family riches.

used since its construction. When you leave, notice that the building is sunken below current street level, showing how the rest of the city has risen on 20 centuries of rubble.

The Pantheon also contains the world's greatest Roman column. There it is, spanning the entire 142 feet from heaven to earth—the pillar of light from the oculus.

CHURCHES NEAR THE PANTHEON

• *Many visitors just see the Pantheon and leave. But consider visiting one or more of these four unique churches, all less than 10 minutes' walk from the Pantheon (see map, page 145). If you're budgeting your energy, here's a quick rundown on what each has to offer: San Luigi houses several stunning Caravaggio paintings. The Gesù is packed with ornate art and Jesuit history. Santa Maria sopra Minerva, Rome's only Gothic church, has a Michelangelo sculpture and St. Catherine's tomb. Finally, San Ignazio is full of Baroque perspective illusions that will leave your head spinning.*

Churches near the Pantheon

N

100 YARDS
100 METERS

TO
PIAZZA
DEL POPOLO

TO M
BARB.

VIA TRITONE

STELL.

UFF.

VICARIO

PARL.

P.
MONTE.

P.
COL.

SABRINA

TO
TREVI

VACC.

COPPELLE

MURATTE

POZZO CORN.

AQUIRO

P.
PIETRA

SAN
LUIGI

SALV.

GIUST.

PIAZZA
ROTUNDA

SEMINARIO

SAN
IGNAZIO

CRESC.

CARA.

CORSO

TO
PIAZZA
NAVONA

S.
EUST.

PANTHEON

CESTARI

STA. MARIA

SOPRA
MINERVA

S. APOST.

TIME
ELEVATOR
ROMA

GALLERIA
DORA
PAMPHILJ

VIA VITTORIO

TORRE ARGEN.

GESU

EMANUELE

DCH

LARGO
ARGENTINA

RUINS

FLOR.

BOTT. OSC.

CAMERE OF
ST. IGNATIUS

TO
CAPITOL
HILL

T TAXI STAND
M METRO STATION
B BUS STOP

ENTRY POINT
TO SIGHTS

PANTHEON TOUR

Church of San Luigi dei Francesi

This is the French national church in Rome. Outside, check out the salamander, symbol of François I, the French king who brought Leonardo (and the Renaissance) north to France. The stylized *fleur-de-lis* symbols found all over the interior are the emblem of French royalty. The one truly *magnifique* sight is the chapel in the far left corner, which was decorated by Caravaggio. This church makes a great little detour between the Pantheon and nearby Piazza Navona.

• *In the Caravaggio chapel, first look to the left wall.*

The Calling of St. Matthew

Matthew (old man with beard) and his well-dressed, tax-collecting cronies sit in a dingy bar and count the money they've extorted. Suddenly, two men in robes and bare feet enter from the right—Jesus and Peter. Jesus' "Creation-of-Adam" hand emerges from the darkness to point at Matthew. A shaft of light extends the gesture, lighting

up the face of Matthew, who points to himself *Last Supper*–style to ask, "You talkin' to me?" Jesus came to convince Matthew to leave his sleazy job and preach Love. Matthew did.

In this, his first large-scale work, 29-year-old Caravaggio (1571–1610) shocked critics and clerics by showing a holy scene in a down-to-earth location. Lower-class people in everyday clothes were his models; his setting was a dive bar (which he knew well). Christ's teeny gold halo is the only hint of the supernatural, as Caravaggio makes a bold proclamation—that miracles are natural events experienced in a profound way.

• *Now look to the center wall.*

The Inspiration of St. Matthew

Matthew followed Christ's call, traveled with him, and (supposedly) wrote Jesus' life story (the Gospel according to Matthew). Here, Matthew is hard at work when he's interrupted by an angel with a few suggestions. This sets the scene in motion. Matthew kneels on a stool, which is just about to fall out of the painting and into our zone. Matthew's bald head, wrinkled face, and grizzled beard make him an all-too-human saint. Even the teen angel lacks a holy glow—he just hangs there. Caravaggio paints a dark background, then shines a dramatic spotlight on the few things that tell the story.

• *Finally, check out the right wall.*

The Martyrdom of St. Matthew

Matthew lies prone, while a truly scary man straddles him and brandishes a sword. The bystanders shrink away from this angry executioner. Caravaggio shines his harsh third-degree spotlight on Matthew and the killer, who are the focus of the painting. The other figures swirl around them in a circle (with the executioner's arm as the radius). Matthew, who thought he had given up everything to follow Christ, now gives up his life as well. He is as open as a crucifix, accepting his fate, and reaching for a palm frond—symbolic of victory over death. The bearded face in the background (to the left of the executioner's shoulder) is a self-portrait of Caravaggio, observing the violence without getting involved.

When the chapel was unveiled in 1600, Caravaggio's ultrarealism shocked Rome. Although he died only 10 years later, his uncompromising details, emotional subjects, odd compositions, and dramatic lighting set the tone for later Baroque painters.

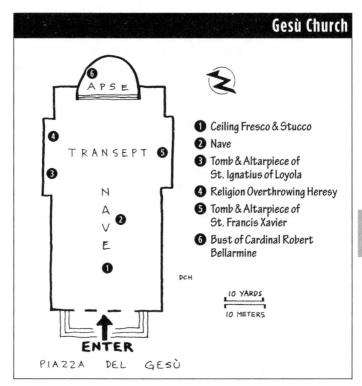

Gesù Church

Gesù Church

1. Ceiling Fresco & Stucco
2. Nave
3. Tomb & Altarpiece of St. Ignatius of Loyola
4. Religion Overthrowing Heresy
5. Tomb & Altarpiece of St. Francis Xavier
6. Bust of Cardinal Robert Bellarmine

APSE

TRANSEPT

NAVE

DCH

10 YARDS
10 METERS

ENTER

PIAZZA DEL GESÙ

PANTHEON TOUR

Gesù Church

The center of the Jesuit order and the best symbol of the Catholic Counter-Reformation, the Gesù (jay-zoo) is packed with overblown art and underappreciated history. Consider seeing this church en route to Capitol Hill.

Exterior

The facade looks ho-hum, like a thousand no-name Catholic churches scattered from Europe to Southern California...until you realize that this was the first, the model for the others. Its scroll-like shoulders

were revolutionary, breaking up the rigid rectangles of Renaissance architecture and signaling the coming of Baroque. The travertine stone facade was recently cleaned but—with its sponge-like properties and Rome's pollution—it will be black again soon enough.

The building to the right of the church—called Camere of St. Ignatius—is where Ignatius of Loyola, the founder of the Jesuits, lived, worked, and died (Mon–Sat 16:00–18:00, Sun 10:00–12:00).

• *Step inside the Gesù Church, grab a seat, and look up at the huge painting on the ceiling.*

Interior

❶ Ceiling Fresco and Stucco—
The Triumph of the Name of Jesus (by Il Baciccio)

The church's sunroof opens, and we can see right up to heaven. A glowing cross with Jesus' initials, "I.H.S." (adopted as the seal of the Society of Jesus), astounds the faithful and sends the infidels plunging downward. The twisted tangle of bodies—the damned—spills over the edge of the painting's frame on their way to hell. The painted bodies mingle with 3-D stucco bodies and a riot of decoration in a classic example of Baroque multimedia.

During the Counter-Reformation, when Catholics fought Protestants for the hearts and minds of the world's Christians, art became propaganda. The moral here is clear—this is the fate of Protestant heretics who dared to pervert the true teachings of Jesus.

❷ The Nave

When the church was originally built (1568), the walls were white and the decor was simple. It was designed for what the Jesuits did best—teaching. The Jesuits wanted to educate Catholics to prepare them for the onslaught of probing Protestant questions. The church's nave is like one big lecture hall, with no traditional side aisles.

In the 1500s, the best way to keep Protestants from stealing your church members was to reason with them. By the 1600s, it was easier to kill them, and so the Thirty Years' War raged across Europe. The church became crusted over with the colorful, bombastic, jingoistic Baroque we see today.

• *Now look toward the left transept.*

❸ Tomb and Altarpiece of St. Ignatius of Loyola (left transept)

The gleaming statue of Ignatius (which may be missing, as it's being restored) spreads his arms wide and gazes up, receiving a vision from on high. Ignatius (1491–1556) was a Spanish soldier during the era of conquistadors. Then, at age 30, he was struck down by a cannonball. While convalescing, he was seized by the burning desire to change his life. He wandered Europe and traveled to Jerusalem. He meditated with monks. He lived in a cave. At 33, he enrolled in a school for boys to fill in the knowledge he'd missed. He studied in Paris and in Rome. Finally, after almost two decades of learning and seeking, he found a way to combine his military training with his spiritual aspirations.

In 1540, the pope gave approval to Ignatius and his small band of followers—the Society of Jesus (Jesuits). These monks, organized like a military company, vowed complete obedience to their "General," and placed themselves at the service of the pope. Their mission: To be intellectual warriors doing battle with heretics. They were in the right place at the right time—Ignatius and Martin Luther were almost exact contemporaries.

Ignatius' body lies in the small coffin beneath the statue (near ground level). This simple, intense man might have been embarrassed by the lavish memorial to him, with its silver, gold, green marble, and lapis lazuli columns. Above Ignatius, a statue of God stands near a lapis lazuli globe (the biggest in the world) and gestures as though to say, "Go and spread the Word to every land"...which the Jesuits tried to do.

• *Look at the marble statue group to the right of Ignatius.*

❹ *Religion Overthrowing Heresy*

This statue (and a similar one to the left of Ignatius) shows the Church as an angry nun hauling back with a whip and just spanking a bunch of miserable Protestants. The serpent (Luther) is being stepped upon

while the angry cherub rips pages out of a heretical book. Not too subtle.

Yes, the Jesuits got a reputation for unfeeling dedication to truth above all else, but their weapons were words, ideas, and critical reasoning. They taught and defended the recently revamped doctrines of the Council of Trent (1545–1563).

• *Now view the right transept.*

❺ **Tomb and Altarpiece of St. Francis Xavier**

This was also the Age of Discovery, when Spain and Portugal were colonizing and Christianizing the world, using force if necessary. Francis Xavier joined a Portuguese expedition and headed out to convert the heathens. He touched down in Africa, India, Indonesia, China, and Japan. Along the way, he learned new languages and customs, trying to communicate a strange, monotheistic religion to puzzled polytheists.

He had been on the road for more than a decade (1552) when he died on an island off China (see the dim painting over the altar). Thanks largely to zealous Jesuits such as Francis, Catholicism became a truly worldwide religion.

• *In the apse, find the...*

❻ Bust of Cardinal Robert Bellarmine
(by Gian Lorenzo Bernini)

The great sculptor Bernini attended this church and honored Bellarmine with a bust. Robert Bellarmine (1542–1621), a theologian at the height of Catholic-Protestant differences, was a voice of reason in the often bitter controversy. He's best known as the man who ordered Galileo to stop teaching the Copernican theory, though he was actually a moderating influence in the debate.

The Jesuits produced some great, open-minded thinkers like Bellarmine, from the poet Gerard Manley Hopkins to modern mystic Pierre Teilhard de Chardin. But they also caught flak for being closed-minded. In the 1700s, several countries expelled them, and finally the pope even banned the Society (1773). Chastened, they were brought back (1814), and today they fill the staff of many a Catholic college.

Church of Santa Maria sopra Minerva

From the outside, survey the many layers of Rome: An Egyptian obelisk sits on a Baroque elephant (by Bernini) in front of a Gothic church built over *(sopra)* a pre-Christian, pagan Temple of Minerva.

Before stepping in, notice the high-water-mark plaques *(alluvione)* on the wall to the right of the door. Inside, you'll see that the lower parts of some frescoes were lost to floods. After the last great flood, in 1870, Rome built the present embankments along the river, finally breaking the spirit of the mighty Tiber.

Nave

This is the only Gothic church you'll see in Rome. The ceiling has pointed, crisscross arches in a starry, luminous blue sky. When this Dominican church was built, Gothic was the rage in northern Europe, with large windows to let in the light—though churches in sunny Italy don't require big expanses of glass. During the Middle Ages, Rome was almost a ghost town, and what little was built during this time was later gussied up in the Baroque style. The simplicity of this church is a refreshing exception.

Main Altar

The body of St. Catherine of Siena lies under the altar (her head is in Siena). In the 1300s, this Italian nun was renowned for her righteousness and her visions of a mystical marriage with Jesus. Her impassioned letters convinced the pope to return from France to Rome, thus saving Italy from untold chaos. Behind her are buried two Medici popes: Leo X, the son of Lorenzo the Magnificent and the man who excommunicated Martin Luther, and his cousin Clement VII.

In 1634, a frail, 70-year-old Galileo knelt at this altar on the way to his trial before the Inquisition in the church's monastery. Facing the fierce Dominican lawyers, he renounced his heretical belief that the earth moved around the sun. (Legend has it that as he walked out, he whispered, "But it *does* move.")

• *Left of the altar stands a little-known Michelangelo statue...*

Christ Bearing the Cross (1519–1520)

Note Jesus' athletic body, a striking contrast to the docile Jesus of medieval art. This sculpture shares the same bulging biceps as

the Christ in Michelangelo's *The Last Judgment* in the Sistine Chapel. Christ's pose is slightly twisted, with one leg forward in typical *contrapposto* style, leaning on a large cross along with the symbols of the Crucifixion. Originally, Christ was buck naked, but later prudish Counter-Reformation censors gave him his bronze girdle. A bronze shoe was later added to protect the right toe from the kisses of the faithful. This statue was Michelangelo's second attempt—he was forced to abandon a first effort due to a flaw in the block  of Carrara marble. In this version, he left parts including the face to be finished by an apprentice, who took the liberty of working on and botching the feet and hands. This ineptitude led him to be replaced by yet another sculptor who finally finished the job. Michelangelo, disturbed that anyone would mess up his work, offered to redo the sculpture, but apparently the patrons were pleased. One contemporary said, "The knees alone are worth more than all of Rome together."

The tomb of the great early Renaissance painter (and Dominican brother) Fra Angelico ("Beato Angelico 1387–1455") is farther to the left, just up the three stairs.

Over in the right (south) transept, pop in a coin for light, and enjoy a Filippino Lippi fresco showing scenes of the life of the great Dominican scholar St. Thomas Aquinas (big man in blue and white). In the central scene, Thomas presents the chapel's patron to Mary, while on the right wall, he displays a book to show everyone the true dogma, causing a heretic to slump defeated at his feet.

• *Exit the church via its rear door (behind the Michelangelo statue), walk down tiny Fra Angelico lane, turn left, and walk to the next square. On your right, you'll find the...*

Church of San Ignazio

This church is a riot of Baroque illusions. Find a seat in the nave and look up at the large, colorful ceiling fresco. St. Ignatius, whom we met

in the Gesù Church, was the founder of the Jesuits, a disciplined Catholic teaching order charged with spreading the word of God around a world that was rapidly being "discovered." Here you see him (a small figure perched on a cloud in the center) having a vision of Christ with the Cross. Heavenly light from the vision bounces off his chest, and the rays beam to the four corners of the earth (including America, to the left, depicted as a bare-breasted Native American maiden spearing naked men). This fresco epitomizes pure Baroque drama, with perspective illusions that fool the eye into thinking the fresco is an extension of the church architecture. Note how the actual columns of the church are extended into the two-dimensional fresco. Now fix your eyes on the arch at the far end of the painting. Walk up the nave, and watch the arch grow and tower over you.

Before you reach the center of the church, stop at the small yellow disk on the floor and look up into the central (black) dome. Watching the dome, walk under and past it. Building project runs out of money? Hire a painter to paint a fake, flat dome. Postcards are sold in the Sacristy, off to the left as you face the altar.

Back outside, the church faces the headquarters of the Carabinieri police force, forming Piazza San Ignazio, a square with several converging streets that has been compared to a stage set. Sit on the church steps, admire the theatrical yellow backdrop, and watch the "actors" enter one way and exit another, in the human opera that is modern Rome.

• *From here it's a short walk to the left down Via della Seminario back to the Pantheon. Or go right, cross busy Via del Corso, and follow the crowds to the Trevi Fountain.*

BATHS OF DIOCLETIAN TOUR

Terme di Diocleziano

Of all the marvelous structures built by the Romans, their public baths were arguably the grandest, and the Baths of Diocletian were the granddaddy of them all. These baths sprawled over 10 acres—roughly twice the area of the entire Forum—and could cleanse 3,000 Romans at once. Today, there are several sections you can visit.

The **Church of Santa Maria degli Angeli,** housed in the former main hall of the baths, is the single most impressive sight of the bunch. The entrance is on Piazza Repubblica (free, Mon–Sat 7:00–18:30, Sun 7:00–19:30, closed to sightseers during Mass).

The **Octagonal Hall** (Aula Ottagona), also facing Piazza Repubblica, is a well-preserved rotunda that displays sculpture from the baths. As you face the church entrance, the Octagonal Hall is 100 yards to your left (free, open sporadically Sun 9:00–13:00 only).

The **Museum of the Bath** (Museo Nazionale Romano Terme di Diocleziano) has a shaded garden with Roman tombstones outside, and early Roman jewelry, masks, burial items, and Roman inscriptions on tombs and tablets inside. The entrance faces the Termini train station (€10, includes entry within three days to three other National Museum branches, including nearby National Museum of Rome—see page 167, open Tue–Sun 9:00–19:45, last entry 45 min before closing, closed Mon, audioguide-€4, Viale E. de Nicola 79, tel. 06-487-730).

Energetic architecture wonks can even walk the perimeter of the baths: from Via Torino to Piazza dei Cinquecento to Via Volturno to Via XX Settembre.

THE TOUR BEGINS

• Start just outside the church of...

Santa Maria degli Angeli

From noisy Piazza Repubblica, step through the curved brick wall of the ancient baths and into the vast and cool church built upon the remains of a vast and steamy Roman bath complex.

The Church's Entry Hall—The Baths' Tepidarium

This round-domed room with an oculus (open skylight, now with modern stained glass) was once the cooling-off room of the baths where medium, "tepid" tem-

peratures were maintained. Romans loved to sweat out last night's indulgences at the baths. After stripping in the locker rooms, they'd enter the steam baths of the *caldarium*, located where Piazza Repubblica is today. The *caldarium* had wood furnaces—stoked by slaves— under the raised floors to heat the floors and hot tubs. The ceiling was low to keep the room steamy.

Next, you'd pass into this *tepidarium*, where masseuses would rub you down and scrape you off with a stick (Romans didn't use soap).

Finally, you'd continue on to the central area of the baths...

The Church's Large Transept— The Baths' Central Hall

This hall retains the grandeur of the ancient baths. It's the size of a football field and seven stories high—once even higher, since the original ancient floor was about 15 feet below its present level. The ceiling's crisscross arches were an architectural feat unmatched for a thousand years. The eight red granite columns are original, from ancient Rome—stand next to one and feel its five-foot girth. (Only the eight in the transept proper are original. The others are made of plastered-over brick.) In Roman times, this hall was covered with mosaics, marble, and gold, and lined with statues.

From here, Romans could continue (through what is now the apse, near the altar) into a vast, open-air courtyard to take a dip in the vast 32,000-square-foot swimming pool (in the *frigidarium*) that paralleled this huge hall. Many other rooms, gardens, and courtyards extended beyond what we see here. The huge complex was built in only 10 years (around A.D. 300)—amazing when you think of the centuries it took builders of puny medieval cathedrals, such as Paris' Notre-Dame.

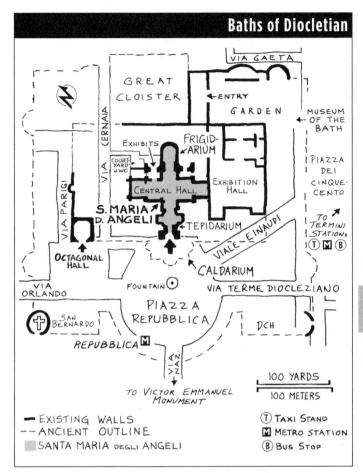

Baths of Diocletian

VIA GAETA

GREAT
CLOISTER
←ENTRY

GARDEN

MUSEUM
←OF THE
BATH

Exhibits

FRIGID-
←ARIUM

VIA CERNAIA

COURT-
YARD
& WC

Exhibition
Hall

PIAZZA
DEI
CINQUE-
CENTO

CENTRAL HALL

S. MARIA
D. ANGELI

TO
TERMINI
STATION,
Ⓣ Ⓜ Ⓑ

←TEPIDARIUM

VIALE EINAUDI

VIA PARIGI

OCTAGONAL
HALL

CALDARIUM

VIA
ORLANDO

FOUNTAIN ⊙

VIA TERME DIOCLEZIANO

PIAZZA
REPUBBLICA

SAN
BERNARDO

DCH

REPUBBLICA Ⓜ

< N
< A
> Z

TO VICTOR EMMANUEL
MONUMENT

100 YARDS

100 METERS

━ EXISTING WALLS
-- ANCIENT OUTLINE
▓ SANTA MARIA DEGLI ANGELI

Ⓣ TAXI STAND
Ⓜ METRO STATION
Ⓑ BUS STOP

BATHS OF DIOCLETIAN

Mentally undress your fellow tourists and churchgoers, and imagine hundreds of naked or toga-clad Romans wrestling, doing jumping jacks, singing in the baths, networking, or just milling about.

The baths were more than washrooms. They were health clubs with exercising areas, equipment, and swimming pools. They had gardens for socializing. Libraries, shops, bars, fast-food vendors, pedicurists, depilatories, and brothels catered to every Roman need. Most important, perhaps, the baths offered a spacious, cool-in-summer/warm-in-winter place for Romans to get out of their stuffy apartments, schmooze, or simply hang out.

Admission was virtually free, requiring only the smallest coin. Baths were open to men and women—and during Nero's reign, coed bathing was popular—but generally there were either separate rooms or separate entry times. Most Romans went daily.

The church we see today was (at least partly) designed by Michelangelo (1561), who used the baths' main hall as the nave. Later, when Piazza Repubblica became an important Roman intersection, another architect renovated the church. To allow people to enter from the grand new piazza, he spun it 90 degrees, turning Michelangelo's nave into a long transept.

• *Embedded in the floor of the right transept (roped off) is a brass rod called...*

La Meridiana (1702)

This is a meridian, pointing due north. It acts as a sundial. As the sun arcs across the southern sky, a ray of light beams into the church through a tiny hole high in the wall and a cut in the cornice of the right transept. (To find the hole, follow the rod to the right to the wall and look up 65 feet.) The sunbeam sweeps across the church floor, crossing the meridian rod at exactly noon. (Allow for variances due to Daylight Saving Time and the approximate time zones of Greenwich Mean Time.)

This celestial clock is also a calendar. In summer, when the sun is high overhead, the sunbeam strikes the southern end of the rod. With each passing day, the sun travels up the rod (toward the apse), passing through the signs of the zodiac (the 28-day months of the moon's phases) marked alongside the rod. Many of the meridian's markings were intended for its other use, charting the movement of the stars. However, the tiny window that once let in light from the North Star (originally above the archway of the entrance to the apse) has been filled in.

Find some key dates in the Christian calendar, particularly the spring equinox and Easter (near Aries the Ram). Most Christians agree that Easter is the first Sunday after the first full moon after the vernal equinox (established with the Nicene Creed, A.D. 325). It took large meridians like this to measure the sun's movements accurately enough to predict Easter and other holidays years in advance.

La Meridiana was the city of Rome's official timekeeper until 1846, when it was replaced by the cannon atop Gianicolo Hill, which is still fired every day at exactly noon.

In the left transept (opposite end), you'll find a monumental organ built for the Jubilee Year of 2000. Free concerts are held regularly; check the schedule posted near the organ.

• *Step into the small room to the left of the main altar.*

Exhibits

Read the English explanation of the church's architectural history, and peruse the copies of Michelangelo's drawings. Notice the immensity and height of the ancient Roman brickwork in this room (just outside in the courtyard is a towering ancient brick wall and a WC). Large building projects like this were political security: They provided employment and fed the masses.

Diocletian (ruled A.D. 285–305) struggled with a system to rule his unwieldy empire. He broke it into zones ruled by four "tetrarchs." During Diocletian's "tetrarchs" period, architecture and art were grandiose, but almost a caricature of greatness—meant to proclaim to Romans that their city was still the power it had once been.

The baths were one of the last great structures built before Rome's 200-year fall. They functioned until A.D. 537, when barbarians cut the city's aqueducts, plunging Rome into a thousand years of poverty, darkness, and B.O.

• *Exit where you entered. If you're feeling lucky, turn right and walk 100 yards to the entrance of the rarely open...*

Octagonal Hall (Aula Ottagona)

This octagonal building, capped by a dome with a hole in the top, may have served as a cool room *(frigidarium)*, with small pools of cold water for plunging into. Or, because of its many doors, it may simply have been a large intersection, connecting other parts of the baths. Originally, the floor was 25 feet lower—as you can see through the glass-covered hole in the floor. The graceful iron grid overhead supported the canopy of a 1928 planetarium.

Piazza della Repubblica

The piazza, shaped like an exedra (a semicircular recess in a wall or building), echoes the wall of a stadium adjoining the original baths. It was called Piazza Esedra until Italian unification (and is still called that by many Romans). The thundering Via Nazionale starts at what was an ancient door. Look down it (past the erotic nymphs of the Naiad fountain) to the Victor Emmanuel Monument. The Art Nouveau fountain of the four water nymphs created quite a stir when unveiled in 1911. The nymphs were modeled after a set of twins, who kept coming to visit as late as the 1960s to remind themselves of their nubile youth.

ANCIENT APPIAN WAY TOUR

Via Appia Antica

The wonder of its day, the Appian Way (named after Appius Claudius Caecus, a Roman official) was the largest, widest, fastest road ever, called the "Queen of Roads." Built in 312 B.C., it connected Rome with Capua (near Naples), running in a straight line for much of the way, ignoring the natural contour of the land. Eventually, this most important of Roman roads stretched 430 miles to the port of Brindisi—the gateway to the East—where boats sailed for Greece and Egypt. Twenty-nine such roads fanned out from Rome. Just as Hitler built the Autobahn system in anticipation of empire maintenance, the expansion-minded Roman government realized the military and political value of a good road system.

Hollywood created the famous image of the Appian Way lined with the crucified bodies of Spartacus and his gang of slave rebels. This image is only partially accurate—Spartacus was killed in battle. But historians do believe there were 6,000 slaves on crosses spaced about 30 yards apart for over 100 miles. Imagine the eerie welcome this provided visitors arriving in Rome.

Today the road and the landscape around it are preserved as a cultural park. For the tourist, the ancient Appian Way offers three attractions: the road itself with its ruined monuments; the two best Christian catacombs open to visitors; and the peaceful atmosphere, which provides a respite from the city. Be aware, however, that the road today is busy with traffic—and actually quite treacherous in spots. I recommend following this tour's route, which lets you avoid the worst of the traffic (between Via di San Sebastiano and Domine Quo Vadis Church—except on Wednesdays, when the pedestrian path is closed). On this walk, you'll find the area a pleasant place for strolling or biking.

ORIENTATION

Tomb of Cecilia Metella: €6, includes entry to adjoining museum, Tue–Sun 9:00–18:30, closed Mon.

Circus and Villa of Maxentius: €3, Tue–Sun 9:00–13:00, closed Mon.

Catacombs of San Sebastiano: Guided tours leave 2/hr, €6, Mon–Sat 8:30–12:00 & 14:00–17:30, last tour at 17:00, closed Sun and mid-Nov–mid-Dec, closes at 17:00 in winter, Via Appia Antica 136, tel. 06-785-0350.

Catacombs of San Callisto: Guided tours leave frequently, €6, Thu–Tue 9:00–12:00 & 14:00–17:30, closed Wed and Feb, closes at 17:00 in winter, Via Appia Antica 110, tel. 06-5130-1580.

Domine Quo Vadis Church: Free, daily 8:00–12:30 & 14:30–19:00.

San Sebastiano Gate and Museum of the Walls: €2.60, Tue–Sun 9:00–14:00, closed Mon, tel. 06-7047-5284.

Information: The **Via Appia Antica TI** gives out maps and information on the entire park, which stretches east and south of the visit outlined here (daily April–Oct 9:30–17:30, Nov–March 9:30–16:30, Via Appia Antica 58/60, tel. 06-513-5316). The Archeobus map (available free from the TI) shows everything clearly. Appia Antica Caffè has good maps (see "Bike Rental," page 161).

When to Go: Visit in the morning or late afternoon, since many of the sights—including the catacombs—shut down from 12:00–14:30. All of the recommended sights are open on Tuesday, Thursday, Friday, and Saturday. The Tomb of Cecilia Metella is closed Monday; the Catacombs of San Callisto and the pedestrian path through the park are closed Wednesday; and the Catacombs of San Sebastiano are closed Sunday. On Sundays, the road is closed to car traffic and opened to people, making it a great day for walking or biking.

Getting There: The tour outlined below begins near the Tomb of Cecilia Metella, at the far (southern) end of the key sights, and works back (downhill) toward central Rome.

The easiest way to get from Rome to the Tomb of Cecilia Metella is by **taxi** (€11). However, to return by taxi, you'll have to telephone for one, as there are no taxi stands on the Appian Way (though bus #118 can easily get you back to Rome).

Your cheapest option for getting to the Tomb of Cecilia Metella is **public bus #660:** In Rome, take Metro line A to the Colli Albani stop, where you catch bus #660 (along Via Appia Nuova) and ride 10 minutes to the last stop—Cecilia Metella/Via Appia Antica. This drops you off right at the intersection of Via Appia Antica and Via Cecilia Metella.

If you want to visit just a few sights (without following the exact tour route outlined below), consider **bus #118.** In Rome,

Ancient Appian Way

TO SAN SEBASTIANO GATE,
MUSEUM OF THE WALLS
& DOWNTOWN ROME

DOMINE QUO
VADIS CHURCH
— ANOTHER ENTRY TO
SAN CALLISTO CATACOMBS

¼ MILE

.5 KM

VIA ARDEATINA

PEDESTRIAN WALKWAY (CLOSED WED.)

N

COLUMBARIUM

SECOND
MILESTONE

VIA APPIA

CATACOMBS
OF SAN
CALLISTO

TO
FOSSE
ARDEANTINE

VIA D. SETTE CHIESE

VILLA
OF
MAXENTIUS

CIRCUS
OF
MAXENTIUS

CATACOMBS
OF
SAN SEBASTIANO
+ WC

VIA PLATONIA

VIA DI SAN SEB.

VIA APPIA ANTICA

TOMB OF
CECILIA
METELLA

VIA CECILIA METELLA

TO
AQUEDUCT
PARK

THIRD
MILESTONE

ANTICA APPIA CAFFE
+ BIKE RENTAL

ALIMENTARI

TORRE DI
CAPO DI BOVE

VIA CAPO DI BOVE

SCENIC
SECTION

A Bus #660 Stop
B Bus #118 Stops
C Archeobus Stops

TO 4TH THROUGH 11TH
MILESTONES & BRINDISI

DCH

take Metro line B to the Piramide stop, then catch the #118 heading south; it will stop at the San Sebastiano Gate, Quo Vadis Church, Catacombs of San Callisto, and Catacombs of San Sebastiano. The #118 does not stop at the Tomb of Cecilia Metella (though the Catacombs of San Sebastiano are only 300 yards away from the tomb).

No matter how you arrive at the Appian Way, bus #118 is the easiest and cheapest way to return to Rome.

The other option for getting to the Appian Way sights is to ride the **Archeobus** from the Termini train station (see "Tours," page 34). It stops at all the key attractions—you can hop off, tour the sights, and pick up a later bus (runs hourly).

Bike Rental: At the Cecilia Metella bus stop (for bus #660) is **Appia Antica Caffè,** where you can rent a bike (€3.50/hr or €12/4 hrs, includes free info map, handy €1 map, Tue–Sun 10:00–18:00, closed Mon, at corner of the Appian Way and Via Cecilia Metella, near Tomb of Cecilia Metella at Via Appia Antica 175, mobile 338-3465-440, www.appiaanticacaffe.it). You can also rent a bike from the **Via Appia Antica TI** (€3/hr or €10/day, see "Information," above). If you don't mind heavy traffic, you could even bike from the Colosseum or Santa Maria Maggiore out past the wall and down the Appian Way. For bike rental in the city center, see "By Bike," on page 30.

Length of This Tour: Budget four hours to get to and from the Appian Way, walk or bike the stretch of sights, and visit one of the catacombs.

Cuisine Art: Appia Antica Caffè (see "Bike Rental," above) makes big salads and abundant sandwiches and has a shady, restful seating area in back. South of the café, just before the Torre di Capo di Bove mausoleum, is a hole-in-the-wall *alimentari* (market), perfect for assembling a picnic. Great picnic spots are just a half-mile uphill (south) of here. The stretch between Cecilia Metella and the Catacombs of San Sebastiano has several restaurants.

Starring: An old road, crumbling tombs, and underground Christian cemeteries.

Overview

The sightseeing core is a mile-and-a-half stretch between the Tomb of Cecilia Metella and Quo Vadis Church. Here you'll find the two catacombs and several Roman sights. See it on foot, by rental bike, or by bus (public bus #118 or the Archeobus), hopping on and off at key stops. Sightseers share the road with speeding drivers talking on mobile phones (except on traffic-free Sunday), but we'll avoid the worst of it by taking a pedestrian path through part of the park (except on Wednesdays, when the path is closed). The self-guided tour below starts at the far (southern) end of the sightseeing highlights and works back northward—mostly downhill—toward the center of Rome. At the walk's end, you can catch bus #118 into Rome.

THE TOUR BEGINS

• *From the café near the Tomb of Cecilia Metella, head downhill 100 yards, where you walk (or rattle your bike) over a stretch of the...*

APPIAN WAY TOUR

Original Paved Road

Huge basalt stones formed the sturdy base of a road 14 feet across. In its heyday, a central strip accommodated animal-powered vehicles, and elevated sidewalks served pedestrians. The first section (near Rome) was perfectly straight, and lined with tombs and funerary monuments.

Nearby (left side) is the original **mile marker III,** one of more than 400 such stones that counted the distance from Rome to Brindisi. Emperors knew a fine network of roads was key to expanding and administering the empire. This road, from c. 312 B.C., kicks off the expansion period.

• *You can't miss (on the right side) the...*

Tomb of Cecilia Metella
(Mausoleo di Cecilia Metella)

This massive cylindrical tomb, one of the best preserved of the many tombs of prominent Romans that line the road, was built in the time

of Augustus (c. 30 B.C.) for the daughter-in-law of Crassus, Rome's richest man. Faced with white travertine and situated on the crest of a hill, the tomb was an imposing sight. This grand tomb in the suburbs rivaled Augustus' own round mausoleum in the city center (near the Ara Pacis, see page 59).

Since no one was allowed to be

buried inside the city walls, the Appian Way was a popular place to have a tomb where everyone could admire it. Later, Christians were buried here, though not in tombs (they preferred to be buried underground). Picture a funeral procession passing under the pines and cypresses, past a long line of pyramids, private mini-temples, altars, and tombs.

• *Just past the tomb on the right are the ruins of the...*

Circus and Villa of Maxentius
(Circo e Villa di Massenzio)

This was the suburban home of the emperor who was eventually

defeated by Constantine in A.D. 312. The main sight to see here is a whole lot of nothing—that is, the expansive stretch of open space contained by this huge former chariot race track. You can see essentially all of it for free from the road. If you pay the admission, you can walk between the

APPIAN WAY TOUR

Sebastiano vs. Callisto

Which of the two catacombs is the best? They're actually quite similar. Both include a half-hour tour, where you go underground, seeing the niches where early Christians were buried (but no bones). Both have some faded frescoes and graffiti with Christian symbols. Both have small chapels and a few memorial statues. Most people pick one catacomb to visit, and either will fit the bill. I lean slightly in favor of San Callisto, but only because of its historical importance, not because it's inherently more interesting.

(Note that the **Catacombs of Priscilla**—more intimate and less crowded than these two more famous ones—can be found at the other end of town, northeast of the Villa Borghese Gardens; see page 61.)

entrance towers to the long central spine, and imagine chariots racing around it while 10,000 fans cheered. Maxentius watched from the building rising up above the bleachers, where the chariots made their hairiest turn. At the far end of the 260-yard track is the triumphal arch under which the winner rode to receive his reward.

Just down the Appian Way from this circus (behind the modern building and single palm tree), the big square ruins contained the circular mausoleum of Maxentius' son, Romulus.

• *About 300 yards farther down the road (on the left) are the...*

APPIAN WAY TOUR

▲▲Catacombs of San Sebastiano

This underground cemetery is named for the Christian soldier who was tied to a column and shot through with arrows because of his faith—a subject depicted by many artists through history. A guide takes you below ground to see burial niches, frescoes, and graffiti. It's said that the bodies of Peter and Paul were kept here for a while in the third century.

Besides the catacombs, the site also has a basilica containing various relics, including St. Sebastian's supposed remains, some arrows, and the column he was tied to.

• *The stretch of the Appian Way past the Catacombs of San Sebastiano is the least interesting and most crowded (even dangerous). Avoid it by taking the pedestrian and bike path (open daily except Wed), which begins just past the Catacombs of San Sebastiano, at the intersection with Via delle Sette Chiese. This quiet path parallels the Appian Way and takes you directly to the Catacombs of San Callisto (described next). To reach the path, go through the arch at #126. On Wednesdays, when the gate is closed, you'll have to stay straight on Via Appia Antica, being careful of traffic. A detour to the left down Via delle Sette Chiese brings you to the evocative Fosse Ardeatine, a memorial tomb to 335 Italians gunned down by Nazis during World War II, to avenge a bomb attack in Rome that killed 32 German soldiers.*

Catacombs

The catacombs are burial places for (mostly) Christians who died in ancient Roman times. By law, no one was allowed to be buried within the walls of Rome. While pagan Romans were into cremation, Christians preferred to be buried (so that they could be resurrected when the time came). But land was expensive, and most Christians were poor. A few wealthy, landowning Christians allowed their properties to be used as burial places.

The 40 or so known catacombs are scattered outside the ancient walls of Rome. From the first through the fifth centuries, Christians dug an estimated 375 miles of tomb-lined tunnels, with networks of galleries as many as five layers deep. The volcanic tufa stone that Rome sits atop—soft and easy to cut, but which hardens when exposed to air—was perfect for the job. The Christians burrowed many layers deep for two reasons: to get more mileage out of the donated land, and to be near martyrs and saints already buried there. Bodies were wrapped in linen (like Christ's). Since they figured the Second Coming was imminent, there was no interest in embalming the body.

When Emperor Constantine legalized Christianity in A.D. 313, Christians had a new, interesting problem: There would be no more recently persecuted martyrs to bind them together and inspire them. Instead, the early martyrs and popes assumed more importance, and Christians began making pilgrimages to their burial places in the catacombs.

In the 800s, when barbarian invaders started ransacking the tombs, Christians moved the relics of saints and martyrs to the safety of churches in the city center. For a thousand years, the catacombs were forgotten. In early modern times, they were excavated and became part of the Romantic Age's Grand

▲▲Catacombs of San Callisto

These are my favorite catacombs, named for the cemetery's first caretaker, St. Callixtus. This was the official cemetery for Rome's early Christians and the burial place of nine third-century popes, other bishops of Rome, and various martyrs. The most famous martyr was St. Cecilia, patron saint of music, a Roman noble who was killed for converting to Christianity. Her tomb is marked with a copy of a famous Maderno statue. (For more on Cecilia and the statue, see page 90 of the Trastevere Walk.)

Buy your €6 ticket and wait for your language to be called. They move lots of people quickly. If one group seems ridiculously large (more than 50 people), wait for the next tour in English. Dig this: The catacombs have a website—www.catacombe.roma.it—that focuses mainly on San Callisto, featuring photos, site info, and history.

• *Continue north (downhill) another half-mile, where the pedestrian path spills out at a busy three-way intersection. There you'll find the small...*

Tour of Europe.

When abandoned plates and utensils from ritual meals were found, 18th- and 19th-century Romantics guessed that persecuted Christians hid out in these candlelit galleries. The popularity of this legend grew—even though it was untrue. By the second century, more than a million people lived in Rome, and the 10,000 early Christians didn't need to camp out in the catacombs. They hid in plain view, melting into obscurity within the city itself.

The underground tunnels, while empty of bones, are rich in early Christian symbolism, which functioned as a secret lan-

guage. The dove represented the soul. You'll see it quenching its thirst (worshipping), with an olive branch (at rest), or happily perched (in paradise). Peacocks, known for their purportedly "incorruptible flesh," embodied immortality. The shepherd with a lamb on his shoulders was the "good shepherd," the first portrayal of Christ as a kindly leader of his flock. The fish was used because the first letters of these words—"Jesus Christ, Son of God, Savior"—spelled "fish" in Greek. And the anchor is a cross in disguise. A second-century bishop had written on his tomb, "All who understand these things, pray for me." You'll see pictures of people praying with their hands raised up—the custom at the time.

APPIAN WAY TOUR

Domine Quo Vadis Church

The ninth-century church (redone in the 17th) was built on the spot where Peter, while fleeing the city to escape Nero's persecution, saw a vision of Christ. Peter asked Jesus, "Lord, where are you going?" (*"Domine quo vadis?"* in Latin), to which Christ replied, "I am going to Rome to be crucified again." This miraculous sign gave Peter faith and courage and caused him to return to Rome. Inside the nave of the church, stumble over the stone that is marked with the supposed footprints of Jesus.

• *The tour is over. "Quo vadis, pilgrim?" To return to central Rome, it's another two miles north along a busy stretch of road, not recommended on foot or bike. Instead, catch bus #118, which stops at the San Sebastiano Gate (see below) on its way to the Piramide Metro stop. (Note that a different bus, the #218, goes from Quo Vadis Church to the San Sebastiano Gate, eventually terminating at San Giovanni in Laterano.)*

For those with more energy, there's more to see, especially if you're renting a bike and want to just get away from it all, consider...

Other Sights on or near the Appian Way

Consider these diversions along the ancient Appian Way.

San Sebastiano Gate and Museum of the Walls: For those heading back to the center of Rome, this is an easy stop—it's at the old city wall, two miles north of Quo Vadis Church (buses #118 and #218). The San Sebastiano Gate offers an interesting look at Roman defense and a chance to scramble along a stretch of the ramparts. The Aurelian wall (c. A.D. 270) was built in five years because of threat of invasions. At 12 miles around, it was the biggest building project ever undertaken within the city of Rome.

More of the Appian Way: Heading south (away from downtown Rome), past the Tomb of Cecilia Metella, you'll find the best-preserved part of the Appian Way—quieter, less touristed, and lined with cypresses, pines, and crumbling tombs. It's all downhill after the first few hundred yards. On a bike, you'll travel over lots of rough paving stones (or dirt sidewalks) for about 30 minutes to reach a big pyramid-shaped ruin on its tiny base, and then five minutes more to the back side of the Villa di Quintilli. You can't enter the villa from here, but you can admire the semi-circular nymphaeum, or fake grotto. Enjoy a picnic, then turn around and pedal up that long hill to return your bike.

Aqueduct Park: Rome's mighty aqueducts kept water flowing into the thriving and thirsty ancient city of one million. (They also

eventually provided a handy Achilles' heel for invading barbarians: Simply break an arch in the aqueduct, and life becomes very tough within the city walls.) This sprawling and evocative park—which seems miles from anywhere but is the last stop on the Archeobus route—is a favorite these days for local joggers. Hardier cyclists not afraid of riding in traffic can also visit.

To get there from the Appia Antica Caffè near the Tomb of Cecilia Metella, go east on Via Cecilia Metella/Almone. Turn right onto busy Via Appia Nuova—there's a sidewalk on the left side—then left onto Via Torre dei Fiscale, to reach a small park with a few ruined aqueducts. To reach a larger park with more ruins, continue south down Via Appia Nuova and turn left onto Via del Quadraro. Go under the tracks, then over, then right onto Via Allesandro Viviani. It's 45 minutes from the café to this farthest point.

NATIONAL MUSEUM OF ROME TOUR

Museo Nazionale Romano
Palazzo Massimo alle Terme

Rome lasted a thousand years...and so do most Roman history courses. But if you want a breezy overview of this fascinating society, there's no better place than the National Museum of Rome.

Rome took Greek culture and wrote it in capital letters. Thanks to this lack of originality, ancient Greek statues were preserved for our enjoyment today. But the Romans also pioneered a totally new form of art—sculpting painfully realistic portraits of emperors and important citizens.

Think of this museum as a walk back in time. As you gaze at the same statues that the Romans swooned over, the history of Rome comes alive—from Julius Caesar's murder to Caligula's incest to Vespasian's Colosseum to the coming of Christianity.

ORIENTATION

Cost: €10 combo-ticket includes entry to three lesser National Museum branches within three days: Museum of the Bath at the nearby Baths of Diocletian (see page 153), Palazzo Altemps (lackluster sculptures), and Crypta Balbi (medieval art).

Hours: Tue–Sun 9:00–19:45, last entry 45 min before closing, closed Mon.

Getting There: The museum is about 100 yards from the Termini train station (Metro: Termini). As you leave the station, it's the sandstone-brick building on your left. Enter at the far end, at Largo di Villa Peretti.

Information: Tel. 06-3996-7700.

Tours: An audioguide costs €4.50 (rent at ticket counter).

Length of This Tour: Allow two hours.

Starring: Roman emperor busts, *The Discus Thrower*, original Greek statues, and fine Roman copies.

THE TOUR BEGINS

Overview

The Palazzo Massimo is the permanent home of major Greek and Roman statues that were formerly scattered in other national museums around town.

The museum is rectangular, with rooms and hallways built around a central courtyard. The ground-floor displays follow Rome's history as it changes from a democratic republic to a dictatorial empire. The first-floor exhibits take Rome from its peak through its slow decline. The second floor houses rare frescoes and fine mosaics, and the basement displays coins and everyday objects. As you tour this museum, note that in Italian, "room" is *sala* and "hall" is *galleria*.

GROUND FLOOR—
FROM SENATORS TO CAESARS

• *Buy your ticket and pass through the turnstile, where you'll find...*

Minerva

It's big, it's gaudy, it's a weird goddess from a pagan cult. Welcome to the Roman world. The statue is also a good reminder that all the statues in this museum—now missing limbs, scarred by erosion, or weathered down to bare stone—were once whole, and painted to look as lifelike as possible.

• *Turning to the right, you'll find Gallery I; this hallway is lined with portrait busts.*

Gallery I—Portrait Heads from the Republic (500–1 B.C.)

Stare into the eyes of these stern, hardy, no-nonsense, farmer-stock people who founded Rome. The wrinkles and crags of these original "ugly republicans" tell the story of Rome's roots as a small agricultural tribe, fighting for survival with neighboring bands.

These faces are brutally realistic, unlike more idealized Greek statues. Romans honored their ancestors and worthy citizens in the "family" *(gens)* of Rome. They wanted lifelike statues to remember them by, and to instruct the young with their air of moral rectitude.

In its first 500 years, Rome was a republic ruled by a Senate of wealthy landowners. But as Rome expanded throughout Italy and the economy shifted from farming to booty, changes were needed.

• *Enter Room I (Sala I). Along the wall between the doorways, find the portrait bust that some scholars think may be Julius Caesar.*

National Museum—Ground Floor

ROOM III
ROOM II
ROOM I
3
BAGGAGE CHECK
STAIRS
ELEV.
6 **7**
GALLERY I
2
WC
5
1
TICKETS
ROOM IV
ROOM V
STEPS
OPEN-AIR COURTYARD
ENTRY
DCH
4
GALLERY III
9
8
ROOM VI
10
ROOM VII
11
ROOM VIII
STAIRS UP TO FIRST FLOOR

VIA
VIMINALE

← TO TERMINI TRAIN STATION

TO PIAZZA REPUBBLICA →

1 Minerva

2 Portrait Heads

3 Julius Caesar

4 Augustus as Pontifex Maximus

5 Livia

6 Tiberius

7 Caligula

8 Alexander the Great

9 Socrates

10 Niobid

11 The Boxer at Rest & Hellenistic Prince

Room I

Julius Caesar
(Rilievo con Ritratto dalla collezione Von Bergen)

Julius Caesar (c. 100–44 B.C.)—with his prominent brow, high cheekbones, and male-pattern baldness with the forward comb-over—changed Rome forever.

When this charismatic general swept onto the scene, Rome was in chaos. Rich landowners were fighting middle-class plebs, who wanted their slice of the plunder. Slaves such as Spartacus were picking up hoes and hacking up masters. And renegade generals—the new providers of wealth and security in an economy of plunder—were becoming dictators. (Notice the **life-size statue** of an unknown but obviously once-renowned general.)

Caesar was a people's favorite. He conquered Gaul (France), then sacked Egypt, then impregnated Cleopatra. He defeated rivals and made them his allies. He gave great speeches. Chicks dug him.

With the army at his back and the people in awe, he took the reins of government, instituted sweeping changes, made himself the center of power...and antagonized the Senate.

A band of republican assassins surrounded him in a Senate meeting. He called out for help as one by one they stepped up to take turns stabbing him. The senators sat and watched in silence. One of the killers was his adopted son, Brutus, and Caesar—astonished that even Brutus joined in—died saying, *"Et tu, Brute?"*

• *At the end of Gallery I, turn left, then left again, into the large glassed-in Room V, with a life-size statue of Augustus.*

Room V—
Augustus and Rome's Legendary Birth

Statue of Augustus as Pontifex Maximus
(Ritratto di Augusto in Vesta di Offerente)

Julius Caesar died, but his family name, his politics, and his flamboyance lived on. Julius had adopted his grandnephew, Octavian, who united Rome's warring factions.

Here, Emperor Augustus has taken off his armor and laurel-leaf crown, donning the simple hooded robes of a priest. He's retiring to a desk job after a lifetime of fighting to reunite Rome. He killed Brutus and eliminated his rivals, Mark Antony and Cleopatra. For the first time in almost a century of fighting, one general reigned supreme. Octavian took the title "Augustus" and became the first of the emperors who would rule Rome for the next 500 years.

In fact, Augustus was a down-to-earth man who lived simply, worked hard, read books, listened to underlings, and tried to restore traditional Roman values after the turbulence of Julius Caesar's time. He outwardly praised the Senate, while actually reducing it to a rubber-stamp body. Augustus' reign marked the start of 200 years of peace and prosperity, the Pax Romana.

See if the statue matches a description of Augustus by a contemporary—the historian Suetonius: "He was unusually handsome. His expression was calm and mild. He had clear, bright eyes, in which was a kind of divine power. His hair was slightly curly and somewhat golden." Any variations were made by sculptors who idealized features to make him almost godlike.

Augustus proclaimed himself a god—not arrogantly or blasphemously, as Caligula later did, but as the honored "father" of the "family" of Rome. As the empire expanded, the vanquished had to worship statues like this one as a show of loyalty.

NATIONAL MUSEUM

• *Cross the hallway into Room IV. Near the doorway, find the bust of the empress Livia.*

Room IV—The Julio-Claudian Family: Rome's First Emperors (c. 50 B.C.–A.D. 68)

Julius Caesar's descendants ruled Rome for a century after his death, turning the family surname "Caesar" into a title.

Livia

Augustus' wife, Livia, was a major power behind the throne. Her stern, thin-lipped gaze withered rivals at court. Her hairstyle—bunched up in a peak, braided down the center, and tied in back—became the rage throughout the empire, as her face appeared everywhere in statues and on coins. Notice that by the next generation (Antonia Minore, Livia's daughter-in-law, next to Livia), a simpler bun was chic. And by the following generation, it was tight curls. Empresses dictated fashion the way that emperors dictated policy.

Livia bore Augustus no sons. She lobbied hard for Tiberius, her own son by a first marriage, to succeed as emperor. Augustus didn't like him, but Livia was persuasive. He relented, ate some bad figs, and died—the gossip was that Livia poisoned him to seal the bargain. The pattern of succession was established—adopt a son from within the extended family—and Tiberius was proclaimed emperor. (The fine frescoed walls of Livia's Anzio villa are upstairs on the second floor.)

• *In the corner of the room, find the well-worn bust of...*

Tiberius (*Tiberio*, ruled A.D. 14–37)

Scholars speculate that acne may have soured Tiberius to the world (but this statue is pocked by erosion). Shy and sullen but diligent, he worked hard to be the easygoing leader of men that Augustus had been. Early on, he was wise and patient, but he suffered personal setbacks. Politics forced him to divorce his only beloved and marry a slut. His favorite brother died, then his son. Embittered, he let subordinates run things and retired to Capri, where he built a villa with underground dungeons. There he hosted orgies of sex, drugs, torture, really loud music, and execution. At his side was his young grandnephew, whom he adopted as next emperor.

• *To your right, in the glass case, is the small bust of...*

Caligula (*Caligola*, ruled A.D. 37–41)

This emperor had sex with his sisters, tortured his enemies, made off with friends' wives during dinner parties and then returned to rate their performance in bed, crucified Christians, took cuts in line at

NATIONAL MUSEUM

the Vatican Museum, and ordered men to kneel before him as a god. Caligula has become the archetype of a man with enough power to act out his basest fantasies.

Politically, he squandered Rome's money, then taxed and extorted from the citizens. Perhaps he was made mad by illness, perhaps he was the victim of vindictive historians, but still, no one mourned when assassins ambushed him and ran a sword through his privates. Rome was tiring of this family dynasty's dysfunction.

• *Continue down Gallery II and turn left. Busts line Gallery III. Find Alexander the Great and Socrates flanking the entrance to Room VII. (Socrates may be displayed a bit farther down the hall, outside Room VIII.)*

Gallery III—Rome's Greek Mentors

Rome's legions easily conquered the less-organized but more-cultured Greek civilization that had dominated the Mediterranean for centuries. Romans adopted Greek gods, art styles, and fashions, and sophisticated Romans sprinkled their conversation with Greek phrases.

Alexander the Great *(Alessandro Magno)*

Alexander the Great (356–323 B.C.) single-handedly created a Greek-speaking empire by conquering, in just a few short years, lands from Greece to Egypt to Persia. Later, when the Romans conquered Greece (c. 200 B.C.), they inherited this pre-existing collection of cultured Greek cities ringing the Mediterranean.

Alexander's handsome statues set the standard for those of later Roman emperors. His features were chiseled and youthful, and this statue was adorned with pompous decorations, like a golden sunburst aura (fitted into the holes). The greatest man of his day, he ruled the known world by the age of 30.

Alexander's teacher was none other than the philosopher Aristotle. Aristotle's teacher was Plato, whose mentor was...

Socrates *(Socrate)*

This nonconformist critic of complacent thinking is the father of philosophy. The Greeks were an intellectual, introspective, sensitive, and artistic people. The Romans were practical, no-nonsense soldiers, salesmen, and bureaucrats. Many a Greek slave was more cultured than his master, reduced to the role of warning his boss not to wear a plaid toga with a polka-dot robe.

• *Backtrack and enter Room VI.*

Room VI— Greek Beauty in Originals and Copies

Niobid *(Niobide Ferita*, 440 B.C.)

The Romans were astonished by the beauty of Greek statues. Niobid's smooth skin contrasts with the rough folds of her clothing. She twists naturally around an axis running straight up and down. This woman looks like a classical goddess awakening from a beautiful dream, but...

Circle around back. The hole bored in her back, right in that itchy place you can't quite reach, once held a golden arrow. The woman has

been shot by Artemis, goddess of hunting, because her mother dared to boast to the gods about her kids. Niobid reaches back in vain, trying to remove the arrow before it drains her of life.

Romans ate this stuff up: the sensual beauty, the underplayed pathos, the very Greekness of it. They crated up centuries-old statues like this and brought them home to their gardens and palaces. Soon there weren't enough old statues to meet the demand. Crafty Greeks began cranking out knock-offs of Greek originals for mass consumption. In Rooms VII and VIII are originals (like *Niobid*) and copies—some of extremely high quality—while others were more like cheesy fake *David*s in a garden store. Appreciate the beauty of the world's rare, surviving Greek originals.

Rome conquered Greece, but culturally the Greeks conquered the Romans.

• *Move next door to see...*

Room VII—Hellenistic and Classical Bronzes
The Boxer at Rest (*Pugilatore*, first century B.C.)

An exhausted boxer sits between rounds and gasps for air. Check out the brass-knuckle-type Roman boxing gloves. Textbook Hellenistic, this pugilist is realistic and full of emotion. His face is scarred, his back muscles are knotted, and he's got cauliflower ears. He's losing.

Slumped over, he turns with a questioning look ("Why am I losing again?"), and eyes that once held glass now make him look empty indeed. "I coulda been a contender."

Hellenistic Prince *(Principe Elenistico)*

Back then, everyone wanted to be like Alexander the Great. This newly restored bronze statue—naked and leaning on a spear—shows a prince (probably Attalus II of Pergamon) in the style of a famous statue of his hero from the second century B.C.

• *We've covered Rome's first 500 years. At the end of the hall are the stairs up to the first floor.*

FIRST FLOOR—
ROME'S PEAK AND SLOW FALL

As we saw, Augustus' family did not always rule wisely. Under Nero (ruled A.D. 54–68), the debauchery, violence, and paranoia typical of the Julio-Claudians festered to a head. When the city burned in the great fire of 64, the Romans suspected Nero of torching it himself to clear land for his enormous luxury palace.

Enough. Facing a death sentence, Nero committed suicide with the help of a servant. An outsider was brought in to rule—Vespasian, from the Flavian family.

• *At the top of the stairs, enter Room I. To your right is Vespasian.*

Room I—The Flavian Family
Vespasian (*Vespasianus*, ruled A.D. 69-79)

Balding and wrinkled, with a big head, a double chin, and a shy smile, Vespasian was a common man. The son of a tax collector, he rose through the military ranks with a reputation as a competent drudge. As emperor, he restored integrity, raised taxes, started the Colosseum, and suppressed the Jewish rebellion in Palestine.

• *In the center of the room is...*

Domitian (*Domitianus*, ruled A.D. 81-96)
Vespasian's son, Domitian, used his father's tax revenues to construct the massive Imperial Palace on Palatine Hill, home to emperors for the next three centuries. Shown with his lips curled in a sneer, he was a moralistic prude who executed several Vestal ex-Virgins, while in private he took one mistress after another. Until...

• *Over your left shoulder, find...*

Domitia
...his stern wife found out and hired a servant to stab him in the groin. Domitia's hairstyle is a far cry from the "Livia" cut, with a high crown of tight curls.

• *In the corner diagonally opposite Domitia is...*

Nerva (ruled A.D. 96-98)
Nerva realized that the Flavian dynasty was no better than its predecessors. Old and childless, he made a bold, far-sighted move—he adopted a son from outside of Rome's corrupting influence.

• *Entering Room II, Trajan is on the left wall.*

National Museum—First Floor

- ❶ Vespasian
- ❷ Domitian
- ❸ Domitia
- ❹ Nerva
- ❺ Trajan
- ❻ Hadrian
- ❼ Aphrodite Crouching
- ❽ Apollo
- ❾ The Discus Thrower
- ❿ Hermaphrodite Sleeping
- ⓫ Septimius Severus
- ⓬ Caracalla
- ⓭ Gordianus III
- ⓮ Sarcophagus of a Procession
- ⓯ Christ Teaching

Room II—A Cosmopolitan Culture

Trajan (*Traianus-Hercules,* ruled A.D. 98–117)

Born in Spain, this conquering hero pushed Rome's borders to their greatest extent, creating a truly worldwide empire. The spoils of three continents funneled into a city of a million-plus people. Trajan could dress up in a lion's skin, presenting himself as a "new Hercules," and no one found it funny. Romans felt a spirit of Manifest Destiny: "The gods desire that the City of Rome shall be the capital of all the countries of the world" (Livy).

• *On the opposite wall is...*

Hadrian (*Hadrianus,* ruled A.D. 117–138)

Hadrian was a fully cosmopolitan man. His beard—the first we've seen—shows his taste for foreign things; he poses like the Greek philosopher he imagined himself to be.

Hadrian was a voracious tourist, personally visiting almost every corner of the vast empire, from Britain (where he built Hadrian's Wall) to Egypt (where he sailed the Nile), from Jerusalem (where he suppressed another Jewish revolt) to Athens (where he soaked up classical culture). He scaled Sicily's Mount Etna just to see what made a volcano tick. Back home, he beautified Rome with the Pantheon and his villa at Tivoli, a microcosm of places he'd visited.

Hadrian is flanked here by the two loves of his life. His wife,

Sabina (left), with modest hairstyle and scarf, kept the home fires burning for her traveling husband. Hadrian was 50 years old when he became captivated by a teenage boy named **Antinous** (right), with his curly hair and full, sensual lips. Together they traveled the Nile, where Antinous drowned. Hadrian wept. Statues of Antinous subsequently went up through the Empire, much to the embarrassment of the stoic Romans.

Hadrian spent his last years at his lavish villa outside Rome, surrounded by buildings and souvenirs that reminded him of his traveling days (see Tivoli Day Trip, page 344).

• *Backtrack through Room I and turn right, down a hall that leads into the large Room V.*

Rooms V and VI—Rome's Grandeur

Pause at Rome's peak to admire the things the Romans found beautiful. Imagine these statues in their original locations, in the pleasure gardens of the Roman rich—surrounded by greenery, with the splashing sound of fountains, the statues all painted in bright, lifelike colors. Though executed by Romans, the themes are mostly Greek, with godlike humans and human-looking gods.

• *In the center of Room V is...*

Aphrodite Crouching *(Afrodite Accovacciata)*

The goddess of beauty crouches while bathing, then turns to admire herself. This sets her whole body in motion—one thigh goes down, one up; her head turns clockwise while her body goes reverse—yet she's perfectly still. The crouch creates a series of symmetrical love handles, molded by the sculptor into the marble-like wax. Hadrian had good taste—he ordered a copy of this Greek classic for his bathroom.

• *Two statues down, find the large statue of...*

Apollo

The god of light appears as a slender youth, not as some burly, powerful, autocratic god. He stands *contrapposto*—originally he was leaning against the tree—in a relaxed and very human way. His curled hair is tied with a headband, with strands that tumble down his neck. His muscles and skin are smooth. (The rusty stains come from the centuries the statue spent submerged in the Tiber.) Apollo is in a reflective mood, and the serenity and intelligence in his face show off classical Greece as a nation of thinkers.

• *At the far end, the room connects into Room VI, with...*

The Discus Thrower *(Discobolo)*

An athlete winds up, about to unleash his pent-up energy and hurl the discus. The sculptor has frozen the moment for us, so that we can examine the inner workings of the wonder called Man. The perfect pecs and washboard abs make this human god-like. Geometrically, you could draw a perfect circle around him, with his hipbone at the center. He's natural yet ideal, twisting yet balanced, moving while at rest. For the Greeks, the universe was a rational place, and the human body was the perfect embodiment of the order found in nature.

This statue is the best-preserved Roman copy (not one member is missing—I checked) of the original Greek work by Myron (450 B.C.). (The subtle nubs on his head were aids for a measuring device used when making copies.) Statues of athletes like this commonly stood in the baths, where Romans cultivated healthy bodies, minds, and social skills, hoping to live well-rounded lives. *The Discus Thrower,* with his geometrical perfection and godlike air, sums up all that is best in the classical world.

• *Continue into Room VII, where you'll run into a sleeping statue.*

Room VII

Hermaphrodite Sleeping *(Ermafrodito Dormiente)*

After leaving the baths, a well-rounded Roman may head post-haste to an orgy, where he might see a reclining nude like this, be titillated, circle around for a closer look, and say, "Hey! *(Insert your own reaction here)*!"

• *Exit Room VII at the far end and turn left. Then turn right into Room XIII and look to the right to find the bust of Septimius Severus.*

Room XIII—Beginning of the End

Septimius Severus (ruled A.D. 193–211)

Rome's sprawling empire was starting to unravel, and it took a disciplined, emperor-warrior like this African to keep it together. Severus' victories on the frontier earned him a grand triumphal arch in the Forum, but here he seems to be rolling his eyes at the chaos growing around him.

• *Near Severus is his son...*

Caracalla (ruled A.D. 211–217)

The stubbly beard, cruel frown, and glaring eyes tell us that Severus' son was bad news. He murdered his little brother to seize power, then proceeded to massacre thousands of loyal citizens on a whim. The army came to distrust rulers whose personal agenda got in their way, and Caracalla was stabbed in the back by a man whose brother had just been executed. Rome's long slide had begun.

Room XIV—The Fall

There are a lot of serious faces in this room. People who grew up in the lap of luxury and security were witnessing the unthinkable—the disintegration of a thousand years of tradition. Rome never recovered from the chaos of the third century. Disease, corruption, revolts from within, and "barbarians" pecking away at the borders were body blows that sapped Rome's strength.

• *Immediately after entering this long room, find...*

Gordianus III (ruled A.D. 238–244)

By the third century, the Roman army could virtually hand-pick an emperor to be their front man. At one point, the office of emperor was literally auctioned to the highest bidder.

Thirteen-year-old Gordianus, with barely a wisp of facial hair, was naive and pliable, the perfect choice—until he got old enough to question the generals. He was one of some 15 emperors in the space of 40 years who was saluted, then murdered, at the whim of soldiers of fortune. His assassins had no problem sneaking up on him because, as you can see, he had no ears.

Sarcophagus of a Procession
(*Sarcofago con Corteo, etc.*, A.D. 270)

A parade of dignitaries, accompanying a new Roman leader, marches up Capitol Hill. They huddle together, their backs to the wall, look-

ing around suspiciously for assassins. Their faces reflect the fear of the age. Rome would stagger on for another 200 years, but the glory of old Rome was gone. The city was becoming a den of thugs, thieves, prostitutes, barbarians... and Christians.

• *Farther along, on the right-hand wall, find the small...*

Seated Statuette of Christ Teaching
(*Cristo Docente*, A.D. 350)

Christ sits like a Roman senator—in a toga, holding a scroll, dispensing wisdom like the law of the land. The statue comes from those delirious days when formerly persecuted Christians could now "come out" and worship in public. Emperor Constantine (ruled 306–337) legalized Christianity, and within two generations it was Rome's official religion.

Whether Christianity invigorated or ruined Rome is debated, but the fall was inevitable. Rome's once-great legions backpedaled, until even the city itself was raped and plundered by foreigners (410). In 476, the last emperor sold his title for a comfy pension plan, "Rome" became just another dirty city with a big history, and the artistic masterpieces now in this museum were buried under rubble.

THE REST OF THE MUSEUM

• *For extra credit, consider exploring two more parts of the National Museum.*

Second Floor

This floor contains frescoes and mosaics that once decorated the walls and floors of Roman villas. They're remarkably realistic and un-

stuffy, featuring everyday people, animals, flowery patterns, and geometrical designs. The frescoes taken from the Villa Farnese—in black, red, yellow, and blue—are mostly architectural designs, with fake columns and "windows" that "look out" on landscape scenes.

In Room II, look for the **Four Frescoes of Rome's Mythical Origins** (*Fregio Pittorico*, etc.). These cartoon-strip frescoes (read right to left) tell the story of Augustus' legendary forebears:

1. Upper right fresco: Aeneas (red skin and sword) arrives in Italy from Troy and fights the locals for a place to live.

2. Upper left: His wife (far left, seated, in purple) and son build a city wall around Rome to protect the womenfolk from battles raging outside.

3. Lower right: Several generations later, the God of War (lounging in center, with red skin) lies in wait to rape and impregnate a Vestal Virgin.

4. Lower left: Her disgraced babies, Romulus and Remus, are placed in a basket (center) and set adrift on the Tiber River. They wash ashore, are suckled by a she-wolf, and finally (far left) taken in by a shepherd. These legendary babies, of course, grow up to found the city that makes real history. The chisel marks were a preparation designed to help a later fresco (which was never applied) stick.

Basement (Floor -2)

The **"Luxury in Rome"** rooms give a peek into the lives of Rome's well-to-do citizens, featuring fine jewelry, common everyday objects, and an eight-year-old girl's mummy.

Next, enter the **coin collection.** Find your favorite emperor or empress on the coins by using remote-controlled magnifying glasses: Julius Caesar (case 8, #41–44), Augustus (case 8, #65–69, and case 9, #1–38), Augustus' system of denars (case 10), Tiberius (case 10, #1–16), Caligula (case 10, #17–28), and Nero (case 11, #2–33). Evaluate Roman life by studying Diocletian's wage and price controls (glass case 21). In A.D. 300, one denar bought one egg.

The rest of the displays trace Europe's money from denars to euros, including a monetary unit that is now history—the Italian *lire*.

NATIONAL MUSEUM

CAPITOLINE MUSEUMS TOUR

Musei Capitolini

This enjoyable museum complex claims to be the world's oldest, founded in 1471 when a pope gave ancient statues to the citizens of Rome. Perched on the top of Capitol Hill Square, its two buildings (Palazzo dei Conservatori and Palazzo Nuovo) are connected by an underground passage that leads to the Tabularium and panoramic views of the Roman Forum.

ORIENTATION

Cost: €8; €10 combo-ticket includes Montemartini Museum (museum described on page 71; combo-ticket good for 7 days). Admission includes mandatory temporary exhibits.

Hours: Tue–Sun 9:00–20:00, last entry one hour before closing, closed Mon.

Getting There: From Piazza Venezia or the Forum, walk uphill to the square on top of Capitol Hill (Campidoglio in Italian). Enter at the Palazzo dei Conservatori (on your right as you face the equestrian statue).

Information: You'll find some English descriptions within the museum. Tel. 06-8205-9127, www.museicapitolini.org.

Tour: The €5 audioguide is good.

Length of This Tour: Allow two hours.

Baggage Check: Free (mandatory for large bags).

Cuisine Art: There's a great view café, called **Caffè Capitolino,** upstairs in Palazzo dei Conservatori (Tue–Sun 9:00–19:30, closed Mon, enter from inside museum; also has exterior entrance for the public—facing museum entrance, go to your right around the building to Piazza Caffarelli and through door #4; see map). The tent on the terrace outside offers full service; inside is self-service (pay first, then take receipt to bar; good

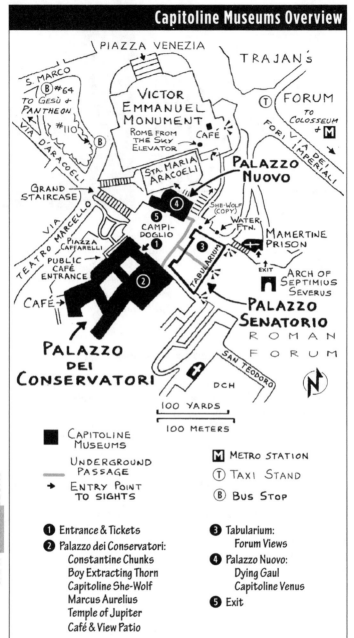

Capitoline Museums Overview

PIAZZA VENEZIA

TRAJAN'S

S. MARCO

Ⓑ #64

TO GESÙ &
PANTHEON

#110

VIA D'ARACOELI

VICTOR
EMMANUEL
MONUMENT

ROME FROM
THE SKY
ELEVATOR

Ⓣ FORUM

TO
COLOSSEUM
& Ⓜ

CAFÉ

VIA DEI
FORI IMPERIALI

STA. MARIA
ARACOELI

PALAZZO
NUOVO

GRAND
STAIRCASE

VIA TEATRO MARCELLO

PIAZZA
CAFFARELLI

PUBLIC
CAFÉ
ENTRANCE

CAFÉ

④

⑤

CAMPI-
DOGLIO

①

②

SHE-WOLF
(COPY)

WATER
FTN.

③

TABULARIUM

MAMERTINE
PRISON

EXIT

ARCH OF
SEPTIMIUS
SEVERUS

PALAZZO
DEI
CONSERVATORI

PALAZZO
SENATORIO

ROMAN
FORUM

SAN TEODORO

DCH

Ⓝ

100 YARDS

100 METERS

◼ CAPITOLINE
   MUSEUMS

── UNDERGROUND
   PASSAGE

➜ ENTRY POINT
   TO SIGHTS

Ⓜ METRO STATION

Ⓣ TAXI STAND

Ⓑ BUS STOP

❶ Entrance & Tickets
❷ Palazzo dei Conservatori:
   Constantine Chunks
   Boy Extracting Thorn
   Capitoline She-Wolf
   Marcus Aurelius
   Temple of Jupiter
   Café & View Patio

❸ Tabularium:
   Forum Views
❹ Palazzo Nuovo:
   Dying Gaul
   Capitoline Venus
❺ Exit

salads and toasted sandwiches). Piazza Caffarelli is a fine place for a snooze or a picnic.

Starring: The original *She-Wolf* statue, *Marcus Aurelius*, the *Dying Gaul*, the *Boy Extracting a Thorn*, and Forum views.

THE TOUR BEGINS

• *Begin at the square on top of Capitol Hill.*

Overview

Capitol Hill's main square (Campidoglio), home to the museum, began in ancient Rome as a religious center, the site of temples to

the gods Jupiter, Juno, and Minerva. In the 16th century, Michelangelo transformed the square from pagan to papal, while adding a harmonious and refined Renaissance touch. (For more on the square, see page 39.)

To identify the museum's two buildings, face the equestrian statue (with your back to the grand stairway). You'll enter at the Palazzo dei Conservatori (on your right), cross underneath the square (beneath the Palazzo Senatorio, or mayoral palace, not open to public—see photo), and exit from the Palazzo Nuovo (on your left).

The museum's layout—with two different buildings connected by an underground passage—can be confusing, but this self-guided tour is easy to follow.

Palazzo dei Conservatori

• *After your ticket is checked, enter the courtyard.*

In the courtyard, enjoy the massive chunks of Constantine: his head, hand, and foot. When intact, this giant held the place of honor in the Basilica of Constantine in the Forum. Also in the courtyard are reliefs of conquered peoples—not in chains, but new members of an expansive empire.

• *Go up the staircase (the one to the left of the entrance, not the one in the courtyard). On the landing, find...*

Reliefs of Second-Century Imperial Grandeur

These four fine reliefs show great moments in an emperor's daily grind. Find Marcus Aurelius overseeing preparations to sacrifice a

bull (with even the bull looking on curiously) on Capitol Hill. Also find Marcus Aurelius in an equestrian pose (like the bronze statue in Capitol Hill Square), with his hand out, offering clemency to his vanquished foes. The detail, with expressive faces and banners blowing in the wind, is impressive. In the relief showing Marcus Aurelius in his chariot, someone's missing...it's Commodus, his wicked son (Russell Crowe's nemesis in *Gladiator*). After the assassination of Commodus, his memory was damned, so images of him were erased (or, in this case, chiseled out).

• *Continue up the stairs to the first floor. Go through two large frescoed rooms and through the doorway on the right of the far wall to find...*

Boy Extracting a Thorn *(Spinario)*

He's just a boy, intent only on picking a thorn out of his foot. As he bends over to reach his foot, his body sticks out at all angles, like a bony chicken wing. He's even scuffed up, the way small boys get. At this moment, nothing matters to him but that splinter. Our lives are filled with these mundane moments (when we'd give anything for tweezers) rarely captured in art.

Art scholars speculate that the boy's head, tilted unnaturally down, and his body are from two separate statues spliced together.

• *In the next room...*

Capitoline *She-Wolf*

The original bronze *She-Wolf* suckles the twins Romulus and Remus.

This symbol of Rome is ancient, though the wolf statue itself (long thought to be Etruscan from the fifth century B.C.) was made in medieval times and the boys are an invention of the Renaissance. Look into the eyes of the wolf. An animal looks back, with ragged ears, sharp teeth, and staring eyes. This wild animal, teamed with the wildest creatures of all—hungry babies—makes a powerful symbol for the tenacious city/empire of Rome.

• *In the next room...*

From Michelangelo to Medusa

Along with a bust of Michelangelo, this room contains Bernini's anguished bust of Medusa—with writhing snakes on her head. This goes way beyond a bad hair day.

• *Pass through three small rooms containing the* Artemis of Efenina, *followed by Greek red-figured vases (and the elevator up to the café). Continue straight to a set of stairs to the next room to discover the remarkable bust of...*

Commodus as Hercules

This arrogant emperor brat used to run around the palace in animal skins. Here, he wears a lion's head over his own, and drapes the lion's paws over his chest. This lion king made a bad emperor (ruled A.D. 180–192).

• *As you are looking at Commodus, directly behind you is his dad, the Emperor...*

Marcus Aurelius (c. A.D. 176)

This is the greatest surviving equestrian statue of antiquity. Marcus Aurelius was a Roman philosopher-emperor (ruled A.D. 161–180) known more for his *Meditations* than his prowess on the battlefield. Notice that he doesn't use stirrups. An Asian invention, those newfangled devices wouldn't arrive in Europe for another 500 years.

Christians in the Dark Ages thought that the statue's hand was

raised in blessing, which probably led to their misidentifying him as Constantine, the first Christian emperor. While most pagan statues were destroyed by Christians, "Constantine" was spared. It has graced several prominent locations in medieval Rome, including the papal palace at San Giovanni in Laterano.

In 1538, this gilded bronze statue was placed in the center of Capitol Hill Square (directly outside the museum), and Michelangelo was hired to design the buildings around it with the statue as the centerpiece. A few years ago, the statue was moved inside and restored, while the copy you see outside today was placed on the square.

Also in the room are a gilded *Hercules* and more hunks—head, finger, and a globe—of another statue of Constantine. (Or was it the Emperor Sylvestrus Stalloneus?)

• *Descend the ramp to the wall of blocks from the...*

Temple of Jupiter

This is part of the foundation of the ancient Temple of Jupiter (or Giove), once the most impressive in Rome. Study the scale model reconstruction (1:40) to get a sense of the temple's size and where you stand in relation to the ruins.

The King of the Gods resided atop Capitol Hill in this once-classy 10,000-square-foot temple, which was perched on a podium and lined with Greek-style columns, overlooking downtown Rome. The most important rites were performed here, and victory parades through the Forum ended here. The famous temple, known as the Capitolium, gave the hill its name. Replicas of this building were erected in every Roman city. The temple was begun by Rome's last king (the Tarquin), and its dedication in 509 B.C. marks the start of the Roman Republic.

All that remains today of the temple are these ruined foundation stones, made of volcanic tufa, an easily carved rock commonly used in Roman construction. Although there are hundreds of these blocks here, they represent only a portion of the immense foundation, which is only a fraction of the temple itself. In its prime, the temple rose two stories above our heads. Inside stood a statue of the god of thunder wielding a lightning bolt. The temple was refurbished a number of

times over the centuries, often after damage by...lightning bolts.

• *Before heading for the Tabularium and Palazzo Nuovo, consider a break in the café. To do this, backtrack to the room with the Greek red-figured vases (near Michelangelo and Medusa), where you'll find the elevator up to the second floor. The café's huge, outdoor view patio overlooks the domes of Rome, representing the religion that remained after Rome fell. When you're ready, go back downstairs to Marcus Aurelius.*

If Marcus trotted a few steps forward, turned left, and went to the end of the hall, he'd find the staircase. Go downstairs two flights, to the base-ment—the piano sotteraneo—*and cross underneath the square through this long passageway. Near the far end, turn right and climb a set of stairs into the...*

Tabularium

Built in the first century B.C., these sturdy vacant rooms once held the archives of ancient Rome. The word Tabularium comes from "tablet," on which laws were written.

The rooms offer a stunning head-on view over the Forum, giving you a more complete picture of the sprawl of ancient Rome. Panning left to right, find the following landmarks: the Arch of Septimius Severus, the Arch of Titus (in the distance), the lone Column of Phocas, the three columns of the Temple of Castor and Pollux, the three columns (closer to you) of the Temple of Vespasiano, and the eight columns of the Temple of Saturn.

Now do an about-face and look up to see a huge white hunk of carved marble, an overhang from the Temple of Vespasiano.

• *Find more views from this vantage point, plus the remains of another temple, then leave the Tabularium by going back down the stairs. Turn right and go up two flights of stairs. You're now on the first floor of the...*

Palazzo Nuovo

• *From the top of the stairs, the first room you encounter is Room VIII—the "Hall of the Gaul"—with one of the museum's most famous pieces.*

Dying Gaul

A first-century B.C. copy of a Greek original, this was sculpted to cel-

ebrate the Greeks' victory over the Galatians. It may have been part of a larger sculpture group (long since lost).

Wounded in battle, the dying Gaul holds himself upright, but barely. Minutes earlier, before he was stabbed in the chest, he'd been in his prime. Now he can only watch helplessly as his life ebbs away. His sword is useless against this last battle. With his messy hair, downcast eyes, and crumpled position, he poignantly reminds us that every victory also means a defeat.

• *In the next few rooms, take a quick look at...*

CAPITOLINE MUSEUMS

Ancient Roman Statues and Busts

A reddish faun glories in grapes and life, oblivious to the loss of his penis (at least he still has his tail). The statue, found in a couple dozen pieces in Hadrian's Villa, was skillfully restored. Check out the chandeliered ceilings in this room and elsewhere; this building is truly a *palazzo* (palace).

The next room, the large hall, features more sculpture from Hadrian's Villa (and elsewhere). Notice the *Wounded Amazon* (near the window) undoing her delicate dress. This is a Roman copy of a fifth-century B.C. Greek original by Polycletus. Watch the progress of restorers who have set up shop in this room.

Roll through two rooms lined with busts—the Hall of Philosophers (Socrates, Homer, Euripides, Cicero, and many more)

and the Hall of Emperors (Constantine's mom Helena sits center stage, resting after her journey to Jerusalem to find Christ's cross). In this 3-D yearbook of ancient history, there are few labels. The only purple bust is Caracalla. Infamous for his fervent brutality, he instructed his portraitists to stress his meanness. Directly across on the lower shelf, the smallest bust—of Emperor Gordiano (238–244 A.D.)—is one of the finest of late antiquity. His expression shows the concerns and consternation of a ruler whose empire is in decline. In this room you can find classic expressions of confidence, brutality, and anguish—human drama through the ages. Don't miss the delicate elegance of the first-century A.D. woman with the complex hairdo by the window.

• *Enter the hallway and start down the hall. The small octagonal room on your right contains one of the museum's treasures.*

Capitoline *Venus*

This is a Roman copy of a fourth-century B.C. Greek original by the master Praxiteles. Venus, leaving the bath, is suddenly aware that someone is watching her. As she turns to look, she reflexively covers up (nearly). Her blank eyes hold no personality or emotion. Her fancy hairstyle is the only complicated thing about her. She is simply beautiful—generically erotic.

• *After viewing the rooms on this end of the hallway, turn back toward where you entered and head to the last room on the left before the stairs. Displayed on the wall is the...*

Mosaic of Doves

Four doves perch on the rim of a bronze bowl as one drinks water from the bowl. Minute bits make up this small, exquisite work. Found in the center of a floor in one of the rooms in Hadrian's Villa, this second-century A.D. mosaic was based on an earlier work done, of course, by the Greeks.

We all know that ancient Rome was grand. But the art in this museum tells us that its culture was exquisite as well.

• *To exit, head down the stairs to the ground floor, and follow signs to the* uscita.

BORGHESE
GALLERY TOUR

Galleria e Museo Borghese

More than just a great museum, the Borghese Gallery is a beautiful villa set in the greenery of surrounding gardens. You get to see art commissioned by the luxury-loving Borghese family displayed in the very rooms for which it was created. Frescoes, marble, stucco, and interior design enhance the masterpieces. This is a place where—regardless of whether you learn a darn thing—you can sit back and enjoy the sheer beauty of the palace and its art.

ORIENTATION

Cost: €8.50, or €12.50 during special exhibits; both prices include €2 reservation fee (see "Reservations" below). Credit cards are accepted.

Hours: Tue–Sun 9:00–19:00, closed Mon.

Reservations: Reservations are mandatory and easy to get in English by booking online (www.ticketeria.it or www.pierreci.it) or calling 06-32810 (if you get an Italian recording, press 2 for English; office hours: Mon–Fri 9:00–18:00, Sat 9:00–13:00, office closed Sat in Aug and Sun year-round). Every two hours, 360 people are allowed to enter the museum. Entry times are 9:00, 11:00,  13:00, 15:00, and 17:00. Reserve a *minimum* of several days in advance for a weekday visit, at least a week ahead for weekends. Reservations are tightest at 11:00 and 15:00, on Tuesdays, and on weekends. On off-season weekdays (but not on weekends), you can generally get a same-day reservation if you're flexible about the entry time.

When you reserve, request a day and time, and you'll get a claim number; you'll be advised to come 30 minutes before your appointed time. The ticket office is located on the lower level. If you're paying with a credit card, you can skip the ticket pick-up line and head directly to the computer kiosks. Enter your reservation number, swipe your credit card, and *pronto*—your tickets are ready.

If you don't have a reservation, you can try arriving near the top of the hour, when they sell unclaimed tickets to those standing by. Generally, out of 360 reservations, a few will fail to show (but more than a few may be waiting to grab them). You're most likely to land a stand-by ticket at 13:00 or 17:00.

Getting There: The museum is set idyllically but inconveniently in the vast Villa Borghese Gardens. To avoid missing your appointment, allow yourself plenty of time to find the place. A taxi drops you 100 yards from the museum. Your destination is the Galleria Borghese (gah-leh-REE-ah bor-GAY-zay). Be sure *not* to tell the cabbie "Villa Borghese"—which is the park, not the museum.

The best public-transportation service is bus #910, which goes from the Termini train station to the Via Pinciana stop (a few steps from the villa). If you're coming from the Campo de' Fiori or from the TI on Via del Corso (at Via Minghetti), bus #116 drops you off inside the park.

By Metro, you have two options. From the Spagna Metro stop (or the Spanish Steps), it's a 15-minute walk: From inside the Metro station, the quickest route is to follow signs to Via Veneto (not Villa Borghese). You'll continue on an underground labyrinth of escalators and moving sidewalks. Once you hit the supermarket, take a right up the stairs of the exit marked *uscita Villa Borghese*. At the top, turn left and head straight ahead—you'll see signs to the Gallery.

From the Barberini Metro stop, walk up Via Veneto, enter the park, and turn right, following signs. From Largo Argentina, bus #63 drops you at the American Embassy on Via Veneto (where you can follow the directions from the Barberini Metro stop mentioned above).

Information: Tel. 06-32-810, www.galleriaborghese.it. For info on the park or Rome sights in general, visit the nearby park TI (April–Sept Mon–Thu 9:00–17:00, Fri–Sun 9:00–19:00; Oct–March daily 9:00–17:00; facing Borghese Gallery, turn left, walk 30 yards down, turn right toward the gate and find the poorly signed TI immediately on the left).

Tours: Excellent €7 guided English tours are offered at 10 minutes past each entry time except 17:00; Jan–March only at 9:10 and

11:10 (book tour when you make your museum reservation). Or consider the fine 90-minute audioguide tour for €5.

Length of This Tour: Two hours is all you get…and you'll want every minute.

Museum Strategy: Visits are strictly limited to two hours. Budget most of your time for the more interesting ground floor, but set aside 30 minutes for the paintings of the Pinacoteca upstairs (highlights are marked by the audioguide icons). Avoid the crowds by seeing the Pinacoteca first. The fine bookshop and cafeteria are best visited outside your two-hour entry window.

Checkroom: Baggage check is free, mandatory, and strictly enforced. Even small purses must be checked. The checkroom does not take coats.

Cuisine Art: A café is on-site. A picnic-friendly park with benches is just in front of the museum (you can check your picnic and feast after your visit).

Photography: No photos allowed; you must check your camera.

Starring: Sculptures by Bernini, Canova's *Venus,* and paintings by Caravaggio, Raphael, and Titian.

THE TOUR BEGINS

Exterior

As you visit this palace-in-a-garden, consider its purpose. Cardinal Scipione Borghese wanted to create a place just outside of the city where he could showcase his fine art while wining and dining the VIPs of his age. He had the villa built, collected ancient works, and hired the best artists of his day. In pursuing the optimistic spirit of the Renaissance, they invented Baroque.

The cardinal was controversial because he was not religious. But as nepotism was routine in the 17th century, just being a nephew of the pope was justification enough to be made a cardinal. And the power of a cardinal could be parlayed into great wealth, still on incredible display here in the gallery.

Main Entry Hall

The first room that guests would see upon entry is a "theater of the arts"—a multi-media and multi-era extravaganza of art treasures. Baroque frescoes on the ceiling, Greek statues along the walls, and ancient Roman mosaics on the floor capture the essence of the collection—a gathering of beautiful objects from every age and culture inside a lavish 17th-century villa.

Five second- and third-century mosaics from a private Roman villa adorn the floor with colorful, festive scenes of slaughter. Gladiators—as famous in their day as the sports heroes of our age— fight animals and each other with swords, whips, and tridents. The

Greek letter Θ marks the dead. Notice some of the gladiators' pro-wrestler nicknames: "Cupid(-o)," "Serpent(-ius)," "Licentious(-us)." On the far left a scene shows how "Alumnusvic" killed "Mazicinus" and left him lying upside down in a pool of blood.

High up on the wall is a thrilling first-century Greek sculpture of a horse falling. The Renaissance-era rider was added by Pietro Bernini, father of the famous Gian Lorenzo Bernini.

Room I

Antonio Canova—*Pauline Bonaparte as Venus* (*Paolina Borghese Bonaparte*, 1808)

Napoleon's sister went the full monty for the sculptor Canova, scandalizing Europe. ("How could you have done such a thing?!" she was asked.

She replied, "The room wasn't cold.") With the famous nose of her conqueror brother, she strikes the pose of Venus as conqueror of men's hearts. Her relaxed afterglow and slight smirk say she's already had her man. The light dent she puts in the mattress makes this goddess human.

Notice the contrasting textures that Canova (1757–1822) gets out of the pure white marble: the rumpled sheet versus her smooth skin. The satiny-smooth pillows and mattress versus the creases in them. Her porcelain skin versus the hint of a love handle. Canova polished and waxed the marble until it looked as soft and pliable as cloth.

The mythological pose, the Roman couch, the ancient hairdo, and the calm harmony make Pauline the epitome of the Neoclassical style.

Room II

Gian Lorenzo Bernini—*David* (1624)

Duck! David twists around to put a big rock in his sling. He purses his lips, knits his brow, and winds his body like a spring as his eyes lock onto the target—Goliath, who's somewhere behind us, putting us right in the line of fire.

In this self-portrait, 25-year-old Bernini (1598–1680) is ready to take on the world. He's charged with the same fighting energy that fueled the missionaries and conquistadors of the Counter-Reformation.

Compared with Michelangelo's *David*, this is unvarnished realism—an unbalanced pose, bulging veins, unflattering face, and armpit hair. Michelangelo's *David* thinks, whereas Bernini's acts—with pursed lips, eyes concentrating, and sling stretched. Bernini slays the pretty-boy *David*s of the Renaissance and prepares to invent Baroque.

Flanking David are two ancient sarcophagi carved with scenes from the *Labors of Hercules* (A.D. 160; find Hercules with his club). The twisting bodybuilders' poses were the Hellenistic inspiration for Bernini's Baroque. The painting behind them, by a follower of Caravaggio, shows a triumphant David with the giant's head.

Room III

Bernini—*Apollo and Daphne* (*Apollo e Dafne,* 1625)

Apollo—made stupid by Cupid's arrow of love—chases after Daphne, who has been turned off by the "arrow of disgust." Just as he's about

to catch her, she calls to her father to save her. Magically, her fingers begin to sprout leaves, her toes become roots, her skin turns to bark, and she transforms into a tree. Frustrated Apollo will end up with a handful of leaves.

Stand behind the statue to experience it as Bernini originally intended. It's only when you circle around to the front that he reveals the story's surprise ending.

Walk slowly around the statue. Apollo's back leg defies gravity. Bernini has chipped away more than half of the block of marble, leaving airy, open spaces. The statue was two years in restoration

(described to me as similar to dental work). The marble leaves at the top ring like crystal when struck. Notice the same scene, colorized, painted on the ceiling above.

Bernini carves out some of the chief features of Baroque art: He makes a supernatural event seem realistic. He freezes it at the most dramatic, emotional moment. The figures move and twist in unusual poses. He turns the wind machine on, sending Apollo's cape billowing behind him. It's a sculpture group of two, forming a scene, rather than a stand-alone portrait. And the subject is classical. Even in strict Counter-Reformation times, there was always a place for groping, if the subject matter had a moral—this one taught you not to pursue fleeting earthly pleasures. And, besides, Bernini tends to show a lot of skin, but no genitals.

The cardinal's private chapel (between Rooms III and IV) is the only purely religious room in the palace. It's relatively humble, a reminder that the cardinal probably didn't usually stop in here for much longer than tourists do today.

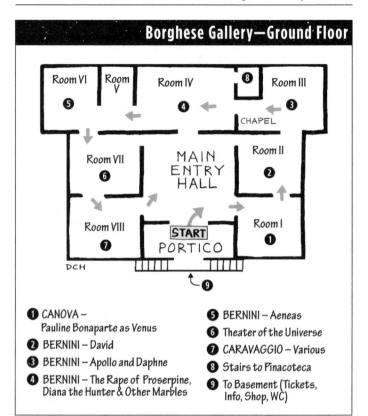

Borghese Gallery—Ground Floor

Room VI ⑤
Room V
Room IV ④
⑧
Room III ③
CHAPEL
Room VII ⑥
MAIN ENTRY HALL
Room II ②
Room VIII ⑦
START
PORTICO
Room I ①
DCH
⑨

① CANOVA – Pauline Bonaparte as Venus
② BERNINI – David
③ BERNINI – Apollo and Daphne
④ BERNINI – The Rape of Proserpine, Diana the Hunter & Other Marbles
⑤ BERNINI – Aeneas
⑥ Theater of the Universe
⑦ CARAVAGGIO – Various
⑧ Stairs to Pinacoteca
⑨ To Basement (Tickets, Info, Shop, WC)

Room IV

Bernini—*The Rape of Proserpine* (*Il Ratto di Proserpina,* 1622)

Pluto, King of the Underworld, strides into his realm and shows off his catch—the beautiful daughter of the earth goddess. His three-

headed guard dog, Cerberus (who guards the gates of Hell), barks triumphantly. Pluto is squat, thick, and uncouth, with knotted muscles and untrimmed beard. He's trying not to hurt her, but she pushes her divine molester away and twists to call out for help. Tears roll down her cheeks. She wishes she could turn into a tree.

Bernini was the master of marble. With this work, at the age of 24, he had discovered his Baroque niche. While Renaissance works were designed to be seen from the front, Baroque is theater-in-the-round—full of action, designed to be experienced as you walk around it. Look how Pluto's fingers dig into

Gian Lorenzo Bernini
(1598–1680)

A Renaissance man in Counter-Reformation times, Bernini almost personally invented the Baroque style, transforming the city of Rome. If you're visiting Rome, you will see Bernini's work, guaranteed.

Bernini was a child prodigy in his father's sculpting studio, growing up among Europe's rich and powerful. His flamboyant personality endeared him to his cultured employers—the popes in Rome, Louis XIV in France, and Charles I in England. He was extremely prolific, working fast and utilizing an army of assistants.

Despite the fleshiness and sensuality of his works, Bernini was a religious man, seeing his creativity as an extension of God's. In stark contrast to the Protestant world's sobriety, Bernini shamelessly embraced pagan myths and nude goddesses, declaring them all part of the "catholic"—that is, universal—Church.

Bernini, a master of multimedia, was a...

- Sculptor (Borghese Gallery and *St. Teresa in Ecstasy*—page 51)
- Architect (elements of St. Peter's—see "Bernini Blitz," page 249, and the Church of Sant'Andrea al Quirinale)
- Painter (Borghese Gallery)
- Interior decorator (the *baldacchino* canopy and other stuff in St. Peter's, page 249)
- Civic engineer (he laid out St. Peter's Square—page 239, and he designed and renovated Rome's fountains in Piazza Navona—page 81, Piazza Barberini, Piazza di Spagna, and more).

Even works done by other artists a century later (such as the Trevi Fountain) can be traced indirectly to Bernini, the man who invented Baroque, the "look" of Rome for the next two centuries.

her frantic body like it was real flesh. Bernini picked out this Carrara marble, knowing that its relative suppleness and ivory hue would lend itself to a fleshy statue.

• *In a niche over Pluto's right shoulder, find...*

Artist Unknown—*Diana the Hunter (Artemide)*

The goddess has been running through the forest. Now she's spotted her prey, and slows down, preparing to string her (missing) bow with an arrow. Or is she smoking a (missing) cigarette? Scholars debate it.

The statues in the niches are classical originals. *Diana the Hunter* is a rare Greek original, with every limb and finger intact, from the second century B.C. The traditional *contrapposto* pose (weight on one leg) and idealized grace were an inspiration for artists such as Canova, who grew tired of Bernini's Baroque bombast.

The Marbles in Room IV

The many ancient Roman statues and portrait busts of Roman emperors in this room were intended as a reminder that the pope was essentially a king, the successor to ancient Roman rulers of the past. (Up until around 1800, popes held vast political—and even military—power.)

Appreciate the beauty of the different types of marble in the room: Bernini's ivory Carrara, *Diana*'s translucent white, purple porphyry emperors, granite-like columns that support them, wood-grained pilasters on the walls, and the different colors on the floor—green, red, gray, lavender, and yellow, some grainy, some "marbled" like a steak. Some of the world's most beautiful and durable things have been made from the shells of sea creatures layered in sediment, fossilized into limestone, then baked and crystallized by the pressure of the earth—marble.

Room VI

Bernini—*Aeneas* (*Enea che fugge*, etc., 1620)

Aeneas' home in Troy is in flames, and he escapes with the three most important things: his family (decrepit father on his shoulder, baby boy), his household gods (the statues in dad's hands), and the Eternal Flame (carried by son). They're all in shock, lost in thought, facing an uncertain future. Aeneas isn't even looking where he's going; he just puts one foot in front of the other. Little do they know that eventually they'll wind up in Italy, where—according to legend—Aeneas will found the city of Rome and house the flame in the Temple of Vesta.

Bernini was just 20 when he started this, his first major work for Cardinal Borghese. He was probably helped by his dad, who nurtured the child prodigy much like Leopold mentored Mozart, but without the rivalry. Bernini's portrayal of human flesh—from baby fat to middle-aged muscle to sagging decrepitude—is astonishing. Still, the flat-footed statue just stands there—it lacks the Baroque energy of his more mature work. More lively are the reliefs up at the ceiling, with their dancing, light-footed soldiers with do-si-do shields.

Room VII

The "Theater of the Universe"

The room's decor sums up the eclectic nature of the villa. There are Greek statues and Roman mosaics. There are fake "Egyptian" sphinxes and hieroglyphs (perfectly symmetrical, in good Neoclassical style). Look out the window past the sculpted gardens at the mesh domes of the aviary, once filled with exotic birds. Cardinal Borghese's vision was to make a place where art, history, music, nature, and science from every place and time would come together..."a theater of the universe."

Room VIII

Caravaggio

This room holds the greatest collection of Caravaggio paintings anywhere. Michelangelo Merisi (1571–1610), nicknamed Caravaggio after his hometown (near Milan), brought Christian saints down to earth with gritty realism. In each of these paintings you see the Baroque innovator Caravaggio's unique style: His saints are balding and wrinkled. His Bacchus (a self-portrait) is pale and puffy-faced. David sticks Goliath's severed head (a self-portrait of the artist) right in your face. The Madonnas scarcely glow. The boy Jesus is buck naked. Ordinary people were his models. People emerge from a dark background, lit by a harsh, unflattering light, which highlights part of the figure, leaving the rest in deep shadows. Caravaggio's straightforwardness can be a refreshing change in a museum full of (sometimes overly) refined beauty.

The painting of *La Madonna dei Palafrenieri* was removed from St. Peter's for its lack of decorum. Jesus and Mary step on the snake of evil (i.e., Protestantism). The pope had no problem with that...but the face of Mary is the face of Rome's most famous prostitute of the day. Cardinal Borghese didn't care; he bought it and hung it here.

David with Head of Goliath was painted after Caravaggio killed a man and was forced to flee Rome. By portraying himself as Goliath, he symbolically gives his head to the pope as request for forgiveness. The pope accepted, but Caravaggio died of yellow fever on his way home.

• *To reach the Pinacoteca, head through the main entry hall back to Room IV, find the entry to the staircase in the far right corner, and spiral up to the...*

Pinacoteca (Painting Gallery)

You must visit the Pinacoteca within the two-hour window of time printed on your ticket for the Borghese Gallery. Most visitors wait until the last half-hour to see the Pinacoteca, so that's when it's most crowded (and the ground floor is less crowded). If you see the paintings first, remember that during a two-hour visit, the ground floor with the sculpture is worth most of that time.

• *Along the long wall of Room XIV, you'll find the following statues and paintings by Bernini. First, find the two identical white busts set on columns.*

Room XIV
Bernini—*Busts of Cardinal Borghese* (*Ritr. del Card. Scipione Borghese*, 1632)

Say *grazie* to the man who built this villa, assembled the collection, and hired Bernini to sculpt masterpieces. The cardinal is caught turning as though to greet someone at a party. There's a twinkle in his eye, and he opens his mouth to make a witty comment. This man of the cloth was, in fact, a sophisticated hedonist.

Notice that there are two identical versions of this bust. The first one started cracking along the forehead (visible) just as Bernini was finishing it. *No problema*—Bernini whipped out a replacement in just three days.

• *On the left wall above the middle table, find these paintings...*

Two Bernini Self-Portraits (*Autoritratto Giovanile,* 1623, and *Autoritratto in età Matura,* 1630–1635)

Bernini was a master of many media, including painting. The younger Bernini (age 25) looks out a bit hesitantly, as if he's still finding his way in high-class society. His jet-black eyes came from his Southern Italian mother who, it's said, also gave him his passionate personality.

In his next self-portrait (age 35), with a few masterpieces under his belt, Bernini shows himself with more confidence and facial hair—the dashing, flamboyant man who would rebuild Rome in Baroque style, from St. Peter's Square to the fountains that dot the piazzas.

• *On the table below, find the smaller...*

Bust of Pope Paul V

The cardinal's uncle was a more sober man, but he was also a patron of the arts with a good eye for talent who hired Bernini's father. When Pope Paul V saw sketches made by little Gian Lorenzo, he announced, "This boy will be the Michelangelo of his age."

• *To the right of the Borghese busts, find a small statue of...*

Two Babies Milking a Goat

Bernini was 11 years old when he did this. That's about the age when I mastered how to make a Play-Doh snake.

• *Room IX is back near the top of the staircase you ascended to get here.*

Room IX
Raphael (Raffaello Sanzio)—*Deposition* (*Deposizione di Cristo,* 1507)

Jesus is being taken from the cross. The men support him while the women support Mary (in purple), who has fainted. Mary Magdalene rushes up to take Christ's hand. The woman who commissioned the painting had recently lost her son. She wanted to show the death of a son and the grief of a mother. We see two different faces of grief—mother Mary faints at the horror, while Mary Magdalene still can't quite believe he's gone.

In true Renaissance style, Raphael (1483–1520) orders the scene with geometrical perfection. The curve of Jesus' body is echoed by the swirl of Mary Magdalene's hair, and then by the curve of Calvary Hill, where Christ met his fate.

Room X

Correggio—*Danaë* (c. 1531)

Cupid strips Danaë as she spreads her legs, most unladylike, to receive a trickle of gold from the smudgy cloud overhead—this was Zeus' idea

of intercourse with a human. The sheets are rumpled, and Danaë looks right where the action is with a smile on her face. It's hard to believe that a supposedly religious family would display such an erotic work. But the Borgheses felt that the Church was truly "catholic" (universal), and that all forms of human expression—including physical passion—glorified God.

• *Backtrack through the room of the two cardinal busts, then turn left and travel to the farthest room.*

Room XX

Titian (Tiziano Vecellio)—*Sacred and Profane Love* (*Amor Sacro e Amor Profano,* c. 1515)

While you might guess that the naked woman on the right represents profane love, that's actually represented by the material girl on the

left—with her box of treasures, fortified castle, and dark, claustrophobic landscape. Sacred love is represented by the naked woman who has nothing to hide

and enjoys open spaces filled with light, life, a church in the distance, and even a couple of lovers in the field.

The clothed woman at left has recently married, and she cradles a vase filled with jewels representing the riches of earthly love. Her naked twin on the right holds the burning flame of eternal, heavenly love. Baby Cupid, between them, playfully stirs the waters.

Symbolically, the steeple on the right points up to the love of heaven, while on the left, soldiers prepare to "storm the castle" of the new bride. Miss Heavenly Love looks jealous.

This exquisite painting expresses the spirit of the Renaissance—that earth and heaven are two sides of the same coin. And here in the Borghese Gallery, that love of earthly beauty can be spiritually uplifting—as long as you feel it within two hours.

VATICAN
MUSEUM TOUR

Musei Vaticani

The glories of the ancient world displayed in a lavish papal palace, decorated by the likes of Michelangelo and Raphael...the Musei Vaticani. Unfortunately, many tourists see the Vatican Museum only as an obstacle between them and its grand finale, the Sistine Chapel. True, this huge, confusing, and crowded megamuseum can be a jungle—but with this book as your vine, you should swing through with ease, enjoying the highlights and getting to the Sistine just before you collapse. On the way, you'll see some of the less-appreciated but equally important sections of this warehouse of Western civilization.

ORIENTATION

Cost: €14; except on the last Sun of each month (when it's free, packed, and open 8:30–14:00, last entry at 12:30).

Dress Code: Modest dress (no short shorts or bare shoulders) is required. While this dress code may not be strictly enforced here, it is at St. Peter's Basilica.

Hours: Mon–Sat 8:30–17:30, last entry at 16:00 (the official closing time is 18:00, but the staff starts ushering you out at 17:30). Hours are notoriously subject to constant change.

The museum is closed on many holidays (mainly religious ones) including, for 2009: Jan 1 (New Year's), Jan 6 (Epiphany), Feb 11 (Vatican City established), March 19 (St. Joseph), April 12 and 13 (Easter Sunday and Monday), May 1 (Labor Day), May 21 (Ascension Thursday), May 22 (Corpus Christi), June 29 (Saints Peter and Paul), Aug 15 plus either Aug 14 or 16—it varies year to year (Assumption of the Virgin), Nov 1 (All Saints' Day), Dec 8 (Immaculate Conception), and Dec 25 and 26 (Christmas). Other holidays and changes in opening hours may pop up—check the hours and calendar at www.vatican.va.

The Sistine Chapel closes before the museum. Individual rooms may close at odd hours, especially in the afternoon. TV screens inside the entrance list closures. The rooms described here are usually open.

Avoiding Lines: The best entry time is 12:30 or later, since tour groups tend to come to the museum early in the morning or right before lunchtime. Another good time to go is during the papal audience on Wednesday after 10:30, when many tourists are at St. Peter's Basilica.

The museum is generally hot and crowded, especially on Saturdays, the last Sunday of the month (when it's free), Mondays, rainy days, and any day before or after a holiday closure. There's little advantage to arriving early in the morning, as the place is already mobbed with early-bird tour groups when it opens—which keeps the whole line moving slowly.

Most mornings, particularly if you arrive before the opening time, the line to get in stretches around the block. (Stuck in the line? Figure about a 10-minute wait for every 100 yards. If the line stretches all the way to St. Peter's Square, count on waiting nearly two hours.) If you do arrive before the museum opens, be sure to line up against the Vatican City wall (to the left of the entrance as you face it); the other line (to the right of the entrance) is for guided tours. To skip the long line for individuals (and just wait in the sometimes shorter line for groups), consider taking a guided tour offered through a tour company—see "Tours," next page.

Getting There: The nearest Metro stop, Cipro, is a 10-minute walk from the entrance, including a climb up a big flight of stairs. The Ottaviano Metro stop is slightly farther away from the entrance, but if the museum line is long (as it often is), this may be a closer and more level walk than from Cipro. Bus #23 from Trastevere hugs the west bank of the Tiber and stops on Via Leone IV, just downhill from the entrance. The bus #64 stop is on the other side of St. Peter's Square. From St. Peter's Square, it's about a 15- to 20-minute walk (facing the church from the obelisk, take a right through the colonnade and follow the Vatican Wall). Taxis are reasonable (hop in and say, "moo-ZAY-ee vah-tee-KAH-nee").

Information: The info window, marked by an "i," is to the left next to the group-ticket windows. As you enter, you'll immediately see the electronic reader boards that tell you what rooms are open or closed. The baggage check upstairs takes only big bags; you'll need to carry your day bag with you. Note that you can't bring a pocket knife inside. You'll find a bookstore kiosk in the lobby, another up the stairs, and others scattered throughout the museum. Some exhibits have English explanations. Tel. 06-6988-3860 or 06-6988-1662. For information on tours, the museum, and hours, visit www.vatican.va. For more on Vatican City, see page 62. The post office, with stamps that make collectors drool, is upstairs.

Tours: Both **private tour companies** and **private guides** offer guided English tours of the museum, usually allowing you to skip the long ticket-buying line. If going with a tour, look for the tour entrance (to the right of the individuals entrance), which sometimes has a shorter line. For a listing of several companies, see page 31. These tours can be expensive—shop around for the best deal.

The Vatican offers English tours, but these are extremely difficult to join—they can book up as much as a year in advance (for details, see www.vatican.va). If you don't hear back—which you likely won't—it means they're full. If you do sign up, you'll enter through the group-tours entrance.

Audioguide Tours: If you rent a €6 **audioguide** (available at the top of the ramp/escalator), you lose the option of taking the shortcut from the Sistine Chapel to St. Peter's (audioguides must be returned at museum entrance). You can also download a free **audiotour** at www.ricksteves.com.

Length of This Tour: Until you expire, the museum closes, or 2.5 hours, whichever comes first.

Museum Strategies: There are two exits from the museum, and you'll want to decide which you'll take before you enter. The main exit is right near the entrance. Use this one if you plan on renting an audioguide (which you must return at the entrance) or if you plan on following this self-guided tour exactly as laid out, visiting the Pinacoteca at the end.

The other exit is a shortcut that leads from the Sistine Chapel directly to St. Peter's Basilica. This route saves you a 30-minute walk (15 minutes back to the Vatican Museum entry/exit, then 15 minutes to St. Peter's) and lets you avoid the often-long security line at the Basilica's main entrance. If you take this route, you'll have to do the following: adhere to St. Peter's stricter dress code (no shorts, miniskirts, or bare shoulders), forego an audioguide, skip the Pinacoteca (or tour it earlier), and be prepared for the odd chance that the shortcut is simply closed (which sometimes happens).

To see the Sistine Chapel with fewer crowds, visit at the end of the day (on days when the museum closes at 18:00, the closing bell rings at 16:30). Add to the experience by slipping directly into St. Peter's Basilica afterward for Mass.

Cuisine Art: A cafeteria is upstairs, above the entrance. Cheaper choices: The great Via Andrea Doria produce market is three blocks north of the entrance (head across the street, down the stairs, and continue straight), and inexpensive "Pizza Rustica" shops (which sell pizza to go) line Viale Giulio Cesare. Good restaurants are nearby (see page 311).

Photography: No photos are allowed in the Sistine Chapel. Elsewhere in the museum, photos without a flash are permitted.

Starring: World history, Michelangelo, Raphael, *Laocoön*, the Greek masters, and their Roman copyists.

THE TOUR BEGINS

Overview

With the Fall of Rome, the Catholic (or "universal") Church became the great preserver of civilization, collecting artifacts from cultures dead and dying. Renaissance popes (15th and 16th centuries) collected most of what we'll see, using it as furniture to decorate their palace (today's museum). Combining the classical and Christian worlds, they found the divine in the creations of man.

We'll concentrate on classical sculpture and Renaissance painting. But along the way (and there's a lot of along-the-way here), we'll stop to leaf through a few yellowed pages from this 5,000-year-old scrapbook of humankind.

This heavyweight museum is shaped like a barbell—two buildings connected by a long hall. The entrance building covers the ancient world (Egypt, Greece, Rome). The one at the far end covers its "rebirth" in the Renaissance (including the Sistine Chapel). The halls there and back are a mix of old and new. Move quickly—don't burn out before the Sistine Chapel at the end—and see how each civilization borrows from and builds on the previous one.

• *Leave Italy by entering the doors. Once you clear the security checkpoint, go upstairs (or take the elevator) to buy your ticket, punch it in the turnstiles, then take the long escalator or spiral stairs up, up, up.*

At the courtyard up top: To your right is the cafeteria and the Pinacoteca painting gallery (consider touring the Pinacoteca now—skip over to page 198—if you want the option of taking the Sistine-to-St.-Peter's shortcut at the end). To your left is the beginning of our tour. Go left, then take another left up a flight of stairs to reach the first-floor Egyptian Rooms (Museo Egizio) on your right. Don't stop until you find your mummy.

Note: Occasionally, the stairs up to Egypt are closed off, and crowds are routed through a spacious open-air courtyard, the Cortile della Pigna (see map on page 206). Just keep following the masses until you reach the Apollo Belvedere *and* Laocoön *(page 208). Tour the museum from there until the "Sarcophagi" (page 212), where you'll find the entrance to the Egyptian rooms.*

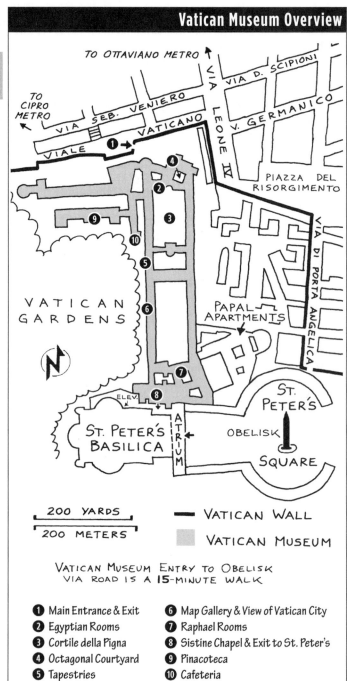

Vatican Museum Overview

TO OTTAVIANO METRO

VIA D. SCIPIONI

VIA LEONE IV

V. GERMANICO

TO CIPRO METRO

VIA SEB. VENIERO

VIALE VATICANO

PIAZZA DEL RISORGIMENTO

VIA DI PORTA ANGELICA

VATICAN GARDENS

PAPAL APARTMENTS

N

ELEV.

ST. PETER'S BASILICA

ATRIUM

ST. PETER'S

OBELISK

SQUARE

200 YARDS

200 METERS

━━━ VATICAN WALL

▨ VATICAN MUSEUM

VATICAN MUSEUM ENTRY TO OBELISK VIA ROAD IS A 15-MINUTE WALK

❶ Main Entrance & Exit
❷ Egyptian Rooms
❸ Cortile della Pigna
❹ Octagonal Courtyard
❺ Tapestries
❻ Map Gallery & View of Vatican City
❼ Raphael Rooms
❽ Sistine Chapel & Exit to St. Peter's
❾ Pinacoteca
❿ Cafeteria

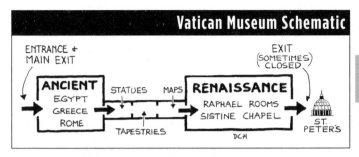

EGYPT (3000–1000 B.C.)

Egyptian art was for religion, not decoration. A statue or painting preserved the likeness of someone, giving him a form of eternal life. Most of the art was for tombs, where they put the mummies.

• *Pass beyond the imitation Egyptian pillars to the left of the case in the center of the room, and you'll find...*

Mummies

This woman died three millennia ago. Her corpse was disemboweled, and her organs were placed in a jar like those you see nearby. Then

the body was refilled with pitch, dried with natron (a natural sodium carbonate), wrapped in linen, and placed in a wood coffin, which went inside a stone coffin, which was placed in a tomb. (Remember that the pyramids were just big tombs.) Notice the henna job on her hair— in the next life, your spirit needed a body to be rooted to—and you wanted to look your best.

Painted inside the coffin lid is a list of what the deceased "packed" for the journey to eternity. The coffins were decorated with magical spells to protect the body from evil and to act as crib notes for the confused soul in the netherworld.

• *In the next room are...*

Egyptian Statues

Egyptian statues walk awkwardly, as if they're carrying heavy buckets, with arms straight down at their sides. Even these Roman reproductions (made for Hadrian's Villa) are stiff, two-dimensional, and schematic—the art is only realistic enough to get the job done. In Egyptian belief, a statue like this could be a stable refuge for the wandering soul of a dead man. Each was made according to an established set of proportions. Little changed over the centuries—these had a function, and they worked.

• *Walk through the next small room and into the curved hallway, and look for...*

Various Egyptian Gods as Animals

Before technology made humans top dogs on earth, it was easier to appreciate our fellow creatures. Egyptians saw the superiority of animals and worshipped them as incarnations of the gods. Wander through a pet store of Egyptian animal gods. Find Anubis, a jackal in a toga. The lioness portrays the fierce goddess Sekhmet. The clever baboon is the god of wisdom, Thot. At the end of the curved hall on your right is Bes (the small white marble statue), the patron of pregnant women (and beer-bellied men).

• *Continue left to Room VIII (the third room), pausing at the glass case, which contains brown clay tablets.*

Sumerian Writing

Even before Egypt, civilizations flourished in the Middle East. The Sumerian culture in Mesopotamia (the ancestors of the ancient Babylonians and of Saddam Hussein) invented writing in about 3000 B.C. People wrote on clay tablets by pressing into the wet clay with a wedge-shaped (cuneiform) pen. The Sumerians also rolled cylinder seals into soft clay to make an impression used to seal documents and mark property.

• *Pass through the next room, and then turn left, to a balcony with a view of Rome through the window. Then turn around and go into an octagonal courtyard.*

SCULPTURE—GREECE AND ROME (500 B.C.–A.D. 500)

This palace wouldn't be here, this sculpture wouldn't be here, and our lives would likely be quite different if it weren't for a few thousand Greeks in a small city about 450 years before Christ. Athens set the tone for the rest of the West. Democracy, theater, economics, literature, and art all flourished in Athens during a 50-year "Golden Age." Greek culture was then appropriated by Rome, and revived again 1,500 years later, during the Renaissance. The Renaissance popes built and decorated these papal palaces, re-creating the glory of the classical world.

Apollo Belvedere

Apollo, the god of the sun and of music, is hunting. He's been running through the woods, and now he spots his prey. Keeping his eye on the animal, he slows down and prepares to put a (missing) arrow into

The Ancient World

❶ Mummies
❷ Egyptian Statues
❸ Anubis
❹ Sumerian Writing
❺ Apollo Belvedere
❻ Laocoön
❼ Belvedere Torso
❽ Hercules
❾ Porphyry Basin
❿ Sarcophagi

his (missing) bow. The optimistic Greeks conceived of their gods in human form...and buck naked.

The Greek sculptor Leochares, following the style of the greater Greek sculptor Praxiteles, has fully captured the beauty of the human form. The anatomy is perfect, his pose is natural. Instead of standing at attention, face-forward with his arms at his sides (Egyptian-style), Apollo is on the move, coming to rest, with his weight on one leg.

The Greeks loved balance. A well-rounded man was both a thinker and an athlete, a poet and a warrior. In art, the *Apollo Belvedere* balances several opposites. He's moving, but not out of control. Apollo eyes his target, but hasn't attacked yet. He's realistic, but with idealized, godlike features. And the smoothness of his muscles is balanced by the rough folds of his cloak. The only sour note: his recently added left hand. Could we try a size smaller?

During the Renaissance, when this Roman copy of the original Greek work was discovered, it was considered the most perfect work of art in the world. The handsome face, eternal youth, and body that seems to float just above the pedestal made *Apollo Belvedere* seem superhuman, divine, and godlike, even for devout Christians.

• *In the neighboring niche to the right, a bearded old Roman river god lounges in the shade. This pose inspired Michelangelo's* Adam, *in the Sistine Chapel (coming soon). While there are a few fancy bathtubs in this courtyard, most of the carved boxes you see are sarcophagi—Roman coffins and relic holders, carved with the deceased's epitaph in picture form.*

Laocoön

Laocoön (lay-AWK-oh-wahn), the high priest of Troy, warned his fellow Trojans: "Beware of Greeks bearing gifts." The attacking

Greeks had brought the Trojan Horse to the gates as a ploy to get inside the city walls, and Laocoön tried to warn his people not to bring it inside. But the gods wanted the Greeks to win, so they sent huge snakes to crush him and his two sons to death. We see them at the height of their terror, when they realize that, no matter how hard they struggle, they—and their entire race—are doomed.

The figures (carved from four blocks of marble pieced together seamlessly) are powerful, not light and graceful. The poses are as twisted as possible, accentuating every rippling muscle and bulging vein. Follow the line of motion from *Laocoön's* left foot, up his leg, through his body, and out his right arm (which some historians used to think extended straight out—until the elbow was dug up early in the 1900s). Goethe would stand here and blink his eyes rapidly, watching the statue flicker to life.

Laocoön was sculpted four centuries after the Golden Age, after the scales of "balance" had been tipped. Whereas *Apollo* is a balance between stillness and motion, this is unbridled motion. *Apollo* is serene, graceful, and godlike, while *Laocoön* is powerful, emotional, and gritty.

Laocoön—the most famous Greek statue in ancient Rome and considered "superior to all other sculpture or painting"—was lost for more than a thousand years. Then, in 1506, it was unexpectedly unearthed in the ruins of Nero's Golden House near the Colosseum.

The discovery caused a sensation. They cleaned it off and paraded it through the streets before an awestruck populace. No one had ever seen anything like its motion and emotion, having been raised on a white-bread diet of pretty-boy *Apollo*s. One of those who saw it was the young Michelangelo, and it was a revelation to him. Two years later, he started work on the Sistine Chapel, and the Renaissance was about to take another turn.

• *Leave the courtyard to the right of* Laocoön *and swing around the Hall of Animals, a jungle of beasts real and surreal, to the limbless torso in the middle of the next large hall.*

Belvedere Torso

My experience with sculpting statues ends with snowmen. But standing face to face with this hunk of shaped rock makes you appreciate the sheer physical labor involved in chipping a figure out of solid stone. It takes great strength, but at the same time, great delicacy.

This is all that remains of an ancient statue of Hercules seated on a lion skin. Michelangelo loved this old rock. He knew that he was the best sculptor of his day. The ancients were his only peers—and his rivals. He'd caress this statue lovingly and tell people, "I am the pupil of the *Torso*." To him, it contained all the beauty of classical sculpture. But it's not beautiful. Compared with the pure grace of the *Apollo*, it's downright ugly.

But Michelangelo, an ugly man himself, was looking for a new kind of beauty—not the beauty of idealized gods, but the innate beauty of every person, even so-called ugly ones. With its knotty lumps of muscle, the *Torso* has a brute power and a distinct personality despite—or because of—its rough edges. Remember this *Torso*, because we'll see it again later on.

• *Enter the next, domed room.*

Round Room

This room, modeled on the Pantheon interior, gives some idea of Roman grandeur. Romans took Greek ideas and made them bigger, like the big bronze statue of Hercules with his club, found near the Theater of Pompey (by modern-day Campo de' Fiori). The mosaic floor once decorated the bottom of a pool in an ancient Roman bath. The enormous Roman basin/hot tub/birdbath/vase decorated Nero's place. It was made of a single block of purple porphyry stone imported from the desert of Egypt. Purple was a rare, royal, expensive, and prestigious color in pre-Crayola days. This was the stone of emperors...and then of popes. Now it's all been quarried out, and the only porphyry available to anyone has been recycled.

• *Enter the next room.*

Sarcophagi

These two large porphyry marble coffins were made (though not used) for the Roman emperor Constantine's mother (Helena, on left) and daughter (Constanza, on right). Helena's coffin depicts a battle game

showing dying victims in their barbarian dress. Constanza's is decorated with a mix of Christian and pagan themes. Helena and Constanza were Christians—and therefore outlaws—until Constantine made Christianity legal in A.D. 312, and they became

saints. Both sarcophagi were quarried and worked in Egypt. The technique for working this extremely hard stone (a special tempering of metal was required) was lost after this, and porphyry was not chiseled again until Renaissance times in Florence.

• *We've come full circle in this building—the Egyptian Rooms are to the left. Go upstairs and prepare for The Long March down the hall lined with statues, toward the Sistine Chapel and Raphael Rooms.*

THE LONG MARCH—SCULPTURE, TAPESTRIES, MAPS, AND VIEWS

This quarter-mile walk gives you a sense of the scale that Renaissance popes built on. Remember, this building was originally a series of papal palaces. The popes loved beautiful things—statues, urns, marble floors, friezes, stuccoed ceilings—and, as heirs of imperial Rome, they

felt they deserved such luxury. The palaces and art represent both the peak and the decline of the Catholic Church in Europe. It was extravagant spending like this that inspired Martin Luther to rebel, starting the Protestant Reformation.

Gallery of the Candelabra: Classical Sculpture

In the second "room" of the long hall, stop at the statue *Diana the Huntress* on the left. Here, the virgin goddess goes hunting. Roman hunters would pray and give offerings to statues like this to get divine help in their search for food.

Farmers might pray to another version of the same goddess, *Artemis,* on the opposite wall. This billion-breasted beauty stood for fertility. "Boobs or bulls' balls?" Some historians say that bulls were sacrificed and castrated, with the testicles draped over the statues as symbols of fertility.

• *Shuffle along to the next "room." On the left is* Bacchus, *with a baby on his shoulders.*

Fig Leaves

Why do the statues have fig leaves? Like *Bacchus,* many of these statues originally looked much different than they do now. First off, they were painted, often in gaudy colors. *Bacchus* may have had brown hair, rosy cheeks, purple grapes, and a leopard-skin sidekick at his feet. Even the *Apollo Belvedere,* whose cool gray tones we now admire as "classic Greek austerity," may have had a paisley pink cloak for all we know. Also, many statues had glass eyes like *Bacchus.*

And the fig leaves? Those came from the years 1550 to 1800, when

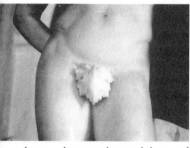

the Church decided that certain parts of the human anatomy were obscene. (Why not the feet?) Perhaps Church leaders associated these full-frontal statues with the outbreak of Renaissance humanism that reduced their power in Europe. Whatever the cause, they reacted by covering classical crotches with plaster fig leaves, the same leaves Adam and Eve had used when the concept of "privates" was invented.

Note: The leaves could be removed at any time if the museum officials were so motivated. There are suggestion boxes around the museum. Whenever I see a fig leaf, I get the urge to pick-it. We could start an organ-ized campaign...

• *Cover your eyes in case they forgot a fig leaf or two, and continue to the* tapestries.

Tapestries

Along the left wall are tapestries designed by Raphael's workshop and made in Brussels. They show scenes from the life of Christ: Baby Jesus in the manger, being adored by shepherds, and presented in the temple. The Resurrection tapestry, with Jesus coming out of the tomb, is curiously interactive...as you walk, Jesus' eyes, feet, knee, and even the stone square follow you across the room.

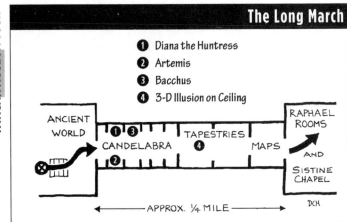

The Long March

❶ Diana the Huntress
❷ Artemis
❸ Bacchus
❹ 3-D Illusion on Ceiling

ANCIENT WORLD

RAPHAEL ROOMS

❶❸ CANDELABRA

TAPESTRIES ❹

MAPS AND

❷

SISTINE CHAPEL

← APPROX. ¼ MILE →

DCH

Check out the beautiful sculpted reliefs on the ceiling. Admire the workmanship of this relief, then realize that it's not a relief at all—it's painted on a flat surface! Illusions like this were proof that painters had mastered the 3-D realism of ancient statues.

Map Gallery and View of Vatican City

This gallery still feels like a pope's palace. The crusted ceiling of color-

ful stucco and paint is pure papal splendor. The 16th-century maps on the walls show the regions of Italy. Popes could take visitors on a tour of Italy, from the toe (entrance end) to the Alps (far end), with east Italy on the right wall, west on the left. The scenes in the ceiling portray exciting moments in Church history in each of those regions.

The windows give you your best look at the tiny country of Vatican City, formed in 1929. It has its own radio station, as you see from the tower on the hill. What you see here is pretty much all there is—these gardens, the palaces you're in, and St. Peter's.

If you have the chance to lean out and look left, you'll see the dome of St. Peter's the way Michelangelo would have liked you to see it—without the bulky Baroque facade.

At the far end, maps show Italy's four ports of entry (including Venice). Also look for maps

of Antique Italy (names in Latin, Roman political boundaries in gold) and New Italy.

• *Exit the map room, and take a breather in the next small tapestry hall before turning left into the crowded rooms that lead to the Raphael Rooms.*

These grand, painting-filled rooms are crowded for good reason. The art is well worth seeing—but tired visitors who want to make a beeline to the Sistine Chapel could go straight ahead (unless this route is roped off) to get to the Chapel instead of turning left into the Raphael Rooms.

RENAISSANCE ART

Raphael Rooms: Papal Wallpaper

We've seen art from the ancient world; now we'll see its rebirth in the Renaissance. We're entering the living quarters of the great Renaissance popes—where they slept, worked, and worshipped. The rooms reflect the grandeur of their position. They hired the best artists—mostly from Florence—to paint the walls and ceilings, combining classical and Christian motifs.

Entering, you'll immediately see a huge (non-Raphael) painting that depicts Sobieski liberating Vienna from the Ottomans in 1683, finally tipping the tide in favor of a Christian Europe. See the Muslim tents on the left and the spires of Christian Vienna on the right.

The second room's paintings celebrate the doctrine of the Immaculate Conception, establishing that Mary herself was conceived free from original sin. This medieval idea wasn't actually made dogma until a century ago. The largest fresco shows how the inspiration came straight from heaven (upper left) in a thin ray of light directly to the pope.

• *Next, you'll pass along an outside walkway that overlooks a courtyard (is that the pope's Fiat?), finally ending up in the first of the Raphael Rooms, the...*

Constantine Room

The frescoes (which after Raphael's death were finished by his assistants, notably Giulio Romano) celebrate the passing of the baton from one culture to the next. Remember, Rome was a pagan empire persecuting a new cult from the East—Christianity.

Then, on the night of October 27, A.D. 312 (left wall), as General Constantine (in gold, with crown) was preparing his troops for a coup d'état, he looked up and saw something strange. A cross appeared in the sky with the words, "You will conquer in this sign."

The next day (long wall), his troops raged victoriously into battle with the Christian cross atop their Roman eagle banners. There's Constantine in the center with a smile on his face, slashing through the enemy, while God's warrior angels ride shotgun overhead.

Constantine even stripped (right wall) and knelt before the pope to be baptized a Christian (some say). As emperor, he legalized Christianity and worked hand in hand with the pope (window wall). When Rome fell, its glory lived on through the Dark Ages in the pomp, pageantry, and learning of the Catholic Church.

Look at the ceiling painting. A classical statue is knocked backward, crumbling before the overpowering force of the cross. Whoa! Christianity triumphs over pagan Rome. (This was painted, I believe, by Raphael's surrealist colleague, Salvadorus Dalio.)

• *While viewing these frescoes, ponder the life and times of...*

Raphael

Raphael was only 25 when Pope Julius II invited him to paint the walls of his personal living quarters. Julius was so impressed by Raphael's talent that he had the work of earlier masters scraped off and gave Raphael free rein to paint what he wanted.

Raphael lived a charmed life. He was handsome and sophisticated, and soon became Julius' favorite. He painted masterpieces effortlessly. In a different decade, he might have been thrown out of the Church as a great sinner, but his love affairs and devil-may-care personality seemed to epitomize the optimistic pagan spirit of the Renaissance. His works are graceful but never lightweight or frilly—they're strong, balanced, and harmonious in the best Renaissance tradition. When he died young in 1520, the High Renaissance died with him.

• *Continue through the next room and bookshop. In the following room, block the sunlight with your hand to see...*

The Liberation of St. Peter

Peter, Jesus' right-hand man, was thrown into prison in Jerusalem for his beliefs. In the middle of the night, an angel appeared and rescued him from the sleeping guards (Acts 12). The chains miraculously fell away (and were later brought to the St. Peter-in-Chains

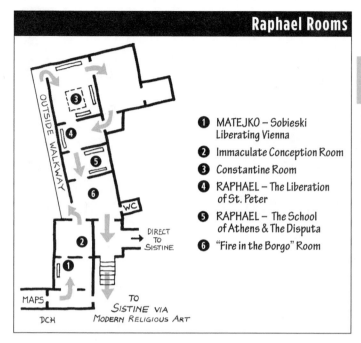

Raphael Rooms

❶ MATEJKO – Sobieski Liberating Vienna

❷ Immaculate Conception Room

❸ Constantine Room

❹ RAPHAEL – The Liberation of St. Peter

❺ RAPHAEL – The School of Athens & The Disputa

❻ "Fire in the Borgo" Room

Church in Rome), and the angel led him to safety (right), while the guards took hell from their captain (left). This little "play" is neatly divided into three separate acts that make a balanced composition.

Raphael makes the miraculous event even more dramatic with the use of four kinds of light illuminating the dark cell—half-moon-light, the captain's torch, the radiant angel, and the natural light spilling through the museum's window. Raphael's mastery of realism, rich colors, and sense of drama made him understandably famous.

Find Pope Julius II (who also commissioned Michelangelo to do the Sistine ceiling) in the role of Peter in *The Liberation,* and as the bearded and kneeling pope in *The Mass of Bolsena* (opposite wall).

• *Enter the next room. Here in the pope's private study, Raphael painted...*

The School of Athens

In both style and subject matter, this fresco sums up the spirit of the Renaissance, which was not only the rebirth of classical art, but a rebirth of learning, discovery, and the optimistic spirit that man is a rational creature. Raphael pays respect to the great thinkers and scientists of ancient Greece, gathering them together at one time in a mythical school setting.

In the center are Plato and Aristotle, the two greatest Greeks. Plato points up, indicating his philosophy that mathematics and pure ideas are the source of truth, while Aristotle points down, showing

his preference for hands-on study of the material world. There's their master, Socrates (midway to the left, in green), ticking off arguments on his fingers. And in the foreground at right, bald Euclid bends over a slate to demonstrate a geometrical formula.

Raphael shows that Renaissance thinkers were as good as the ancients. There's Leonardo da Vinci, whom Raphael worshipped, in

the role of Plato. Euclid is the architect Donato Bramante, who designed St. Peter's. Raphael himself (next to last on the far right, with the black beret) looks out at us. And the "school" building is actually an early version of St. Peter's Basilica (under construction at the time).

Raphael balances everything symmetrically—thinkers to the left, scientists to the right, with Plato and Aristotle dead center—showing the geometrical order found in the world. Look at the square floor tiles in the foreground. If you laid a

ruler over them and extended the line upward, it would run right to the center of the picture. Similarly, the tops of the columns all point down to the middle. All the lines of sight draw our attention to Plato and Aristotle, and to the small arch over their heads—a halo over these two secular saints in the divine pursuit of knowledge.

While Raphael was painting this room, Michelangelo was at

work down the hall in the Sistine Chapel. Raphael had just finished *The School of Athens* when he got a look at Michelangelo's powerful figures and dramatic scenes. He was astonished. From this point on, Raphael began to beef up his delicate, graceful style to a more heroic level. He returned to *The School of Athens* and added one more figure to the scene—Michelangelo, the brooding, melancholy figure in front, leaning on a block of marble.

• *On the opposite wall...*

The Disputa

As if to underline the new attitude that pre-Christian philosophy and Church thinking could coexist, Raphael painted *The Disputa* facing

The School of Athens. Christ and the saints in heaven are overseeing a discussion of the Eucharist (the communion wafer) by mortals below. The classical-looking character in blue and gold looks out as if to say, "The pagans had their *School of Athens*, but we Christians (pointing up) have the School of Heaven."

These rooms were the papal library, so themes featuring learning, knowledge, and debate were appropriate.

In Catholic terms, the communion wafer miraculously becomes the body of Christ when it's consecrated by a priest, bringing a little bit of heaven into the material world. Raphael's painting also connects heaven and earth, with descending circles: Jesus in a halo, down to the dove of the Holy Spirit in a circle, which enters the communion wafer in its holder. Balance and symmetry reign, from the angel trios in the upper corners to the books littering the floor. Find Dante wearing his poet's laureate in the lower right. (Hint: He's the guy on your €2 coin, modeled after this detail of *The Disputa*.)

Moving along, the last Raphael Room (called the "Fire in the Borgo" Room) shows work done mostly by Raphael's students, who were influenced by the bulging muscles and bodybuilder poses of Michelangelo.

• *Get ready. It's decision time. From here, there are two ways to get to the Sistine Chapel. Leaving the final Raphael Room, you'll soon see two arrows—one pointing to the far left to the Sistine (Cappella Sistina) and one pointing right to the Sistine. Left goes directly to the Sistine (depending on the volume of visitors, however, this direct route may be cut off).*

But bearing right (a five-minute walk and a few staircases longer) leads to quiet rooms at the foot of the stairs, with benches where you can sit in peace and read ahead before entering the hectic Sistine Chapel. Also, you get to stroll through the impressive Modern Religious Art collection on the way (signs will direct you to the Sistine). Your call.

THE SISTINE CHAPEL

The Sistine Chapel contains Michelangelo's ceiling and his huge *The Last Judgment*. The Sistine is the personal chapel of the pope and the place where new popes are elected. When Pope Julius II asked Michelangelo to take on this important project, he said, "No, *grazie.*"

Michelangelo insisted he was a sculptor, not a painter. The Sistine ceiling was a vast undertaking, and he didn't want to do a half-vast job. But the pope pleaded, bribed, and threatened until Michelangelo finally consented, on the condition that he be able to do it all his own way.

Julius had asked for only 12 apostles along the sides of the ceiling, but Michelangelo had a grander vision—the entire history of the world until Jesus. He spent the next four years (1508–1512) craning his neck on scaffolding six stories up, covering the ceiling with frescoes of biblical scenes.

In sheer physical terms, it's an astonishing achievement: 5,900 square feet, with the vast majority done by his own hand. (Raphael only designed most of his rooms, letting assistants do the grunt work.)

First, he had to design and erect the scaffolding. Any materials had to be hauled up on pulleys. Then, a section of ceiling would be plastered. With fresco—painting on wet plaster—if you don't get it right the first time, you have to scrape the whole thing off and start over. And if you've ever struggled with a ceiling light fixture or worked underneath a car for even five minutes, you know how heavy your arms get. The physical effort, the paint dripping in his eyes, the creative drain, and the mental stress from a pushy pope combined to almost kill Michelangelo.

But when the ceiling was finished and revealed to the public, it simply blew 'em away. Like the *Laocoön* statue discovered six years earlier, it was unlike anything seen before. It both caps the Renaissance and turns it in a new direction. In perfect Renaissance spirit, it mixes Old Testament prophets with classical figures. But the style is more dramatic, shocking, and emotional than the balanced Renaissance works before it. This is a very personal work—the Gospel according to Michelangelo—but its themes and subject matter are universal. Many

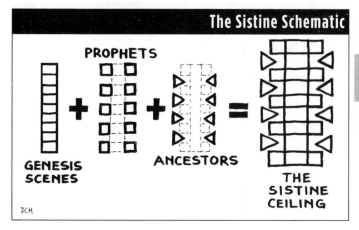

The Sistine Schematic

PROPHETS

ANCESTORS

GENESIS SCENES

THE SISTINE CEILING

DCH

art scholars contend that the Sistine ceiling is the single greatest work of art by any one human being.

The Sistine Ceiling: Understanding What You're Standing Under

The ceiling shows the history of the world before the birth of Jesus. We see God creating the world, creating man and woman, destroying the earth by flood, and so on. God himself, in his purple robe, actually appears in the first five scenes. Along the sides (where the ceiling starts to curve), we see the Old Testament prophets and pagan Greek prophetesses who foretold the coming of Christ. Dividing these scenes and figures are fake niches (a painted 3-D illusion) decorated with nude, statuelike figures with symbolic meaning.

The key is to see three simple divisions in the tangle of bodies:
1. The central spine of nine rectangular biblical scenes;
2. The line of prophets on either side; and
3. The triangles between the prophets showing the ancestors of Christ.

• *Ready? Within the chapel, grab a seat along the side (if there's room). Face the altar with the big* The Last Judgment *on the wall (more on that later). Now look up to the ceiling and find the central panel of...*

The Creation of Adam

God and man take center stage in this Renaissance version of creation. Adam, newly formed in the image of God, lounges dreamily in perfect naked innocence. God, with his entourage, swoops in with a swirl of activity (which—with a little imagination—looks like a cross-section of a human brain...quite a strong humanist statement). Their reaching hands are the center of this work. Adam's is limp and passive; God's is strong and forceful, his finger twitching upward with energy. Here is the very moment of creation, as God passes the spark of life to man,

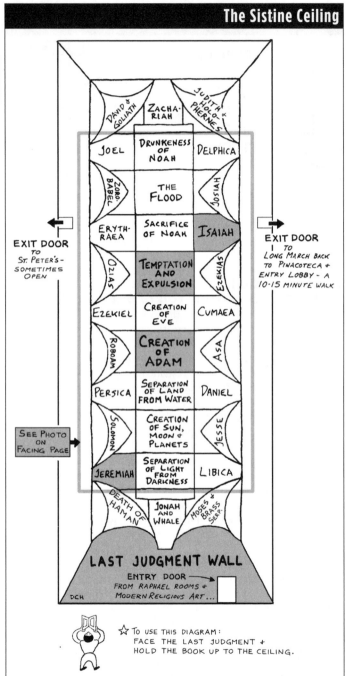

The Sistine Ceiling

the crowning work of his creation.

This is the spirit of the Renaissance. God is not a terrifying giant reaching down to puny and helpless man from way on high. Here

they are on an equal plane, divided only by the diagonal patch of sky. God's billowing robe and the patch of green upon which Adam is lying balance each other. They are like two pieces of a jigsaw puzzle, or two long-separated continents, or like the yin and yang symbols finally coming together—uniting, complementing each other, creating wholeness. God and man work together in the divine process of creation.

• *This celebration of man permeates the ceiling. Notice the Adonises-come-to-life on the pedestals that divide the central panels. And then came woman.*

The Garden of Eden: Temptation and Expulsion

In one panel, we see two scenes from the Garden of Eden. On the left is the leafy garden of paradise where Adam and Eve lie around blissfully. But the devil comes along—a serpent with a woman's torso—and winds around the forbidden Tree of Knowledge. The temptation to gain new knowledge is too great for these Renaissance people. They eat the forbidden fruit.

At right, the sword-wielding angel drives them from Paradise into the barren plains. They're grieving, but they're far from helpless. Adam's body is thick and sturdy, and we know they'll survive in the cruel world. Adam firmly gestures to the angel, like he's saying, "All right, already! We're going!"

The Nine Scenes from Genesis

Take some time with these central scenes to understand the story that the ceiling tells. They run in sequence, starting at the front:

1. God, in purple, divides the light from darkness.
2. God creates the sun (burning orange) and the moon (pale white, to the right). Oops, I guess there's another moon.
3. God bursts toward us to separate the land and water.
4. *The Creation of Adam.*
5. God creates Eve, who dives into existence out of Adam's side.

6. *The Garden of Eden: Temptation and Expulsion.*
7. Noah kills a ram and stokes the altar fires to make a sacrifice to God.
8. The great Flood, sent by God, destroys the wicked, who desperately head for higher ground. In the distance, the Ark carries Noah's family to safety. (The blank spot dates to 1793, when a nearby gunpowder depot exploded, shaking the building.)
9. Noah's sons see their drunken father. (Perhaps Michelangelo chose to end it with this scene as a reminder that even the best of men are fallible.)

Prophets

You'll notice that the figures at the far end of the chapel are a bit smaller than those over *The Last Judgment.*

Michelangelo started at the far end, with the Noah scenes. By 1510, he'd finished the first half of the ceiling. When they took the scaffolding down and could finally see what he'd been working on for two years, everyone was awestruck—except Michelangelo. As powerful as his figures are, from the floor they didn't look dramatic enough for Michelangelo. For the other half, he pulled out all the stops.

Compare the Noah scenes (far end) with their many small figures to the huge images of God at the other end. Similarly, Isaiah (near the lattice screen, marked "Esaias") is stately and balanced, while Jeremiah ("Hieremias," in the corner by *The Last Judgment*) is a dark, brooding figure. This prophet who witnessed the destruction of Israel slumps his chin in his hand and ponders the fate of his people. Like the difference between the stately *Apollo Belvedere* and the excited *Laocoön,* Michelangelo added a new emotional dimension to Renaissance painting.

The Last Judgment

When Michelangelo returned to paint the altar wall 23 years later (1535), the mood of Europe—and of Michelangelo—was completely different. The Protestant Reformation had forced the Catholic Church to clamp down on free thought, and religious wars raged. Rome had recently been pillaged by roving bands of mercenaries. The Renaissance spirit of optimism was fading. Michelangelo himself had begun to question the innate goodness of mankind.

It's Judgment Day, and Christ—the powerful figure in the center, raising his arm to spank the wicked—has come to find out who's naughty and who's nice.

The Last Judgment

HEAVEN

THE **GOOD,**

THE **BAD,**

& THE **UGLY**

HELL

DCH

ENTRY DOOR TO SISTINE →

❶ Christ with Mary
❷ Trumpeting Angels
❸ Righteous Dead Ascending
❹ Damned Man
❺ Charon the Ferryman
❻ Demon/Critic Wrapped in Snakes
❼ St. Bartholomew Holding Flayed Skin (Michelangelo's Face)

Beneath him, a band of angels blows its trumpets Dizzy Gillespie–style, giving a wake-up call to the sleeping dead. The dead at lower left leave their graves and prepare to be judged. The righteous, on Christ's right hand (the left side of the picture), are carried up to the glories of heaven. The wicked on the other side are hurled down to hell, where demons wait to torture them. Charon, from the underworld of Greek mythology, waits below to ferry the souls of the damned to hell.

It's a grim picture. No one, but no one, is smiling. Even many

of the righteous being resurrected (lower left) are either skeletons or cadavers with ghastly skin. The angels have to play tug-of-war with subterranean monsters to drag them from their graves.

Over in hell, the wicked are tortured by gleeful demons. One of the damned (to the right of the trumpeting angels) has an utterly lost expression, as if saying, "Why did I cheat on my wife?!" Two demons grab him around the ankles to pull him down to the bowels of hell, condemned to an eternity of constipation.

But it's the terrifying figure of Christ that dominates this scene. He raises his arm to smite the wicked, sending a ripple of fear through everyone. Even the saints around him—even Mary beneath his arm (whose interceding days are clearly over)—shrink back in terror at loving Jesus' uncharacteristic outburst. His expression is completely closed, and he turns his head, refusing to even listen to the whining alibis of the damned. Look at Christ's bicep. If this muscular figure looks familiar to you, it's because you've seen it before—the *Belvedere Torso*.

When *The Last Judgment* was unveiled to the public in 1541, it caused a sensation. The pope is said to have dropped to his knees and

The Cleaning Project

The ceiling and *The Last Judgment* have been cleaned, removing centuries of preservatives, dirt, and soot from candles, oil lamps, and the annual Papal Barbecue (just kidding). The bright, bright colors that emerged are a bit shocking, forcing many art experts to reevaluate Michelangelo's style. Notice the very dark patches left in the corner above *The Last Judgment,* and imagine how dreary and dark it was before the cleaning.

cried, "Lord, charge me not with my sins when thou shalt come on the Day of Judgment."

And it changed the course of art. The complex composition, with more than 300 figures swirling around the figure of Christ, was far beyond traditional Renaissance balance. The twisted figures shown from every imaginable angle challenged other painters to try and top this master of 3-D illusion. And the sheer terror and drama of the scene was a striking contrast to the placid optimism of, say, Raphael's *School of Athens.* Michelangelo had Baroque-en all the rules of the Renaissance, signaling a new era of art.

With the Renaissance fading, the fleshy figures in *The Last Judgment* aroused murmurs of discontent from Church authorities. Michelangelo rebelled by painting his chief critic into the scene—in hell. He's the jackassed demon in the bottom right corner, wrapped in a snake. Look at how Michelangelo covered his privates. Sweet revenge.

(After Michelangelo's death, prudish Church authorities painted the wisps of clothing that we see today.)

Now move up close. Study the details of the lower part of the painting from right to left. Charon, with Dr. Spock ears and a Dalí moustache, paddles the damned in a boat full of human turbulence. Look more closely at the J-Day band. Are they reading music, or is it the Judgment Day tally? Before the cleaning, these details were lost in murk.

The Last Judgment marks the end of Renaissance optimism epitomized in *The Creation of Adam,* with its innocence and exaltation of man. There, he was the wakening man-child of a fatherly God. Here, man cowers in fear and unworthiness before a terrifying, wrathful deity.

Michelangelo himself must have wondered how he would be judged—had he used his God-given talents wisely? Look at St.

Bartholomew, the bald, bearded guy at Christ's left foot (our right). In the flayed skin he's holding is a barely recognizable face—the twisted self-portrait of a self-questioning Michelangelo.

• *There are two exits from the Sistine Chapel. To return to the main entrance/exit, leave the Sistine through the side door next to the screen. You'll soon find yourself facing The Long March back to the museum's entrance (about 15 minutes away) and the Pinacoteca. You're one floor below the long corridor that you walked to get here.*

Or, if you're planning to take the shortcut directly to St. Peter's Basilica (see "Museum Strategies," page 204), exit out the far-right corner of the Sistine Chapel (with your back to the altar). (When the cardinals use this room to elect a new pope, this is where they put the small old-fashioned stove for ballot burning. White smoke signals that a pope has been chosen.) This route saves you a 30-minute walk and the wait in the St. Peter's security line, but you can't get back to the Pinacoteca. Though this corner door is likely labeled "Exit for private tour groups only," you can usually just slide through with the crowds (or protest that your group has left you behind). This door can be closed when big shots are moving within the Vatican. If it's closed, hang out in the Sistine Chapel for a few more minutes—it'll likely reopen shortly.

The Long March Back

Along this corridor, you'll see some of the wealth amassed by the popes, mostly gifts from royalty. Find your hometown on the 1529 map of the world—look in the land labeled "Terra Incognita." The elaborately decorated library that branches off to the right contains rare manuscripts.

• *The corridor eventually spills out back outside. Follow signs to the...*

PINACOTECA

Like Lou Gehrig batting behind Babe Ruth, the Pinacoteca (Painting Gallery) has to follow the mighty Sistine & Co. But after the Vatican's artistic feast, this little collection of paintings is a delicious, 15-minute after-dinner mint.

See this gallery of paintings as you'd view a time-lapse blossoming of a flower, walking through the evolution of painting from medieval to Baroque with just a few stops.

• *Enter, passing a model of Michelangelo's* Pietà *(offering a handy close-up look), and stroll up to Room IV.*

Melozzo da Forli—*Musician Angels*

Salvaged from a condemned church, this playful series of frescoes shows the delicate

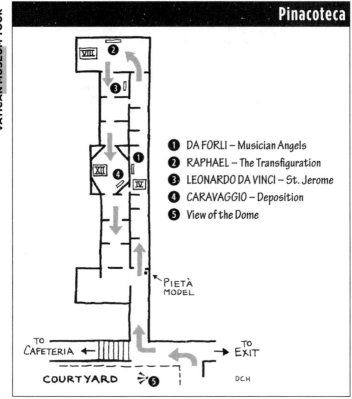

Pinacoteca

❶ DA FORLI – Musician Angels
❷ RAPHAEL – The Transfiguration
❸ LEONARDO DA VINCI – St. Jerome
❹ CARAVAGGIO – Deposition
❺ View of the Dome

PIETÀ MODEL

TO CAFETERIA ←

TO EXIT →

COURTYARD ❺

DCH

grace and nobility of Italy during the time known fondly as the Quattrocento (1400s). Notice the detail in the serene faces; the soothing primary colors; the bright and even light; and the classical purity given these religious figures. Rock on.

• *Walk on to the end room (Room VIII), where precious Raphael-designed tapestries that once hung in the Sistine Chapel now surround the highlight of this collection. They've turned on the dark to let Raphael's* Transfiguration *shine. Take a seat.*

Raphael—*The Transfiguration*

Christ floats above a stumpy mountaintop, visited in a vision by the prophets Moses and Elijah. Peter, James, and John, who wanted visual proof that Jesus was Lord, cower in awe under their savior, "transfigured before them, his face shining as the sun, his raiment white as light" (as described by the evangelist Matthew—who can be seen taking notes in the painting's lower left).

Raphael composes the scene in three descending tiers: Christ, the

holiest, is on top, then Peter-James-John, and finally, the nine remaining apostles surround a boy possessed by demons. They direct him and his mother to Jesus for healing.

Raphael died in 1520, leaving this final work to be finished by his pupils. The last thing Raphael painted was the beatific face of Jesus, perhaps the most beautiful Christ in existence. When Raphael was buried (in the Pantheon, at age 37), this work accompanied the funeral.

• *Heading back down the parallel corridor, stop in Room IX at the brown, unfinished work by Leonardo.*

Leonardo da Vinci—*St. Jerome* (c. 1482)

Jerome squats in the rocky desert. He's spent too much time alone, fasting and meditating on his sins. His soulful face is echoed by his friend, the roaring lion.

This unfinished work gives us a glimpse behind the scenes at Leonardo's technique. Even in the brown undercoating, we see the psychological power of Leonardo's genius. Jerome's emaciated body on the rocks expresses his intense penitence, while his pleading eyes hold a glimmer of hope for divine forgiveness. Leonardo wrote that a good painter must paint two things: "man and the movements of his spirit." (The patchwork effect is due to Jerome's head having been cut out and used as the seat of a stool in a shoemaker's shop.)

• *Roll on through the sappy sweetness of the Mannerist rooms into the gritty realism of Caravaggio (Room XII).*

Caravaggio—*Deposition* (1604)

Christ is being buried. In the dark tomb, the faces of his followers emerge, lit by a harsh light. Christ's body has a deathlike color. We see Christ's dirty toes and Nicodemus' wrinkled, sunburned face.

Caravaggio was the first painter to intentionally shock his viewers. By exaggerating the contrast between light and dark, shining a brutal third-degree-interrogation light on his subjects, and using everyday models in sacred scenes, he takes a huge leap away from the Raphael-pretty past and into the "expressive realism" of the modern world.

A tangle of grief looms out of the darkness as Christ's heavy, dead body nearly pulls the whole group with him from the cross into the tomb. After this museum, I know how he feels.

• *Walk through the rest of the gallery's canvas history of art, enjoy one last view of the Vatican grounds and Michelangelo's dome, then follow the grand spiral staircase down. Go in peace.*

ST. PETER'S BASILICA TOUR

Basilica San Pietro

St. Peter's is the greatest church in Christendom. It represents the power and splendor of Rome's 2,000-year domination of the Western world. Built on the memory and grave of the first pope, St. Peter, this is where the grandeur of ancient Rome became the grandeur of Christianity.

ORIENTATION

Cost: Free (€7 for elevator to roof, plus €5 to climb 323 steps to the top of the dome).

Dress Code: No shorts or bare shoulders (applies to men, women, and children), and no miniskirts. This dress code is strictly enforced.

Hours of Church: Daily April–Sept 7:00–19:00, Oct–March 7:00–18:00. The church closes on Wednesday mornings during papal audiences. The best time to visit the church is early or late; I like to be here at 17:00, when the church is fairly empty, sunbeams can work their magic, and the late-afternoon Mass fills the place with spiritual music.

Mass is held daily (Mon–Sat at 8:30, 10:00, 11:00, 12:00, and 17:00; Sun and holidays at 9:00, 10:30—in Latin, 11:30, 12:10, 13:00, 16:00, and 17:00, confirm schedule locally, www.saintpetersbasilica.org).

You can go downstairs into the **Crypt** underneath the church (follow *Tombe* signs), featuring part of the foundations of the old St. Peter's, as well as the tombs of St. Peter and John Paul II (entrance point varies; the line usually starts outside near the front steps, to the left as you exit). For specifics, see the end of this chapter.

Vatican City

This tiny independent country of little more than 100 acres, contained entirely within Rome, has its own postal system, armed guards, helipad, mini-train station, and radio station (KPOP). Politically powerful, the Vatican is the religious capital of 1.1 billion Roman Catholics. If you're not a Catholic, become one for your visit.

The pope is both the religious and secular leader of Vatican City. For centuries, locals referred to him as "King Pope." Italy and the Vatican didn't always have good relations. In fact, after unification (in 1870), when Rome's modern grid plan was built around the miniscule Vatican, it seemed as if the new buildings were designed to be just high enough so no one could see the dome of St. Peter's from street level. Modern Italy was created in 1870, but the Holy See didn't recognize it as a country until 1929, when the pope and Mussolini signed the Lateran Pact, giving sovereignty to the Vatican and a few nearby churches.

Like every European country, Vatican City has its own versions of the euro coin (with a portrait of Pope Benedict XVI, and before him, of Pope John Paul II). You're unlikely to find one in your pocket, though, as they are snatched up by collectors before falling into actual circulation.

Small as it is, Vatican City has two huge sights: St. Peter's Basilica (with Michelangelo's *Pietà*) and the Vatican Museum (with the Sistine Chapel). The Vatican **post office,** with offices on St. Peter's Square (next to TI) and in the Vatican Museum, is famous for its stamps (Mon–Sat 8:30–18:30, closed Sun). Vatican stamps are good throughout Rome, but to use the Vatican's mail service, you need to mail your cards from the Vatican; write your postcards ahead of time. (Note that the Vatican won't mail cards with Italian stamps.)

Seeing the Pope: Your best chances for a sighting are on Sunday and Wednesday. The pope usually gives a blessing at noon on Sunday from his apartment on St. Peter's Square (except in July and August, when he speaks at his summer residence at Castel Gandolfo, 25 miles from Rome, reachable by train from Rome's Termini station). St. Peter's is easiest (just show up) and, for most, enough of a "visit." Those interested in a more formal appearance (but not more intimate) can get a ticket for the Wednesday general audience (at 10:30) when the pope, arriving in his bulletproof Popemobile, greets and blesses the crowds at St. Peter's from a balcony or canopied platform on the square (except in winter, when he speaks at 10:30 in the 7,000-seat Aula Paolo VI Auditorium, next to St. Peter's Basilica). If you only want to see St. Peter's—but not the pope—minimize crowd problems by avoiding these times.

For the Wednesday general audience, while anyone can observe from a distance, you need a ticket to actually get close to the papal action. To find out the pope's schedule, call 06-

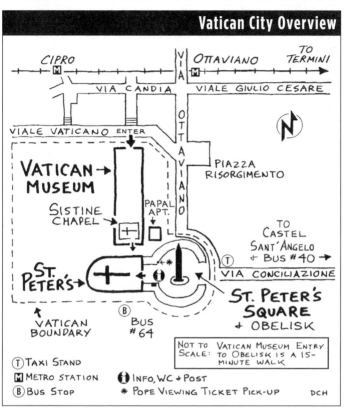

Vatican City Overview

CIPRO — Ⓜ — TO TERMINI
OTTAVIANO — Ⓜ

VIA CANDIA
VIALE GIULIO CESARE

VIA OTTAVIANO

VIALE VATICANO ENTER

VATICAN → MUSEUM

PIAZZA RISORGIMENTO

SISTINE CHAPEL →

PAPAL APT.

TO CASTEL SANT'ANGELO + BUS #40 →

ⓉVIA CONCILIAZIONE

ST. PETER'S →

ST. PETER'S SQUARE
+ OBELISK

↑ VATICAN BOUNDARY

Ⓑ BUS #64

NOT TO SCALE: VATICAN MUSEUM ENTRY TO OBELISK IS A 15-MINUTE WALK

ⓉTAXI STAND
ⓂMETRO STATION
ⒷBUS STOP

🛈 INFO, WC + POST
✳ POPE VIEWING TICKET PICK-UP

DCH

6988-4631. Tickets are free and easy to get, but must be picked up on Tuesday for the Wednesday service. You can get tickets from Santa Susanna Church or the papal guard (at the Vatican).

Santa Susanna Church hands out tickets Tuesdays between 17:00 and 18:45 (Via XX Settembre 15, near recommended Via Firenze hotels, Metro: Repubblica, tel. 06-4201-4554, www.santa susanna.org). While they have lots of tickets, the sure way to have a ticket held for you is to email your request to tickets @santasusanna.org. Their hours are timed in the hopes that you'll stay for the English Mass at 18:00.

Probably less convenient—because of the long line—is picking up a ticket at St. Peter's Square from the Vatican guard at their station at the bronze doors (under the "elbow" of Bernini's colonnade, on the right side of the square as you face the basilica) Tuesdays 12:00–19:30; just join the line.

While many visitors come hoping for a more intimate audience, private audiences ended with the death of Pope John Paul II. Pope Benedict doesn't do them.

Hours of Dome: Daily April–Sept 8:00–17:45, Oct–March 8:00–16:45. Allow one hour for the full trip up and down, or a half hour to go only to the roof. Even after the elevator, it's a 323-step climb all the way to the top. The entry to the elevator is just outside the basilica on the north side of St. Peter's (near the secret Sistine exit—described on page 204). Look for signs to the cupola. For more on the dome, see the end of the chapter.

Getting There: Take the Metro to Ottaviano, then walk 10 minutes south on Via Ottaviano. Two city buses stop near St. Peter's Square. The #40 express bus drops off at Piazza Pio, next to Castel Sant'Angelo. The more crowded bus #64 is convenient for pickpockets and stops just outside St. Peter's Square to the south (after crossing the Tiber, take the first stop past the tunnel; backtrack toward the tunnel and turn left when you see the rows of columns). Taxis are reasonable (Termini train station to St. Peter's is about €12).

Avoiding the Line: To bypass the long security-checkpoint line, visit the Vatican Museum first (though it has its own long lines and checkpoint), then take the shortcut from the Sistine Chapel directly to St. Peter's. (Note, though, that this shortcut isn't always open—see page 204.) If you visit the museum first, remember that St. Peter's dress code is stricter than the Vatican Museum's.

Information: The TI on the left (south) side of the square is excellent (Mon–Sat 8:30–18:30, closed Sun, free Vatican and church map, tel. 06-6988-1662). WCs are to the right and left (near TI) of the church, near baggage storage past the security checkpoint, and on the roof. Drinking fountains are at the obelisk and near WCs. The post office is next to the TI.

Tours: The Vatican TI conducts free 90-minute tours of St. Peter's (depart Mon–Fri from TI, confirm schedule at TI, tel. 06-6988-1662). Audioguides can be rented near the checkroom (€5, daily 9:00–17:00). You can download a free audiotour at www.ricksteves.com (see page 382).

Tours are the only way to see the Vatican Gardens. Book at least two weeks in advance by faxing 06-6988-5100 or emailing visiteguidate.musei@scv.va; no response means they're booked up (€18; Tue, Thu, and Sat; verify times when you reserve; tours start at Vatican Museum tour desk and finish on St. Peter's Square).

Length of This Tour: Allow one hour, plus another hour if you climb the dome (elevator plus 323 steps one-way).

Checkroom: The free, usually mandatory bag check is outside the basilica (to the right as you face the entrance), and just inside the security checkpoint.

Starring: Michelangelo, Bernini, St. Peter, a heavenly host...and, occasionally, the pope.

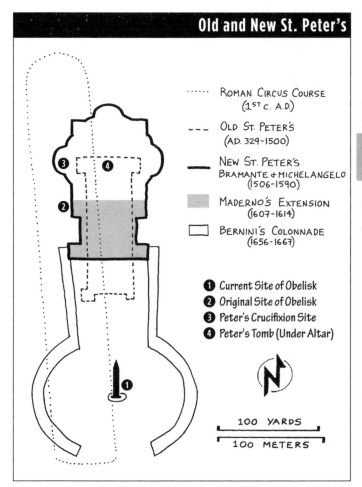

Old and New St. Peter's

······ ROMAN CIRCUS COURSE
(1ST C. A.D.)

--- OLD ST. PETER'S
(A.D. 329-1500)

— NEW ST. PETER'S
BRAMANTE & MICHELANGELO
(1506-1590)

░ MADERNO'S EXTENSION
(1607-1614)

▢ BERNINI'S COLONNADE
(1656-1667)

❶ Current Site of Obelisk
❷ Original Site of Obelisk
❸ Peter's Crucifixion Site
❹ Peter's Tomb (Under Altar)

100 YARDS

100 METERS

THE TOUR BEGINS

• *Find a shady spot where you like the view under the columns around St. Peter's oval-shaped "square." If the pigeons left a clean spot, sit on it.*

Background

Nearly 2,000 years ago, this area was the site of Nero's Circus—a huge, cigar-shaped Roman chariot racecourse. The tall obelisk you see in the middle of the square once stood about 100 yards from its current location, in the center of the circus course (to the left of where St. Peter's is today). The Romans had no marching bands, so for half-time entertainment they killed Christians. This persecuted minority was forced to fight wild animals and gladiators, or they were simply crucified. Some were tarred up, tied to posts, and burned—human torches to light up the evening races.

One of those killed here, in about A.D. 65, was Peter, Jesus' right-hand man, who had come to Rome to spread the message of love. At his own request, Peter was crucified upside-down, because he felt unworthy to die as his master had. His remains were buried in a nearby cemetery located where the main altar in St. Peter's is today. For 250 years, these relics were quietly and secretly revered.

Peter had been recognized as the first "pope," or bishop of Rome, from whom all later popes claimed their authority as head of the Church. When Christianity was finally legalized in 313, the Christian emperor Constantine built a church on the site of Peter's martyrdom. "Old St. Peter's" lasted 1,200 years (A.D. 329–1500).

By the time of the Renaissance, old St. Peter's was falling apart and was considered unfit to be the center of the Western Church. The new, larger church we see today was begun in 1506 by the architect Bramante. He was succeeded by Michelangelo and a number of other architects, each with his own designs. Carlo Maderno took Michelangelo's Greek-cross-shaped church and lengthened it, adding a long nave. As the construction proceeded, they actually built the new church around the old one (see diagram on page 237). The project was finally finished 120 years later, and Old St. Peter's was dismantled and carried out of the new church. (A few bits survive from the first church: the central door, some columns in the atrium, eight spiral columns around the tomb from the Jerusalem Temple, the venerated statue of Peter, and Michelangelo's *Pietà*.)

Michelangelo designed the magnificent dome. Unfortunately, although it soars above St. Peter's, it's barely visible from the center of the square due to Maderno's extended nave. To see the entire dome, you'll need to step outside the open end of the square, where in the 1930s Benito Mussolini opened up the broad boulevard, finally letting people see the dome that had been hidden for centuries by the facade. Though I don't make a habit of thanking fascist dictators, in this case I'll make an exception: *"Grazie, Benito."*

• *More on the church later—for now, let's talk about the square. Ideally, you should head out to the obelisk to view the square and read this. But let me guess—it's 95 degrees outside, right? OK, read on in the shade of these stone sequoias.*

ST. PETER'S SQUARE

St. Peter's Square, with its ring of columns, symbolizes the arms of the church welcoming everyone—believers and non-believers—with its motherly embrace. It was designed a century after Michelangelo by the Baroque architect Gian Lorenzo Bernini, who did much of the work that we'll see inside. Numbers first: 284 columns, 56 feet high, in stern Doric style. Topping them are Bernini's 140 favorite saints, each 10 feet tall. The "square" itself is actually elliptical, 660 by 500 feet. Though large, it's designed like a saucer, a little higher around the edges, so that even when full of crowds (as it often is), it allows those on the periphery to see above the throngs.

The obelisk in the center is 90 feet of solid granite weighing more than 300 tons. Think for a second about how much history this monument has seen. Originally erected in Egypt more than 2,000 years ago, it witnessed the fall of the pharaohs to the Greeks and then to the Romans. It was then moved to imperial Rome by the emperor Caligula, where it stood impassively watching the slaughter of Christians at the racecourse and the torture of Protestants by the Inquisition (in the yellow-and-rust building just outside the square, to the left of the church). Today, it watches over the church, a reminder that each civilization builds on the previous ones. The puny cross on top reminds us that Christian culture has cast but a thin veneer over our pagan origins.

• *Now venture out across the burning desert to the obelisk, which provides a narrow sliver of shade.*

As you face the church, the gray building to the right at two o'clock, rising up behind Bernini's colonnade, is where the pope lives.

The last window on the right of the top floor is his bedroom. To the left of that window is his study window, where he appears occasionally to greet the masses. If you come to the square at night as a Poping Tom, you might see the light on—the pope burns much midnight oil.

On more formal occasions (which you may have seen on TV), the pope appears from the church itself, on the small balcony above the central door.

The Sistine Chapel is just to the right of the facade—the small gray-brown building with the triangular roof, topped by an antenna. The tiny chimney (the pimple along the roofline midway up the left side) is where the famous smoke signals announce the election of each new pope. If the smoke is black, a two-thirds majority hasn't been reached. White smoke means a new pope has been selected.

Walk to the right, five pavement plaques from the obelisk, to one marked *Centro del Colonnato*. From here, all of Bernini's columns on

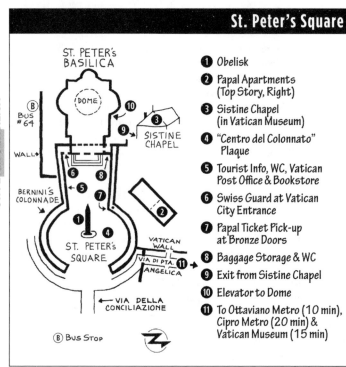

St. Peter's Square

ST. PETER's
BASILICA

(DOME)

B
BUS
#64

WALL→

BERNINI'S
COLONNADE

ST. PETER's
SQUARE

SISTINE
CHAPEL

VATICAN
WALL

VIA DI PTA.
ANGELICA

← VIA DELLA
CONCILIAZIONE

B BUS STOP

❶ Obelisk

❷ Papal Apartments
(Top Story, Right)

❸ Sistine Chapel
(in Vatican Museum)

❹ "Centro del Colonnato"
Plaque

❺ Tourist Info, WC, Vatican
Post Office & Bookstore

❻ Swiss Guard at Vatican
City Entrance

❼ Papal Ticket Pick-up
at Bronze Doors

❽ Baggage Storage & WC

❾ Exit from Sistine Chapel

❿ Elevator to Dome

⓫ To Ottaviano Metro (10 min),
Cipro Metro (20 min) &
Vatican Museum (15 min)

the right side line up. The curved Baroque square still pays its respects to Renaissance mathematical symmetry.

• *Climb the gradually sloping pavement past crowd barriers, the security checkpoint, and the huge statues of St. Paul (with his two-edged sword) and St. Peter (with his bushy hair and keys). Along the way, you'll pass by the dress-code enforcers and a gaggle of ticked-off guys in shorts.*

On the square are two entrances to Vatican City: one to the left of the facade, and one to the right in the crook of Bernini's "arm"—head for this one (it's also the same entrance that hands out pope-viewing tickets). Guarding this small but powerful country's border crossing are the mercenary guards from Switzerland. You have

to wonder if they really know how to use those pikes. Their colorful uniforms are said to have been designed by Michelangelo, though he was not known for his sense of humor.

· *Enter the atrium (entrance hall) of the church.*

THE BASILICA

The Atrium

The atrium is itself bigger than most churches. The huge white columns on the portico date from the first church (fourth century). Five famous bronze doors lead into the church.

Made from the melted-down bronze of the original door of old St. Peter's, the central door was the first Renaissance work in Rome (c. 1450). It's only opened on special occasions. The panels (from the top down) feature Jesus and Mary, Paul and Peter, and (at the bottom) how each was martyred: Paul decapitated, Peter crucified upside-down.

The far-right entrance is the **Holy Door,** opened only during Holy Years. On Christmas Eve every 25 years, the pope knocks three times with a silver hammer and the door opens, welcoming pilgrims to pass through. After Pope John Paul II opened the door on Christmas Eve, 1999, he bricked it up again with a ceremonial trowel a year later to wait another 24 years. (A plaque above the door fudges a bit for effect: it says that Pope "IOANNES PAULUS II" opened the door in the year "MM"—2000—and closed it in "MMI.") On the door itself, note crucified Jesus' shiny knees, polished by pious pilgrims who touch them for a blessing.

· *Now for one of Europe's great "wow" experiences. Enter the church. Gape for a while. But don't gape at Michelangelo's famous* Pietà *(on the right). That's this tour's finale. I'll wait for you at the round maroon pavement stone on the floor near the central doorway.*

The Church

This church is appropriately huge. Size before beauty: The golden window at the far end is two football fields away. The dove in the window has the wingspan of a 747 (OK, maybe not quite, but it *is* big). The church covers six acres. The babies at the base of the pillars along the main hall (the nave) are adult-size. The lettering in the gold band along the top of the pillars is seven feet high. Really. The church has a capacity of 60,000 standing worshippers (or 1,200 tour groups).

The church is huge and it feels huge, but everything is designed to make it seem smaller and more intimate than it really is.

For example, the statue of St. Teresa near the bottom of the first pillar on the right is 15 feet tall. The statue above her near the top looks the same size, but is actually six feet taller, giving the impression that it's not so far away. Similarly, the fancy bronze canopy over the altar at the far end is as tall as a seven-story building. That makes the great height of the dome seem smaller.

Looking down the nave, we get a sense of the splendor of ancient Rome that was carried on by the Catholic Church. The floor plan is based on the ancient Roman basilica, or law-court building, with a central aisle (nave) flanked by two side aisles. In fact, many of the stones used to build St. Peter's were scavenged from the ruined law courts of ancient Rome.

On the floor near the central doorway is a round slab of porphyry stone in the maroon color of ancient Roman officials. This is the spot where, on Christmas night in A.D. 800, the French king Charlemagne was crowned Holy Roman Emperor. Even in the Dark Ages, when Rome was virtually abandoned and visitors reported that the city had more thieves and wolves than decent people, its imperial legacy made it a fitting place to symbolically establish a briefly united Europe.

St. Peter's was very expensive to build and decorate. The popes financed it by selling "indulgences," allowing the rich to buy forgiveness for their sins from the Church. This kind of corruption inspired an obscure German monk named Martin Luther to rebel and start the Protestant Reformation.

The ornate, Baroque-style interior decoration—a riot of marble, gold, stucco, mosaics, columns of stone, and pillars of light—was part of the Church's "Counter-" Reformation. Baroque served as cheery propaganda, impressing followers with the authority of the Church, and giving them a glimpse of the heaven that awaited the faithful.

• *Now, walk straight up the center of the nave toward the altar.*

"Michelangelo's Church"—The Greek Cross

The plaques on the floor show where other, smaller churches of the world would end if they were placed inside St. Peter's: St. Paul's Cathedral in London (Londinense), Florence's Duomo, and so on.

You'll also walk over circular golden grates. Stop at the second one (at the third pillar from the entrance). Look back at the entrance and realize that if Michelangelo had had his way, this whole long section of the church wouldn't exist. The nave was extended after his death.

ST. PETER'S BASILICA

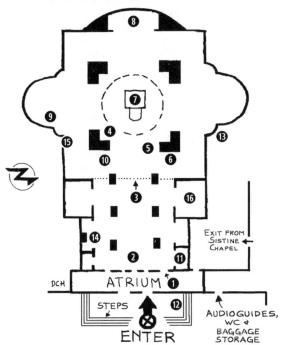

St. Peter's Basilica

EXIT FROM SISTINE CHAPEL

DCH   ATRIUM ➊

STEPS   ➓

AUDIOGUIDES, WC & BAGGAGE STORAGE

ⓧ ENTER

ST. PETER'S SQUARE

➊ Holy Door

➋ Charlemagne's Coronation Site

➌ Extent of Original "Greek Cross" Church Plan

➍ St. Andrew Statue & View of Dome

➎ St. Peter Statue (With Kissable Toe)

➏ Pope John XXIII

➐ Main Altar (Directly Over Peter's Tomb)

➑ BERNINI – Dove Window & "Throne of Peter"

➒ St. Peter's Crucifixion Site

➓ RAPHAEL – The Transfiguration (Mosaic Copy)

⑪ MICHELANGELO – Pietà

⑫ Line for Crypt & Dome Visits

⑬ Elevator to Roof & Dome-Climb

⑭ Roof & Dome-Climb Exit

⑮ Museum-Treasury

⑯ Blessed Sacrament Chapel

From Pope to Pope

On March 30, 2005, 84-year-old Pope John Paul II appeared at his apartment window overlooking St. Peter's Square, and—frail

JOAN. PAULUS II

and unable to speak—he silently blessed the crowd. It was his final public appearance. He died three days later.

For four days, John Paul II's body lay in state in front of St. Peter's main altar. Outside, hundreds of thousands of pilgrims lined up all the way down Via della Conciliazione, waiting up to 24 hours for one last look at their pope. Some five million people converged on Vatican City during the week.

On the day of the funeral, some 300,000 mourners, dignitaries, and security personnel gathered in windblown St. Peter's Square. As John Paul II's coffin was carried out—decorated with an "M" for Mary—the crowd broke into applause, and many shouted *"Santo subito!"* insisting he be made a saint *(santo)* right now *(subito)*. During the eulogy, Cardinal Josef Ratzinger pointed to the pope's apartment window and told the crowd, "We can be sure that our beloved pope is standing today at the window of the Father's house."

John Paul II was buried in St. Peter's Basilica in the Crypt, near the tomb of St. Peter and next to the shrine of another

Michelangelo was 71 years old when the pope persuaded him to take over the church project and cap it with a dome. He agreed, intending to put the dome over Donato Bramante's original "Greek Cross" floor plan, with four equal arms. In optimistic Renaissance times, this symmetrical arrangement symbolized perfection—the orderliness of the created world and the goodness of man (who was created in God's image). But Michelangelo was a Renaissance man in Counter-Reformation times. The Church, struggling against Protestants and its own corruption, opted for a plan designed to impress the world with its grandeur—the Latin cross of the Crucifixion, with its nave extended to accommodate the grand religious spectacles of the Baroque period.

• *Continue toward the altar, entering "Michelangelo's Church." Park yourself in front of the statue of St. Andrew to the left of the altar, the guy holding an X-shaped cross. Like Andrew, gaze up into the dome, and also like him, gasp. (Never stifle a gasp.)*

popular 20th-century pope, John XXIII. The tomb has no monument—just a simple stone slab with the inscription: Joannes Paulus II (1920–2005).

Then came nine days of mourning—punctuated by a Mass each day in St. Peter's—as cardinals representing the globe's 1.1 billion Catholics arrived to elect a new pope.

On April 18, 115 cardinals dressed in crimson were stripped of their mobile phones, given a vow of secrecy, and locked inside the Sistine Chapel for the "conclave" (from Latin *cum clave,* with key). Finally, at 17:50 on April 19, an anxious crowd in St. Peter's Square looked up to see a puff of white smoke emerging from the Sistine Chapel's chimney. The bells in St. Peter's clock towers rang out gloriously (a new tradition) confirming that, indeed, a pope had been elected. The crowd erupted in cheers, and Romans watching on their TVs hailed taxis to hurry to the Square.

On the balcony of St. Peter's facade, a cardinal addressed the crowd below. "Brothers and sisters," he said in several languages, *"Habemus Papam."* We have a pope. As thousands chanted *"Viva il Papa,"* 78-year-old Josef Ratzinger of Germany stepped up, raised his hands, and was introduced as Pope Benedict XVI.

The Dome

The dome soars higher than a football field on end, 430 feet from the floor of the cathedral to the top of the lantern. It glows with light from its windows, the blue and gold mosaics creating a cool, solemn atmosphere. In this majestic vision of heaven (not painted by Michelangelo), we see (above the windows) Jesus, Mary, and a ring of saints, more rings of angels above them, and, way up in the ozone, God the Father (a blur of blue and red without binoculars).

When Michelangelo died (1564), he'd completed only the drum of the dome—the base up to the windows flanked by half-columns—but the next architects were guided by his designs.

Listen to the hum of visitors echoing through St. Peter's and reflect on our place in the cosmos: half animal, half angel, stretched between heaven and earth, born to live only a short while, a bubble of foam on a great cresting wave of humanity.

• *But I digress.*

Peter

The base of the dome is ringed with a gold banner telling us in massive blue letters why this church is so important. According to Catholics, Peter was selected by Jesus to head the church. The banner in Latin quotes from the Bible where Jesus says to him, "You are Peter *(Tu es Petrus)* and upon this rock I will build my church, and to you I will give the keys of the kingdom of heaven" (Matthew 16:18). (Every quote from Jesus to Peter found in the Bible is written out in seven-foot-tall letters that continue around the entire church.)

Peter was the first bishop of Rome. His prestige and that of the city itself made this bishopric more illustrious than all others, and Peter's authority has supposedly passed in an unbroken chain to each succeeding bishop of Rome—that is, the 250-odd popes that followed.

Under the dome, under the bronze canopy, under the altar, some 23 feet under the marble floor, rest the bones of St. Peter, the "rock" upon which this particular church was built. You can't see the tomb, but go to the railing and look down into the small, lighted niche below the altar with a box containing bishops' shawls—a symbol of how Peter's authority spread to the other churches. Peter's tomb (not visible) is just below this box.

Are they really the bones of Jesus' apostle? According to a papal pronouncement: definitely maybe. The traditional site of his tomb was sealed up when Old St. Peter's was built on it in A.D. 326, and it remained sealed until 1940, when it was opened for archaeological study. Bones were found, dated from the first century, of a robust man who died in old age. His body was wrapped in expensive cloth. Various inscriptions and graffiti in the tomb indicate that second- and third-century visitors thought this was Peter's tomb. Does that mean

it's really Peter? Who am I to disagree with the pope? Definitely maybe.

If you line up the cross on the altar with the dove in the window, you'll notice that the niche below the cross is just off-center compared with the rest of the church. Why? Because Michelangelo built the church around the traditional location of the tomb, not the actual location—about two feet away—discovered by modern archaeology.

Back in the nave sits a bronze statue of Peter under a canopy. This is one of a handful

Benedict XVI

When Josef Ratzinger became the 265th pope, he introduced himself as "a simple, humble worker in the vineyard

of the Lord." But the man has a complex history, a reputation for intellectual brilliance, a flair for the piano, and a penchant for controversy for his unbending devotion to traditional Catholic doctrine.

Born in small-town Bavaria in 1927, he lived life under Nazi rule as many Germans did—outwardly obeying leaders while inwardly conflicted. Like all 14-year-old boys, he joined the Hitler Youth and, like most German men, was drafted into the Army. During World War II, he trained to spray flak from anti-aircraft guns, saw Jews transported to death camps, and, like many Germans in the final days of the war, he deserted his post.

After the war, he completed his studies in theology and became a rising voice of liberal Catholicism, serving as an advisor at the Second Vatican Council (1962–1965). But after the May 1968 student revolts rocked Europe's Establishment, he became increasingly convinced that Church tradition was needed to offset the growing chaos of the world.

Pope John Paul II appointed him to several positions, and Ratzinger became John Paul II's closest advisor and good friend. Every Friday afternoon for two decades, they met for lunch, intellectual sparring, and friendly conversation.

Under John Paul II, Ratzinger served as the Church's "enforcer" of doctrine, earning the nickname "God's Rottweiler." He spoke out against ordaining women, chastised Latin American priests for fomenting class warfare (Liberation theology), reassigned bishops who were soft on homosexuality, reaffirmed opposition to birth control, and wrote thoughtful papers challenging the secular world's moral relativism. He also punished pedophile priests, though critics charged him with glossing over the issue to preserve the Church's image.

Ratzinger chose the name of "Benedict" to recall both Pope Benedict XV (who tried to bring Europeans together after World War I) and the original St. Benedict (c. 480–543), the monk who symbolizes Europe's Christian roots. A true pan-European who speaks many languages, Ratzinger heads a Church that thrives everywhere except Europe, which is becoming increasingly secular (with the notable exception of an increasing Muslim population). In 2006, Benedict stirred controversy among many Muslims with some unguarded remarks. Generally, Benedict XVI has continued John Paul II's two priorities: defending Catholic doctrine in a changing world and building bridges with fellow Christians.

of pieces of art that was in the earlier church. In one hand he holds the keys, the symbol of the authority given him by Christ, while with the other hand he blesses us. He's wearing the toga of a Roman senator. It may be that the original statue was of a senator and that the bushy head and keys were added later to make it Peter. His big right toe has been worn smooth by the lips of pilgrims and foot-fetishists. Stand in line and kiss it, or, to avoid foot-and-mouth disease, touch your hand to your lips, then rub the toe. This is simply an act of reverence with no legend attached, though you can make one up if you like.

• *Circle to the right around the statue of Peter to find another popular stop among pilgrims: the lighted glass niche with the red-robed body of...*

Pope John XXIII

Pope John XXIII, who reigned 1958–1963, is nicknamed "the good pope." He is best known for initiating the landmark Vatican II Council (1962–1965) that instituted major reforms, bringing the Church into the modern age. The Council allowed Mass to be conducted in the vernacular rather than in Latin. Lay people were invited to participate more in services, Church leadership underwent some healthy self-criticism, and a spirit of ecumenism flourished. Pope John was a populist, referring to people as "brothers and sisters"...a phrase popular today among popes. In 2000, during the beatification process (a stop on the way to sainthood), Church authorities checked his body, and it was surprisingly fresh. So they moved it upstairs, put it behind glass, and now old Catholics who remember him fondly enjoy another stop on their St. Peter's visit.

The Main Altar

The main altar beneath the dome and canopy (the white marble slab with cross and candlesticks) is used only when the pope himself says Mass. He sometimes conducts the Sunday morning service when he's in town, a sight worth seeing. I must admit, though, it's a little strange being frisked at the door for weapons at the holiest place in Christendom.

The tiny altar would be lost in this enormous church if it weren't for Gian Lorenzo Bernini's seven-story bronze canopy (God's "four-poster bed"), which "extends" the altar upward and reduces the perceived distance between floor and ceiling. The corkscrew columns echo the marble ones that surrounded the altar/tomb in Old St. Peter's. Some of the bronze used here was taken and melted down from the ancient Pantheon. On the marble base of the columns are three bees on a shield, the symbol of the Barberini family, who

Bernini Blitz

Nowhere is there such a conglomeration of works by the flamboyant genius who remade the church—and the city—in the Baroque style. Here's your scavenger-hunt list. You have 20 minutes. Go!

1. St. Peter's Square: design and statues
2. Constantine equestrian relief (right end of atrium)
3. Decoration (stucco, gold leaf, marble, etc.) of side aisles (flanking the nave)
4. Tabernacle (the temple-like altarpiece) inside Blessed Sacrament Chapel
5. Much of the marble floor throughout church
6. Bronze canopy over the altar
7. St. Longinus statue (holding a lance) near altar
8. Balconies (above each of the four statues) with corkscrew, Solomonic columns
9. Dove window, bronze sunburst, angels, "Throne," and Church Fathers (in the apse)
10. Tomb of Pope Urban VIII (far end of the apse, right side)
11. Tomb of Pope Alexander VII (between the apse and the left transept, over a doorway, with the gold skeleton smothered in jasper poured like maple syrup)

Bizarre...Baroque...Bernini.

commissioned the work and ordered the raid on the Pantheon. As the saying went, "What the barbarians didn't do, the Barberini did."

Starting from the column to the left of the altar, walk clockwise around the canopy. Notice the female faces on the marble bases, about

eye level above the bees. Someone in the Barberini family was pregnant during the making of the canopy, so Bernini put the various stages of childbirth on the bases. Continue clockwise to the last base to see how it came out.

Bernini (1598–1680), the Michelangelo of the Baroque era, is the man most responsible for the interior decoration of the church. The altar area was his masterpiece, a "theater" for holy spectacles. Bernini did: 1) the bronze canopy; 2) the dove window in the apse, surrounded by bronze work and statues; 3) the statue of lance-bearing St. Longinus ("The hills are alive..."), which became the model for the other three statues; 4) much of the marble floor decoration; and 5) the balconies above the four statues, incorporating some of the actual corkscrew columns from Old St. Peter's, said to have been looted by the Romans from the Temple of Herod (called "Solomon's

Temple") in Jerusalem. Bernini, the father of Baroque, gave an impressive unity to an amazing variety of pillars, windows, statues, chapels, and aisles.

• *Approach the apse, the front area with the golden dove window.*

The Apse

Bernini's dove window shines above the smaller front altar used for everyday services. The Holy Spirit, in the form of a six-foot-high dove, pours sunlight onto the faithful through the alabaster windows, turning into artificial rays of gold and reflecting off swirling gold clouds, angels, and winged babies. During a service, real sunlight passes through real clouds of incense, mingling with Bernini's sculpture. This is the epitome of Baroque—an ornate, mixed-media work designed to overwhelm the viewer.

Beneath the dove is the centerpiece of this structure, the so-called "Throne of Peter," an oak chair built in medieval times for a king. Subsequently, it was encrusted with tradition and encased in bronze by Bernini as a symbol of papal authority. Statues of four early Church Fathers support the chair, a symbol of how bishops should support the pope in troubled times—times like the Counter-Reformation.

Remember that St. Peter's is a church, not a museum. In the apse, Mass is said daily (Mon–Sat at 17:00, Sun at 17:30) for pilgrims, tourists, and Roman citizens alike. Wooden confessional booths are available for Catholics to tell their sins to a listening ear and receive forgiveness and peace of mind. The faithful renew their faith, and the faithless gain inspiration. Look at the light streaming through the windows, turn and gaze up into the dome, and quietly contemplate your deity (or lack thereof).

• *To the left of the main altar is the south transept. At the far end, left side, find the dark "painting" of St. Peter crucified upside-down.*

South Transept—Peter's Crucifixion Site

This marks the exact spot (according to tradition) where Peter was killed 1,900 years ago. Peter had come to the world's greatest city to preach Jesus' message of love to the pagan, often hostile Romans. During the reign of Nero, he was arrested and brought to Nero's Circus so all Rome could witness his execution. When the authorities told Peter he was to be crucified just like his Lord, Peter said "I'm not worthy," and insisted they nail him on the cross upside-down.

The Romans were actually quite tolerant of other religions, but they required their conquered peoples to worship the Roman emperor as a god. For most religions, this was no problem, but monotheistic

Christians refused to worship the emperor even when burned alive, crucified, or thrown to the lions. Their bravery, optimism in suffering, and message of love struck a chord among slaves and members of the lower classes. The religion started by a poor carpenter grew, despite occasional pogroms (persecution of minorities) by fanatical emperors. In three short centuries, Christianity went from a small Jewish sect in Jerusalem to the official religion of the world's greatest empire.

This and all the other "paintings" in the church are actually mosaic copies made from thousands of colored chips the size of your little fingernail. Smoke and humidity would damage real paintings. Around the corner on the right (heading back toward the central nave), pause at the copy of Raphael's huge "painting" (mosaic) of *The Transfiguration*, especially if you won't be seeing the original in the Vatican Museum.

• *Back near the entrance to the church, in the far corner, behind bullet-proof glass is the...*

Pietà

Michelangelo was 24 years old when he completed this *Pietà* (pee-ay-TAH) of Mary with the dead body of Christ taken from the cross. It was Michelangelo's first major commission (by the French ambassador to the Vatican), done for Holy Year 1500.

Pietà means "pity." Michelangelo, with his total mastery of the real world, captures the sadness of the moment. Mary cradles her crucified son in her lap. Christ's lifeless right arm drooping down lets us know how heavy this corpse is. His smooth skin is accented by the rough folds of Mary's robe. Mary tilts her head down, looking at her dead son with sad tenderness. Her left hand turns upward, asking, "How could they do this to you?"

Michelangelo didn't think of sculpting as creating a figure, but as simply freeing the God-made figure from the prison of marble around it. He'd attack a project like this with an inspired passion, chipping away to find what God put inside.

The bunched-up shoulder and rigor-mortis legs show that Michelangelo learned well from his studies of cadavers. But realistic as this work is, its true power lies in the subtle "unreal" features. Life-size Christ looks childlike compared with larger-than-life Mary. Unnoticed at first, this accentuates the subconscious impression of Mary enfolding Jesus in her maternal love. Mary—the mother of a 33-year-old man—looks like a teen-ager, emphasizing how Mary was the eternally youthful "handmaiden" of the

Lord, always serving him, even at this moment of supreme sacrifice. She accepts God's will, even if it means giving up her son.

The statue is a solid pyramid of maternal tenderness. Yet within this, Christ's body tilts diagonally down to the right and Mary's hem flows with it. Subconsciously, we feel the weight of this dead God sliding from her lap to the ground.

At 11:30 on May 23, 1972, a madman with a hammer entered St. Peter's and began hacking away at the *Pietà*. The damage was repaired, but that's why there's now a shield of bulletproof glass.

This is Michelangelo's only signed work. The story goes that he overheard some pilgrims praising his finished *Pietà*, but attributing it to a second-rate sculptor from a lesser city. He was so enraged he grabbed his chisel and chipped "Michelangelo Buonarroti of Florence did this" in the ribbon running down Mary's chest.

On your right (covered in gray concrete with a gold cross) is the inside of the Holy Door. It won't be opened until Christmas Eve, 2024, the dawn of the next Jubilee Year. If there's a prayer inside you, ask that St. Peter's will no longer need security checks or bulletproof glass when this door is next opened.

Up to the Dome (Cupola)

A good way to finish a visit to St. Peter's is to go up to the dome for the best view of Rome anywhere (daily April–Sept 8:00–17:45, Oct–March 8:00–16:45).

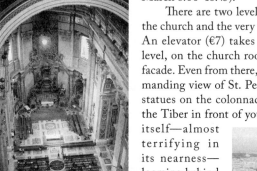

There are two levels: the rooftop of the church and the very top of the dome. An elevator (€7) takes you to the first level, on the church roof just above the facade. Even from there, you have a commanding view of St. Peter's Square, the statues on the colonnade, Rome across the Tiber in front of you, and the dome itself—almost terrifying in its nearness—looming behind you.

From here, you can also go inside to the gallery ringing the interior of the dome, where you can look down inside the church. Notice the dusty top of Bernini's seven-story-tall canopy far below. Study the mosaics up close—and those huge letters! It's worth the elevator ride for this view alone.

From this level, if you're energetic, continue all the way up to the top of the dome.

The staircase (€5) actually winds between the outer shell and the inner one. It's a sweaty, crowded, claustrophobic, 15-minute, 323-step climb, but worth it. The view from the summit is great, the fresh air even better. Admire the arms of Bernini's colonnade encircling St. Peter's Square. Find the big, white Victor Emmanuel Monument with the two statues on top and the Pantheon with its large, light, shallow dome. The large rectangular building to the left of the obelisk is the Vatican Museum, stuffed with art. Survey the Vatican grounds, with its mini-train system and lush gardens. Look down into the square on the tiny pilgrims buzzing like electrons around the nucleus of Catholicism.

THE REST OF THE CHURCH

The Crypt (a.k.a. Grottoes, or *Tombe*)

Visitors can go down to the foundations of Old St. Peter's, containing tombs of popes and memorial chapels. Exit the basilica and turn left to head down the steps (back out the way you entered, unless you took the Vatican Museum shortcut). You'll see people here lined up to visit the Crypt, and to ride up to the dome. Once you're in the Crypt, descend to the floor level of the previous church, look at St. Peter's tomb and walk by the simple tomb of Pope John Paul II. Out of 265 popes, two have been given the title "Great." That elite group may soon grow by 50 percent, as there's talk of calling the pope who died in 2005 "John Paul the Great."

The walk through the Crypt is free and easy—but you won't see St. Peter's original grave unless you take a "Scavi" ("excavations") tour. Excellent Vatican guides take groups of 15 to the excavations in the well-lit pagan Necropolis (€10, 2 hours, ages 15 and older only, book well in advance by emailing scavi@fsp.va, fax to 06-6987-3017, or ask directly by calling the Excavations Office—Mon–Sat 9:00–17:00, closed Sun and holidays, tel. 06-6988-5318). Follow the detailed instructions at www.vatican.va to submit a request. No response to your fax or email means they're booked up.

The Museum-Treasury (Museo-Tesoro)

The museum, located on the left side of the nave near the altar, contains an original corkscrew column from Old St. Peter's, the room-size tomb of Sixtus IV by Antonio Pollaiuolo, a big pair of Roman pincers used to torture Christians, and assorted jewels, papal robes, and golden reliquaries—a marked contrast to the poverty of early Christians (€6, daily April–Sept 8:00–18:00, Oct–March 8:30–17:30).

Blessed Sacrament Chapel

You're welcome to step through the metalwork gates into this oasis of peace reserved for prayer and meditation. It's located on the right-hand side of the church, about midway to the altar.

ST. PETER-IN-CHAINS TOUR

San Pietro in Vincoli

Michelangelo—Earth's greatest sculptor—died having failed to complete his greatest work, the tomb of Pope Julius II. Today, you can visit the powerful remains of that unfinished masterpiece, including the famous statue of Moses, housed in a historic church that also contains Peter's chains.

ORIENTATION

Cost: Free.

Dress Code: Modest dress is required.

Hours: Daily 8:00–12:30 & 15:00–19:00, until 18:00 in winter.

Getting There: The church is a 15-minute uphill walk north of the Colosseum (Metro stop: Colosseo, exit Metro stop to the left and climb the staircase that's roughly 50 yards away, then work your way slowly uphill; or get off at Metro: Cavour, exit Metro and go up steep flight of steps, take a right at the top, and walk a block). There are several churches in the area—if asking for directions, say "San Pietro in Vincoli" (sahn pee-AY-troh een VEEN-koh-lee).

Length of This Tour: Allow 30 minutes.

Cuisine Art: See the recommended eateries listed on page 308.

THE TOUR BEGINS

The Art

• *In the far-right corner of the church, you'll find a wall full of marble statues. In the center sits...*

Michelangelo's *Moses* (1515)

Moses has just returned from meeting face-to-face with God. Now he senses trouble back home. Slowly he turns to see his followers worshipping a golden calf. As his anger builds, he glares at them. His physical strength is symbolic of his moral and spiritual fortitude as a leader of his people. His powerful left leg tucks under and tenses, as he's just about to spring up out of his chair and punish the naughty Children of Israel with the Ten Commandments under his arm. Enjoy the cascading beard, one of the greatest in art history.

And if he did stand up, this statue would be 13 feet tall, nearly the height of Michelangelo's famous *David*. This Charlton Heston-with-horns is interesting in photographs...and awe-inspiring when confronted in person. His bare, muscular arms exude power. Michelangelo completed the statue after practicing for four years painting the seated prophets on the Sistine ceiling.

Like other Michelangelo statues, *Moses* is both at rest (seated) and in motion (his tensed leg, turning head, and nervous fingers). This restlessness may reflect Michelangelo's neo-Platonic belief that the soul is the claustrophobic prisoner of the body. Or it's the statue itself fighting to emerge from the stone around it. A frustrated Michelangelo, working to bring God's statue into existence, reportedly threw his chisel at the thing (some say causing a scar on *Moses'* right knee), yelling at it, "Speak, damn it, speak!"

The horns are the crowning touch. In medieval times, the Hebrew word for "rays of light" (halo) was mistranslated as "horns." Michelangelo knew better but wanted to give the statue an air of *terribilità*, a kind of scary charisma possessed by Moses, Pope Julius II...and Michelangelo. This Moses radiates the smoldering *terribilità* of a borderline-abusive father.

The Tomb Today

In 1542, some of the remnants of the tomb project were brought to St. Peter-in-Chains and pieced together by Michelangelo's assistants. What we see today is a far cry from the original design, which was to have been fully three-dimensional and five times as big. Some of the best statues ended up elsewhere, like the *Prisoners* in Florence, and the *Slaves* in the Louvre. Though the assistants had Michelangelo's original instruction manual, they were trying to assemble it with most of the parts missing.

Moses and the Louvre's *Slaves* are the only statues Michelangelo personally completed for the project. Flanking *Moses* are the Old Testament sister-wives of Jacob, Leah (to our left) and Rachel, both begun by Michelangelo but probably finished by pupils. On the second story, a Madonna and Child stand above a reclining, thoughtful-looking Pope Julius II on a coffin.

The sheer variety of decoration we see here gives us a glimpse of the tomb's original scope—nearly 50 statues laced together with Pompeii-esque garlands and proto-Baroque scrolls.

Michelangelo went to his grave thinking that he'd wasted the

The Tomb of Pope Julius II

Moses sits on the bottom level of a three-story marble wall filled with statues. This is a puny, cobbled-together version of what was to have been a grand tomb for Pope Julius II.

In 1505, Pope Julius II hired young Michelangelo to build his tomb, a huge monument to be placed in St. Peter's Basilica. An excited Michelangelo sketched designs for a three-story, wedding-cake mountain of marble studded with 48 statues and bronze reliefs, and topped with a huge statue of the egomaniacal pope. *Moses* was to have been placed on an upper level on the right-hand corner, looking away from the monument.

Michelangelo traveled to Carrara, selected 100 tons of marble for the project, and started working. Then Julius changed his mind. He ordered Michelangelo to work on painting the Sistine Chapel instead. Michelangelo knocked it off in a mere four years so that he could return to his true masterwork. Michelangelo would spend 30 years of his life working in fits and starts on the tomb. But when Julius died (1513), the funding for the project petered out, and Michelangelo eventually moved on to other things. Julius was buried in a simple grave in St. Peter's Basilica at the Vatican.

best years of his life on the tomb. Today, we can only reconstruct it in our minds, imagining a monument intended to exceed (according to Giorgio Vasari) "every ancient or imperial tomb ever made."

The Church

Founded in 440, it's one of Rome's oldest, built to house Peter's chains. Though the church was greatly changed in 1475, the 20 Doric columns flanking the wide nave are from the original church. The central ceiling painting (c. 1700) shows the chains—with their miraculous curative powers in action—healing someone possessed by demons, on the steps of St. Peter's Basilica in the Vatican.

• *On the altar is a gold-and-glass case, containing what tradition claims are...*

Peter's Chains

There are actually two different sets of chains, linked together. One set held Peter (it's said) when he and Paul were in the Mamertine Prison in Rome (near the Forum).

The other dates from when Herod jailed Peter in Jerusalem (Acts 12; see the scene frescoed on the left wall of the apse). During the night, "Peter was sleeping between two soldiers, bound with chains, while sentries were guarding the doors. And behold, an angel of the Lord appeared and a light shone in the cell. The angel struck Peter on the side and woke him, saying, 'Get up quickly.' And the chains fell off his hands." The angel led Peter, who thought he was dreaming, out of the prison to safety. (Raphael depicted this in the Vatican, page 216.)

In the waning days of ancient Rome, the Jerusalem chains ended up here as a gift from the Eastern empress to her son-in-law, the Western emperor. When they arrived and were paired with the Mamertine chains, the two sets—chink!—joined together miraculously.

PILGRIM'S ROME TOUR

Pilgrimage Churches

Rome is the "capital" of the world's 1.1 billion Catholics. In Rome, you'll rub elbows with religious pilgrims from around the world—Nigerian nuns, Bulgarian theology students, extended Mexican families, and everyday Catholics returning to their religious roots.

The pilgrim industry helped shape Rome after the fall of the empire. Ancient Rome's population peaked at about 1.2 million. When Rome fell in A.D. 476, barbarians cut off the water supply by breaking the aqueducts, Romans fled the city, and the Tiber filled with silt. During the Dark Ages, mosquitoes ruled over a pathetic village of 50,000...bad news for pilgrims, bad news for the Vatican. Back then, the Catholic Church was the Christian Church. Because popes needed a place fit for pilgrimages, the Church revitalized the city. Owners of hotels and restaurants cheered.

In 1587, Pope Sixtus V reconnected aqueducts and built long, straight boulevards connecting the great churches and pilgrimage sites. Obelisks served as markers. As you explore the city, think like a pilgrim. Look down long roads and you'll see either a grand church or an obelisk (from which you'll see a grand church).

ORIENTATION

Church of San Giovanni in Laterano: Free, daily 7:00–18:30, €5 audioguide available at info desk near statue of Constantine (show your Rick Steves guidebook in 2009 for a €1 discount, leave ID as a deposit, last rental 30 min before closing), Piazza San Giovanni in Laterano, Metro: San Giovanni, or bus #85 or #87, tel. 06-6988-6392. For hours for Holy Stairs, see page 264.

Church of Santa Maria Maggiore: Free, daily 8:00–18:30, skip the €4 audioguide, Piazza Santa Maria Maggiore, Metro: Termini or Vittorio Emanuele, tel. 06-48-3058.

Pilgrim's Rome

TERMINI — TERMINI TRAIN STATION

SANTA MARIA MAGGIORE

CAVOUR

STA. PRASSEDE

CAVOUR

VIA G. LANZA

PIAZZA VITTORIO EM.

VITTORIO EMANUELE

ST. PETER-IN-CHAINS

VIA ANNI.

COLOSSEO

MERULANA

SAN CLEMENTE

VIA L.

MANZONI

VIA

LABICANA

COLOSSEUM

S. GIOVANNI LAT.

HOLY STAIRS

→ ENTRY POINT TO SIGHTS

M METRO STATION

SAN GIOVANNI IN LATERANO

¼ MILE

400 METERS

CITY WALLS →

VIA SANNIO

S. GIO.

DCH

PILGRIM'S ROME TOUR

Church of Santa Prassede: Free, bring €0.50 and €1 coins for lights, daily 7:00–12:00 & 16:00–18:30, 100 yards from Santa Maria Maggiore.

Church of San Clemente: Upper church—free, lower church—€5, both open Mon–Sat 9:00–12:30 & 15:00–18:00, Sun 12:00–18:00, Via di San Giovanni in Laterano, Metro: Colosseo, or bus #85 or #87, tel. 06-7045-1018.

Getting There: Metro line A stops at San Giovanni in Laterano and Piazza Vittorio. Bus #87 runs from Largo Argentina to Piazza Venezia to the Colosseum to the Church of San Clemente to the Church of San Giovanni in Laterano. Bus #85 does the same route but skips Largo Argentina.

THE TOUR BEGINS

Overview

Pilgrims to Rome try to visit four great basilicas: St. Peter's, of course (page 233), St. Paul's Outside the Walls (page 72), San Giovanni in Laterano, and Santa Maria Maggiore. The last two are covered in this chapter, as well as two other "honorable mentions": For the best Byzantine-style mosaics in Rome, visit the Church of Santa Prassede (near Santa Maria Maggiore). And the fascinating and central San Clemente is not far from San Giovanni in Laterano.

SAN GIOVANNI IN LATERANO

Imagine the jubilation when this church—the first Christian church in the city of Rome—was opened in about A.D. 318. Christians could finally "come out" and worship openly without fear of reprisal. (Still, most Romans were pagan, so this first great church was tucked away from the center of things, near the wall.) After that glorious beginning, the church served as the center of Catholicism and the home of the popes up until the Renaissance renovation of St. Peter's. Until 1870, all popes were "crowned" here. Even today, it's the home church of the Bishop of Rome—the pope.

The church is located on Piazza San Giovanni in Laterano (Metro: San Giovanni). From the Metro station, go through the old city walls and look left.

The **Via Sannio** market, selling clothing and some handicrafts every morning except Sunday, is a couple of blocks south of the church.

Exterior

The massive facade is 18th century, with Christ triumphant on the top. The blocky, peach-colored building adjacent on the right is the Lateran Palace, standing on the site of the old Papal Palace—residence of popes until about 1300. Across the street to your right are the pope's private chapel and the Holy Stairs (Scala Santa), popular with pilgrims (we'll see the stairs later). To the left is a well-preserved chunk of the ancient Roman wall. Pass the one-meter high granite posts surrounding the church to leave Italy and enter the Vatican State—Carabinieri must leave their guns at the door.

• *Step inside the portico and look left.*

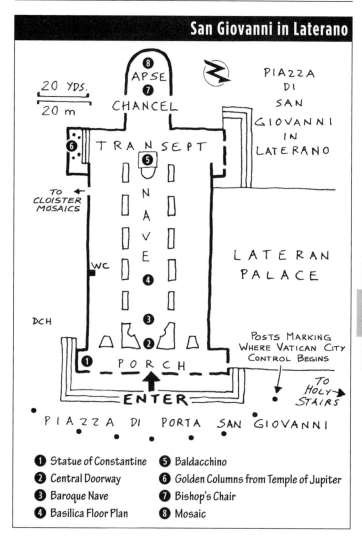

San Giovanni in Laterano

20 YDS.
20 m

❽ APSE
❼ CHANCEL

PIAZZA DI SAN GIOVANNI IN LATERANO

❻

T R A N S E P T

❺

TO CLOISTER MOSAICS

N A V E

❹

WC

❸

DCH

❷

❶ P O R C H

LATERAN PALACE

POSTS MARKING WHERE VATICAN CITY CONTROL BEGINS

TO HOLY STAIRS

ENTER

P I A Z Z A   D I   P O R T A   S A N   G I O V A N N I

❶ Statue of Constantine
❷ Central Doorway
❸ Baroque Nave
❹ Basilica Floor Plan
❺ Baldacchino
❻ Golden Columns from Temple of Jupiter
❼ Bishop's Chair
❽ Mosaic

❶ Statue of Constantine
(inside the portico, far left end)

It's October 28, A.D. 312, and Constantine—sword tucked under his arm and leaning confidently on a (missing) spear—has conquered Maxentius and liberated Rome. Constantine marched to this spot where his enemy's personal bodyguards lived, trashed their pagan idols, and dedicated the place to the god who gave him his victory— Christ. The holes in Constantine's head once held a golden, halo-like crown for the emperor who legalized Christianity. In the relief above the statue, you'll see a beheaded John the Baptist.

❷ Central Doorway (in the portico)

These tall green bronze doors, with their floral designs and acorn studs, are the original doors from ancient Rome's Senate House (Curia) in the Forum. The Church moved these here in the 1650s to remind people that from now on, the Church was Europe's lawmaker. The star borders were added to make these big doors bigger. Imagine, those cool little acorns date to the third century.

• *Now go inside the main part of the church. Stand in the back of the nave.*

❸ Baroque Nave

Very little survives from the original church—most of what you see was built after 1600. In preparation for the 1650 Jubilee, Pope Innocent X commissioned architect Francesco Borromini (rival to Bernini) to remake the interior. He redesigned the basilica in the Baroque style, reorganizing the nave, and adding the huge statues of the apostles (they are stepping out of niches...symbolically bringing celestial Jerusalem to our world). The relief panels above the statues depict parallel events from the Old Testament (on the left) and New Testament (on the right). For instance, in the very back you'll see two resurrections: Jonah escaping the whale and Jesus escaping death. Only the ceiling (which should have been a white vault) breaks from the Baroque style—it's Renaissance and the pope wanted it to stay.

❹ Basilica Floor Plan

San Giovanni was the first public church in Rome and the model for all later churches, including St. Peter's. The floor plan—a large central hall (nave) flanked by two side aisles—was based on the ancient Roman basilica (law courts) floor plan. These buildings were big enough to accommodate the large Christian congregations. Note that Roman basilicas came with two apses. You came in through the main entrance, which was designed to stress the authority of the place by slightly overwhelming and intimidating those who entered. When the design was adapted for use as a church, a grand and welcoming entry (the west portal) replaced one of the apses. Upon entering, the worshipper could take in the entire space instantly, and the rows of columns welcomed him to proceed to the altar.

❺ Baldacchino (canopy over altar)

In the upper cage are two silver statues of Saints Peter (with keys) and Paul (sword), which contain pieces of their...heads.

The gossip buzzing among Rome's amateur archaeologists is that the Vatican tested DNA from Peter's head (located here) and from his body (located at St. Peter's)...and they didn't match.

❻ **Golden Columns from Temple of Jupiter**
(left transept)

Tradition says that these gilded bronze columns once stood in pagan Rome's holiest spot—the Temple of Jupiter, dedicated to the King of all Gods, on the summit of Capitol Hill (c. 50 B.C.); for information on the temple, see page 186. Now they support a triangular pediment inhabited by a bearded, Jupiter-like God the Father.

❼ **Bishop's Chair** (in apse)

The chair (or "cathedra") reminds visitors that this is the cathedral of Rome...and the pope himself is the bishop that sits here. Once elected, the new pope must actually sit in this chair to officially become the pope. The ceremonial sitting usually happens within one month of election—Pope Benedict XVI took his seat on May 3, 2005.

❽ **Mosaic** (in semicircular dome of apse)

The original design dates from about 450 (although it was made in the 13th century and heavily restored in the 19th century). Pop in a coin

for light. You'll see a cross, animals, plants, and the River Jordan running along the base. Mosaic, of course, was an ancient Roman specialty adapted by medieval Christians. The head of Christ (above the cross) must have been a glorious sight to early worshippers. It was one of the first legal images of Christ ever seen in formerly pagan Rome.

• Fans of Cosmatesque marble inlay floor (c. 1100–1300) may want to visit the cloister (€2, free with €5 basilica audioguide rental, enter near left transept).

The Holy Stairs are outside the church in a building across the street.

Holy Stairs (Scala Santa)

In 326, Emperor Constantine's mother (Sta. Helena) brought home the 28 marble steps of Pontius Pilate's residence. Jesus climbed these steps on the day he was sentenced to death. Each day, hundreds of faithful penitents climb these steps on their knees (reciting a litany of prayers, available at the desk to the right of the entry). Covered with walnut wood with small glass-covered holes showing stains from Jesus' blood, the steps lead to the "Holy of Holies" (Sancta

Sanctorum), the private chapel of the popes in the Middle Ages. With its world-class relics, this chapel was considered the holiest place on earth. While the relics were moved to the Vatican in 1905, and the chapel is open only a few hours a week, you can climb the tourist staircases along the sides and look inside through the grated windows.

On September 20, 1870, as nationalist forces unifying Italy took Rome and ended the pope's temporal power, Pope Pius IX left his Quirinal Palace home for the last time. He stopped here to climb the steps, pray in his chapel, and bless his supporters from the top of the steps. Then he fled to the Vatican, where he spent the rest of his days.

The building housing the **Holy Stairs** is free and open daily (April–Sept 6:30–12:00 & 15:30–18:30, Oct–March 6:30–12:00 & 15:00–18:00).

SANTA MARIA MAGGIORE

The basilica of Santa Maria celebrates Holy Mary, the mother of Jesus. One of Rome's oldest and best-preserved churches, it was built (A.D. 432) while Rome was falling around it. The city had been sacked by Visigoths (410), and the emperors were about to check out (476). Increasingly, popes stepped in to fill the vacuum of leadership. The fifth-century mosaics give the church the feel of the early-Christian community. The general ambience of the church really takes you back to ancient times.

The church is at Piazza Santa Maria Maggiore (Metro: Termini or Vittorio Emanuele).

Exterior

Mary's column originally stood in the Forum's Basilica of Constantine. The fifth-century church built in her honor proclaims she was indeed the Mother of God—a fact disputed by hair-splitting theologians of the day. When you step inside the church, you'll be exiting Italy and entering the Vatican—the Maggiore indicates that this church, a Vatican possession, was much more important than other churches dedicated to the Virgin Mary.

Interior

Despite the Renaissance ceiling and Baroque crusting, you still feel like you're walking into an early-Christian church. The stately rows of columns, the simple basilica layout, the cheery colors, the spacious nave—it's easy to imagine worshipers finding an oasis of peace here as the Roman Empire crashed around them. (The 15th-century coffered

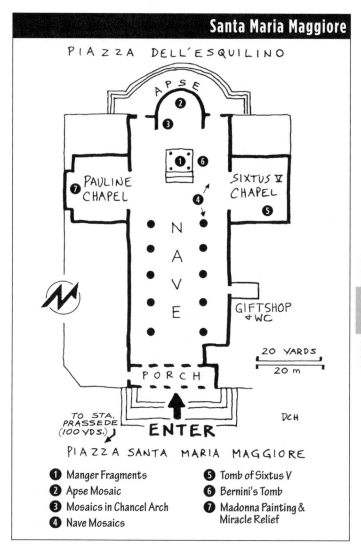

Santa Maria Maggiore

PIAZZA DELL'ESQUILINO

APSE

❷

❸

❶ **❻**

PAULINE CHAPEL
❼

SIXTUS Ⅴ CHAPEL

❹

❺

N A V E

GIFTSHOP & WC

20 YARDS
20 m

PORCH

TO STA. PRASSEDE (100 YDS.)

DCH

ENTER

PIAZZA SANTA MARIA MAGGIORE

❶ Manger Fragments
❷ Apse Mosaic
❸ Mosaics in Chancel Arch
❹ Nave Mosaics
❺ Tomb of Sixtus V
❻ Bernini's Tomb
❼ Madonna Painting & Miracle Relief

ceiling is gilded with gold perhaps brought back from America by Columbus.)

• *In the center of the church is the main altar, under a purple and gold canopy. Underneath the altar, in a lighted niche, are...*

❶ Manger Fragments

A kneeling Pope Pius IX (who established the dogma of the Immaculate Conception in the 19th century) prays before a glass case with an urn that contains several pieces of wood, bound by iron—these pieces are said to be from Jesus' crib. The church, dedicated to Mary's motherhood, displays these relics as physical evidence that Mary was indeed the mother of Christ. (The church is also built on the site of a former pagan temple dedicated to Rome's mother goddess, Juno.) Is the manger the real thing? Look into the eyes of pilgrims who visit.

• *In the apse, topped with a semicircular dome, find the...*

❷ Apse Mosaic

This 13th-century mosaic shows Mary being crowned by Jesus, both on the same throne. They float in a bubble representing heaven, borne aloft by angels. By the Middle Ages, Mary's cult status was secure.

• *Up in the arch that frames the outside of the apse, you'll find some of the church's oldest mosaics.*

❸ Mosaics in Chancel Arch

Colorful panels tell Mary's story in fifth-century Roman terms. Haloed senator-saints in white togas (top panel on left side) attend to Mary, who sits on a throne, dressed in gold and crowned like an empress. The angel Gabriel swoops down to announce to Mary that she'll conceive Jesus, and the Dove of the Holy Spirit follows. Below (the panel in the bottom left corner) are sheep representing the apostles, entering the city of Jerusalem ("Hiervsalem").

❹ Nave Mosaics
(right side of nave, starting near altar)

The church contains some of the world's oldest and best-preserved mosaics from Christian Rome. If the floodlights are on (it doesn't hurt to ask someone), those with good eyesight or binoculars will enjoy watching the story of Moses unfold in a series of surprisingly colorful and realistic scenes—more sophisticated than anything that would be seen for a thousand years.

The small, square mosaic panels are above all the columns, on the right side of the nave. Start at the altar and work back toward the entry.

1. It's a later painting—skip it.
2. Pharaoh's daughter (upper left) and her maids take baby Moses from the Nile.
3. Moses (lower half of panel) sees a burning bush that reconnects him with his Hebrew origins.
4. A parade of Israelites (left side) flee Egypt through a path in the Red Sea, while Pharaoh's troops drown.
5. Moses leads them across the Sinai desert (upper half), and God provides for them with a flock of quail (lower half).
6. Moses (upper half) sticks his magic rod in a river to desalinate it.
7. The Israelites battle their enemies while Moses commands from a hillside.
8. Skip it.

9. Moses (upper left) brings the Ten Commandments, then goes with Joshua (upper right) to lie down and die.
10. Joshua crosses the (rather puny) Jordan River...
11. ...and attacks Jericho...
12. ...and then the walls come a-tumblin' down.

• *If the gate is open, enter the chapel in the right transept (otherwise skip ahead to Bernini's Tomb). On the right wall of the chapel is a statue of a praying pope, atop the...*

❺ Tomb of Sixtus V

The Rome we see today is due largely to Pope Sixtus V (or was it Fiftus VI?). This energetic pope (1585–1590) leveled shoddy medieval Rome and erected grand churches connected by long, broad boulevards spiked with obelisks as focal points (such as the obelisk in Piazza dell'Esquilino behind Santa Maria Maggiore). The city of Rome has 13 Egyptian obelisks—all of Egypt has only five. The white, carved-marble relief panels (especially the one in the upper right) show some of the obelisks and buildings he commissioned.

• *Walk back toward the main altar. On a roped-off step between two pillars, you'll find an inscription on the ground marking...*

❻ Bernini's Tomb

The plaque reads, "Ioannes Laurentivs Bernini"—Gian Lorenzo Bernini (1598–1680)—"who brought honor to art and the city, here humbly rests." Next to it is another plaque to the "Familia Bernini." It's certainly humble…a simple memorial for the man who grew up in this neighborhood, then went on to remake Rome in the ornate Baroque style. (For more on Bernini, see page 196.)

• *In the left transept, over the altar, you'll see a...*

❼ Madonna Painting and Miracle Relief

The altar, a geologist's delight, is adorned with jasper, agate, amethyst, lapis lazuli, and gold angels. Amid it all is a simple icon of the lady this church is dedicated to: Mary.

Above the painting is a bronze relief panel showing a pope, with amazed bystanders, shoveling snow. One hot August night in the year 432, Mary appeared to Pope Liberius in a dream, telling him: "Build me a church where the snow falls." The next morning, they discovered a small patch of snow here on the Esquiline Hill—on August 5—and this church, dedicated to Santa Maria, was begun.

• *After looking around Santa Maria Maggiore, fans of mosaics, Byzantines, and the offbeat should consider a visit to the nearby church of Santa Prassede, about 100 yards away.*

Exiting Santa Maria Maggiore, walk away from the church, past Mary on her column, cross the street, and turn right down the small street Via S. Giovanni Gualberto.

CHURCH OF SANTA PRASSEDE

The mosaics at the Church of Santa Prassede, from A.D. 822, are the best Byzantine-style mosaics in Rome. The Byzantine Empire, with its capital in Constantinople (modern Istanbul), was the eastern half of the Roman Empire. Unlike the western half, it didn't "fall," and its inhabitants remained Christian, Greek-speaking, and cultured for a thousand years while their distant cousins in Italy were fumbling for the light switch in the Dark Ages. Byzantine craftsmen preserved the techniques of ancient Roman mosaicists (who decorated floors and walls of villas and public buildings), then reinfused this learning into Rome during the city's darkest era. Take the time to let your eyes adjust, and appreciate the Byzantine glory glowing out of the dark church.

Bring €0.50 and €1 coins to buy floodlighting. (While €1 feels like a lot for five minutes of light, consider it a donation to maintain the church and treat all those visiting to the full sparkle of the mosaics.) Popping a coin into the box in the Chapel of St. Zeno (described below) saves you a trip to Ravenna.

• *The best mosaics are in the apse (behind the main altar) and in the small Chapel of St. Zeno along the right (north) side of the nave.*

Apse Mosaics

On a blue background is Christ, standing in a rainbow-colored river, flanked by saints. Christ has commanded Peter (to our right of Christ, with white hair and beard) to spread the Good News to all the world. Beneath Christ, 12 symbolic sheep leave Jerusalem's city gates to preach to the world. Peter came here to the world's biggest city to preach love...and was met with a hostile environment. He turns his palm up in a plea for help. Persecuted Peter was taken in by a hospitable woman named Pudentia (next to him) and her sister, Praxedes (to the left of Christ, between two other saints), whose house was located on this spot. (The church is named for Praxedes.)

The saint on the far left (to left of Praxedes) is Pope Paschal I, who built the church in the 800s in memory of these early sisters, hiring the best craftsmen in the known world to do the mosaics.

Chapel of St. Zeno

The ceiling is gold, representing the Byzantine heaven. An icon-like Christ emerges from the background, supported by winged angels in white. On the walls are saints walking among patches of flowers. In the altar niche, Mary and the child Jesus are flanked by the sisters Praxedes and Pudentia. On the side wall, the woman with the square blue halo (indicating she was alive at the time this was made) is Theodora, the mom of the pope who built this.

The chapel, covered completely with mosaics, may be underwhelming to our modern eyes, but in the darkness of Rome's medieval era, it was known as the "Garden of Paradise."

SAN CLEMENTE

Here, like nowhere else, you'll enjoy the layers of Rome—a 12th-century basilica sits atop a fourth-century Christian basilica, which sits atop a second-century Mithraic Temple and some even earlier Roman buildings.

The church is on Via di San Giovanni in Laterano (Metro: Colosseo). Bus #85 or #87 connects San Clemente and San Giovanni in Laterano, saving a 10-minute walk.

Upper Church—12th Century

The church (at today's ground level) is dedicated to the fourth pope, Clement, who shepherded the small Christian community when the

religion was, at best, tolerated, and at worst, a capital offense. Clement himself was martyred by drowning in about A.D. 100—tied to an anchor by angry Romans and tossed overboard. You'll see his symbol, the anchor, around the church. The painting on the ceiling shows Clement being carried aloft to heaven.

While today's main entry is on the side, the original entry was through the courtyard in back, a kind of defensive atrium common in medieval times. To reach the original entry, enter the church through today's main entrance, walk diagonally toward the right, and exit again into this courtyard. Turn around and face the original entry. (This courtyard is inviting for a cool quiet break, as I imagine it was for a visiting medieval pilgrim.)

Back inside the church, step up to the carved marble choir—an enclosure in the middle of the church (Schola Cantorum) where the cantors sat. About 1,200 years ago, it stood in the old church beneath us, before that church was looted and destroyed by invading Normans.

In the apse (behind the altar), study the fine 12th-century mosaics. The delicate Crucifixion—with Christ sharing the cross with a dozen apostles as doves—is engulfed by a Tree of Life richly inhabited by deer, birds, and saints. The message is clear: All life springs from God in Christ. Above it all, a triumphant Christ, one hand on the Bible, blesses the congregation.

St. Catherine Chapel

The chapel near the side (tourists') entrance—considered one of the first great Renaissance masterpieces—is dedicated to St. Catherine of Alexandria, a noblewoman martyred for her defense of persecuted Christians. The fresco on the left wall—which shows an early Renaissance three-dimensional representation of space—is by the Florentine master Masolino (1428), perhaps aided by his young assistant, Masaccio. Studying the left wall, working from left to right, you can follow her story:

1. Catherine (lower left panel), in black, confronts an assembly of the pagan Emperor Maxentius and his counselors. She bravely ticks off arguments on her fingers why Christianity should be legalized. Her powerful delivery silences the crowd.

2. Under the rotunda of a pagan temple (above, on the upper left panel), Catherine, in blue, points up at a statue and tells a crowd of pagans, "Your gods are puny compared to mine."

3. Catherine, in blue (upper right panel, left side), is thrown in prison, where she's visited by the emperor's wife (in green). Catherine converts her.

4. Emperor Maxentius, enraged, orders his own wife killed. The executioner (upper panel, right side), standing next to the empress' decapitated corpse, impassively sheathes his sword.

5. In the most well-known scene (the middle panel on the bottom), Maxentius, in black, looks down from a balcony and condemns Catherine (in black) to be torn apart between two large, spiked wheels turned by executioners. But suddenly, an angel swoops in with a sword to cut her loose.

6. Catherine is eventually martyred (lower right panel). Now dressed in green, she kneels before the executioner, who raises his sword to finish the job.

7. Finally, on the top of holy Mount Sinai (lower right panel, upper right side), two angels bear Catherine's body to its final resting place.

Taking a few steps back, look up at the arch that frames the chapel, topped by the delightful Annunciation fresco (top of the arch) by Masolino. Also notice the big St. Christopher, patron saint of travelers (left pillar), with 500-year-old graffiti scratched in by pilgrims.

Lower Church—Fourth Century

Buy a €5 ticket in the bookshop, and descend 1,700 years to the time when Christians were razzed on their way to church by pagan neighbors. The first room you enter was the original atrium (entry hall)—the nave extends to the right. (Everything you'll visit from here on was buried until the 19th century.)

Pagan Inscription
(flippable stone in atrium)

This two-sided, marble, recycled burial slab—one side (with leafy decorations) for a Christian, the other for a pagan (you can turn it)—shows how the two Romes lived side by side in the fourth century.

Fresco of St. Clement and Sisinnius
(in nave, five yards before altar, on left wall)

Clement (center) holds a secret Mass for early Christians back when it was a capital crime. Theodora, a prominent Roman (in yellow, to the right), is one of the undercover faithful. Her pagan husband, Sisinnius, has come to retrieve and punish her when—zap!—he's struck blind and has to be led away (right side).

But Sisinnius is still unconvinced. When Clement cures his blindness, Sisinnius (very faded, lower panel, far right) orders two servants to drag Clement off to the authorities. But through a miraculous intervention, the servants mistake a column for Clement (see the shadowy black log) and drag that out of the house instead. The inscription (crossword-style on right, waist-high, very faded) is famous among Italians because it's one of the earliest examples of the transition from Latin to Italian. Sisinnius encourages his servants by yelling *"Fili dele pute, traite!"* ("You sons of bitches, pull!")

• *In the far left corner of the lower church (in the room behind the fresco you just saw), near the staircase leading down, is the...*

Presumed Burial Place of St. Cyril

Cyril, who died in A.D. 869 (see the modern iconlike mosaic of him), was an inveterate traveler who spread Christianity to the Slavic lands and Russia—today's Russian Orthodox faithful. Along the way, he introduced the Cyrillic alphabet still used by Russians and many other Slavs.

Temple of Mithras (Mithreum)— Second Century

Now descend (through a door immediately to the right of the altar and down steps) farther to the dark, dank Mithraic Temple (Mithreum). Nowhere in Rome is there a better place to experience this weird cult.

Worship Hall (the barred room to the left)

Worshippers of Mithras—men only—reclined on the benches on either side of the room. At the far end is a small statue of the god Mithras, in a billowing cape. In the center sits an altar carved with a relief showing Mithras fighting with a bull that contains all life. A scorpion, a dog, and a snake try to stop Mithras, but he wins, running his sword through the bull (see photo at bottom of page). The blood spills out, bringing life to the world.

Mithras' fans gathered here, in this tiny microcosm of the universe (the ceiling was decorated with stars), to celebrate the victory

with a ritual meal. Every spring, Mithras brought new life again, and so they ritually kept track of the seasons—the four square shafts in the corners of the ceiling represent the seasons, the seven round ones were the great constellations. Initiates went through hazing rituals representing the darkness of this world, then emerged into the light-filled world brought by Mithras.

Rome's official pagan religion had no real spiritual content and did not offer any concept of salvation. As the empire slowly crumbled, people turned more and more to Eastern religions (including Christianity), in search of answers and comfort. The cult of Mithras, stressing loyalty and based on the tenuousness of life, was popular among soldiers. Part of its uniqueness and popularity (in this very class-conscious society) was due to its belief that all were equal before God. It dates back to the time of Alexander the Great, who brought it from Persia. In 67 B.C., soldiers who had survived the bloody conquest of Asia Minor returned to Rome swearing by Mithras. When Christians gained power, they banished the worship of Mithras.

Facing the barred room are two Corinthian columns supporting three arches of the temple's entryway, decorated with a fine stucco, coffered ceiling. At the far end of the hallway, another barred door marks the equivalent of a Mithraic Sunday School room. Peeking inside, see a faded fresco of bearded Mithras (right wall) and seven niches carved into the walls representing the seven stages a novice had to go through. Exit signs direct you down. You'll pass a very narrow ancient alleyway separating Roman walls barely three feet across. Step into this and imagine the first Western city to reach one million. Forget the two churches above you, and imagine standing on this exact spot and looking up at the sky 2,000 years ago. Now climb back through the centuries to today's street level.

SLEEPING

For hassle-free efficiency, I favor accommodations and restaurants handy to your sightseeing activities. Rather than listing hotels scattered throughout Rome, I describe my favorite neighborhoods and recommend the best-value accommodations in each, ranging from hotels to less expensive hostels and convents. (For additional listings, see www.ricksteves.com/andyrome.)

Hotels in Rome are generally pricey, the cheaper hotels can be depressing, and the TI isn't allowed to rate quality. A major feature of this book is its extensive listing of good-value rooms (for more listings, see www.ricksteves.com/andyrome). I like places that are clean, small, central, quiet at night, traditional, inexpensive, and friendly, with firm beds—and those not listed in other guidebooks. In Rome, for me, a hotel with at least six of these attributes is a keeper.

As you look over the listings, you'll notice that many hotels promise special prices to my readers who book direct (without using a room-finding service or hotel-booking website, which take a commission). To get these rates, mention this book when you reserve, then show the book upon arrival. During slow times, rooms might be offered for even less than listed. To get the best price, first ask the price, then request the discount with the book. Many places prefer hard cash. "Rack rates" (the highest rates a hotel charges, usually to travel agencies and Web-booking services) are much higher.

Reserve your hotel room well in advance if you'll be in Rome over a holiday (see list of "Major Holidays and Weekends" on page 4).

TYPES OF ACCOMMODATIONS

Hotels

Double rooms listed in this book will range from about €60 (very simple, toilet and shower down the hall) to €480 (maximum plumbing and more), with most clustering around €150 (with private bathrooms).

and more), with most clustering around €150 (with private bathrooms). I've favored these pricier options, because intense and grinding Rome is easier to enjoy with air-conditioning and a welcoming oasis to call home.

Three or four people economize by sharing larger rooms. Solo travelers find that the cost of a *camera singola* is often only 25 percent less than a *camera doppia*. Most listed hotels have rooms for anywhere from one to five people. If there's room for an extra cot, they'll cram it in for you. English works in all but the cheapest places.

Prices are fairly standard. Shopping around earns you a better location and more character, but rarely a better price. However, prices at many hotels get soft if you do any of the following: offer to pay cash, mention this book, stay at least three nights, and/or arrive late in the day during off-season (roughly mid-July through August and November through mid-March) and haggle. It's common for hotels in Rome to lower their prices 10–35 percent during the off-season, although prices at hostels and the cheaper hotels won't fluctuate much. Room rates are lowest in sweltering August. Unless otherwise indicated, breakfasts are included.

Traffic in Rome roars. With the recent arrival of double-paned windows and air-conditioning, night noise is not the problem it once was. Even so, light sleepers who ask for a *tranquillo* room will likely get a room in the back...and sleep better.

Nearly all places offer private bathrooms. Generally rooms with a bath or shower also have a toilet and a bidet (which Italians use for quick sponge baths). The cord that dangles over the tub or shower is not a clothesline. You pull it when you've fallen and can't get up.

Double beds are called *matrimoniale,* even though hotels aren't interested in your marital status. Twins are *due letti singoli.*

Many hotel rooms have a TV and phone. Rooms in fancier hotels usually come with a small safe, air-conditioning (sometimes you pay an extra per-day charge for this, and often the air-con is turned on only in summer), and a small fridge called a *frigo bar* (FREE-goh bar) stocked with drinks that aren't free.

When you check in, the receptionist will normally ask for your passport and keep it for a couple of hours. Hotels are legally required to register each guest with the local police. Relax. Americans are notorious for making this chore more difficult than it needs to be.

Rooms are safe. Still, zip cameras and keep money out of sight. More pillows and blankets are usually in the closet or available on request. In Italy, towels and linen aren't always replaced every day. Hang your towel up to dry.

Your hotel can point you to the nearest Internet café or launderette; also see page 22.

Most hotels are eager to connect you with a shuttle service to the airport. It's reasonable and easy for departure, but upon arrival, I just catch a cab or the train into the city.

Almost no hotels have parking, but nearly all have a line on spots in a nearby garage (about €24/day).

Bed-and-Breakfasts (B&Bs)

B&Bs offer double the cultural intimacy for a good deal less than most hotel rooms, and help compensate for the low value of the dollar. Roman B&Bs are small—most have no more than three rooms, and the owner generally lives on-site. (Be aware that small hotels sometimes erroneously use the term "B&B.") You'll pay in cash rather than by credit card. Expect few services and no amenities such as public lounges, in-room phones, private bathrooms, and daily bed-sheet changes (though the basics, such as sheets and towels, are provided). After picking up your keys, you can come and go as you wish. When reserving, confirm what kind of breakfast is included—some less-expensive B&Bs simply give you a voucher for a pastry and coffee at a nearby bar.

Doubles with breakfast start at €60, with prices increasing along with the number of amenities. B&B prices are often advertised "per person," making them a good value for singles. Due to the large volume of our readers and the small size of Roman B&Bs, it isn't practical to include many B&B listings here. To find a B&B in Rome, start your search with a website such as www.bedandbreakfast.com or www.b-b.rm.it. You'll get better prices, however, by booking directly with the B&B. These websites connect you directly with the B&B owner: www.romanrooms.com, www.wheninromeaccommodation .com, and www.gulliversplace.com (see listing on page 281).

Convents

Although I list only four, Rome has many convents that rent out rooms. See the Church of Santa Susanna's website for a long list (www.santa susanna.org, select "Coming to Rome"). At convents, the beds are twins and English is often in short supply, but the price is right.

Consider these nun-run places, all listed in this chapter: the expensive but divine **Casa di Santa Brigida** (near Campo de' Fiori), the **Suore di Santa Elisabetta** (near Santa Maria Maggiore), the **Istituto Il Rosario** (near Piazza Venezia), and the most user-friendly of all, **Casa per Ferie Santa Maria alle Fornaci dei Padri Trinitari** (near the Vatican).

Hostels and Dorms

For easy communication with young, friendly entrepreneurs, €20 dorm beds, and some inexpensive doubles—within a 10-minute hike of the Termini train station—consider the following places (see pages 281–282 for descriptions): **The Beehive** (with the best €70 doubles in town, two blocks from train station) and **Casa Olmata** (near Santa Maria Maggiore). Check www.backpackers.it for more listings.

Apartments

Many locals rent out their apartments in downtown Rome, a great value for families or multiple couples traveling together. Rentals are generally by the week, with prices around €120 per day. Apartments typically offer a couple of bedrooms, a sitting area, and a teensy *cucinetta* (kitchenette), usually stocked with dishes and flatware. After you check in, you're basically on your own. While you won't have a doorman to carry your bags or a maid to clean your room each day, you will get an inside peek at a Roman home, and you can save lots of money—especially if you take advantage of the cooking facilities—with no loss of comfort. Most places are rented through booking agencies, the TI, or websites. Browse through www.craigslist.org (select "Rome," then "Vacation Rentals") and www.wantedinrom.com (select "Housing," then "Short Lets"). Steve and Linda of The Beehive also run a booking service for private rooms and apartments in the old centers of Rome, Florence, and Venice; rates start at €30 per person (see listing on page 282, www.cross-pollinate.com).

PRACTICALITIES

Phoning

To call Italy from the US or Canada, dial 011-39 (the country code) and then the local number. If calling Italy from another European country, dial 00-39-local number. For more tips on calling, see page 386.

Making Reservations

Given the quality of the gems I've found for this book, I'd recommend that you reserve your rooms in advance, particularly if you'll be traveling during peak season. Book several weeks ahead, or as soon as you've pinned down your travel dates. Note that some national holidays jam things up and merit your making reservations far in advance (see "Major Holidays and Weekends" on page 4).

To make a reservation, contact hotels directly by email, phone, or fax. Don't use a website unless it is the hotel's official site—otherwise you may pay higher rates than you should (and you won't be able to ask for the Rick Steves discount).

The recommended hotels are accustomed to English-only travelers. Email is the clearest and most economical way to make a reservation. If phoning from the US, be mindful of time zones (see page 7). To ensure you have all the information you need for your reservation, use the form in this book's appendix (also at www.ricksteves.com/reservation). If you don't get a reply to your email or fax, it usually means the hotel is already fully booked.

When you request a room for a certain time period, use the European style for writing dates: day/month/year. Hoteliers need to know your arrival and departure dates. For example, a two-night stay in July would be "2 nights, 16/07/09 to 18/07/09." Consider in advance

Sleep Code

(€1 = about $1.50)

To help you easily sort through these listings, I've divided the rooms into three categories based on the price for a standard double room with bath:

$$$ **Higher Priced**—Most rooms €200 or more.

$$ **Moderately Priced**—Most rooms between €130-200.

$ **Lower Priced**—Most rooms €130 or less.

To give maximum information in a minimum of space, I use the following code to describe accommodations. Prices listed are per room, not per person. Unless I note otherwise, the staff speaks English and breakfast is included. You can assume a hotel takes credit cards unless you see "cash only" in the listing.

S = Single room (or price for one person in a double).

D = Double or Twin room. "Double beds" are often two twins sheeted together and are usually big enough for nonromantic couples.

T = Triple (generally a double bed with a single).

Q = Quad (usually two double beds).

b = Private bathroom with toilet and shower or tub.

s = Private shower or tub only (toilet is down the hall).

According to this code, a couple staying at a "Db-€140" hotel would pay a total of €140 (about $210) for a double room with a private bathroom.

how long you'll stay; don't just assume you can extend your reservation for extra days once you arrive.

If the response from the hotel gives its room availability and rates, it's not a confirmation. You must tell them that you want that room at the given rate.

The hotelier will sometimes request your credit card number for a one-night deposit. While you can email your credit card information (I do), it's safer to share that personal info via phone, fax, or secure online reservation form (if the hotel has one on its website).

If you must cancel your reservation, it's courteous to do so with as much advance notice as possible (simply make a quick phone call or send an email). Hotels, which are often family-run, lose money if they turn away customers while holding a room for someone who doesn't show up. Understandably, some hotels bill no-shows for one night. Hotels sometimes have strict cancellation policies (for example, you might lose a deposit if you cancel within two weeks of your reserved stay, or you might be billed for the entire visit if you leave early); ask about cancellation policies before you book.

Always reconfirm your room reservation a few days in advance from the road. If you'll be arriving after 17:00, let them know. Don't have the tourist office reconfirm rooms for you; they'll take a commission.

On the small chance that a hotel loses track of your reservation, bring along a hard copy of their emailed or faxed confirmation.

ACCOMMODATIONS IN ROME

Near Termini Train Station

While not as atmospheric as other areas of Rome, the hotels near Termini train station are less expensive, restaurants are plentiful, and the many public-transportation options link it easily with the entire city. The city's two Metro lines intersect at the station, and most buses leave from here. Piazza Venezia is a 20-minute walk down Via Nazionale.

Via Firenze

Via Firenze is safe, handy, central, and relatively quiet. It's a 10-minute walk from Termini train station and the airport shuttle, and two blocks beyond Piazza della Repubblica and the TI. The Defense Ministry is nearby, so you've got heavily armed guards watching over you all night.

Getting Around: The neighborhood is well-connected by public transportation (with the Repubblica Metro stop nearby). Virtually all the city buses that rumble down Via Nazionale (#64, #70, #115, #640, and the #40 express) take you to Piazza Venezia (Forum) and Largo Argentina (Pantheon). From Largo Argentina, the #64 bus (jammed with people and thieves) and the #40 express bus both continue to the Vatican. Or, at Largo Argentina, you can transfer to electric trolley #8 to Trastevere (get off at first stop after crossing the river).

Services: Phone and Internet Center is a cute little hole-in-the-wall within a block or so of several recommended hotels that's handy for getting online (€2/hr, daily 8:30–22:00, Via Modena 48, tel. 06-4890-5224). To stock your closet pantry, the **Despar Supermarket** is handy (daily 8:00–21:00, Via Nazionale 211, at the corner of Via Venezia). A 24-hour **pharmacy** near the recommended hotels is Farmacia Piram (Via Nazionale 228, tel. 06-488-4437).

$$ Hotel Oceania is a peaceful slice of air-conditioned heaven. This 19-room, manor house–type hotel is spacious and quiet, with spotless, tastefully decorated rooms, run by a pleasant father-and-son team. While Armando (the dad) serves world-famous coffee, Stefano (the son) works to maintain a caring family atmosphere with a fine staff and provides lots of thoughtful extra touches (Sb-€125, Db-€158, Tb-€190, Qb-€212, these prices good through 2009 with this book and cash, large roof terrace, family suite, Internet access, videos in the

TV lounge, Via Firenze 38, third floor, tel. 06-482-4696, fax 06-488-5586, www.hoteloceania.it, info@hoteloceania.it; Anna and Radu round out the staff).

$$ Hotel Aberdeen, which perfectly combines high quality and friendliness, is warmly run by Annamaria, with support from cousins Sabrina and Cinzia and sister Laura. The 37 comfy, modern, air-conditioned rooms are a terrific value. Enjoy the frescoed breakfast room (Sb-€102, Db-€160, Tb-€170, Qb-€200, check website for deals,  Via Firenze 48, tel. 06-482-3920, fax 06-482-1092, www.hotelaberdeen.it, hotel.aberdeen@travel.it).

$$ Residenza Cellini is a gorgeous 11-room place that feels like the guest wing of a Neoclassical palace. It offers "ortho/anti-allergy beds," four-star comforts and service, and a breezy breakfast terrace (Db-€175, larger Db-€195, Tb-€200–220, prices good through 2009 with this book and cash, air-con, elevator, Internet access, Via Modena 5, tel. 06-4782-5204, fax 06-4788-1806, www.residenzacellini.it, residenzacellini@tin.it; Barbara, Gaetano, and Donato).

$$ Residence Adler, which will serve you breakfast on its garden patio, has wide halls and eight quiet, simple, air-conditioned rooms in a good location (plus more rooms in their slightly pricier Bellesuite wing). It's run the old-fashioned way by a charming family (Db-€130, Tb-€170, Qb-€195, Quint/b-€220, these prices good through 2009 with this book, additional 5 percent off with cash, elevator, Internet access, Via Modena 5, second floor, tel. 06-484-466, fax 06-488-0940, www.hoteladler-roma.com, info@hoteladler-roma.com, Alessandro).

$ Hotel Nardizzi Americana, with 33 pleasant, air-conditioned rooms and a delightful rooftop terrace, is an excellent value (Sb-€95, Db-€123, Tb-€155, Qb-€175, email them for instructions on getting these special Rick Steves rates in 2009, 15 percent discount for stays of 5 days or more, additional 10 percent off any time with cash, elevator, Internet access, Via Firenze 38, fourth floor, tel. 06-488-0035, fax 06-488-0368, www.hotelnardizzi.it, info@hotelnardizzi.it, Stefano, Fabrizio, Mario, and Samy).

Between Via Nazionale and Santa Maria Maggiore

$$ Hotel Opera Roma, brand-spanking new with contemporary furnishings and marble accents, boasts 15 fresh, spacious, but somewhat dark rooms. It's located a stone's throw from the Opera House (Db-€165, Tb-€190, these prices good through 2009 with this book,

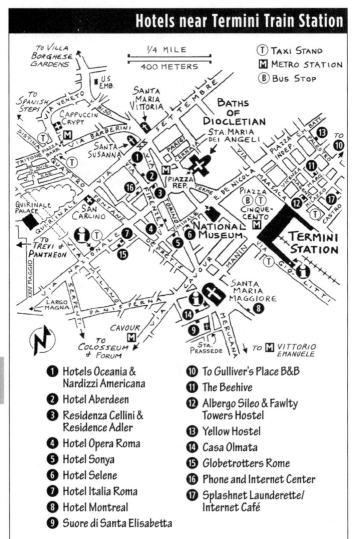

Hotels near Termini Train Station

- (T) TAXI STAND
- (M) METRO STATION
- (B) BUS STOP

1/4 MILE
400 METERS

1 Hotels Oceania & Nardizzi Americana

2 Hotel Aberdeen

3 Residenza Cellini & Residence Adler

4 Hotel Opera Roma

5 Hotel Sonya

6 Hotel Selene

7 Hotel Italia Roma

8 Hotel Montreal

9 Suore di Santa Elisabetta

10 To Gulliver's Place B&B

11 The Beehive

12 Albergo Sileo & Fawlty Towers Hostel

13 Yellow Hostel

14 Casa Olmata

15 Globetrotters Rome

16 Phone and Internet Center

17 Splashnet Launderette/ Internet Café

air-con, elevator, Internet access, Via Firenze 11, www.hotelopera roma.it, info@hoteloperaroma.it, tel. 06-487-1787, Rezza).

$$ Hotel Sonya is small and family-run but impersonal, with 23 well-equipped rooms, a central location, and decent prices (Sb-€90, Db-€140, Tb-€160, Qb-€180, Quint/b-€195, 5 percent discount in 2009 with this book and cash, air-con, elevator, faces the opera at Via Viminale 58, Metro: Repubblica or Termini, tel. 06-481-9911, fax 06-488-5678, www.hotelsonya.it, info@hotelsonya.it, Francesca and Ivan).

$$ Hotel Selene spreads its rooms out on a few floors of a big palazzo. With elegant tapestry details and room to breathe, its 40 rooms are a great value (Db-€135, Tb-€155, these prices good through 2009 with this book, air-con, elevator, Via del Viminale 8, tel. 06-482-4460, www.hotelseleneroma.it, reception@hotelseleneroma.it, Federico).

$ Hotel Italia Roma, in a busy, interesting, and handy locale, is placed safely on a quiet street next to the Ministry of the Interior. Thoughtfully run by Andrea, Sabrina, Nadine, and Gabriel, it has 31 comfortable, clean, and bright rooms (Sb-€80, Db-€120, Tb-€160, Qb-€180, air-con—€10 extra per day, elevator, Internet access, Via Venezia 18, just off Via Nazionale, Metro: Repubblica or Termini, tel. 06-482-8355, fax 06-474-5550, www.hotelitaliaroma.it, info@hotel italiaroma.it). While you must secure your reservation with a credit card, they accept only cash for payment. They also have eight decent annex rooms across the street.

$ Hotel Montreal, run with care, is a bright, solid, business-class place with 27 rooms on a big street a block southeast of Santa Maria Maggiore (Sb-€95, Db-€120, Tb-€150, these prices good through 2009 with this book, air-con, elevator, Internet access, communal garden terrace, good security, Via Carlo Alberto 4, 1 block from Metro: Vittorio Emanuele, 3 blocks west of Termini train station, tel. 06-445-7797, fax 06-446-5522, www.hotelmontrealroma.com, info @hotelmontrealroma.com, Pasquale).

$ Suore di Santa Elisabetta is a heavenly Polish-run convent with a peaceful garden and tidy twin-bedded (only) rooms. Often booked long in advance, with such tranquility, it's a super value (S-€40, Sb-€48, D-€66, Db-€85, Tb-€106, Qb-€128, Quint/b-€142, elevator, fine view roof terrace and breakfast hall, 23:00 curfew, a block southwest of Santa Maria Maggiore at Via dell'Olmata 9, Metro: Termini or Vittorio Emanuele, tel. 06-488-8271, fax 06-488-4066, ist.it.s.elisabetta@libero.it, Anna).

$ Gulliver's Place B&B has five fun, nicely decorated rooms in a large, secure building next to the university (D-€90, Db-€100, Tb-€130, less off-season, air-con, elevator, east of Termini train station, 100 yards from Metro: Castro Pretorio at Viale Castro Pretorio 25, tel. 06-4470-4012, mobile 393-917-3040, www.gulliversplace.com, stay @gulliversplace.com, Simon and Sara). They run another B&B on Via Cavour (Db-€115). Their prices at both places are good through 2009 if you show this book.

Sleeping Cheaply, Northeast of the Train Station

The cheapest beds in town are northeast of the Termini train station (Metro: Termini). Some travelers feel this area is weird and spooky after dark, but these hotels feel plenty safe. With your back to the train tracks, turn right and walk two blocks out of the station. **Splashnet** launderette/Internet café is handy if you're staying in this area (just off Via Milazzo at Via Varese 33, €6 full-serve wash and dry, Internet access-€1.50/hr, €2 luggage storage per day—or free if you wash and go online, daily 8:30–24:00, mobile 3906-4938-0450).

$ The Beehive gives vagabonds—old and young—a cheap, clean, and comfy home in Rome, thoughtfully and creatively run by a friendly young American couple, Steve and Linda. They offer six great-value, artsy-mod double rooms (D-€80) and an eight-bed dorm (€25 bunks, Internet access, private garden terrace, cheery café, 2 blocks north of Termini train station at Via Marghera 8, tel. 06-4470-4553, www .the-beehive.com, info@the-beehive.com).

$ Albergo Sileo, with shiny chandeliers in dim rooms, has a contract to house train conductors who work the night shift—so its two single rooms are rentable only from 19:00 to 9:00. The rest of their rooms are available any time of day (D-€55, Db with air-con-€75, Tb-€75, elevator, Via Magenta 39, fourth floor, tel. & fax 06-445-0246, www.hotelsileo.com, info@hotelsileo.com; friendly Alessandro and Maria Savioli don't speak English, but their daughter Anna does).

Hostels and Backpacker Dorm Beds near the Station

$ Yellow Hostel rents 130 beds in 4-, 6-, and 12-bed co-ed dorms ranging from about €24 to €34 per bed, depending on plumbing, size, and season. It's well-run with fine facilities, including lockers (reserve via email—no telephone reservations accepted, no breakfast, laptop rental available, 6 blocks from the station, just past Via Vicenze at Via Palestro 44, tel. 06-493-82682, www.the-yellow.com).

$ Casa Olmata is a homey, ramshackle, laid-back backpack-ers' haven with 50 beds a block southwest of Santa Maria Maggiore, midway between Termini train station and the Colosseum (dorm beds-€22, S-€38, D-€57, Qb-€100, sack breakfast, elevator, commu-nal kitchen, rooftop terrace with views and twice-weekly spaghetti parties, Via dell'Olmata 36, tel. 06-483-019, fax 06-486-819, www .casaolmata.com, info@casaolmata.com, Mirella and Marco).

$ Globetrotters Rome is a fun little hostel in a safe and handy location. Its 22 beds in cramped quarters work fine for backpackers (€20 per bunk in 8-bed dorm, €22 per bunk in 6-bed dorm, lockers, air-con, small kitchen, closed 12:00–15:00, Via Palermo 36, tel. 06-481-7680, info@backpackers.it).

$ Fawlty Towers Hostel is well-run and ideal for backpackers arriving by train. It offers 50 beds and lots of fun, games, and extras (4-bed dorms-€24 per person, S-€55, D-€65, Db-€80, Q-€90, includes sheets, from station walk a block down Via Marghera and turn right to Via Magenta 39, tel. & fax 06-445-0374, www.fawltytowers.org, info@fawltytowers.org). Their nearby annex, **Bubbles,** offers similar beds and rates and shares the same reception desk.

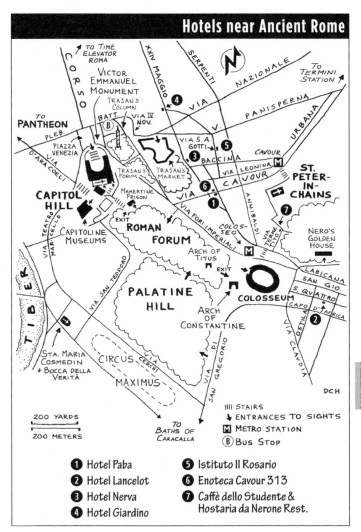

Hotels near Ancient Rome

TO TIME ELEVATOR ROMA
VICTOR EMMANUEL MONUMENT
TRAJAN'S COLUMN
TO PANTHEON
PLEB.
PIAZZA VENEZIA
BATT.
VIA IV NOV.
VIA S.A. GOTTI
BACCINA
CORSO
XXIV MAGGIO
SERPENTI
NAZIONALE
TO TERMINI STATION
VIA
PANISPERNA
URBANA
CAVOUR
VIA LEONINA
ST. PETER-IN-CHAINS
TRAJAN'S FORUM
TRAJAN'S MARKET
VIA CAVOUR
CAPITOL HILL
TEATRO MARCELLO
CAPITOLINE MUSEUMS
MAMERTINE PRISON
EXIT
ROMAN FORUM
VIA FORI IMPERIALI
COLOSSEO
ANNIBALDI
VIA TERME TITO
NERO'S GOLDEN HOUSE
ARCH OF TITUS
EXIT
TIBER
VIA SAN TEODORO
PALATINE HILL
ARCH OF CONSTANTINE
COLOSSEUM
LABICANA
SAN GIO.
S. QUATTRO
CAPO D'AFRICA
VIA CLAUDIA
STA. MARIA COSMEDIN + BOCCA DELLA VERITÀ
CIRCUS MAXIMUS
VIA DI CERCHI
SAN GREGORIO
VIA DI
D'ARA COELI
VIA
TO BATHS OF CARACALLA

200 YARDS
200 METERS

IIII STAIRS
↓ ENTRANCES TO SIGHTS
Ⓜ METRO STATION
Ⓑ BUS STOP

DCH

❶ Hotel Paba
❷ Hotel Lancelot
❸ Hotel Nerva
❹ Hotel Giardino
❺ Istituto Il Rosario
❻ Enoteca Cavour 313
❼ Caffè dello Studente & Hostaria da Nerone Rest.

Near Ancient Rome

Stretching from the Colosseum to Piazza Venezia along the barren boulevard called Via dei Fori Imperiali, this area is central. Sightseers are a short walk from the Colosseum, Roman Forum, and Trajan's Column. Busy Piazza Venezia—the geographical center of the city—is a major hub for city buses.

Near the Colosseum

$$ Hotel Paba has seven fresh rooms, chocolate-box-tidy and lovingly cared for by Alberta Castelli. Though it overlooks busy Via Cavour just two blocks from the Colosseum, it's quiet enough (Db-€135, extra bed-€40, 5 percent cash discount, huge beds, breakfast served in room, air-con, elevator, Via Cavour 266, Metro: Cavour, tel. 06-4782-4902, fax 06-4788-1225, www.hotelpaba.com, info@hotelpaba.com).

$$ Hotel Lancelot is a homey yet elegant refuge—a 60-room hotel with the ambience of a B&B. It's quiet and safe, with a shady courtyard, restaurant, bar, and tiny communal sixth-floor terrace. Well-run by Faris and Lubna Khan, it's popular with returning guests (Sb-€115, Db-€180, Tb-€200, Qb-€240, €10 extra for first-floor terrace room, €15 extra for sixth-floor room with big terrace, air-con, elevator, wheelchair-accessible, parking-€10/day, 10-min walk behind Colosseum near San Clemente Church at Via Capo d'Africa 47, tel. 06-7045-0615, fax 06-7045-0640, www.lancelot hotel.com, info@lancelothotel.com, Lubna speaks the Queen's English).

Near Piazza Venezia

To locate these hotels, see the map on page 283.

$$$ Hotel Nerva is a three-star slice of tranquility on a surprisingly quiet back street just steps away from the Roman Forum. Its 19 rooms come with elegant touches—yours may have exposed-beam ceilings, a balcony, or floor-to-ceiling windows. It's run by brothers Umberto and Amelio, with the help of daughter Anna (Sb-€150, Db-€180, Qb with loft-€350, extra bed-€45, ask for Rick Steves discount, rates very soft—especially off-season, they also have three rooms in a nearby apartment for the same prices, big breakfast, air-con, elevator, Via Tor de' Conti 3, tel. 06-678-1835, fax 06-6992-2204, www.hotel nerva.com, info@hotelnerva.com).

$$ Hotel Giardino, thoughtfully run by kind Englishwoman Kate, offers 11 pleasant rooms in a central location three blocks northeast of Piazza Venezia. With a tiny central lobby and a small breakfast room, it suits travelers who prize location over big-hotel amenities (March–mid-July and Sept–mid-Nov: Sb-€85, Db-€130; mid-July–Aug and mid-Nov–Feb: Sb-€60, Db-€90, one smaller Db for 15 percent less; these prices good through 2009 with this book and cash, check website for specials, air-con, effective double-paned windows, on a busy street off Piazza di Quirinale at Via XXIV Maggio 51, tel. 06-679-4584, fax 06-679-5155, www.hotel-giardino-roma.com, info @hotel-giardino-roma.com).

$ Istituto Il Rosario is a peaceful, well-run Dominican convent renting 40 rooms to both pilgrims and tourists in a good neighborhood (reserve several months in advance, S-€42, Sb-€54, Db-€92, Tb-€122, roof terrace, 23:00 curfew, midway between the Quirinale and Colosseum near bottom of Via Nazionale at Via Sant'Agata dei Goti 10, bus #40 or #170 from Termini, tel. 06-679-2346, fax 06-6994-1106, irodopre@tin.it).

In the Pantheon Neighborhood
(The Heart of Rome)

Winding, narrow lanes filled with foot traffic and lined with boutique shops and tiny trattorias...this is village Rome at its best. You'll pay for the atmosphere, but this is where you want to be—especially at night, when Romans and tourists gather in the floodlit piazzas for the evening stroll, the *passeggiata*.

Near Campo de' Fiori

You'll pay a premium (and endure a little extra night noise) to stay in the old center. But each of these places is romantically set deep in the tangled back streets near the idyllic Campo de' Fiori and, for many, worth the extra money.

$$$ Casa di Santa Brigida overlooks the elegant Piazza Farnese. With soft-spoken sisters gliding down polished hallways and pearly gates instead of doors, this lavish 20-room convent makes exhaust-stained Roman tourists feel like they've died and gone to heaven. If you don't need a double bed, it's worth the splurge (Sb-€110, twin Db-€190, 3 percent extra if you pay with credit card, can pay with personal check for no extra charge, air-con, elevator, Internet access, tasty €25 dinners, roof garden, plush library, Monserrato 54, tel. 06-6889-2596, fax 06-6889-1573, piazzafarnese@brigidine.org, many of the sisters are from India and speak English). If you get no response to your fax or email within three days, consider that a "no."

$$ Hotel Smeraldo, with 50 rooms, is strictly run, clean, and a great deal (Sb-€100, Db-€130, Tb-€150, buffet breakfast-€7, centrally controlled air-con, elevator, flowery roof terrace, midway between Campo de' Fiori and Largo Argentina at Vicolo dei Chiodaroli 9, tel. 06-687-5929, fax 06-6880-5495, www.smeraldoroma.com, albergo smeraldoroma@tin.it, Massimo). Their **Dipendenza Smeraldo,** 10 yards around the corner at Via dei Chiavari 32, is more bare and basic, and €10 less per night (same contact info).

In the Jewish Ghetto

To locate this hotel, see map on page 286.

$$ Hotel Arenula, with 50 decent rooms, is the only hotel in Rome's old Jewish ghetto. While it has the ambience of a gym and attracts lots of students, it's a good value in the thick of old Rome (Sb-€95, Db-€130, 5 percent off with this book in high season of 2009, extra bed-€21, air-con, just off Via Arenula at Via Santa Maria de' Calderari 47, tel. 06-687-9454, fax 06-689-6188, www.hotelarenula.com, info@hotelarenula.com, Rosanna).

Near the Pantheon

These places are buried in the pedestrian-friendly heart of ancient Rome, each within a four-minute walk of the Pantheon. You'll pay

Hotels in the Heart of Rome

TO PIAZZA
DEL POPOLO

TO SPANISH STEPS

TO M BARB.

PONTE UMBERTO

TIBER

LUNGOTEVERE MARZIO

BRIANEO

ANCIENT STADIUM ENTRANCE
CORONARI

❼

SAN LUIGI (CARAVAGGIO)

PIAZZA COLONNA

GIOLITTI

PARL.

UFF. VIC

❺

T

TRITONE

VIA

T

TREVI

DATARIA

P. QUIRINALE

VIA QUIRINALE

PIAZZA NAVONA

PIAZZA PASQUINO

CITY MUSEUM

T

SALV.

GIUST.

AQUIRO

PIETRA

PIAZZA ROTUNDA

SEMINARIO

SABINA

MURATTE

SAN IGNAZIO

PANTHEON

❻

STA. MARIA SOPRA MINERVA

GALLERIA DORA PAMPHILJ

IV NOV.

CAMPO DE' FIORI

❶

VITTORIO

CHIAVARI

V. M. FARINA

GIUBBO.

NARI

EMANUELE

B T

ARG

CESTARI

GESÙ

PIAZZA VENEZIA

T

FORI IMPERIALI

TO COLOSSEUM

M

❸

V. BOTT. OSC.

ARENULA

LARGO ARGENTINA RUINS (+ CAT HOSPICE)

V.E. MON.

CAPITOL HILL

PALAZZO FARNESE

❷

DCH

MARCELLO

❹

GHETTO

FORUM

LUNGOTEVERE SITO

PONTE

TO TRASTEVERE

200 YARDS
200 METERS

N

Ⓣ - TAXI STAND
Ⓜ - METRO STATION
Ⓑ - BUS STOP

❶ Casa di Santa Brigida
❷ Hotel Smeraldo
❸ Dipendenza Smeraldo
❹ Hotel Arenula

❺ Hotel Nazionale
❻ Albergo Santa Chiara
❼ Hotel Due Torri

more here—but you'll save time and money by being exactly where you want to be for your early and late wandering.

$$$ Hotel Nazionale, a four-star landmark, is a 16th-century palace that shares a well-policed square with the Parliament building. Its 92 rooms are accentuated by lush public spaces, fancy bars, a uniformed staff, and a marble-floored restaurant. It's a big, stuffy hotel with a revolving front door, but it's a worthy splurge if you want security, comfort, and ancient Rome at your doorstep (Sb-€200, Db-€350, giant deluxe Db-€480, extra person-€70, ask for 10 percent Rick Steves discount in 2009; check online for summer and weekend discounts; air-con, elevator, Piazza Montecitorio 131, tel. 06-695-001, fax 06-678-6677, www.hotelnazionale.it, info@hotelnazionale.it).

$$$ Albergo Santa Chiara is big, solid, and hotelesque. Flavia, Silvio, and their fine staff offer marbled elegance (but basic furniture) and all the hotel services in the old center. Its ample public lounges are dressy and professional, and its 99 rooms are quiet and spacious (Sb-€140, Db-€217, Tb-€262, book online direct and request these special Rick Steves rates, check website for better slow-time deals, elevator, behind Pantheon at Via di Santa Chiara 21, tel. 06-687-2979, fax 06-687-3144, www.albergosantachiara.com, info @albergosantachiara.com).

$$$ Hotel Due Torri, hiding out on a tiny, quiet street, is a beautifully located, high-class affair. It feels professional yet homey, with an accommodating staff, generous public spaces, and 26 comfortable rooms scattered by a higgledy-piggledy floor plan (Sb-€120, Db-€200, family apartment-€255 for 3 and €280 for 4, air-con, Internet access, elevator, a block off Via della Scrofa at Vicolo del Leonetto 23, tel. 06-6880-6956, fax 06-686-5442, www.hotelduetorriroma.com, hotelduetorri@mclink.it, Cinzia).

In Trastevere

Colorful and genuine in a gritty sort of way, Trastevere is a treat for travelers looking for a less touristy and more bohemian atmosphere. Choices are few here, but by trekking across the Tiber, you can have the experience of being comfortably immersed in old Rome. To locate the following two places, see the map on page 88.

$$$ Hotel Santa Maria sits like a lazy hacienda in the midst of Trastevere. Surrounded by a medieval skyline, you'll feel as if you're on some romantic stage set. Its 19 small but well-equipped, air-conditioned rooms—former cells in a cloister—are all on the ground floor, as are a few suites for up to six people. The rooms circle a gravelly courtyard of orange trees and stay-awhile patio furniture (Db-€180, Tb-€220; prices good through 2009 with this book, cash, and minimum stay of three nights; family rooms, free loaner bikes and Internet access, face church on Piazza Maria Trastevere and go right down Via della Fonte d'Olio 50 yards to Vicolo del Piede 2, tel. 06-589-4626, fax 06-589-4815, www.htlsantamaria.com, hotelsantamaria@libero .it, Stefano). Some rooms come with family-friendly fold-down bunks for €30 extra per person. Their freshly renovated, six-room **Residenza Santa Maria** is a couple of blocks away (same prices and contact info).

$$ Casa San Giuseppe is down a characteristic, laundry-strewn lane with views of Aurelian walls. While convent-owned, it's a secular place renting 29 plain but peaceful, spacious, and spotless rooms (Sb-€110, Db-€150, Tb-€180, Qb-€210, garden-facing rooms are quiet, air-con, elevator, parking-€15, just north of Piazza Trilussa at Vicolo Moroni 22, tel. 06-5833-3490, fax 06-5833-5754, info@casasan giuseppe.it, Germano).

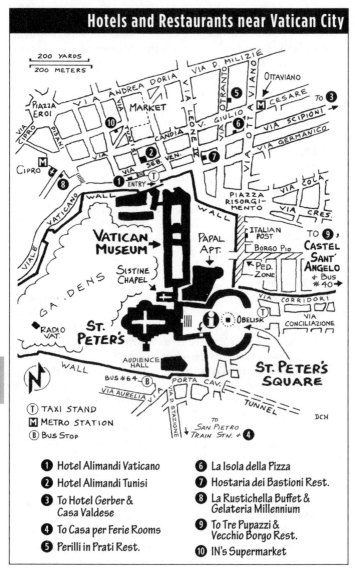

Hotels and Restaurants near Vatican City

1 Hotel Alimandi Vaticano
2 Hotel Alimandi Tunisi
3 To Hotel Gerber &
   Casa Valdese
4 To Casa per Ferie Rooms
5 Perilli in Prati Rest.

6 La Isola della Pizza
7 Hostaria dei Bastioni Rest.
8 La Rustichella Buffet &
   Gelateria Millennium
9 To Tre Pupazzi &
   Vecchio Borgo Rest.
10 IN's Supermarket

Near Vatican City

Sleeping near the Vatican is expensive, but some enjoy calling this neighborhood home. Even though it's handy to the Vatican (when the rapture hits, you're right there), everything else is a long ways away. The first two hotels listed here offer free airport transfers for guests, though you must reserve when you book your room and wait for a scheduled shuttle (every two hours).

$$$ Hotel Alimandi Vaticano, facing the Vatican Museum, is beautifully designed. Run by the Alimandi family (Enrico, Irene, Germano), it features four stars, 24 spacious rooms, and all the modern comforts you can imagine (Sb-€170, standard Db-€200, big Db with 2 double beds-€260, Tb-€280, 5 percent discount if you pay cash, air-con, elevator, Viale Vaticano 99, Metro: Cipro, tel. 06-397-45562, fax 06-397-30132, www.alimandi.it, alimandi@hotelalimandie.191.it).

$$ Hotel Alimandi Tunisi is a good value, run by other members of the friendly and entrepreneurial Alimandi family—Paolo, Grazia, Luigi, Marta, and Barbara. Their 35 perfumed rooms are air-conditioned, modern, and marbled in white (Sb-€90, Db-€175, 5 percent cash discount, elevator, grand buffet breakfast served in great roof garden, small gym, pool table, piano lounge, down the stairs directly in front of Vatican Museum, Via Tunisi 8, Metro: Cipro, reserve by phone at tel. 06-3972-3941, toll-free in Italy tel. 800-122-121, fax 06-3972-3943, www.alimandi.it, alimandi@tin.it).

$$ Hotel Gerber, set in a quiet residential area, is family-run with 27 businesslike, air-conditioned rooms (two S without air-con-€60, Sb-€120, Db-€160, Tb-€180, Qb-€190; 10 percent discount in 2009 with this book in high-season, 15 percent in low-season, Via degli Scipioni 241, at intersection with Ezio, a block from Metro: Lepanto, tel. 06-321-6485, fax 06-321-7048, www.hotelgerber .it, info@hotelgerber.it; Peter and Simonetta).

$ Casa Valdese is an efficient church-run hotel just over the Tiber River and near the Vatican, with 35 big, quiet, and well-run rooms. It feels safe if a bit institutional, with the bonus of two breezy, communal roof terraces with incredible views (two external Sb-€50, Db-€120, €10/night less for 3-night stays, Internet access, 100 yards from Lepanto Metro station, just off Viale Pompeo Magno at Via Alessandro Farnese 18, tel. 06-321-5362, fax 06-321-1843, www.casa valdeseroma.it, reception@casavaldeseroma.it).

$ Casa per Ferie Santa Maria alle Fornaci dei Padri Trinitari houses pilgrims and secular tourists with simple class just a short walk south of the Vatican in 54 stark, identical, utilitarian, mostly twin-bedded rooms. This is the most user-friendly convent-type place I've found. Reserve at least three months in advance (Sb-€70, Db-€95, Tb-€130, air-con, elevator; take bus #64 from Termini train station to San Pietro train station, then walk 100 yards north along Via della Stazione di San Pietro to Piazza Santa Maria alle Fornaci 27; tel. 06-393-67632, fax 06-393-66795, www.trinitaridematha.it, cffornaci@tin.it).

EATING

The Italians are masters of the art of fine living. That means eating... long and well. Lengthy, multi-course lunches and dinners and endless hours sitting in outdoor cafés are the norm. Americans eat on their way to an evening event and complain if the check is slow in coming. For Italians, the meal is an end in itself, and only rude waiters rush you. When you want the bill, mime-scribble on your raised palm or ask for it: *"Il conto?"*

Even those of us who liked dorm food will find that the local cafés, cuisine, and wines become a highlight of our Italian adventure. Trust me: This is sightseeing for your palate, and even if the rest of you is sleeping in cheap hotels, your taste buds will relish an occasional first-class splurge. You can eat well without going broke. But be careful: You're just as likely to blow a small fortune on a disappointing meal as you are to dine wonderfully for €20.

Restaurants

When restaurant-hunting, choose places filled with locals, not the place with the big neon signs boasting, "We speak English and accept credit cards." Restaurants parked on famous squares generally serve bad food at high prices to tourists. Locals eat better at lower-rent locales. Family-run places operate without hired help and can offer cheaper meals.

The word *osteria* (traditionally a simple, local-style restaurant) stokes my appetite. For unexciting but basic values, look for a *menù turistico,* a three- or four-course, set-price menu. Galloping gourmets order à la carte with the help of a menu translator. (*The Marling Italian Menu-Master* is excellent. *Rick Steves' Italian Phrase Book & Dictionary* has a menu decoder with enough phrases for intermediate eaters.) When going to an especially good restaurant with an approachable staff, my favorite strategy is to simply say, "Make me happy" (in this case, it's just fine to set a price limit).

Tipping

Tipping is an issue only at restaurants that have waiters and waitresses. If you order your food at a counter, don't tip. (Many Italians don't ever tip.)

In Italy, the service charge *(servizio)* is usually included and figured at 10 or 15 percent of your total bill. There's no need to tip beyond that. If service is included, the prices listed in the menu will either have this charge built in (the menu will say *servizio incluso*) or the service might show up as a separate line item at the end of your bill. (In this case, the menu might say *servizio non incluso*.) Fixed-price tourist deals include service.

If service is not included, you could tip 5-10 percent by rounding up or leaving the change from your bill. Leave the tip on the table, or hand it to your server. It's best to tip in cash, even if you pay with your credit card; otherwise, the tip may never reach your server.

A full meal consists of an appetizer (antipasto, €3–6), a first course (*primo piatto,* pasta or soup, generally €5–12), and a second course (*secondo piatto,* an expensive meat or fish dish, typically €6–15). Vegetables *(contorni, verdure)* rarely come with the *secondo* and cost extra (€4–5) as a side dish (an ample size for two people). The euros can add up in a hurry. Light and budget eaters get a *primo piatto* each and share an antipasto. Another good option is sharing an array of *antipasti*—either several specific dishes or a big plate of mixed delights assembled from a buffet. Italians admit that the *secondo* is the least-interesting aspect of the local cuisine.

Restaurants often pad the bill with a cover charge (*pane e coperto*—"bread and cover charge," about €1) and the service charge (*servizio,* 10–15 percent, see "Tipping" above); these charges are listed on the menu.

EATING

Wine Bars *(Enoteche)*

An *enoteca* (wine bar) is a popular, fast, and inexpensive option for lunch. Surrounded by the local office crowd, you can get a fancy salad, plate of meats and cheeses, and a glass of good wine (see blackboards for the day's selection and price per glass). The area around the Pantheon and Piazza Parlamento (popular with politicians and bureaucrats) has plenty of *enoteche* handy for a sightseeing lunch break or evening destination (see "Near the Pantheon" on page 304).

Bars/Cafés

Italian "bars" are not taverns but cafés. These local hangouts serve coffee, mini-pizzas, sandwiches, and drinks from the cooler. Many dish up plates of fried cheese and vegetables from under the glass counter, ready to reheat. This budget choice is the Italian equivalent of English pub grub.

For quick meals, bars usually have trays of cheap, ready-made sandwiches (*panini* or *tramezzini*). Some kinds are delightful grilled. To save time for sightseeing and room for dinner, consider a ham-and-cheese *panino* at a bar (called *toast,* have it grilled twice if you want it really hot) for lunch. To get food "to go," say, *"Da portar via"* (for the road). All bars have a WC *(toilette, bagno)* in the back, and customers (and the discreet public) can use it.

Coffee: Coffee is as important as wine in Rome, and Italian coffee is some of the world's best. If you ask for *"un caffè,"* you'll get espresso. If you ask for a latte, you'll get just that—a glass of hot milk. Cappuccino is served to locals before noon and to tourists any time of day. (To an Italian, cappuccino is a breakfast drink and a travesty after eating anything with tomatoes.) Italians like it only warm. To get it hot, request *"Molto caldo"* (MOHL-toh KAHL-doh; very hot) or *"Più caldo, per favore"* (pew KAHL-doh pehr fah-VOH-ray; hotter, please).

Romans like iced coffee in the summer. It's slightly diluted, sugared espresso, called *caffè freddo;* to get it with ice, say *"con ghiaccio"* (kohn ghee-AH-choh, with a hard g). *Cappuccino freddo* is cold cappuccino served in a tall glass.

Experiment with a few of the hot options:
- *Cappuccino:* Espresso with foamed milk on top
- *Caffè latte:* Tall glass with espresso and hot milk mixed
- *Caffè hag:* Instant decaf (you can order decaffeinated versions of any coffee drink—ask for it *decaffeinato*)
- *Macchiato* (mah-kee-AH-toh): Espresso with only a little milk
- *Caffè americano:* Espresso diluted with water
- *Caffè corretto:* Espresso with a shot of liqueur

Juice: *Spremuta* means freshly squeezed as far as *succo* (fruit juice) is concerned; it's usually orange juice, and February through April it's almost always made from blood oranges. (Note: *Spumante* means champagne.)

Beer: Beer on tap is *alla spina.* Get it *piccola* (33 cl, 11 oz), *media* (50 cl, 17 oz), or *grande* (a liter, 34 oz).

Wine: To order a glass (*bicchiere;* bee-kee-AY-ree) of red *(rosso)* or white *(bianco)* wine, say, *"Un bicchiere di vino rosso/bianco."* *Corposo* means full-bodied. House wine *(vino della casa)* often comes in a quarter-liter carafe *(un quarto).* For more on wine, see *"Vini,"* later in this chapter.

Other Drinks: A common *digestivo* in Rome is an *amaro,* which means "bitter." These alcoholic brews are often homemade by restaurants from a secret combination of herbs to aid digestion. Popular commercial brands are *Fernet Branca* and *Montenegro.* If your tastes run sweeter, try an anise-flavored liqueur called *Sambuca,* served *con moscha* (with three "flies"—coffee beans).

Prices: You'll notice a two-tiered price system. Drinking a cup of coffee while standing at the bar is cheaper than drinking it at a table. If you're on a budget, don't sit without first checking out the financial consequences. Ask, "Same price if I sit or stand?" by saying, *"Costa uguale al tavolo o al banco?"* (KOH-stah oo-GWAH-lay ahl TAH-voh-loh oh ahl BAHN-koh?).

If the bar isn't busy, you'll often just order and then pay when you leave. Otherwise: 1) Decide what you want; 2) Find out the price by checking the price list on the wall, the prices posted near the food, or by asking the barista; 3) Pay the cashier; and 4) Give the receipt to the barista (whose clean fingers handle no dirty euros) and tell him or her what you want.

Delis, Cafeterias, Pizza Shops, and *Tavola Calda* (Hot Table) Bars

Rome offers many cheap alternatives to restaurants. Stop by a *rosticceria* for great cooked deli food; a self-service cafeteria (called "free flow" in Italian) that feeds you without the add-ons; a *tavola calda* bar for an assortment of veggies; or a Pizza Rustica shop for stand-up or take-out pizza by the slice.

Pizza is cheap and everywhere. Key pizza vocabulary: *capricciosa* (generally ham, mushrooms, olives, and artichokes), *funghi* (mushrooms), *marinara* (tomato sauce, oregano, garlic, no cheese), *quattro formaggi* (four different cheeses), and *quattro stagioni* (different toppings on each of the four quarters, for those who can't choose just one menu item). If you ask for *peperoni* on your pizza, you'll get green or red peppers, not sausage. Kids like the simple *margherita* (cheese with tomato sauce) or *diavola* (the closest thing in Italy to American pepperoni). At Pizza Rustica take-out shops, slices are sold by weight (100 grams, or *un etto*, is a hot and cheap snack; 200 grams, or *due etti*, makes a light meal).

For a fast, cheap, and healthy lunch, find a *tavola calda* bar with a buffet spread of meat and vegetables, and ask for a mixed plate of vegetables with a hunk of mozzarella *(piatto misto di verdure con mozzarella)*. Don't be limited by what you can see. If you'd like a salad with a slice of cantaloupe and a hunk of cheese, they'll whip that up for you in a snap. Belly up to the bar and, with a pointing finger and key words in the chart in this chapter, you can get a fine mixed plate of vegetables. If something's a mystery, ask for a small taste (*un assaggio;* oon ah-SAH-joh).

Many places sell sandwiches of rustic bread and roasted pork with herbs (look for *porchetta,* por-KET-ah).

Beware of cheap eateries sporting big color photos of pizza and piles of different pastas. They have no kitchens and simply microwave disgusting prepackaged food. Unless you like lasagna with ice in the center, avoid these.

Ordering Food at *Tavola Caldas*

plate of mixed veggies	*piatto misto di verdure*	pee-AH-toh MEES-toh dee vehr-DOO-ray
"Heated, please."	*"Scaldare, per favore."*	skahl-DAH-ray, pehr fah-VOH-ray
"A taste, please."	*"Un assaggio, per favore."*	oon ah-SAH-joh, pehr fah-VOH-ray
artichoke	*carciofi*	kar-CHOH-fee
asparagus	*asparagi*	ah-spah-RAH-jee
beans	*fagioli*	fah-JOH-lee
breadsticks	*grissini*	gree-SEE-nee
broccoli	*broccoli*	BROH-koh-lee
cantaloupe	*melone*	may-LOH-nay
carrots	*carote*	kah-ROT-ay
green beans	*fagiolini*	fah-joh-LEE-nee
ham	*prosciutto*	proh-SHOO-toh
mushrooms	*funghi*	FOONG-ghee
potatoes	*patate*	pah-TAH-tay
rice	*riso*	REE-zoh
spinach	*spinaci*	speen-AH-chee
tomatoes	*pomodori*	poh-moh-DOH-ree
zucchini	*zucchine*	zoo-KEE-nay

(Excerpted from *Rick Steves' Italian Phrase Book & Dictionary*)

Picnics

In Rome, picnicking saves lots of euros and is a great way to sample local specialties. For a colorful experience, gather your ingredients in the morning at one of Rome's open-air produce markets (see page 317); you'll probably visit several small stores or market stalls to put together a complete meal. A local *alimentari* is your one-stop corner grocery store. A *supermercato* gives you more efficiency with less color

for less cost. You'll find handy late-night supermarkets near the Pantheon (Via Giustiniani), Spanish Steps (Via della Vittoria), Trevi Fountain (Via del Bufalo), and Campo de' Fiori (Via di Monte della Farina). Many *alimentari* and even supermarkets will gladly make you a fresh sandwich, charging you only for the weight of what you take and the piece of bread. And *rosticcerie* sell cheap food to go—you'll find options such as lasagna, rotisserie chicken, and sides like roasted potatoes and spinach.

Juice-lovers can get a liter (34 oz) of O.J. for the price of a Coke or coffee. Look for "100% *succo*" (juice) on the label. Hang on to the half-liter mineral-water bottles (sold everywhere for about €1). Buy juice in cheap liter boxes, then drink some and store the extra in your water bottle. Tap water—*acqua del rubinetto*—is fine; I drink water from the public taps found all over the city (often near fountains).

Picnics can be an adventure in high cuisine. Be daring. Try the fresh mozzarella, *presto* pesto, shriveled olives, and any UFOs the locals are excited about.

Shopkeepers are happy to sell small quantities of produce. It is customary to let the merchant choose the produce for you. Say *"Per oggi"* (pehr OH-jee), or "For today," and he or she will grab you something ready to eat, weigh it, and make the sale. A typical picnic for two might be fresh rolls, 100 grams of cheese, 100 grams of meat (*un etto* = 100 grams = about a quarter pound), two tomatoes, three carrots, two apples, yogurt, and a liter box of juice. Total cost: about €10.

ROMAN CUISINE

In ancient times, the dinner party was the center of Roman social life. It was a luxurious affair, set in the *triclinium* (formal dining room). Guest lists were small (3–9 people), and the select few reclined on couches during the exotic multi-course meal. Today the couches are gone, and the fare may not include jellyfish, boiled tree fungi, and flamingo, but the *cucina Romana* influence remains. It's fair to say that while French cuisine makes an art of the preparation, Italian (and Roman) cuisine is simpler and all about the ingredients.

Roman meals are still lengthy social occasions. Simple, fresh, seasonal ingredients dominate the dishes. The *cucina* is robust, strongly flavored, and unpretentious—much like the people who created it over the centuries. It is said that Roman cooking didn't come out of emperors' or popes' kitchens, but from the *cucina povera*—the home cooking of the common people. This may explain the fondness Romans have for meats known as the *quinto quarto* ("fifth quarter"), such as tripe, tail, brain, and pigs' feet, as well as their interest in natural preservatives like chili peppers and garlic. Rome belongs to the warm, southern region of Lazio, which produces a rich variety

Eating with the Seasons

Italian cooks love to serve you fresh produce and seafood at its tastiest. If you must have porcini mushrooms outside of October and November, they'll be frozen. To get the freshest veggies at a fine restaurant, request *"Un piatto di vedure della stagioni, per favore"* ("A plate of veggies in season, please").
Here are a few examples of what's fresh when:

April–May:	Calamari, squid, green beans, asparagus, artichokes, and zucchini flowers
April–May and Sept–Oct:	Black truffles
May–June:	Mussels, asparagus, zucchini, cantaloupe, and strawberries
May–Aug:	Eggplant
Oct–Nov:	Mushrooms, white truffles, and chestnuts
Fresh year-round:	Clams and meats

of flavorful vegetables and fruit that are the envy of American supermarkets. Rome's proximity to the Mediterranean also allows for a great variety of seafood (especially on Fridays) that can be pricey if you're dining out. Beware: On menus, seafood and steak are often priced by the *etto* (100-gram unit, about a quarter pound), rather than by the portion.

Today, eating like a Roman means stopping at the local bar each morning for a pastry and coffee (usually cappuccino or espresso). Lunch (between 13:00 and 15:00) is traditionally the largest meal of the day, eaten at home, although work habits have changed this for many people who don't want to spend time commuting. Instead, they grab a quick meal in a *tavola calda* (cafeteria) buffet or a *panino* or *tramezzino* (sandwich). Dinnertime is generally 20:00 to 22:00, and in restaurants it is a multi-course affair.

When it's hot outside, a *granita* at a *grattachecce* (grah-tah-KAY-chay) cools you down fast. These little booths scrape shavings off ice blocks and then flavor them with syrups. Try the combo-flavors such as *limoncocco*—lemon and coconut syrups with fresh chunks of coconut.

Local specialties you may find on a menu include the following:

Antipasti (Appetizers)

Antipasto misto: A plate of marinated or grilled vegetables (eggplant, artichokes, peppers, mushrooms), cured meats, or seafood (anchovies, octopus).

Bruschetta: Toast brushed with olive oil and garlic or chopped tomatoes.

Fiori di zucca fritti: Squash blossoms filled with mozzarella and anchovies, then battered and fried.

Prosciutto e melone: Thin slices of ham wrapped around pieces of cantaloupe.

Supplí: Fried, oval-shaped rice balls with tomato sauce and mozzarella.

Primi Piatti (First Courses)

Spaghetti alla carbonara: Any type of pasta with a sauce made from beaten eggs, fried *pancetta* (bacon) or *guaniciale* (cured pork cheek), cheese (*pecorino romano* or *parmigiano reggiano*), and black pepper.

Bucatini all'amatriciana: Thin pasta tubes with a sauce of tomatoes, onion, pork, and pecorino cheese on top.

Gnocchi alla romana: Small dumpling-like disks made from semolina, instead of potato, and baked with butter and cheese.

Penne all'arrabbiata: "Angry quills"—quill-shaped pasta topped with a spicy tomato sauce of chili peppers *(pepperoncini)* and garlic.

Rigatoni con la pajata: Medium-size wide pasta tubes topped with a stew of milk-fed calf intestines.

Stacciatella alla romana: Meat broth with whipped eggs, topped with parmesan cheese.

Spaghetti alle vongole veraci: Small clams in the shell sautéed with white wine and herbs, served over pasta.

Secondi Piatti (Second Courses)

Saltimbocca alla romana: "Jump-in-the-mouth"—thinly sliced veal layered with prosciutto and sage, then lightly fried.

Abbacchio alla scottadito: Baby lamb chops grilled and eaten as finger food.

Trippa alla romana: Tripe braised with onions, carrots, and mint.

Coda alla vaccinara: Oxtail braised with garlic, wine, tomato, and celery.

Involtini al sugo: Veal cutlets rolled with prosciutto, celery, and cheese in a tomato sauce.

Anguillette in umido: Stewed baby eels from nearby Lake Bracciano.

Filetti di baccalà: Dried cod fried in a batter.

Contorni (Side Dishes)

Sometimes the second course is not served with a vegetable, and you may want to order a side dish separately. If you get a salad, note that olive oil and wine vinegar are the only dressings.

Carciofi alla giudia: Small artichokes flattened and fried.

Fave al guanciale: Fava beans simmered with *guanciale* (cured pork cheek) and onion.

Misticanza: Mixed green salad of arugula *(rucola)* and curly endive *(puntarelle)* with anchovies.

EATING

Dolci (Desserts)

Dessert can be a seasonal fruit, such as *fragole* (strawberries) or *pesche* (peaches), or even cheese, such as *pecorino romano* (made from ewe's milk) or *caciotta romana* (made from a combination of ewe's and cow's milk).

Crostata di ricotta: A cheesecake-like dessert with ricotta, Marsala wine, cinnamon, and bits of chocolate.

Bignè: Cream-puff-like pastries filled with *zabaglione* (egg yolks, sugar, and Marsala wine).

Tartufo: Rich, dark-chocolate gelato ball with a cherry inside. **Con panna** gets you whipped cream on top.

Gelato: Rather than order dessert in a restaurant, I like to stroll with a cup or cone of gelato picked up at one of Rome's popular *gelaterias.*

Vini (Wines)

No large meal in Italy is complete without wine. Although Lazio is not the most notable wine region in Italy, it produces several pleasant white wines and a few reds.

Frascati, probably the best-known wine of the region, is an inexpensive dry white made from Trebbiano and Malvasia grapes. **Castelli Romani,** from the hills just south of Rome, is also from the Trebbiano grape and is similar to **Marino, Colli Albani,** and **Velletri,** all light and fairly dry. **Torre Ercolana** is known as Lazio's finest red. This dense wine is made from the local Cesanese grape, as well as Cabernet and Merlot. Produced in small quantities, it must be aged for at least five years.

RESTAURANTS

I've listed a number of restaurants I enjoy. While most are in quaint and therefore pricey and touristy areas (Piazza Navona, the Pantheon, Campo de' Fiori, and Trastevere), many are tucked away just off of the tourist crush. If you want to sit on a famous square with a famous view, you'll pay extra and be surrounded by tourists. Noisy English-speakers can negate the pluses of the spot...leaving you with just a forgettable and overpriced meal. I savor a drink or dessert on a famous square, but dine with locals on nearby low-rent streets, where the proprietor needs to serve a good-value meal and nurture a local following to stay in business.

In general, I'm impressed by how small the price difference is from a mediocre restaurant to a fine one. You can pay about 20 percent more for double the quality. If I had $90 for three meals in Rome, I'd spend $50 for one and $20 each for the other two, rather than $30 on all three. For splurge meals, I'd consider Gabriello, Al Bric, Fortunato, and Checco er Carettiere (in that order).

In Trastevere

Colorful Trastevere is now pretty touristy. Still, Romans join the tourists to eat on the rustic side of the Tiber River. Start at the central square (Piazza Santa Maria). Then choose: Eat with tourists enjoying the ambience of the famous square, or wander the back streets in search of a mom-and-pop place with barely a menu. My recommendations are within a few minutes' walk of each other (between Piazza Santa Maria Trastevere and Ponte Sisto; see map on page 88).

Trattoria da Lucia lets you enjoy simple, traditional food at a good price in a great scene. It's the quintessential, rustic, 100 percent Roman Trastevere dining experience, and has been family-run since World War II. You'll meet four generations of the family, including Giuliano and Renato, their uncle Ennio, and Ennio's mom—pictured on the menu in the 1950s. The family specialty is *spaghetti alla Gricia*, with pancetta bacon (€9 pastas, €11 *secondi*, Tue–Sun 12:30–15:30 & 19:30–24:00, closed Mon, cash only, comfy indoor or evocative outdoor seating, just off Via del Mattonato on Vicolo del Mattonato 2, tel. 06-580-3601, some English spoken).

Trattoria da Olindo takes homey to extremes. You really feel like you dropped in on a family that cooks for the neighborhood to supplement their income (€7 pastas, €9 *secondi*, Mon–Sat dinner served 20:00–22:30, closed Sun, cash only, indoor and funky cobbled outdoor seating, on the corner of Vicolo della Scala and Via del Mattonato at #8, tel. 06-581-8835).

Osteria Ponte Sisto, small and Mediterranean, specializes in traditional Roman cuisine, but has frequent Neapolitan specials as well. Just outside the tourist zone, it caters mostly to Romans and offers beautiful desserts and a fine value (daily 12:30–15:30 & 19:30–24:00, Via Ponte Sisto 80, tel. 06-588-3411, Antonio and Adriano). It's easy to find: Crossing Ponte Sisto (pedestrian bridge) toward Trastevere, continue across the little square (Piazza Trilussa) and you'll see it on the right.

Ristorante Checco er Carettiere is a big, classic, family-run place that's been a Trastevere fixture for four generations. With white tablecloths, well-presented food, and dressy local diners, this is *the* place for a special meal in Trastevere. While it's a bit pricey, you'll eat well amidst lots of fun commotion. Reservations are smart, especially on weekends (€16 pastas, €22 *secondi*, daily 12:30–15:00 & 19:30–23:15, Via Benedetta 10/13, tel. 06-580-0985). For a pared-down menu with down-home Roman cooking and cheaper prices, go to their **Osteria Checco er Carettiere** just next door (€11 pastas, €15 *secondi*, same hours and phone number as above).

Pizzeria "Ai Marmi" is a bright and noisy festival of pizza, where the oven and pizza-assembly line are surrounded by marble-slab tables (hence the nickname "the morgue"). It's a classic Roman scene with famously good €8 pizzas and tight seating. Expect a long line between 20:00 and 22:00 (Thu–Tue 18:30–24:00, closed Wed, outdoor seating on busy Viale Trastevere, tram #8 from Largo Argentina to first stop over bridge, just beyond Piazza Sonnino at Viale Trastevere 53, tel. 06-580-0919).

Cantina Paradiso Wine and Cocktail Bar has a simple romantic charm, a block over Viale Trastevere from the touristy action. During happy hour (18:00–20:30), €6 drinks come with a well-made little buffet that can make a cheap, light dinner (daily 12:00–24:00, €8 pastas, lunch buffet as well, Via San Francesco a Ripa 73, tel. 06-5899-799).

And for Dessert: **Gelateria alla Scala** is a terrific little ice-cream shop that dishes up delightful cinnamon *(cannella)* and oh-wow pistachio (daily 12:00–24:00, Piazza della Scala 51, across from the church on Piazza della Scala). Seek this place out.

Jewish Ghetto

The Jewish Ghetto sits just across the river from Trastevere (see map on page 96).

Sora Margherita, hiding without a sign on a cluttered square, has been a neighborhood favorite since 1927. Amid a picturesque commotion, local families chow down on old-time Roman and Jewish dishes for a good price. As it's technically not a real restaurant (it avoids red tape by being officially designated as an *associazione culturale*), you'll need to sign a card to join the "cultural association" when you order (don't worry; membership has no obligations except that you enjoy your meal). The menu's crude term for the fettuccini gives you some idea of the mood of this place: *nazzica culo* ("asses shake while it's made"). Reservations are almost always necessary; to secure a spot for lunch without a reservation, go early or late (April–Oct Tue–Sun 12:30–15:00 for lunch, dinner seatings on Fri and Sat at 20:00 and 21:30, closed Mon; Nov–March Mon–Fri 12:30–15:00, dinner seatings at 20:00 and 21:30 on Fri, closed Sat–Sun; Piazza delle Cinque Scole 30, tel. 06-687-4216, Ivan doesn't speak English).

In the Heart of Rome

On and near Campo de' Fiori

While it is touristy, Campo de' Fiori offers a sublimely romantic setting. And, since it's so close to the collective heart of Rome, it remains popular with locals. For greater atmosphere than food value, circle the square, considering your choices. The square is lined with popular and interesting bars, pizzerias, and small restaurants—all great for people-watching over a glass of wine.

Ristorante la Carbonara is a venerable standby with the ultimate Campo de' Fiori outdoor setting and dressy waiters. While the service gets mixed reviews, the food and Italian ambience are wonderful. Meals on small surrounding streets may be a better value, but they lack that Campo de' Fiori magic. While La Carbonara's on-square dining is classic, the big room upstairs is good, too (€11 pastas, €16

Restaurants in the Heart of Rome

1. Ristorante la Carbonara
2. Osteria da Giovanni ar Galletto
3. Osteria Enoteca al Bric
4. Filetti di Baccalà
5. Trattoria der Pallaro
6. Hostaria Costanza
7. Ristorante Montevecchio & Osteria del Pegno
8. Cul de Sac & L'Insalata Ricca
9. L'Antica Birreria Peroni
10. Rist. Pizzeria Sacro e Profano
11. Gelateria San Crispino

secondi, Wed–Mon 9:00–15:00 & 19:00–23:30, closed Tue, reservations recommended, Campo de' Fiori 23, tel. 06-686-4783).

Osteria da Giovanni ar Galletto is nearby, on the more elegant and peaceful Piazza Farnese. Angelo entertains an upscale local crowd and has magical outdoor seating. Regrettably, service can be horrible and single diners aren't treated very well. Still, if you're in no hurry and ready to savor my favorite *al fresco* setting in Rome (while humoring the waiters), this is a good bet (Mon–Sat 12:15–15:00 & 19:30–23:00, closed Sun, tucked in corner of Piazza Farnese at #102, tel. 06-686-1714).

Osteria Enoteca al Bric is a mod bistro-type place run by Maurizio, a man who loves to cook, serve good wine, and listen to jazz. With only the finest ingredients, and an ambience elegant in its simplicity, he's created the perfect package for a romantic night out. Wine-case lids decorate the wall like happy memories. With candlelit grace and few tourists, it's perfect for the wine snob in the mood for pasta and fine cheese. Aficionados choose their bottle from the huge selection lining the walls near the entrance. Beginners order fine wine by the glass with help from the waiter when they order their meal (daily 12:30–15:00 & from 19:30 for dinner, closed Mon June–Sept, reserve after 20:30, 100 yards off Campo de' Fiori at Via del Pellegrino 51, tel. 06-687-9533). Al Bric offers my readers a special "Taste of Italy for Two" deal (appetizing plate of mixed cheeses and meats with two glasses of full-bodied red wine and a pitcher of water) for €22 from 19:30, but you may need to finish by 20:30. This could be a light meal if you're kicking off an evening stroll, a substantial appetizer, or a way to check this place out for a serious meal later. While Al Bric can be pricey, feel free to establish a price limit (e.g., €40 per person) and trust Maurizio to feed you well.

Filetti di Baccalà is a cheap and basic Roman classic, where nostalgic regulars cram into wooden tables savoring their old-school favorites—hand-held, fried cod fillets and raw *puntarelle* greens (slathered with anchovy sauce in spring and winter). Study what others are eating, and order from your grease-stained server by pointing at what you want. Rather than sit in the fluorescently-lit interior, try to grab a seat out on the little square, a quiet haven a block east of Campo de' Fiori (Mon–Sat 17:30–23:00, closed Sun, cash only, Largo dei Librari 88, tel. 06-686-4018).

Trattoria der Pallaro, a well-worn eatery that has no menu, has a slogan: "Here, you'll eat what we want to feed you." Paola Fazi—with a towel wrapped around her head turban-style—and her family serve up a five-course meal of typically Roman food for €22, including wine, coffee, and a tasty mandarin juice finale. As many locals return every day, each evening features a different menu (Tue–Sun 12:00–15:00 & 19:00–24:00, closed Mon, indoor/outdoor seating on quiet square, a block south of Corso Vittorio Emanuele, down Largo del Chiavari to Largo del Pallaro 15, tel. 06-6880-1488).

Hostaria Costanza has crisp-vested waiters, a local following, and lots of energy. You'll eat traditional Roman cuisine, including grilled meats and fresh fish, on a ramshackle patio or inside under arches from the ancient Pompeo Theater (Mon–Sat 12:30–15:00 & 19:30–23:30, closed Sun, Piazza Paradiso 63, tel. 06-686-1717).

West of Piazza Navona

Romantic **Ristorante Montevecchio** is tucked into the corner of a secluded piazza. Sitting under high wood-beamed ceilings or outside among Renaissance walls, you savor Italian classics with a creative touch—and maybe even some of the chef's little extra offerings of the evening. Start with their delicate *fritti* of lightly battered seasonal vegetables and you'll realize you're in for a memorable meal (€15 pastas, €20 *secondi*, Tue–Sun 12:30–15:30 & 19:15–23:00, reservations recommended, closed Mon, 3 blocks from Piazza Navona off Via dei Coronari—turn left on Via della Pace to Piazza Montevecchio 22a, tel. 06-686-1319, Annamaria).

Osteria del Pegno, across the street from Ristorante Montevecchio, is a lively, atmospheric, soft-focus kind of place, with candlelight shining off wine-bottle-lined walls. Its local clientele enjoys good regional dishes and a fine house wine (pizza at lunch only, €8 pastas, €15 *secondi*, no cover, Thu–Tue 12:30–15:00 & 19:30–23:30, closed Wed, Vicolo di Montevecchio 8, tel. 06-6880-7025).

Piazza Pasquino

Located just a block off Piazza Navona (toward Campo de' Fiori) on Piazza Pasquino, these bustling places have low prices and a happy clientele. As they are neighbors and each is completely different, check both before choosing.

Cul de Sac is a corridor-wide trattoria lined with wine bottles and packed with enthusiastic locals. Come early for an excellent tasting plate of salami and one of their many bottles of wine (they've got more than 1,000), or come later for a full meal of nicely cooked Roman dishes (daily 12:00–16:00 & 18:00–24:00, tel. 06-6880-1094).

L'Insalata Ricca is a popular local chain that specializes in hearty and healthy €7 salads and less healthy pastas (daily 12:00–15:45 & 18:45–24:00, tel. 06-6830-7881).

Near the Trevi Fountain

L'Antica Birreria Peroni is Rome's answer to a German beer hall. Serving hearty mugs of the local Peroni beer and lots of just plain fun beer-hall food, the place is a hit with locals for a cheap night out (Mon–Sat 12:00–24:00, closed Sun, midway between Trevi Fountain and Capitol Hill, a block off Via del Corso at Via di San Marcello 19, tel. 06-679-5310).

Ristorante Pizzeria Sacro e Profano fills an old church with spicy south Italian (Calabrian) cuisine; some pricey, exotic dishes; and satisfied tourists. Run with enthusiasm and passion by Pasquale and friends, this is just far enough away from the Trevi mobs. Their hearty €15 *antipasti* plate is a delightful montage of Calabrian taste treats—plenty of food for a light, but exceptional meal (daily 12:00–15:00 & 18:00–24:00, a block off Via del Tritone at Via dei Maroniti 29, tel. 06-679-1836). And for dessert...

Around the corner, **Gelateria San Crispino,** well-respected by locals, serves particularly tasty gourmet gelato using creative ingredients.

EATING

Because of their commitment to natural ingredients, the colors are muted and they serve cups, but no cones (April–Nov daily 12:00–24:00, Dec–March closed Tue, Via della Panetteria 42, tel. 06-679-3924).

Near the Pantheon

Eating on the square facing the Pantheon is a temptation (there's even a McDonald's that offers some of the best outdoor seating in town), and I'd consider it just to relax and enjoy the Roman scene. But if you walk a block or two away, you'll get less view and better value. Here are some suggestions:

Ristorante da Fortunato is an Italian classic, with fresh flowers on the tables and white-coated, black-tie waiters politely serving good meat and fish to local politicians, foreign dignitaries, and tourists with good taste. Don't leave without perusing the photos of their famous visitors—everyone from former Iraqi Foreign Minister Tariq Aziz to Bill Clinton seems to have eaten here. All are pictured with the boss, Fortunato, who, since 1975, has been a master of simple edible elegance. The outdoor seating is fine for watching the river of Roman street life flow by, but the atmosphere is inside. For a dressy night out, this is a reliable and surprisingly reasonable choice—but be sure to reserve ahead (plan to spend €45 per person, Mon–Sat 12:30–15:00 & 19:30–23:30, closed Sun, a block in front of the Pantheon at Via del Pantheon 55, tel. 06-679-2788).

Ristorante Enoteca Corsi is a wine shop that grew into a thriving lunch-only restaurant. The Paiella family serves straightforward, traditional cuisine at great prices to an appreciative crowd of office workers. Check the blackboard for daily specials (gnocchi on Thursday, fish on Friday, and so on). Friendly Juliana, Claudia, and Manuela welcome diners to step into their wine shop and pick out a bottle. For the cheap take-away price, plus €2, they'll uncork it at your table. With €6 pastas, €9.50 main dishes, and fine wine at a third of the price you'd pay in normal restaurants, this can be a superb value (Mon–Sat 12:00–15:00, closed Sun, a block toward the Pantheon from the Gesù Church at Via del Gesù 87, no reservations possible, tel. 06-679-0821).

Miscellanea is run by much-loved Mikki, who's on a mission to keep foreign students well-fed. You'll find hearty and fresh €3 sandwiches and a long list of €6 salads. Mikki often tosses in a fun little extra, including—if you have this book on the table—a free glass of Mikki's "sexy wine" (homemade from *fragoline*—strawberries). This place is popular with American students on foreign-study programs (daily 11:00–24:00, indoor/outdoor seating, a block toward Via del Corso from the Pantheon at Via delle Paste 110).

Osteria da Mario, a homey little mom-and-pop joint with a no-stress menu, serves traditional favorites in a fun dining room or on tables spilling out onto a picturesque old Roman square (€7 pastas,

Restaurants near the Pantheon

100 YARDS
100 METERS

TO PIAZZA DEL POPOLO
TO M BARB.
VIA TRITONE
TO M STELL.
SCROFA
UFF.
VICARIO
PARL.
VIA. MARIO
P. MONTE.
P. COL.
SABRINA
TO TREVI
MURATTE
SAN LUIGI
VACC.
COPPELLE
POZZO CORN.
SALV.
GIUST.
CRESC.
AQUIRO
ORE.
PASTINI
PIAZZA ROTUNDA
SEMINARIO
P. PIETRA
CARA.
SAN IGNAZIO
CORSO
S. APOST.
TIME ELEVATOR ROMA
TO PIAZZA NAVONA
S. EUST.
PANTHEON
ARGEN
CESTARI
GESÙ
STA. MARIA
SOPRA MINERVA
P. COLL. ROM.
GALLERIA DORA PAMPHILJ
VIA VITTORIO
LARGO ARGENTINA RUINS
EMANUELE
GESÙ
DCH
ARACOELI
FLOR.
BOTT.
OSC.
TO CAPITOL HILL

Ⓣ TAXI STAND
Ⓜ METRO STATION
Ⓑ BUS STOP
→ ENTRY POINT TO SIGHTS

❶ Ristorante da Fortunato
❷ Ristorante Enoteca Corsi
❸ Miscellanea Restaurant
❹ Osteria da Mario & Restaurant Coco
❺ Le Coppelle Taverna
❻ To Trattoria dal Cav. Gino
❼ Pizzeria Zazà
❽ Antica Salumeria
❾ Angelo Feroci Butcher Shop
❿ Super Market Di per Di
⓫ Gelateria Giolitti
⓬ Crèmeria Monteforte

€10 *secondi,* Mon–Sat 13:00–15:30 & 19:00–23:00, closed Sun, from the Pantheon walk 2 blocks up Via Pantheon, go left on Via delle Coppelle, take first right to Piazza delle Coppelle 51, tel. 06-6880-6349, Marco).

Restaurant Coco is good for a quick and atmospheric €10 buffet lunch on weekdays, or a lavish €15 lunch on weekends. After assembling your plate, sit on the square next to a produce market, and watch politicians stroll in and out of their dining hall across the way (daily

12:30–15:30 & 19:30–24:00, classy indoor and rustic outdoor seating, Piazza delle Coppelle 54, tel. 06-6813-6545).

Le Coppelle Taverna is simple, good, and inexpensive—especially for pizza—with a checkered-tablecloth ambience (May–Sept daily 12:30–15:00 & 19:30–23:30, Nov–April closed Mon, Via delle Coppelle 39, tel. 06-6880-6557, Alfonso).

Trattoria dal Cav. Gino, tucked away on a tiny street behind the parliament, has been a local favorite since 1963. Photos on the wall recall the days when it was the haunt of big-time politicians. Grandpa Gino shuffles around grating the parmesan cheese while his sister and son serve up traditional Roman favorites and make sure things run smoothly. Reserve ahead, even for lunch (€7 pastas, €10 *secondi,* fish on Friday, cash only, Mon–Sat 13:00–14:45 & 20:00–22:30, closed Sun, behind Piazza del Parlamento and just off Via di Campo Marzio at Vicolo Rosini 4, tel. 06-687-3434, Fabrizio and Carla—Gino's son and daughter—speak English).

(Discreetly) Picnic near the Pantheon

Pizzeria Zazà is a quick take-out stop for stellar pizza by the slice (with little outdoor seating). With primarily organic ingredients and a doughy, plush crust, this is fast-food gourmet—great for a quick bite in the old center. It's sold by weight—ask for *un etto* (100 grams), or *due etti* if you're really hungry (May–Oct Mon–Sat 10:00–22:00, closed Sun; Nov–April daily 10:00–22:00; facing the back of the Pantheon, head 20 yards to your right to reach Piazza San Eustachio 49, tel. 06-68-80-1357, Alessandro).

Antica Salumeria is an old-time *alimentari* (grocery store) on the Pantheon square. Eduardo speaks English and will help you assemble your picnic: artichokes, mixed olives, bread, cheese, meat (they're proud of their Norcia prosciutto), and wine (with plastic glasses). Their pastries are fresh from their own bakery. While you can create your own (sold by the weight, more fun, and cheaper), they also sell quality ready-made sandwiches. Now take your peasant's feast to an atmospheric spot, find some shade, and munch your meal (daily 8:00–21:00, mobile 334-340-9014).

Angelo Feroci also offers cheap, quick *antipasti* to go. Though it's a butcher shop—from another era—you can pick up seasonal vegetables as well as meats (try the meatballs in sauce). Just point to the size of container you want, then nod and gesture toward what looks tastiest (sold by weight—about €5 for a lunch portion, Mon–Wed and Fri 6:00–13:30 & 17:00–20:00, Thu and Sat 6:00–13:30, closed Sun, one and a half blocks north of the Pantheon at Via della Maddalena 15, tel. 06-6880-1016).

Super Market Di per Di is a convenient place for groceries in the old center (Mon–Sat 8:00–21:00, Sun 9:00–19:30, 50 yards off Via del Plebiscito at Via del Gesù 59).

EATING

Gelato near the Pantheon

Two fine *gelaterias* are within a two-minute walk of the Pantheon.

Gelateria Caffè Pasticceria Giolitti, Rome's most famous and venerable ice-cream joint, has low take-away prices and elegant Old World seating (daily 7:00–24:00, just off Piazza Colonna and Piazza Monte Citorio at Via Uffici del Vicario 40, tel. 06-699-1243).

Crèmeria Monteforte is known for its super-creamy sorbets, traditional quality, and mellow hues; gelato purists consider bright colors a sign of unnatural chemicals used to attract children (Tue–Sun 10:00–24:00, closed Mon, faces the west side of the Pantheon at Via della Rotonda 22).

In North Rome: Near the Ara Pacis and Spanish Steps

Many simple and lively places line Via della Croce. To locate these restaurants, see the "Dolce Vita Stroll" map on page 321.

Ristorante il Gabriello is inviting and small—modern under medieval arches—and provides a peaceful and local-feeling respite from all the top-end fashion shops in the area. Claudio serves with

charisma, while his brother Gabriello cooks creative Roman cuisine using fresh, organic products from his wife's farm. Italians normally just trust the waiter and say, "Bring it on." Tourists are understandably more cautious, but you can be trusting here. Simply close your eyes and point to anything on the menu. Or invest €40 in "Claudio's Extravaganza" (not including wine), and he'll shower you with edible kindness. Specify whether you'd prefer fish, meat, or both. When finished, I stand up, hold my belly, and say, *"La vita è bella"* (€9 pastas, €12 *secondi,* dinner only, Mon–Sat 19:00–23:30, closed Sun, reservations smart, air-con, dress respectfully—no shorts please, 3 blocks from Spanish Steps at Via Vittoria 51, tel. 06-6994-0810).

Osteria Gusto is great for a glass of good wine over an artisanal cheese plate or a complete dinner (daily 12:30–15:30 & 19:00–24:00, opens at 18:30 for drinks and appetizers only, reservations recommended after 20:00 and on weekends, on the corner of Via Soderini at Via della Frezza 16, tel. 06-3211-1482). Don't confuse the *osteria* with its nearby wine bar and *ristorante* sister operations—the *osteria* has better food and warmer ambience (the others are under different management).

Ristorante alla Rampa, just around the corner from the touristy crush of the Spanish Steps, offers Roman cooking, busy but pleasant indoor/outdoor ambience at a moderate price, piles of tourists, and impersonal service. It's a good idea to make reservations if arriving after 19:30. For a simple meal, go with the €10 *piatto misto all'ortolana*—a self-service trip to their antipasto spread with meat, fish, and veggies. Even though you get just one trip to the buffet (and fried items are generally cold), this can be a meal in itself (Mon–Sat 12:00–15:00 & 18:00–23:00, closed Sun, 100 yards east of Spanish Steps at Piazza Mignanelli 18, tel. 06-678-2621).

L'EnotecAntica, an upbeat, 200-plus-year-old *enoteca,* has around 60 Italian-only wines by the glass, and a fresh €12 *antipasti* plate of veggies, salami, and cheese. It's very crowded on summer evenings (Via della Croce 76b, tel. 06-679-0896).

Bar Ripetta is so famous for its cappuccino that the barista is used to tourists ordering it in the evening (Italian coffee purists usually scoff at foreigners who order cappuccinos past noon). Pay for and order your coffee and dessert, then grab a table outside for no extra charge (Mon–Sat 6:00–20:30, closed Sun, Via Ripetta 72, tel. 06-321-0524).

Cesaretto, a casual wine bar with outdoor seating and light, inexpensive appetizers, is run by hospitable, Harley-loving Angelo (€4.50 antipasto buffet plate, daily 12:00–24:00, buffet 18:30–20:30, Via Bocca di Leone 44, tel. 06-6938-0557).

In Ancient Rome:
Eating Cheaply near the Colosseum

You'll find good views but poor value at the restaurants directly behind the Colosseum. To get your money's worth, eat at least a block away. Here are three handy eateries, all shown on the map on page 283: one at the foot of Via Cavour, and two at the top of Terme di Tito (a long block uphill from the Colosseum, near St. Peter-in-Chains church—of Michelangelo's *Moses* fame; for directions, see page 254).

Enoteca Cavour 313 is a wine bar with a mission: to offer good wine and quality food with an old-fashioned commitment to value and friendly service. It's also a convenient place for a good lunch near the Forum and Colosseum. Angelo and his three partners enjoy creating a mellow ambience under lofts of wine bottles (daily specials and fine wines by the glass, daily 12:30–14:45 & 19:30–24:00, 100 yards off Via dei Fori Imperiali at Via Cavour 313, tel. 06-6785-496).

Lively **Caffè dello Studente** is popular with local engineering students attending the nearby University of Rome. Pina, Mauro, and their perky daughter Simona (speaks English, but you can teach her some more) give my readers a royal welcome and serve typical *bar gastronomia* fare—toasted sandwiches and pizzas—and big salads, too (stick to any of the aforementioned fare to avoid frozen dishes). You can get your food to go *(da portar via);* eat standing at the crowded bar; wait for table service outside; or—if it's not busy—show this book when you order at the bar and sit without paying extra at a table (Mon–Sat 7:30–21:00, Sun 9:00–18:00, tel. 06-488-3240).

Hostaria da Nerone, next door, is a more formal restaurant with homemade pasta dishes. Their €8 *antipasti* plate—with a variety of veggies, fish, and maybe meatballs, too—is a good value for a quick lunch (Mon–Sat 12:00–15:00 & 19:00–23:00, closed Sun, indoor/outdoor seating, Via delle Terme di Tito 96, tel. 06-481-7952, run by Teo and Eugenio).

Near Termini Train Station

You have several eating options near my recommended hotels on Via Firenze.

Ristorante del Giglio is a circa-1900 place with a long family tradition of serving traditional Roman dishes (though the quality can be uneven). You'll eat in a big hall of about 20 tables with dressy locals and tourists following the recommendations of nearby hotels (€10 pastas, €15 *secondi,* alluring dessert cart, Tue–Sat 12:00–15:00 & 19:00–23:00, Mon 19:00–23:00, closed Sun, Via Torino 137, tel. 06-488-1606).

La Gallina Bianca, with a classy country villa atmosphere and sprightly service, seems out of place near the Termini station. The wood-fired pizza—surely the best in the area—might distract you from their excellent Roman *fritti, primi, secondi,* and the knockout *tiramisù.* A wait is almost always necessary after 19:30. Come earlier, especially on weekends, as they don't take reservations (€8 pizzas, €11 pastas, €15 *secondi,* Via Antonio Rosmini 9, tel. 06-474-3777, Antonio).

Snack Bar, despite its plain-Jane name, is anything but: The place puts out an impressive lunchtime display of pastas, colorful sandwiches, and fresh fruit. You can even make your own salad. Rub elbows with lunching businesspeople in the afternoon (12:30–15:00), either inside the characterless interior or out on the sidewalk (daily 6:00–24:00, Via Firenze 33, mobile 339-393-1356, Enrica).

Cafeteria Nazionale, with woody elegance, offers light lunches—including salads—at fair prices. It's noisy with local office workers being served by frantic red-vested wait staff. Their lunch buffet is a delight but gets picked over early (small €10 buffet plate, €8 pastas, Mon–Sat 7:00–20:00, closed Sun, Via Nazionale 26–27, near intersection with Via Agostino de Pretis, tel. 06-4899-1716).

The **McDonald's** restaurants on Piazza della Repubblica (free piazza seating outside), Piazza Barberini, and Via Firenze offer air-conditioned interiors, and salads and cappuccino to go.

Flann O'Brien Irish Pub is an entertaining place for a light meal (of pasta...or something *other* than pasta, such as grilled meats and giant salads, served early and late, when other places are closed), Irish beer, live sporting events on TV, and perhaps the most Italian crowd of all. Walk way back before choosing a table (daily 7:30–24:00,

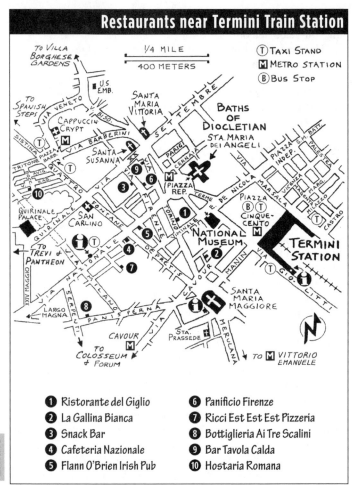

Restaurants near Termini Train Station

Ⓣ Taxi Stand
Ⓜ Metro Station
Ⓑ Bus Stop

❶ Ristorante del Giglio
❷ La Gallina Bianca
❸ Snack Bar
❹ Cafeteria Nazionale
❺ Flann O'Brien Irish Pub
❻ Panificio Firenze
❼ Ricci Est Est Est Pizzeria
❽ Bottiglieria Ai Tre Scalini
❾ Bar Tavola Calda
❿ Hostaria Romana

EATING

Via Nazionale 17, at intersection with Via Napoli, tel. 06-488-0418).

Panificio Firenze has take-out pizza, sandwiches, and an old-fashioned *alimentari* (grocery) with everything you'd need for a picnic. It's such a favorite with locals that it doesn't even need a sign (Mon–Fri 7:00–19:00, Sat until 13:30, closed Sun, Via Firenze 51–52, tel. 06-488-5035).

Ricci Est Est Est Pizzeria, a venerable family-run pizzeria, has plenty of historical ambience, good €8 pizzas, and dangerously tasty *fritti*, such as fried *baccalà* (dried cod) and zucchini flowers (Tue–Sun 19:00–24:00, closed Mon, Via Genova 32, tel. 06-488-1107).

Bottiglieria Ai Tre Scalini is a relaxed and characteristic little wine bar popular with young neighborhood regulars, who pop in to sip a glass of fine wine and munch some light Roman pub grub to jazz or blues music. It's nothing earth-shaking—just a serviceable wine bar with wines by the glass listed on the blackboard (Tue–Sun 15:00–24:00, closed Mon, 100 yards off Via Nazionale at Via Panisperna 251, tel. 06-4782-5881).

Bar Tavola Calda is a local workers' favorite for a quick, cheap lunch. They have good, fresh, hot dishes ready to go for a fine price. Head back past the bar to peruse their enticing display, point at what you want, then grab a seat, and the young waitstaff will serve you (Mon–Sat 12:00–15:30 for lunch, closed Sun, Via Torino 40).

Hostaria Romana is a busy bistro with a hustling and fun-loving gang of waiters and noisy walls graffitied by happy eaters. While they specialize in fish and traditional Roman dishes, their *antipasti* plate can make a good meal in itself (Mon–Sat 12:15–15:00 & 19:15–23:00, closed Sun, a block up the lane just past the entrance to the big tunnel near the Trevi Fountain at Via de Boccaccio 1, tel. 06-474-5284).

Near Vatican City

Avoid the restaurant-pushers handing out fliers near the Vatican: bad food and expensive menu tricks. Try any of these instead (see map on page 288).

Perilli in Prati is bright, modern, and just far enough away from the tourist hordes. While friendly Lucia and Massimo specialize in pizza, fish, and grilled meats, the highlight is their excellent €8 lunch buffet (Mon–Fri 12:30–15:00 & 19:30–23:30, Sat 19:30–23:30, closed Sun, one block from Ottaviano Metro stop, Via Otranto 9, tel. 06-370-0156).

La Isola della Pizza has wood-fired pizzas, sidewalk seating, and home-cooking at its truest: For €10, Adele, Vito, or their son Renzo serve up generous plates of their mixed *antipasti*...and Vito himself hunts the wild boar for the *cinghiale* pasta (Thu–Tue 12:30–15:00 & 19:30–24:00, closed Wed, Via degli Scipioni 41/51, tel. 06-3973-3483).

Hostaria dei Bastioni, run by Emilio, is conveniently located midway on your hike from St. Peter's to the Vatican Museum, with noisy street-side seating and a quiet interior (€7 pastas, €12 *secondi,* no cover charge, Mon–Sat 12:00–15:30 & 19:00–23:00, closed Sun, Via Leone IV 29, at corner of Vatican wall, tel. 06-3972-3034). The *gelateria* three doors away is good.

La Rustichella serves a famous and sprawling *antipasti* buffet (€7 for a single meal-size plate). Arrive when it opens at 19:30 to avoid a line and have the pristine buffet to yourself (Tue–Sun 12:30–15:00 & 19:30–23:00, closed Mon, near Metro: Cipro, opposite church at end of Via Candia, Via Angelo Emo 1, tel. 06-3972-0649). Consider the fun and fruity **Gelateria Millennium** next door.

Viale Giulio Cesare: This street is lined with cheap Pizza Rustica shops, self-serve places, and inviting eateries.

Along Borgo Pio: The pedestrians-only Borgo Pio—a block from Piazza San Pietro—has restaurants worth a look, such as **Tre Pupazzi** (Mon–Sat 12:00–15:00 & 19:00–23:00, closed Sun, at corner of Via Tre Pupazzi and Borgo Pio, tel. 06-686-8371). At **Vecchio Borgo,** across the street, you can get pasta, pizza slices, and veggies to go (Mon–Sat 9:00–21:00, closed Sun, Borgo Pio 27a, tel. 06-6880-6355).

Picnic Supplies: Turn your nose loose in the wonderful **Via Andrea Doria** open-air market, three blocks north of the Vatican Museum (Mon–Sat roughly 7:00–13:30, until 16:30 Tue and Fri except summer, corner of Via Tunisi and Via Andrea Doria). If the market is closed, try the nearby **IN's supermarket** (Mon–Sat 8:00–20:00, Sun 9:00–14:00, a half-block straight out from Via Tunisi entrance of open-air market, Via Francesco Caracciolo 18).

In South Rome's Testaccio Neighborhood

To locate this restaurant, see the map on page 70.

Trattoria "Da Oio" a Casa Mia serves good-quality, traditional cuisine to a local crowd. It's an upbeat little eatery where you understand the Testaccio passion for the "fifth quarter." (Testaccio, dominated for centuries by its slaughterhouses, is noted for restaurants expert at preparing undesirable bits of the animals.) The menu is a minefield of soft meats. Anything that comes with their *pajata* (baby veal intestines) sauce will give you the edible tripe of a lifetime. While having just pasta for lunch is fine, at dinner they expect diners to order two courses (€10 pastas, €12 *secondi,* Mon–Sat 12:30–15:00 & 19:30–23:30, closed Sun, Via Galvani 43, tel. 06-578-2680).

ROME WITH CHILDREN

Sorry, but Rome is not a great place for little kids. Parks are rare. Kid-friendly parks are rarer. Most of the museums are low-tech and lack hands-on fun.

The good news for kids? Pizza and gelato. And Italians are openly fond of kids, so you'll probably get lots of friendly attention from locals.

SIGHTS AND ACTIVITIES

Rome's many squares are traffic-free, with plenty of space to run and pigeons to feed while Mom and Dad enjoy a coffee at an outdoor table.

When visiting the ancient sites, have some fun with *Rome: Past and Present*, a book with plastic overlays showing how the ruins used to look. It's available at stalls near the entrance of ancient sites.

The following sights, which are fun for kids, are covered in more detail elsewhere in this book: the **Montemartini Museum** for ancient statuary (in an old power plant with art at kids' level, and no crowds—see page 71); **Time Elevator Roma** (like a Disney ride trying to teach Roman history—see page 39); the **Planetarium** and **Astrological Museum** (especially the "Machine of Space and Time") at the Museum of Civilization in E.U.R. (see page 75); and the climb to the top of **St. Peter's dome** (it'll tire them out, plus it includes a dizzy railing view into the church from halfway up the dome—see page 252). The topless double-decker **Trambus Open 110 tour** offers a two-hour swing past all of the major sights (see page 34).

Older children may want to **rent a bike** to see the Ancient Appian Way (see page 30); use the bike/pedestrian path to avoid the traffic. The spooky tunnels of the **Catacombs** are goblin-pleasers (the Catacombs of Priscilla offer half-off entry for kids 15 and under; for Catacombs, see pages 61 and 163–164). The macabre **Cappuccin Crypt,** decorated with bones, fascinates children and adults alike (see page 56).

The **Vatican Museum** comes with mummies and cool statues (in particular, my kids were very entertained by the entire hall of statues with their penises broken off). Nearby, **Castel Sant'Angelo**—with Vatican views and weapon displays—appeals to young knights (see page 63).

The **Church of San Ignazio,** with its false dome, fascinates kids and adults (see page 152). Your children can get a whiff of Egypt by visiting Rome's funky little **pyramid** (free and always viewable, Metro: Piramide—see page 69). Check out the cat hospice in the adjacent park and a climb on the chunk of old Roman wall across the street.

The following attractions will help round out your kid-friendly Rome experience.

The **Villa Borghese Gardens** are Rome's sprawling central park. The best kids' zones are near Porta Pinciana, where you'll find rental bikes, pony rides, and other amusements (Metro: Barberini or Spagna). Summer activities at the gardens, sure to be a hit with kids, include hot-air balloon rides—a great way to get the lay of the land and a life-long memory—and classic Roman puppet shows at Teatro dei Burattini (weekends only). Rome's **zoo,** Bioparco, in the northeast section of the park, houses about 900 animals—including the endangered black lemur, pygmy hippopotamus, Gila monster, and painted hunting dog (kids under 3-free, kids 4–12-€8.50, adults-€10, April–Oct 9:30–18:00, Nov–March 9:30–17:00, last entry one hour before closing, café and picnic areas, Piazzale del Giardino Zoologico 1, Metro: Flaminio, tel. 06-360-8211, www.bioparco.it).

Explora, a children's museum, is a hands-on wonderland for kids 12 and under. Descriptions are in Italian, but younger kids probably won't care (kids under 3-free, kids 4–12-€7, adults-€6, parent must accompany child; four 1.75-hour sessions/day: Tue–Sun at 10:00, 12:00, 15:00, and 17:00; closed Mon, confirm session times in advance by checking website—www.mdbr.it—or calling 06-361-3776, helpful English-speaking staff; 10-min walk from Piazza del Popolo at Via Flaminia 82, Metro: Flaminio).

Bocca della Verità, the legendary "Mouth of Truth," draws a young crowd and parents with cameras. Stick your hand in the mouth of the gaping stone face in the porch wall at the Church of Santa Maria in Cosmedin. As the legend goes, if you're a liar, your hand will be gobbled up. The mouth is only accessible when the church gate is open (free, daily 10:00–16:50, Piazza Bocca della Verità, near the north end of Circus Maximus).

Rome has a big water park called **Hydromania** (€14.50 June–Sept Mon–Fri, €16 Sat–Sun, cheaper for kids 14 and under and anyone arriving after 14:00, open Mon–Fri 9:30–19:00, Sat–Sun 9:30–19:00, Vicolo Casal Lumbroso 200, exit 33 off ring freeway west of the city, tel. 06-6618-3183, www.hydromania.it). **Aquapiper,** another water park, is near Tivoli (Via Maremmana Inferiore, in Guidonia, 15-min

Family Travel Tips

- Take advantage of local information. *Roma c'è*, the periodical entertainment guide (€1.50, new edition every Wed, sold at newsstands, www.romace.it), has a children's section in English. Ask at Rome's TIs about kid-friendly activities. TIs often have a helpful "kid's pack."
- Don't overdo it. Tackle only one or two key sights a day (Vatican Museum, or Colosseum and Forum) and mix in a healthy dose of fun activities, like exploring Rome's great public sites (Piazza Navona, Trevi Fountain, and Villa Borghese Gardens).
- Rome's hotels often give price breaks for kids. (Air-conditioning can be worth the splurge.)
- Eat dinner early (around 19:00) and you'll miss the romantic crowd. While kids may do best in self-serve cafeterias or even fast-food places, if you eat early you'll find that kids are comfortable and welcome in better restaurants. Eating *al fresco* is great with kids. For ready-made picnics that can please adults and kids, try the *rosticcerie* (delis). Pizza Rustica shops sell cheap take-out pizza; kids like *margherita* (tomato and cheese) and *diavola* (similar to pepperoni).
- Public WCs are hard to find: Try museums, bars, gelato shops, and fast-food restaurants.
- Follow this book's crowd-beating tips. Kids don't want to stand in a long line for a museum (which they might not even want to see).
- Any person under 39 inches tall travels free on Rome's public transit.
- If you're taking the train to another city, ask for the family discount ("Offerta Familia") when buying tickets at a counter; or, at a ticket machine, click "Yes" to the "Do you want ticket issue?" cue, then click "Familia." With the discount, families of three to five people with at least one kid (age 12 or under) get 50 percent off the kids' tickets, and 20 percent off the adults'. The deal doesn't apply to all trains at all times, but it's certainly worth asking about.

drive east of Rome, tel. 0774-326-538, www.aquapiper.it); ask about the free shuttle bus from the center of Rome.

Rome feels safe at night, and you can easily take your kids on the **walks** suggested in this book, such as the "Dolce Vita Stroll" on page 320. On the Night Walk Across Rome (page 78), children like slurping up chocolaty *tartufo* at the Tre Scalini café on Piazza Navona and tossing coins in the Trevi Fountain. Consider letting your **child act as tour guide** for an hour by actually leading one of the walks. *Buona fortuna!*

SHOPPING

Shops are generally open from 9:00 to 13:00 and from 16:00 to 19:00. They're often closed on summer Saturday afternoons and winter Monday mornings. For information on VAT refunds and customs regulations, see page 11.

If all you need are souvenirs, a surgical strike at any souvenir shop will do. Otherwise, try...

Department Stores

To conveniently peruse clothes, bags, shoes, and perfume at several major Italian chain stores, wander the shopping complex under the Termini train station (most stores open daily 8:00–22:00).

Large department stores offer relatively painless one-stop shopping. A good upscale department store is **La Rinascente** (like Nordstrom or Macy's). Its main branch is on Piazza Fiume, and there's a smaller store on Via del Corso. **UPIM** is the Roman JC Penney (many branches, including inside Termini station, Via Nazionale 111, Piazza Santa Maria Maggiore, and Via del Tritone 172). **Oviesse,** a cheap clothing outlet, is near the Vatican Museum (on the corner of Via Candia and Via Mocenigo, Metro: Cipro).

Shopping Neighborhoods

A good, midrange shopping area is all along **Via del Corso,** with prices increasing as you head toward Piazza di Spagna. **Via Nazionale** also features a range of affordable shops, especially for clothes and shoes. Cheapskates scrounge through the junky but dirt-cheap shops in the gritty area around **Piazza Vittorio.**

Boutiques

For top fashion, stroll the streets around the Spanish Steps, including **Via Condotti, Via Borgognona** (for the big-name shops), and **Via del**

Babuino (trendy design shops and galleries). For antiques, stroll **Via de Coronari** (between Piazza Navona and the bend in the river), **Via Giulia** (between Campo de' Fiori and the river), and **Via Margutta** (classier, with art galleries too, from Spanish Steps to Piazza del Popolo). For funkier, unique items, try **Via Giubbonari**—it's packed with artsy little boutiques—and other streets near Campo de' Fiori.

Flea Markets

For antiques and fleas, the granddaddy of markets is the **Porta Portese** *mercato delle pulci* (flea market). This Sunday morning market is long and spindly, running between the

actual Porta Portese (a gate in the old town wall) and the Trastevere train station. Starting at Porta Portese, walk through the long, tacky parade of stalls selling cheap bras and shoes. Along the way, check out the con artists with the shell games. Each has shills in the crowd "winning big money" to get suckers involved. Hang on to your wallet—literally, in your front pocket. This is a den of thieves. The heart of the market for real flea-market junk (hiding a few little antique treasures) is the square in the center near Via Cesare Pascarella. I find that a slow stroll through the entire market and back to the Porta Portese takes about 90 minutes. While the shopping gets old (and the vendor food will make you sick), the people-watching is endlessly entertaining (6:30–13:00 Sun only, on Via Portuense and Via Ippolito Nievo; to get to the market, catch bus #75 from Termini station or tram #3 from Largo Argentina, get off the bus or tram on Viale Trastevere, and walk toward the river—and the noise).

At the **Via Sannio** market, you'll find new and used clothing, some handicrafts, and random items that were probably stolen. You won't find antiques (Mon–Sat 9:00–13:30, closed Sun, a couple of blocks south of San Giovanni in Laterano, Metro: San Giovanni).

Open-Air Produce Markets

Rome's outdoor markets provide a fun and colorful dimension of the city that even the most avid museum-goer should not miss. Wander through the easygoing neighborhood produce markets, which clog certain streets and squares every morning (7:00–13:00) except Sunday. Consider the huge **Mercato Trionfale** (three blocks in front of Vatican Museum at Via Andrea Doria). Another great food market is the **Mercato Esquilino** (Via Turati near Piazza Vittorio). Smaller but equally charming slices of everyday Roman life are at markets on these streets and squares: **Piazza delle Coppelle** (near the Pantheon),

Via Balbo (near Termini station and recommended hotels off Via Nazionale), and **Via della Pace** (near Piazza Navona). The covered **Mercato di Testaccio** sells mostly produce and is a hit with photographers and people-watchers (Piazza Testaccio, near Metro: Piramide). And **Campo de' Fiori,** while renovated to fit European Union standards, is still a fun scene.

Airport Souvenirs

Fiumicino (a.k.a. Leonardo da Vinci) Airport sells Italian specialty foods vacuum-packed to clear US customs. Most shops are near the departure gates (after you check your bags and pass through security). Try *parmigiano reggiano* cheese, dried porcini mushrooms or peppers, and better olive oil than you can buy at home. Don't bother buying any salami or prosciutto unless it's canned; you're not allowed to bring fresh meat into the US.

NIGHTLIFE

Romans get dressed up and eat out in casual surroundings for their evening entertainment. For most visitors, the best after-dark activity is simply to stroll the medieval lanes that connect the romantic, floodlit squares and fountains. Head for Piazza Navona, the Pantheon, Campo de' Fiori, Trevi Fountain, Spanish Steps, Via del Corso, Trastevere (around the Santa Maria in Trastevere Church), or Monte Testaccio.

✪ See my Night Walk Across Rome, page 78, and "Dolce Vita Stroll," next page.

Performances

Get a copy of one of the entertainment guides, *Roma c'è* (€1.50, new edition every Wed, sold at newsstands, www.romace.it) or *Evento* (free at TIs). Look at the current listings of concerts, operas, dance, and films. Posters around town also advertise upcoming events.

Classical music lovers will seek out the mega-music complex of the Rome Auditorium (Parco della Musica), designed by contemporary architect Renzo Piano (Via Vittorio Veneto 96, or take Metro to Flaminio and then catch tram #2, www.auditorium.com).

The Teatro dell'Opera has an active schedule of opera and classical concerts (near Via Firenze/Via Nazionale hotels at Via Firenze 72, tel. 06-481-60255, www.operaroma.it).

Musical events at the Church of St. Paul's Outside the Walls range from orchestral concerts to full operatic performances (€20; Tue, Thu, Fri, and Sun at 20:00; arrive at least 30 min early for a good seat, performances last 1–2 hours, Via Nazionale 16a).

Movies

Some theaters around town run movies in their original language (look for "V.O."—*versione originale*). Check out www.inromenow.com for current English-language film showings. **Warner Village Moderno** shows some films in English (Piazza Repubblica, near Termini train station and recommended hotels, tel. 06-892-111). Also try Monday nights at the Trastevere's retro **Alcazar** (Via Merry del Val 14, tel. 06-588-0099).

Nightclubs

An interesting place for club-hopping is **Monte Testaccio.** After 21:00, ride the Metro to Piramide and follow the noise. Monte Testaccio, once an ancient trash heap, is now a small hill whose cool caves house funky restaurants and trendy clubs. (It stands amid a pretty rough neighborhood, though.)

Other Evening Activities

Some **museums** have later opening hours (especially on Sat in summer), offering a good chance to see art in a cooler, less-crowded environment. Ask the TI if any museums are currently open late. The **Scuderie del Quirinale** stays open late when it's hosting major art exhibitions (Sun–Thu 10:00–20:00, Fri–Sat 10:00–22:30, last admission one hour before closing, Via XXIV Maggio 16, tel. 06-696-271, www.scuderiequirinale.it).

Pub crawls, offered year-round by several companies, attract a boisterous crowd. I tried one, and had never seen 50 young, drunk people having so much fun. Look for fliers locally. Late on Friday and Saturday evenings, entire quarters of old Rome seem to be overtaken by young beer-drinking revelers. Campo de' Fiori becomes one big, rude street party.

SELF-GUIDED WALK

Dolce Vita Stroll

This is the city's chic stroll, from Piazza del Popolo (Metro: Flaminio) down a wonderfully traffic-free section of Via del Corso, and up Via Condotti to the Spanish Steps each evening around 18:00. Saturdays and Sundays are best; leave earlier than 18:00 if you plan to visit the Ara Pacis, which closes at 19:00.

Shoppers, people-watchers, and flirts on the prowl fill this neighborhood of some of Rome's most fashionable stores (open after siesta 16:30–19:30). While both the crowds and the shops along Via del Corso have gone downhill recently, elegance survives in the grid of streets between this street and the Spanish Steps.

Throughout Italy, early evening is time to stroll. While elsewhere in Italy this is called the *passeggiata,* in Rome it's a cruder, big-city version called the *struscio.* (*Struscio* means "to rub.") Unemployment among Italy's youth is very high; many stay with their parents even into their thirties. They spend a lot of time being trendy and hanging out. Hard-core cruisers from the suburbs, which

NIGHTLIFE

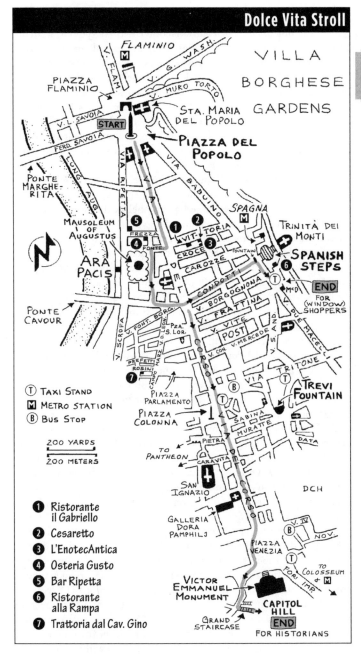

Dolce Vita Stroll

VILLA BORGHESE GARDENS

PIAZZA FLAMINIO

STA. MARIA DEL POPOLO

START

PIAZZA DEL POPOLO

SPAGNA

TRINITÀ DEI MONTI

SPANISH STEPS

END
FOR (WINDOW) SHOPPERS

PONTE MARGHERITA

MAUSOLEUM OF AUGUSTUS

ARA PACIS

PONTE CAVOUR

TREVI FOUNTAIN

PIAZZA PARLAMENTO

PIAZZA COLONNA

TO PANTHEON

SAN IGNAZIO

GALLERIA DORA PAMPHILJ

PIAZZA VENEZIA

TO COLOSSEUM & M

Ⓣ Taxi Stand
Ⓜ Metro Station
Ⓑ Bus Stop

200 YARDS
200 METERS

❶ Ristorante il Gabriello
❷ Cesaretto
❸ L'EnotecAntica
❹ Osteria Gusto
❺ Bar Ripetta
❻ Ristorante alla Rampa
❼ Trattoria dal Cav. Gino

VICTOR EMMANUEL MONUMENT

CAPITOL HILL
END
FOR HISTORIANS

GRAND STAIRCASE

lack pleasant public spaces, congregate on Via del Corso to make the scene. The hot *vroom-vroom* motorscooter is their symbol; haircuts and fashion are follow-the-leader. They are called the *coatto*. In a more genteel small town, the *passeggiata* comes with sweet whispers of *"bella"* and *"bello"* ("pretty" and "handsome"). In Rome, the admiration is stronger, oriented toward consumption—they say *"buona"* and *"buono"*—meaning roughly "tasty." But despite how lusty this all sounds, you'll see as many chunky, middle-aged Italians on this walk as hormone-charged youth. If you get hungry during your stroll, see page 307 for descriptions of the nearby wine bars and restaurants mentioned below.

To get to **Piazza del Popolo,** where the stroll starts, take Metro line A to Flaminio and walk south to the square. Delightfully car-free, Piazza del Popolo is marked by an obelisk that was brought to Rome by Augustus after he conquered Egypt. (It used to stand in the Circus Maximus.) In medieval times, this area was just inside Rome's main entry. For more background on the square, see page 56.

The Baroque church of **Santa Maria del Popolo** is worth popping into (Mon–Sat until 19:00, Sun until 19:30, next to gate in old wall on north side of square). Inside, look for Raphael's Chigi Chapel (KEE-gee, second chapel on left) and two paintings by Caravaggio (the side paintings in the Cerasi Chapel, left of altar). See the listing on page 58 for more information.

From Piazza del Popolo, shop your way down **Via del Corso.** If you need a rest or a viewpoint, join the locals sitting on the steps of various churches along the street. The stroll continues down Via del Corso, but there are some fun detours off the main drag:

If you're up for dinner, or just some wine and appetizers, turn left at Via Vittorio to reach the recommended **Ristorante il Gabriello,** or pass the restaurant and turn right on Via Bocca di Leone for two wine bars: laid-back **Cesaretto,** and, farther down the same street, the more touristy **L'EnotecAntica** (at the corner of Via Bocca di Leone and Via della Croce). If you've taken this detour, take Via della Croce to head back to Via del Corso (you'll turn right out of L'EnotecAntica). Cross the street to Via Pontefici.

Head west on Via Pontefici for sights and more eateries. For the eateries, walk behind the modern building by turning right on Via Soderini; you'll soon see **Osteria Gusto** (nice for a wine-and-cheese break). For a cappuccino that looks and tastes like a work of art, head down Via della Frezza to **Bar Ripetta,** on the corner of Via Ripetta.

Historians continue on Via Pontefici past the fascist architecture to see the massive, rotting, round-brick **Mausoleum of Augustus,** topped with overgrown cypress trees. Beyond it, next to the river, is Augustus' **Ara Pacis** (Altar of Peace), now enclosed within a protective glass-walled museum (described on page 59).

From the mausoleum, return to Via del Corso and the 21st

century, continuing straight until **Via Condotti.** Window shoppers should take a left to join the parade to the **Spanish Steps.** The streets that parallel Via Condotti to the south (Borgognona and Frattini) are more elegant, and filled with high-end boutiques. At the end of the walk is the recommended **Ristorante alla Rampa.** You can catch a taxi home at the taxi stand a block south of the Spanish Steps (at Piazza Mignonelli).

Historians: Ignore Via Condotti and forget the Spanish Steps. (Hungry historians could consider the nearby recommended Trattoria del Car. Gino.) Stay on Via del Corso, which has been straight since Roman times, a half-mile down to the Victor Emmanuel Monument. Climb Michelangelo's stairway to his glorious (especially when flood-lit) square atop Capitol Hill. Whether you zip up the Rome from the Sky elevator, or stand at the balconies flanking the mayor's palace on the square, catch the lovely views of the Forum as the horizon reddens and cats prowl the unclaimed rubble of ancient Rome.

TRANSPORTATION CONNECTIONS

Train Stations

Rome has two major train stations: the more central and larger Termini station and the smaller Tiburtina bus/train station.

Termini Train Station

Termini, Rome's main train station, is a buffet of tourist services: TI (daily 8:00–21:00, poorly marked, 100 yards down track 24 near baggage deposit), train info office (daily 7:00–21:00), ATMs, late-hours banks, 24-hour thievery, cafés (VyTA, on the track 1 side of the station, offers healthful sandwiches), and two good self-service cafeterias (Ciao is upstairs, with fine views and seating; Food Village Chef Express is on the track level, daily 11:00–22:30).

Borri Books, near the front of the station, sells books in English, including popular fiction, Italian history and culture, and kids' books, plus maps upstairs (daily 7:00–23:00).

In the modern mall downstairs, a grocery on the track 1 side of the station also sells useful electronics (daily 7:00–22:00).

There are two pharmacies (both open daily 7:30–22:00, at track 1 and downstairs below track 24).

Baggage deposit is along track 24 downstairs (€4/5 hours, €0.60/hr thereafter, daily 6:00–24:00, follow signs, pass through double doors, and take elevator). The post office is on the ground floor, above the baggage deposit (Mon–Fri 8:00–19:00, Sat 8:00–13:15, closed Sun).

The "Leonardo Express" train to Fiumicino Airport usually runs from track 24 (see "Airports," on page 328).

Termini is also a local transportation hub. The city's two Metro lines (A and B) intersect at the Termini Metro station (downstairs). Buses (including Rome's hop-on, hop-off bus tours—see page 34) leave from the square directly in front of the main station hall. Taxis

Italy's Public Transportation

— RAIL ⊥ PRIVATE RAIL ···· SHIP ––– BUS

✈ AIRPORT (NOT ALL SHOWN)

NOT TO SCALE

queue in front; avoid con men hawking "express taxi" services in unmarked cars (only use ones marked with the word *taxi* and a phone number). To avoid the long taxi line, simply hike out past the buses to the main street and hail one. The station has some sleazy sharks with official-looking business cards; avoid anybody selling anything unless they're in a legitimate shop at the station.

From the Termini train station, most of my accommodation listings are easily accessible by foot (for hotels near the Termini train station) or by Metro (for hotels in the Colosseum and Vatican neighborhoods).

Tiburtina Train Station

Tiburtina, Rome's second-largest train station, is located in the city's northeast corner. In general, slower trains (from Milan, Bolzano, Bologna, Udine, and Reggio di Calabria) and some night trains (from Munich, Milan, Venice, Innsbruck, and Udine) use Tiburtina, as does the night bus to Fiumicino airport. Direct night trains from Paris and Vienna use the Termini station instead. Tiburtina is currently being redeveloped for high-speed rail (expected to begin service in 2009).

Tiburtina is better known as a hub for bus service to destinations all across Italy. Buses depart from the piazza in front of the station. Ticket offices are located in the piazza and around the corner on Circonvallazione Nomentana.

Within the train station are a currency-exchange office and a 24-hour grocery. Tiburtina station is on Metro line B, with easy connections to the Termini train station (a straight shot, four stops away) and the entire Metro system. Or take bus #492 from Tiburtina to various city-center stops (such as Piazza Barberini, Piazza Venezia, and Piazza Cavour) and the Vatican neighborhood.

Types of Trains

You'll encounter several types of trains in Italy. Along with the various pokey, milk-run trains, there are the slow IR (Interregional) and *diretto* trains; the medium *espresso;* and the fast IC (InterCity), IC Plus (InterCity Plus), EC (EuroCity), and bullet-train ES (Eurostar Italia). Railpass holders must purchase a €10–15 seat reservation for ES, IC Plus, and some IC, EC, and international trains (as noted in schedules), while the other trains don't require reservations and are fully covered by a railpass. For point-to-point tickets, you'll pay more the faster you go—but even the fastest trains are still affordable (for example, a second-class ticket on a Rome–Venice express train costs about €50 total). Purchasing seat reservations on the train comes with a nasty penalty. Buying them at the station can be a time-waster unless you use the big blue-and-yellow automatic ticket dispensers, which take cash or credit cards, work well, and also provide schedule information.

You can also buy tickets and make reservations at travel agencies around town, such as the American Express office near the Spanish Steps (Mon–Fri 9:00–17:30, Sat 9:00–12:30, closed Sun, Piazza di Spagna 38, tel. 06-67641). The cost is the same, it can be more convenient (if you find yourself near a travel agency while you're sightseeing), and the language barrier can be smaller than at the station's ticket windows. But many travelers find it's easiest just to buy them at the ticket machines readily available at the station.

TRANSPORTATION

Schedules

At the train station, the easiest way to check schedules is at the handy blue-and-yellow machines; enter the desired date, time, and destination to view all your options. The machines take euros and credit cards, issue tickets, and even make reservations for railpass-holders.

Newsstands usually sell up-to-date regional and all-Italy timetables (€4, ask for the *orario ferroviario*). On the Web, check http://bahn .hafas.de/bin/query.exe/en (Germany's excellent all-Europe website) or www.trenitalia.it. There is a single all-Italy phone number for train information (24 hours daily, tel. 892-021, Italian only, consider having your hotelier call for you).

Study the *partenze*—departure—posters on the walls at the station. Note that the town you're going to may be listed in fine print as an intermediate destination. For example, if you're going from Rome to Orvieto, scan the schedule and you'll notice that trains that go to Florence usually stop in Orvieto en route. Travelers who read the fine print end up with a greater choice of trains.

Strikes are common. They generally last a day, and train employees will simply say *"sciopero"* (strike). Still, sporadic trains—following no particular schedule—lumber down the tracks during most strikes.

Since virtually all of the most convenient connections for travelers depart from the Termini train station, I've listed those below. (But as a precaution, it's always smart to confirm whether your train departs from Termini or Tiburtina.)

From Rome's Termini Train Station by Train to: Venice (roughly hourly, 5–8 hrs, overnight possible), **Florence** (at least hourly, 1.5–2.5 hrs, many stop at Orvieto en route), **Orvieto** (hourly, 50–90 min), **Assisi** (2/hr, 2–3 hrs), **Pisa** (at least hourly, 3–4 hrs), **La Spezia** (10/day, 4 hrs, overnight option), **Milan** (at least hourly, 4.5–8 hrs, overnight possible), **Naples** (at least hourly, 1.5–3 hrs), **Civitavecchia** cruise-ship port (2/hr, 1.25 hrs), **Brindisi** (6/day, 6–9 hrs, overnight possible), **Amsterdam** (7/day, 20 hrs, overnight unavoidable), **Bern** (6/day, 9 hrs, plus several overnight options), **Frankfurt** (7/day, 14 hrs, plus several overnight options), **Munich** (4/day, 11 hrs, plus several overnight options), **Nice** (6/day, 10 hrs), **Paris** (3/day, 13–16 hrs, plus several overnight options, important to reserve ahead), **Vienna** (3/day, 13–15 hrs, plus several overnight options).

Bus Station

Long-distance buses (such as from Siena and Assisi) arrive at Rome's **Tiburtina** station (see "Train Stations," page 324).

Airports

Rome's two airports—Fiumicino (a.k.a. Leonardo da Vinci) and the small Ciampino—share the same website (www.adr.it). Budget flights within Europe (Ryanair, easyJet, Vueling, and Blue Express) use both airports.

Fiumicino Airport

Rome's major airport has TIs in terminals B and C (daily 8:00–19:00, tel. 06-8205-9127, press 2 for English), ATMs, banks, luggage storage, shops, and bars.

A slick, direct **"Leonardo Express" train** connects the airport and Rome's central Termini train station in 30 minutes for €11. Trains run twice hourly in both directions from roughly 6:00 to 23:00 (leaving the airport on the half-hour, double-check train times if you have a late-night or early-morning flight to catch). From the airport's arrival gate, follow signs to *Stazione/Railway Station*. Buy your ticket from a machine or the Biglietteria office. Make sure the train you board is going to the central "Roma Termini" station, not "Roma Orte" or others. However, if you're going to Trastevere, take any train but the Leonardo Express (these cheaper trains cost €4.50, and leave at :00 and :35 past the hour).

Going from the Termini train station to the airport, trains depart at about :22 and :52 past the hour, from track 24. Check the departure boards for "Fiumicino Aeroporto"—the local name for the airport—and confirm with an official or a local on the platform that the train is indeed going to the airport (€11, buy ticket from computerized ticket machines or any *tabacchi* shop in the station, Termini–Fiumicino trains run 5:22–22:52). Read your ticket: If it requires validation, stamp it in the yellow machine near the platform before boarding. Know whether your plane departs from terminal A, B, or C.

Allow plenty of time going in either direction; there's a fair amount of transportation involved, including moving walkways, escalators, and walking (e.g., getting from your hotel to Termini, from Termini to the train platform, the ride to the airport, getting from the airport train station to check-in, etc.).

Shuttle van services run to and from the airport and can be economical for one or two people. Consider Rome Airport Shuttle (€28/1 person from Rome to Fiumicino, extra people-€6 each, €35/1 person from Fiumicino to Rome, extra people-€6 each, 30 percent more from 21:00–7:00, by reservation only, tel. 06-4201-4507 or 06-4201-3469, www.airportshuttle.it).

Rome's **taxis** now have a fixed rate to and from the airport (€40 for up to four people with bags). If your cab driver tries to charge you more than €40 from the airport into town, say, *"Quaranta euro—È la legge"* (kwah-RAHN-tah AY-oo-roh ay lah LAY-jay; which means, "Forty euros is the law"), and they should back off. Your hotel can arrange a taxi to the airport at any hour. To get from the airport into town cheaply by taxi, try teaming up with any tourist also just arriving (most are heading for hotels near yours in the center). Be sure to wait at the taxi stand. Avoid unmarked, unmetered taxis; these guys will try to tempt you away from the taxi stand line-up by offering an immediate (rip-off) ride.

For **airport information,** call 06-65951. To inquire about flights, call 06-6595-3640 (Alitalia: tel. 06-2222; British Airways: tel. 06-5249-2756; Continental: tel. 06-6605-3030; Delta: toll-free tel. 848-780-376, KLM/Northwest: tel. 199-414-199; Swiss International: tel. 848-868-120; United: tel. 02-6963-3707).

Ciampino Airport

Rome's smaller airport (tel. 06-6595-9515) handles some budget airlines, such as easyJet and Ryanair, and charter flights. To get to downtown Rome from the airport, you can take the Cotral bus (2/hr, 40 min) to the Anagnina Metro stop, where you can connect by Metro to the stop nearest your hotel. Rome Airport Shuttle (listed above) also offers service to and from Ciampino. The Terravision Express Shuttle connects Ciampino and Termini, leaving every 20 minutes (€7 one-way, €12 round-trip, www.terravision.it,). The SIT Bus Shuttle also connects the Termini train station to Ciampino (€6, 30–60 min, about 2/hr, runs 8:30–23:30 Ciampino to Termini, 4:30–23:15 Termini to Ciampino, pick-up on Via Marsala just outside the train exit to Ciampino, www.sitbusshuttle.it, tel. 06-591-7844).

Tips for Drivers

The Grande Raccordo Anulare circles greater Rome. This ring road has spokes that lead you into the center. Entering from the north, leave the autostrada at the Settebagni exit. Following the ancient Via Salaria (and the black-and-white *Centro* signs), work your way doggedly into the Roman thick of things. This will take you along the Villa Borghese Gardens and dump you right on Via Veneto in downtown Rome. Avoid rush hour and drive defensively: Roman cars stay in their lanes like rocks in an avalanche.

Parking in Rome is dangerous. Park near a police station or get advice at your hotel. The Villa Borghese underground garage is handy (Metro: Spagna). Garages charge about €24 per day.

Consider this: Your car is a worthless headache in Rome. Avoid a pile of stress and save money by parking at the huge, easy, and relatively safe lot behind the train station in the hill town of Orvieto (follow *P* signs from autostrada) and catching the train to Rome (every 2 hrs, 75 min).

TRANSPORTATION

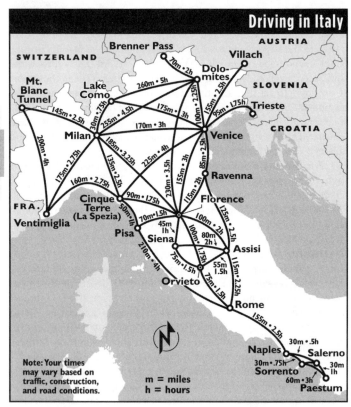

Driving in Italy

AUSTRIA

SWITZERLAND

Brenner Pass
Villach

Mt. Blanc Tunnel

Lake Como

Dolo-mites

SLOVENIA

70m • 2h

260m • 5h

175m
3h

155m • 2.5h

145m • 2.5h

30m•.75h

255m • 4.5h

100m • 2.25h

95m • 1.75h

Trieste

200m • 4h

Milan

170m • 3h

Venice

CROATIA

175m • 2.75h

185m • 3.25h

225m • 3.5h

85m • 2.5h

160m • 2.75h

135m • 2.5h

230m • 4h

Ravenna

90m • 1.75h

155m • 3h

FRA.

Cinque Terre (La Spezia)

50m•1h

70m•1.5h

230m • 3.5h

115m • 2h

Florence

Ventimiglia

Pisa

45m 1h

Siena

100m 2h

125m • 2.5h

80m 2h

55m 1.5h

210m • 4h

75m•1.5h

75m•1.5h

115m • 2.25h

Assisi

Orvieto

75m • 1.5h

Rome

155m • 2.5h

Note: Your times may vary based on traffic, construction, and road conditions.

m = miles
h = hours

Naples

30m • .5h

Salerno

30m•.75h

Sorrento

30m 1h

60m • 3h

Paestum

If you absolutely must drive and park a car in Rome, try to avoid commuter traffic by arriving Friday evening, or anytime during the weekend, and by leaving town during the weekend. Park your car at the Tiburtina station and take a 10-minute ride on the Metro line B into the center (€1/hr, www.atac.roma.it).

Civitavecchia Cruise Ship Port

Hundreds of cruise chips—including Carnival, Royal Caribbean, Princess, and Celebrity lines—dock each year at the Port of Civitavecchia, about 45 miles northwest of Rome. Port facilities include a waiting room, ATMs, bag storage, and snack bar. A **TI** is located between the port and train station at Viale Garibaldi 42 (Mon–Sat 8:00–14:00, Tue also 15:00–18:00, closed Sun, longer hours in summer, tel. 0766-25348).

Getting Between Civitavecchia and Downtown Rome

Twice-hourly **trains** connect Civitavecchia and Rome's Termini station (€5–9, 75 min, regional and pricier IC options).

To reach the Civitavecchia train station from the ship, take the free shuttle bus to the port entrance, and walk about 10–15 minutes straight along the seaside road. Some shuttle buses may take you all the way to the station—ask.

To reach the port from the Civitavecchia station, turn right after you exit and walk 10–15 minutes along the waterfront road. Or you can take either bus #C or #F from in front of the train station; buy your ticket at the *tabacchi* shop before you board. Local taxis also run between the port and the train station (tel. 0766-24251 or 0766-26121).

The road traffic between Civitavecchia and Rome is terrible, making trains faster and more economical than any of your other options. **Taxis** can run €200–400 between Civitavecchia and Rome. A slightly less expensive option is to hire a **private limousine** (figure €150 for up to three people).

Getting Between Civitavecchia and Fiumicino Airport

You'll need to take two **trains** to link Civitavecchia and Fiumicino Airport: one between the airport and Rome's Termini station, and another between Termini and Civitavecchia. See "Airports," above.

Shuttle van services run between the port and Rome's Fiumicino Airport (see page 328). Try **Rome Airport Shuttle** (€140/1–2 people, €160 for up to 6 people, share with others and save, 30 percent more for pick-up between 21:00–7:00, tel. 06-4201-4507 or 06-4201-3469, www.airportshuttle.it).

Day Trips to Rome from Civitavecchia

Do-it-yourselfers will find it easy to visit Rome for a day using the **train** (see details above). Consider disembarking the train at Rome's San Pietro station instead of the more-central Termini station, in order to start your sightseeing with St. Peter's Basilica and the Vatican. Then take the Metro to the Spanish Steps to explore Rome's other sights. If you return to the port from Rome's Termini station, note that Civitavecchia trains generally leave from tracks 27–30, a 10-minute walk from the station entrance.

If your cruise ship stops in Civitavecchia for the day, you may be offered a **shore excursion** to Rome. Many of Civitavecchia's private limousine companies and the Rome Airport Shuttle also offer Rome **tours.** Look for a tour that is a minimum eight hours in length: six hours for sightseeing and two-plus hours of travel time. On shorter tours you'll see most of Rome from the bus window. Plan to spend about €200 per person.

DAY TRIPS
FROM ROME

There's so much to see and do in Rome that you could easily fill a vacation without ever leaving the city limits. But here are several nearby sights that might match your particular interest.

Ostia Antica is similar to Pompeii, but without the crowds. This excavated ancient Roman city is located an easy 45 minutes by Metro and train from Rome.

Tivoli is less accessible (consider seeing it via private tour), but you're rewarded with the ruins of Hadrian's Villa and with the lush

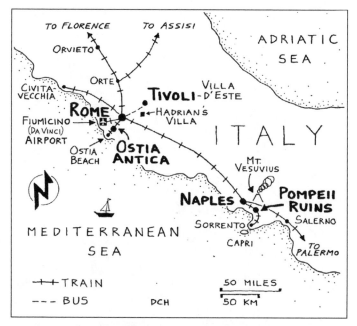

gardens and recently restored fountains of a Renaissance mansion, the Villa d'Este.

Thanks to Italy's excellent train system, **Naples** is a direct 90-minute high-speed-train ride away (or 2–3 hours on cheaper trains), landing you right in the middle of town. Visit Roman statues and mosaics at the wonderful Archaeological Museum, stroll colorful Spaccanapoli street, and have lunch in the city where pizza was born, sampling the exotic chaos of southern Italy.

History hounds can venture an hour farther south of Naples to see the ultimate in ruined Roman cities—**Pompeii**—frozen in time by the eruption of Mt. Vesuvius.

Arrive back in Rome for a late dinner at a sidewalk café to recount your busy day over a glass of wine.

OSTIA ANTICA DAY TRIP

For an exciting day trip, pop down to the Roman port of Ostia, which is similar to Pompeii but a lot closer and, in some ways, more interesting. Because Ostia was a working port town, it shows a more complete and gritty look at Roman life than wealthier Pompeii. Wandering around today, you'll see the remains of the docks, warehouses, apartment flats, mansions, shopping arcades, and baths that served a once-thriving port of 60,000 people.

ORIENTATION

Cost: €6.50 for the site and museum.

Hours: Tue–Sun April–Oct 8:30–19:00, Nov–Feb 8:30–16:00, March 8:30–18:00, last entry one hour before closing, closed Mon.

Getting There: Getting to Ostia Antica from downtown Rome is a snap—it's a 45-minute combination Metro/train ride. It'll cost you just one Metro ticket each way (your €1 Metro ticket also covers the train—so just €2 total round-trip). From Rome, take Metro line B to the Piramide stop (which really *is* next to a pyramid, and several other interesting sights—it's worth a quick stop, see page 69). At Piramide, the train tracks are just a few steps from the Metro tracks—follow signs to *Lido.* All trains depart in the direction of *Lido,* leave every 15 minutes, and stop at Ostia Antica along the way. The lighted schedule at each track will read something like, *"Treno in partenza alle ore 13.25,"* meaning, *"Train departing at 13:25."* Look for the train departing next, hop on, ride for about 30 minutes (keep your Metro ticket handy), and get off at the Ostia Antica stop. (If you don't have a ticket to get back, purchase one at the ticket window at the station, or from the nearby snack bar.)

Leaving the train station in Ostia Antica, cross the road via the blue sky-bridge and walk straight down Via della Stazione di Ostia Antica, continuing straight until you reach the parking lot. The entrance is to your left.

Tip: If you're using the Metro and want to maximize sightseeing efficiency on your Ostia day trip, consider visiting the sights in south Rome—such as St. Paul's Outside the Walls, the Montemartini Museum, and the Testaccio neighborhood—on your return (see page 69).

Information: A map of the site with suggested itineraries is available for €2 from the ticket office. Although you'll see little audio-guide markers at different points throughout the site, there are no audioguides. Tel. 06-5635-8099.

Length of This Tour: Allow two hours.

Cuisine Art: A cafeteria is next to Ostia's museum.

History

Located at (and named for) the mouth *(ostium)* of the Tiber, Ostia was founded about 620 B.C. Its main attraction was the salt gleaned from nearby salt flats, which was a precious preserver of meat in ancient times. Later, as Rome began expanding (around 400 B.C.), Ostia was conquered, and a fort, or *castrum*, was built here. Ostia—often called Rome's first colony—served as a naval base, protecting Rome from any invasion by river. By A.D. 150, when Rome controlled the Mediterranean, Ostia's importance became commercial rather than military. Rome eventually outgrew the port of Ostia, and a vast new port was dug nearby (where Rome's airport now stands). But Ostia remained a key administrative and warehousing center, busy with the big business of keeping more than a million Romans fed and in sandals. With the fall of Rome, the port was abandoned. Over time, the harbor silted up, and the Tiber retreated to about one mile away. The mud that eventually buried Ostia actually protected it from the ravages of time—and stone-scavenging medieval peasants.

THE TOUR BEGINS

Overview

Consider your visit a three-part affair:

1. Follow this tour, which leads you straight down Decumanus Maximus (the town's main drag), with a couple of slight detours, finishing at the forum (the main square).

2. Pop into the museum and consider getting a bite to eat at the cafeteria.

3. Explore the back lanes—going on a visual scavenger hunt—as you wander your way back to the entry point.

• *Find the map (30 yards inside the gate, on the right) for an orientation. Notice how the core of Ostia is a rectangular Roman military camp, with*

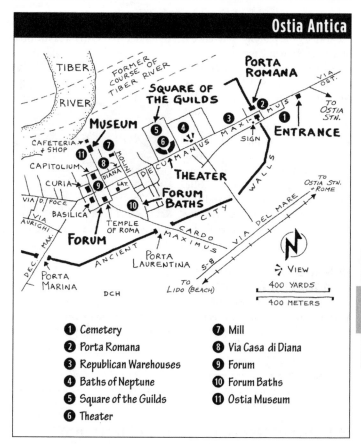

Ostia Antica

- ❶ Cemetery
- ❷ Porta Romana
- ❸ Republican Warehouses
- ❹ Baths of Neptune
- ❺ Square of the Guilds
- ❻ Theater
- ❼ Mill
- ❽ Via Casa di Diana
- ❾ Forum
- ❿ Forum Baths
- ⓫ Ostia Museum

two major roads crossing at the forum. One of four city gates lies ahead, and on your left is the...

❶ Cemetery (Necropolis)

Ancient Romans buried their dead outside the city walls. Detour to find family sepulchres—private open-air rooms lined with niches for ash-filled urns. Until the first century A.D., cremation was common. In the second and third centuries A.D., the Romans here buried their dead in marble and terra-cotta sarcophagi in tombs.

• Ahead (where the road narrows) you enter the ancient city of Ostia through the scant remains of the gate called...

❷ Porta Romana

Just as Rome's Porta Ostiense faced Ostia, Ostia's Porta Romana faced Rome. Just inside to the left (under the big tree), you can see on the gate the bits of the Latin inscription that greeted all who entered. It reads: "The Senate and the people of the colony of Ostia constructed the walls." The "colony" reference is a reminder that Ostia was the first bit of the Roman Empire.

From the gate, Ostia's main street (named Decumanus Maximus) leads straight to the forum, where this walk ends. Note that this road was elevated above some buildings' foundations. Over the centuries, Ostia's ground level rose. You can actually identify buildings from the republic (centuries before Christ) and the empire (centuries after Christ) by  their level. Anything you walk down into is from the earlier period.

· *Just inside the gate and to the right are the...*

❸ Republican Warehouses (Magazzini Repubblicani)

The first century B.C. was busy with activities relating to the river port. Walking along the main street, you pass vast warehouses on the right. The goods of the port—such as grain from Sicily, Egypt, and all of North Africa—were processed and stored in warehouses here before being consumed by Rome.

· *Continue straight ahead about 200 yards. At the little well in the road, you'll see a viewpoint (with railings, above on right). Climb up for a view of the...*

❹ Baths of Neptune (Terme di Nettuno)

Examine the fine mosaic with Neptune riding four horses through the sea. Apart from the cupid riding the dolphin, the sea looks frightening—which it was. The large square to the left of the mosaic would have been busy with people wrestling, stretching, doing jumping jacks, and getting rubdowns. The niches that ring the square housed small businesses.

· *Climb back down, turn right, and immediately take another right. About seven yards in, on your right as you enter a grassy square, you'll see mosaics of ancient Roman boxers (mosaico degli atleti). Continue around the square until you reach an exit directly opposite the entrance. Follow the path to your left (paralleling the main street) as it crosses a typical street lined with apartments (insulae), to reach the...*

❺ Square of the Guilds (Piazzale delle Corporazioni)

This grand square evolved from a simple place—where businessmen would stroll and powwow together—to become a monumental square lined with more than 60 offices of ship owners and traders. This was the bustling center of Rome's import/export industry. Along the sidewalk, second-century A.D. mosaics advertise the services offered by the various shops. Walking counterclockwise, circle the square to "read" the mosaics that advertised in Latin and in pictograms for illiterate or non-Latin-reading sailors. The most common symbol—the lighthouse—was the sign of the port of Ostia. Grain containers are reminders that grain was the major import of Ostia. The elephant marking the office of the Sabratans (a place in present-day Libya) symbolized the sale of ivory or perhaps of exotic animals (great for parties and private spectacles). One shipper advertised dealings with Narbon (Narbonne in present-day France).

In the far corner, you'll see a mosaic that shows porters loading containers from a seagoing ship to a river-going ship and the three-mouthed delta of a river (probably the Nile). Statues of notable local guild members and business leaders decorated the courtyard. The temple in the center was likely related to Ceres, the goddess of harvest and abundance (prosperity from good business). As you leave, notice the small white altar on the right. This would have been used to sacrifice animals—such as the rams carved into the corners—to ask for favor from the gods. The entrails would be read to divine the future, and to determine whether the gods were for or against a particular business venture.

• *Ahead of you, in the direction of the Decumanus Maximus, you can't miss the…*

❻ Theater (Teatro)

Up to 4,000 residents could gather here for entertainment. The three rows of marble steps near the orchestra were for big shots. While this theater seems big, it was twice as high in ancient times. (The upper two-thirds of what you see today is reconstructed.) In its day, a wall rose behind the stage, enclosing the theater. Even today, this place—one of the oldest brick theaters anywhere—is used for concerts. Climb to the top of the theater for a fine view.

• *Continue down the main street. About two blocks down (look for* Tempio Repubblicano *on the corner to the right), Via dei Molini marks the wall of the original military* castrum *(rectangular camp). Before continuing into that oldest part of Ostia, turn right, down Via dei Molini (but don't take the left onto Via Casa di Diana—we'll get to that next). Turn left into the…*

Housing in Ancient Rome

In ancient times, the lower classes lived in miserable, cramped apartment buildings, an average of five floors high (the highest was 10 floors). People living on the higher floors climbed treehouse-type stairs to get to their rooms.

Made cheaply of wood and with weak foundations, many buildings burned or collapsed. The apartments had no heat, no kitchen (food was cooked or purchased elsewhere), and no plumbing. Garbage was tossed out the windows. Chariot and cart traffic were allowed only at night, with the noise (increased by the absence of glass in windows) making sleeping a challenge.

The wealthier classes, on the other hand, lived in sprawling and luxurious homes. These were generally built on one floor, with a series of rooms facing a central open courtyard. Decorative pools collected rainwater. Statues, mosaics, and frescoes were everywhere. Rome's wealthy were as comfortable as the poor were wretched.

❼ Mill (Molino)

This mill building *(panificio)* dates from A.D. 120. Before you are several lava millstones that were used to grind grain. Study the workings: A bowl-like lower structure carefully cupped a moving upper section. Grain would be sprinkled in from a sack hanging from the ceiling. Mules or workers would power the grinding by walking in circles, pushing inserted wood poles. Powdery flour (with not much grit) would eventually tumble out of the bottom of the mill, ready to be made into bread. A nearby room contains two ovens.

• *Now, backtrack down Via dei Molini and take the first right onto…*

❽ Via Casa di Diana

There are three places of interest along this street: the House of Diana, a tavern, and stairs leading to the second floor of an apartment flat for a commanding view.

The **House of Diana** is a great example of an *insula* (a multi-storied tenement complex where the lower-middle class lived). The House of Diana originally had three or four floors (reaching the 66-foot maximum height allowed by Ostia's building codes).

Across the street, and down another 30 yards, is an inn called the **Insula of the Thermopolium.** Belly up to this tavern's bar. You'll see display shelves for food and drinks for sale, a small sink, and scant remains of wall paintings.

Across the street, stairs lead to the top floor of the **Insula of the Paintings.** Climb these for a good view and a chance to imagine life as an apartment dweller in ancient Rome.

• *Now, walk (from street level, of course) to the end of the street, toward the high brick temple that marks Ostia's...*

❾ Forum

Whenever possible, Rome imposed a grid road plan on its conquered cities. After Rome conquered Ostia in about 400 B.C., it built a military camp, or *castrum*—a rectangular fort with east, west, north, and south gates and two main roads converging on the forum. Throughout the empire, Romans found comfort in this familiar city plan.

Ostia's main square became a monumental forum in the imperial period. And dominating this square, like most Roman towns, was the **grand temple** (from A.D. 120). The marble veneer was scavenged in the Middle Ages, leaving only the core brickwork. Note the reinforcement arches in the brick. The temple, called the Capitolium (after the original atop Capitol Hill in Rome), was dedicated to the pagan trinity of Jupiter, Juno, and Minerva. A forum dominated by a Capitolium temple was a standard feature of colonies throughout the empire. The purpose: to transport the Roman cult of Jupiter, Juno, and Minerva to the newly conquered population.

Opposite the Capitolium, and distinguished by its sawed-off column, is the **Temple of Roma and Augustus.** Its position is powerfully symbolic. The power of the emperor stands equal, facing the power of the Capitolium Triad.

At the **basilica,** dating from about A.D. 100, legal activities and commercial business took place (with your back to the forum, it's the building across the street and to your right). Its central nave and two side aisles lead to the "high altar" where the judge sat.

Behind the Capitolium temple—and a little to the right—the pink, modern building houses the fine little **Ostia Museum.** Behind that is a shop and a modern cafeteria (with a tiny Tiber view). And Decumanus Maximus continues through the forum into a vast urban expanse, great for simply wandering (see "Archaeological Scavenger Hunt," page 343).

• *But first, make one more stop. Walk to the front left corner of the Temple of Roma and Augustus. As you're facing it, look left for a street marked by a grand arch. This leads to Ostia's best and largest baths (entrance on right).*

❿ Forum Baths (Terme del Foro)

As you wander around this huge complex, try to imagine it peopled, steaming, and busy. Government-subsidized baths were a popular social and business meeting place in any Roman city. Roman engineers were experts at radiant heat. A huge furnace heated both the water and air that flowed through pipes under the floors and in the walls. Notice the fine marble steps—great for lounging—that led to the pools. People used olive oil rather than soap to wash, so the water needed to be periodically skimmed by servants. The octagonal room (for sunbathing) leads to the elliptical *laconicum* (sweating room), two *tepidaria* (where Romans were rubbed down by masseuses), and the once-steamy *caldarium* with three pools.

From the baths, you can look across the street to the 20-hole **latrine** (across from the entry to the baths). You can still see the pivot hole in the floor that once supported its revolving door. The cutout below the seat was to accommodate the washable sponge on a stick, which was used rather than toilet paper. Rushing water below each seat (brought in by aqueduct) did the flushing.

⓫ Ostia Museum

This small museum offers a delightful look at some of Ostia's finest statuary. Without worrying too much about exactly what's what, just wander and imagine these fine statues—tangled wrestlers, kissing cupids, playful gods—adorning the courtyards of wealthy Ostia families. Most of the statues are second- and third-century A.D. Roman pieces inspired by rare and famous Greek originals. The portrait busts are of real people—the kind you'd sit next to in the baths (or on the toilets).

A forte of Roman sculptors was realistic busts. Roman religion revered the man of the house (and his father and grandfather). A statue of daddy and grandpa was common in the corner of any proper house. Also, with the emperor considered a god, you'd find his bust in classrooms, at the post office, and so on.

The sarcophagi (marble coffins) generally show mythological scenes of Dionysus, the Greek god who relates to the afterlife and immortality. A few humble frescoes give a feeling for how living quarters may have been "wallpapered."

Perhaps the most interesting room (to the left as you enter) features statuary from religions of foreign lands. Being a port town, Ostia accommodated people (and their worship needs) from all over the known world. The large statue of a man sacrificing a bull is a Mithraic altarpiece.

The **cafeteria** and **shop** are in a modern building just behind the museum.

ARCHAEOLOGICAL
SCAVENGER HUNT

As you return to the entry gate, get off the main drag and explore Ostia's back streets. Wandering beyond the forum and then taking the back lanes as you return to the entry, see if you can find:

- Tarp- and sand-protected mosaic flooring.
- White cornerstones put into buildings to fend off wild carts and reflect corners in the dark.
- Fast-food fish joint (on Decumanus Maximus, just beyond the forum).
- Hidden bits of fresco (clue: under hot tin roofs).
- Republican buildings and buildings dating from the empire.
- Stucco roughed up for fresco work (before applying the wet plaster of a fresco, the surface needs to be systematically gouged so the plaster can grip the wall).
- Mill stones for grinding grain (Ostia's big industry).
- Floor patterns made colorful with sliced columns.
- A *domus* (single-family dwellings always faced a fancy, central open-air courtyard).

TIVOLI DAY TRIP

At the edge of the Sabine Hills, 18 miles east of Rome, sits the medieval hill town of Tivoli, a popular retreat since ancient times. Today, it's famous for two very different villas: Hadrian's Villa (the emperor's Versailles-like place of government, which enabled him to rule from outside but still near the capital city), and the recently restored Villa d'Este (the lush and watery 16th-century residence of a cardinal in exile).

The town of Tivoli, with Villa d'Este in its center, is about 2.5 miles from Hadrian's Villa ("Villa Adriana" in Italian). The **TI** is on Largo Garibaldi, near the bus stop (Tue–Sun 10:00–13:00 & 15:00–18:00, closed Mon, tel. 0774-313-536).

Note that Hadrian's Villa is open daily, and Villa d'Este is closed on Monday.

Getting to Tivoli

Reaching the town of Tivoli is easy, and Villa d'Este is in the town center. Getting to Hadrian's Villa is complicated and time-consuming—you'll go into Tivoli and backtrack on another bus—but many find it well worth the trouble (see map on page 333). To return to Rome from Tivoli, simply reverse the connections—*no problema*.

From Rome, take a Metro/bus combination. Ride Metro line B to Ponte Mammolo, and then take the local blue Cotral bus to Tivoli (3/hr, direction: Tivoli).

For **Villa d'Este,** get off in downtown Tivoli, near the central square and the big park with amusements. Cross the road and follow signs (for about a block) that lead to the villa.

To get to **Hadrian's Villa** from downtown Tivoli, catch orange city bus #4X. Buy your ticket at a nearby *tabacchi* shop. When you're ready to leave Hadrian's Villa to go back to Tivoli, catch bus #4 or #4X in the direction of Tivoli. If you're continuing on to Rome, get off at the main road and change to a Cotral bus (ask the bus driver for help—he knows what you need to do). Departures after 16:30 can be sparse.

Several Rome tour companies—including Context Rome, Rome Walks, and Through Eternity—offer private tours of the villas (see their respective websites for specifics; tour companies listed on page 31).

Hadrian's Villa

Built at the peak of Roman Empire by Hadrian (ruled A.D. 117–138), this was a retreat from the political complexity of court life. The

Spanish-born Hadrian—an architect, lover of Greek culture (nicknamed "The Little Greek"), and great traveler—created a microcosm of the lands he ruled as emperor, which at that point stretched from Scotland to the Euphrates and encompassed countless diverse cultures. In the spirit of Legoland, Epcot Center, and Las Vegas, he re-created famous structures from around the world, producing a kind of diorama of his empire in the form of the largest and richest Roman villa anywhere. Just as Louis XIV governed France from Versailles, rather than Paris, Hadrian ruled Rome from this villa of more than 300 evocative acres. He basically spent his last decade here.

Start your visit at the plastic model of the villa (the WC is nearby). Find the Egyptian Canopus (sanctuary of the god Serapis, a canal lined with statues), the Greek Pecile (from Athens), and the Teatro Marittimo (a circular palace, Hadrian's favorite retreat on an island, where he did his serious thinking). Regrettably, this "Versailles of Ancient Rome" was plundered by barbarians. They burned the marble to make lime for cement. The art was scavenged and wound up in the Vatican Museum, the Louvre, and other museums throughout Europe.

Cost and Hours: May–Aug-€10, Sept–April-€6.50, audioguide-€4, May–Aug daily 9:00–19:00, Sept–April daily 9:00–17:00, last entry 90 minutes before closing, tel. 0774-382-733.

Villa d'Este

Ippolito d'Este's grandfather, Alexander VI, was the pope. Ippolito was fast-tracked from birth for church service and became a cardinal. His claim to fame: his pleasure palace at Tivoli. In the 1550s, he destroyed a Benedictine monastery to build this fanciful, late-Renaissance palace. Like Hadrian's Villa, it's a large, residential estate. But this one features hundreds of Baroque fountains, all gravity-powered. The Aniene River, frazzled into countless threads, weaves its way entertainingly through the villa. At the bottom of the garden, the exhausted little streams once again team up to make a sizable river.

The cardinal had a political falling-out with Rome, and was exiled. With this watery wonderland on a cool hill with fine views, he made sure Romans would come to visit. It's symbolic of the luxury and secular interests of the cardinal.

After years of neglect, the villa has been completely restored. All the most eye-popping fountains have been put back in operation, and—with the exception of the two highest jets of the central fountain, which are electric-powered—everything still operates on natural hydraulics. A new terrace restaurant has been installed on the highest level of the garden, opportunely placed to catch cool afternoon sea breezes coming in across the plain of Rome. Expect lots of stairs.

Cost and Hours: €6.50, audio-guide-€4, Tue–Sun 8:30–18:30, closed Mon, closes earlier off-season, last entry one hour before closing, tel. 0774-312-070.

NAPLES AND POMPEII DAY TRIP

While the Eternal City can keep you busy for ages, here are two excuses to leave Rome for a day. The trip south to Naples and Pompeii is demanding (five-plus hours of train travel round-trip). But you'll be rewarded for your time, given the chance to wander ancient Rome's most evocative ruins and go on an urban safari in what is perhaps Europe's most intense city.

If you have a week in Rome and are interested in maximum travel thrills, take a day trip to Naples and Pompeii. (See map on page 333.) Note that Naples' Archaeological Museum is closed on Tuesday. Pompeii is open daily.

Naples (Napoli)

If you like Italy as far south as Rome, go farther south. It gets better. If Italy is getting on your nerves, don't go farther. Italy intensifies as

you plunge deeper. Naples is Italy in the extreme—its best (birthplace of pizza and Sophia Loren) and its worst (home of the Camorra, Naples' "family" of organized crime).

Twenty-five hundred years ago, Neapolis ("new city") was a thriving Greek commercial center. It remains southern Italy's leading city, offering a fascinating collection of museums, churches, and eclectic architecture.

Naples—Italy's third-largest city, with more than two million people—has almost no open spaces or parks, which makes its position as Europe's most densely populated city plenty evident. Watching the police try to enforce traffic sanity is almost comical in Italy's grittiest, most polluted, and most crime-ridden city. But Naples surprises the observant traveler with its impressive knack for living, eating, and raising children in the streets with good humor and decency.

Overcome your fear of being run down or ripped off long enough to talk with people. For a conversation starter, ask a local about the New Year's Eve tradition of tossing chipped dinner plates off of balconies into the streets.

The pulse of Italy throbs in Naples. Like Cairo or Bombay, it's appalling and captivating at the same time, the closest thing to "reality travel" that you'll find in Western Europe. But this tangled mess still somehow manages to breathe, laugh, and sing—with a captivating Italian accent.

Planning Your Time

A blitz visit to Naples and Pompeii looks something like this:

7:30	Catch the express train from Rome to Naples, where you'll transfer to the commuter train to Pompeii
10:30	Tour Pompeii, grab a quick lunch on site, then catch the commuter train back to Naples
14:30	Visit Naples' Archaeological Museum during the heat of the day
15:30	Take my self-guided "Slice of Neapolitan Life" walk
18:30	Finish with a pizza dinner as the city comes to life in the early evening
20:30	Hop on the train back to Rome
22:00	Arrive in Rome

Arrival in Naples

At the central train station (Napoli Centrale), keep your back to the tracks to find a TI to your left (Mon–Sat 9:30–19:00, closed Sun, look for *Ente Provinciale Turismo* sign, tel. 081-268-779, www.inaples.it). To your right are the WCs and a baggage counter (*deposito bagagli*, daily 7:00–23:00). Any train listed on the schedule as leaving Napoli PG departs not from the actual station, but from the Piazza Garibaldi subway station below.

Piazza Garibaldi is straight out the doors. Be on the lookout for thievery (see "Theft Alert," below), especially when hurrying to transfer to the Circumvesuviana commuter train (see below).

If your train does not stop at the central station, other stations such as Campi Flegrei and Mergellina are connected to the central train station by a direct subway route; take the Metro to the Garibaldi stop, which is located beneath the central train station. A railpass or

Naples

ARCHAEOLOGICAL MUSEUM — PIAZZA CAVOUR — PIAZZA CAPUANA MKT. — CENTRAL STATION — NOVARA — VIA FORIA — VIA CARBONARA — CASANOVA — Museo — Cappella Sansevero — DUOMO — PIAZZA GARIBALDI — MONTESANTO METRO + FUNICULAR — PIAZZA DANTE — VIA TARSIA — GESÙ NUOVO — S. BIAGIO — FORCELLA — FISH MKT. — CIRCUMVESUVIANA TERMINUS STATION — VOMERO — VIT. EMAN. — VIA P. SCURA — TOLEDO — VIA B. CROCE — MORG. — S. CHIARA — SPACCA-NAPOLI — CORSO GARI. — VIA PIGNASECCA — PIAZZA CARITA — CORSO — N. MARINA — SPANISH QUARTER — VIA ROMA — VIA DIAZ — DEPRETIS — VIA COLOMBO — PORT — SAN CARLO — GALLERIA UMBERTO I — CASTEL NUOVO — STAZIONE MARITTIMA — PIAZZA PLEBISCITO — BEVE-RELLO — CAR FERRIES TO SICILY & SARDINIA — CHAIA — S. FRAN E PAOLO — VITTORIO TUNNEL — N. SAURO — ROYAL PALACE — TO SORRENTO, CAPRI, ISCHIA & PROCIDA — TO LUNGOMARE — VIA PARTENOPE — 800 YARDS — 800 METERS — CASTEL DELL'OVO — BORGO MARINARO — DCH — N — M METRO STATION — B BUS STOP — View

train ticket to the central train station covers the ride (subway trains depart about every 10 min).

Continuing to Pompeii on the Circumvesuviana

Naples and Pompeii are connected by a **commuter train**—the Ferrovia Circumvesuviana—handy for tourists, commuters, and pickpockets.

Catch it in the basement of Naples' central train station (down the stairs, near track 14). Remember that in 2009, the Circumvesuviana may be on the ground level, past track 24; follow *Circumvesuviana* signs. You'll find the ticket booth, schedules posted on the wall, and a lighted departure board. You're looking for trains whose final destination is Sorrento.

If you're day-tripping, there are two trains per hour to Pompeii. It's a 35-minute trip (€3.20 one-way, not covered by railpasses). The faster, express trains are marked *DD* on the schedule (12/day). When you buy your ticket, purchase a round-trip ticket if you'll be returning to Naples: Ask for *"Pompeii, andata e ritorno"* (ahn-DAH-tah ay ree-TOR-noh). Ask the ticket seller which track your train will depart from (*"Che binario?"*—kay bee-NAH-ree-oh). Before boarding, check the schedule carefully or confirm with a local to make sure the train is going to Pompeii. You want the "Pompei Scavi, Villa dei Misteri" stop.

When returning to Naples' central train station on the Circumvesuviana, get off at the next-to-last stop, called Garibaldi (a.k.a. Napoli Collegamento F.S.). The train station is just upstairs.

For about €70–80, you can take a **taxi** from Naples to Pompeii; agree on a fixed price without the meter and pay upon arrival.

Theft Alert

Err on the side of caution. Don't venture into neighborhoods that make you uncomfortable. Walk with confidence, as if you know where you're going and what you're doing. Assume able-bodied beggars are thieves. Tighten your money belt and keep it completely hidden.

Stick to busy streets and beware of gangs of hoodlums. A third of the city is unemployed, and past local governments set an example that the Mafia would be proud of. Assume con artists are cleverer than you. Any jostle or commotion is probably a thief-team smokescreen. To keep bags safe, it's probably best to check them at the Centrale train station.

Perhaps your biggest risk of theft is while catching or riding the Circumvesuviana commuter train. If you're connecting from a major train, you'll be stepping from a relatively secure compartment into a crowded commuter train filled with thieves hunting disoriented American tourists with luggage. While I ride the Circumvesuviana comfortably and safely, each year I hear of many who get ripped off on this ride. You won't be mugged—just conned or pickpocketed. Con artists may say you need to "transfer" by taxi to catch the Circumvesuviana; you don't. Anyone offering to help you with your bags is likely a thief, despite displayed credentials. There are no porters at the central train station or in the basement where the Circumvesuviana station is located. Wear your money belt, hang on to your bag, and don't display any valuables.

Getting Around Naples

Naples' subway, the Servizio Metropolitano, runs from the central train station (Garibaldi stop) through the center of town (direction: Pozzuoli), stopping at Piazza Cavour (Archaeological Museum),

Piazza Dante, and Montesanto (top of Spanish Quarter and Spacca-napoli). Tickets are €1 and are good for 90 minutes. An all-day ticket costs €3. If you can afford a taxi, don't mess with the buses. A short taxi ride costs about €5 (insist on the meter, €1.50 supplement charged on Sun, €2 supplement after 22:00). For information on getting to the Archaeological Museum, see below.

SIGHTS

▲▲▲Archaeological Museum (Museo Archeologico)

For lovers of antiquity, this museum makes Naples a worthwhile stop. Considering the importance of its collection and its popular-ity, it's remarkable how ramshackle, unkempt, and dumpy its displays are. Still, if you can overlook the dust bunnies, this museum offers the best possible peek into the artistic jewelry boxes of Pompeii and Herculaneum. The actual sights are impressive but barren; the finest art and all the artifacts ended up here.

Cost and Hours: €6.50, often €10 with mandatory charge for special exhibits, Wed–Mon 9:00–20:00, last entry 19:00, closed Tue, tel. 081-440-166. To visit the Secret Room (Gabinetto Segreto), which contains erotic art from Pompeii, you have to make an appoint-ment at the information counter, which is immediately on your right as you enter (included in admission, you get a 15-min window; room described later in this chapter).

Getting There: From the central train station (Napoli Centrale), follow signs to the Metro, called *Servizio Metropolitano* (downstairs). Buy tickets from the yellow kiosk and ask which track—*"Binario?"*—to Piazza Cavour (direction: Pozzuoli). Go through a *solo metropoli-tano* turnstile and ride the subway one stop. As you leave the Metro, you can exit and hike uphill, or follow *Linea 1 Museo* signs through a long series of underground moving sidewalks to the new *Museo* stop (on a different line) closer to the museum. Either way, the museum is a grand old red building located up a flight of stairs at the top of the block.

Information: For a **guided tour,** try to find Pina—look for her licensed guide nametag (€120 for a 2-hour tour, help her assemble a group to split this cost with up to 10 others). **Audioguides** cost €4 (at ticket desk, rentable for 3 hours). Photos are allowed without a flash. The shop sells a worthwhile green *National Archeological Museum of Naples* guidebook for €7.50. Bag check is obligatory and free.

The entire museum is in flux—everything is being moved around and renovated. Try to get an up-to-date floor plan as you enter. If you can't find a particular work, ask a museum custodian, *"Dov'è?"* ("Where?"), followed by the item's name.

Self-Guided Tour: Overview

Entering the museum, stand at the base of the grand staircase. To your right, on the ground floor, are larger-than-life statues from the Farnese

Collection, starring the *Toro Farnese*. Up the stairs on the mezzanine level (turn left at the lion) are mosaics and frescoes from Pompeii, including the *Battle of Alexander* and the Secret Room of erotic art. On the top floor is a scale model of Pompeii and bronze statues from Herculaneum (a nearby town destroyed in the same eruption that devastated Pompeii). You'll find WCs by circling behind the staircase.
• *From the base of the grand staircase, turn right and head to the far end.*

Ground Floor: The Farnese Collection

The museum's ground floor alone has enough Greek and Roman art to put any museum on the map. Its highlight is the Farnese Collection, a grand hall of huge, bright, and wonderfully restored statues excavated from Rome's Baths of Caracalla.

The **Toro Farnese**—a tangled group with a woman being tied to a bull—is the largest intact statue from antiquity. At 13 feet, it's the tallest ancient marble group ever found. A third-century A.D. copy

of a lost bronze Hellenistic original, it was carved out of one piece of marble. Michelangelo and others "restored" it at the pope's request—meaning that they integrated surviving bits into a new work. Panels on the wall show which pieces are actually carved by Michelangelo (in blue on the chart): the head of the woman in back, the torso of the aunt under the bull, and the dog. (Imagine how the statue would stand out if it was thoughtfully lit and not surrounded by white walls.)

Here's the story behind the statue: Once upon an ancient Greek time, King Lycus was bewitched by Dirce. He abandoned his pregnant wife, Antiope (standing regally in the background). The single mom gave birth to twin boys shown here, who grew up to kill their deadbeat dad and tie Dirce to the horns of a bull to be bashed against a mountain. Captured in marble, the action is thrilling: cape flailing, dog snarling, hooves in the air. You can almost hear the bull snorting. And in the back, Antiope oversees this harsh ancient justice with satisfaction.

At the far end of the hall stands **Hercules.** In a small room behind Hercules is a glass case with the sumptuous **Farnese Cup** (*Tazza Farnese,* second century B.C., from Egypt). This large, ancient cameo made of agates looks less like a cup than a cereal bowl. Its decorations are both Egyptian (the Nile toting a lush cornucopia) and, on the flip side, Greek (Medusa's head).

• *Now head up to the mezzanine level.*

Mezzanine: Pompeiian Mosaics and the Secret Room

Most of these mosaics—of animals, musicians, and geometric designs—were taken from Pompeii's House of the Faun (see page 370). The house's delightful centerpiece is a 20-inch-high statue of the *Dancing Faun.* This rare surviving Greek bronze statue (from the fourth century B.C.) is surrounded by some of the best mosaics from the age.

A highlight is the grand *Battle of Alexander,* a second-century B.C. copy of the original Greek fresco, done a century earlier. It

decorated a floor in the House of the Faun. It was found intact; the damage you see occurred as this treasure was moved from Pompeii to the king's collection here. The painting (on left, made before it was moved) shows how it once looked. Alexander (left side of the scene, with curly hair and sideburns) is about to defeat the Persians under Darius (central figure, in chariot with turban and beard). This pivotal victory allowed Alexander to quickly overrun much of Asia (331 B.C.). Alexander is the only one without a helmet...a confident master of the battlefield while everyone else is fighting for their lives, eyes bulging with fear. Notice the shading and perspective, which Renaissance artists later worked so hard to accomplish. (A modern reproduction of the mosaic is now back in the House of the Faun; see page 370.)

The **Secret Room (Gabinetto Segreto),** contains a sizable assortment of erotic frescoes, well-hung pottery, and perky statues that once decorated bedrooms, meeting rooms, brothels, and even shops at Pompeii and Herculaneum. You'll have to make an appointment to view the room (see "Cost and Hours," above), and at those times, you might also be escorted by a local guide (offering a 20-minute tour primarily in Italian but, if you ask nicely, likely in English). Even without a guide, the art speaks for itself (and comes with good printed descriptions in English).

The first room contains big stone penises that once projected over Pompeii's doorways. A massive phallus was not necessarily a sexual symbol, but a magical amulet used against the "evil eye." It symbolized fertility, happiness, good luck, riches, straight A's, and general well-being.

The next room is furnished and decorated as an ancient brothel might have been. The 10 frescoes on the wall functioned as both a menu of services offered and as a kind of *Kama Sutra* of sex positions.

These bawdy statues and frescoes—often found in Pompeii's grandest houses—were entertainment for guests. (By the time they made it to this museum, in 1819, the frescoes could only be viewed with permission from the king—see the letters in the glass case just outside the door.) The Roman nobles commissioned the wildest scenes imaginable. Think of them as ancient dirty jokes: Find the horny pygmies from Africa in action. In a nearby fresco, a faun playfully pulls the sheet off a beautiful woman, only to be grossed out by the plumbing of a hermaphrodite. (Perhaps the original *"Mamma mia!"*) Venus, the patron goddess of Pompeii, was a favorite pin-up girl. In a particularly high-quality statue, a goat and a satyr illustrate the act of sodomy.

• *So, now that your travel buddy is finally showing a little interest in art... let's finish the visit on the top floor.*

Top Floor: Statues, Artifacts, and a Model of Pompeii

Climb the stairs to the top floor, entering a grand, empty hall. This was the great hall of the university (17th and 18th centuries) until the building became the royal museum in 1777. The sundial (from 1791) still works. At noon, a sunray strikes the spot, indicating today's date... if you know your zodiac.

To your right are rooms containing **bronze statues** from Herculaneum—of racers, dancers, and fauns (first-century B.C. copies of fourth-century B.C. originals). They once decorated the holiday home (Villa dei Papyri in Herculaneum) of Julius Caesar's father-in-law. Look into the lifelike blue eyes of the intense *atleta* (athletes)—bent on doing their best. The *Five Dancers,*

with their inlaid ivory eyes and graceful poses, decorated a portico. *Resting Hermes* (with his tired little heel wings) is taking a break. The *Drunken Faun* (singing and snapping his fingers to the beat, with a wineskin at his side) is clearly living for today—true to the *carpe diem* preaching of the Epicurean philosophy. Caesar's father-in-law was an Epicurean philosopher, and his library—with 2,000 papyrus scrolls—supported his outlook.

Return to the grand hall and continue to the other side, passing through several rooms of vases, statuettes, spoons, glassware, and other objects found at Pompeii. Keep going to the far end, where you'll find a **scale model** of the archaeological site of Pompeii, circa 1879 (*plastico di Pompeii*). Belly up to the railing and find the Porta Marina entrance and the large rectangle of the town's forum. Another model on the wall shows the site in 2004, after more excavations.

For extra credit, visit ***Doriforo***. (Ask a guard, *"Dov'è il Doriforo?"* He was last spotted on the ground floor, in the hall to the left, as you face the staircase.) This seven-foot-tall "spear-carrier" (the literal translation of *doriforo*) just stands there, holding a missing spear. What's the big deal about this statue, which looks like so many others? It's a marble copy made by the Romans of one of the most-copied statues of antiquity, a fifth-century B.C. bronze Greek original by Polycletus. This copy once stood in a Pompeii gym, where it inspired ancient athletes with the ideal proportions of Greek beauty. Centuries later, the *Doriforo*—so full of motion, and so realistic in its *contrapposto* pose (weight on one foot)—inspired Donatello and Michelangelo, triggering the Renaissance. And so the glories of ancient Pompeii, once buried and forgotten, live on today.

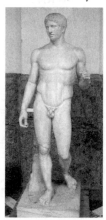

SELF-GUIDED WALK

▲▲▲A Slice of Neapolitan Life

Walk from the Archaeological Museum through the heart of town and back to the station. Allow at least three hours, plus pizza and sightseeing stops. Those on a limited time budget could do a shorter version in an hour by walking briskly and skipping the sights south of Spaccanapoli (i.e., the Royal Palace, Teatro San Carlo, and Galleria Umberto I).

Naples, a living medieval city, is its own best sight. Couples artfully make love on Vespas surrounded by more fights and smiles per cobblestone than anywhere else in Italy. Rather than seeing Naples as a list of sights, visit its one great museum and then capture its essence by taking this walk through the core of the city. Should you become overwhelmed or lost, step into a store and ask for directions: "Where is the central station?" in Italian is *"Dov'è la stazione centrale?"* (DOH-vay lah staht-zee-OH-nay chen-TRAH-lay?). Or point to the next sight in this book.

Part 1: Via Toledo and the Spanish Quarter

Leaving the Archaeological Museum at the top of Piazza Cavour

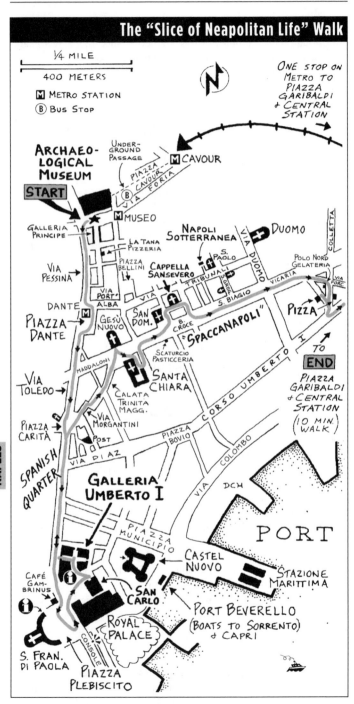

The "Slice of Neapolitan Life" Walk

¼ MILE

400 METERS

Ⓜ METRO STATION
Ⓑ BUS STOP

N

ONE STOP ON METRO TO PIAZZA GARIBALDI & CENTRAL STATION

ARCHAEO-LOGICAL MUSEUM

UNDER-GROUND PASSAGE

PIAZZA CAVOUR A FORIA

Ⓜ CAVOUR

START

GALLERIA PRINCIPE

Ⓑ

Ⓜ MUSEO

NAPOLI SOTTERRANEA

VIA DUOMO

✚ DUOMO

COLLETTA

LA TANA PIZZERIA

S. PAOLO

VIA PESSINA

PIAZZA BELLINI

CAPPELLA SANSEVERO

TRIBUNALI

VICARIA

POLO NORD GELATERIA

VIA FORC

VIA PORT' ALBA

VIA

S. BIAGIO

DANTE

Ⓜ

GESÙ NUOVO

SAN DOM.

B. CROCE

"SPACCANAPOLI"

PIZZA

PIAZZA DANTE

MADDALONI

SCATURCIO PASTICCERIA

END

VIA TOLEDO

SANTA CHIARA

TO PIAZZA GARIBALDI & CENTRAL STATION (10 MIN. WALK)

PIAZZA CARITÀ

CALATA TRINITA MAGG.

VIA MORGANTINI

CORSO UMBERTO I

POST

PIAZZA BOVIO

SPANISH QUARTER

VIA DIAZ

COLOMBO

VIA

DCH

PORT

GALLERIA UMBERTO I

PIAZZA MUNICIPIO

CAFÉ GAM-BRINUS

ⓘ

CASTEL NUOVO

STAZIONE MARITTIMA

ⓘ

SAN CARLO

PORT BEVERELLO (BOATS TO SORRENTO) & CAPRI

CONSOLE

ROYAL PALACE

✚

S. FRAN. DI PAOLA

PIAZZA PLEBISCITO

NAPLES

(Metro: Piazza Cavour), turn right and go one block, to the head of Via Pessina. The first part of this walk is a straight one-mile ramble down this boulevard to Galleria Umberto I near the Royal Palace.

Busy Via Pessina leads downhill to **Piazza Dante**—marked by a statue of Dante. Originally, a statue of a Spanish Bourbon king stood here. The grand red-and-gray building is typical of the Bourbon buildings from that period. In 1861, with the unification of Italy, the king (symbolic of Italy's colonial subjugation) was replaced by Dante—considered the father of the Italian language and a strong symbol of Italian nationalism.

Poor old Dante looks out over the urban chaos with a hopeless gesture. The **Alba Gate,** part of Naples' old wall and the entrance to a small street often lined with street-side book vendors, is to Dante's left. Via Pessina, the long, straight road that we're walking, originated as a military road built by Spain around 1600. It skirted the old town wall to connect the Spanish military headquarters (now the museum) with the Royal Palace (down by the bay).

A new subway station has recently been built here on Piazza Dante. Construction was slowed by the city's rich underground history: 13 feet down are Roman ruins, 23 feet down are Greek ruins.

Continue walking downhill, remembering that here in Naples, red traffic lights are considered "decorations." When crossing a street, try to tag along with a local. The people here are survivors; a long history of corrupt and greedy colonial overlords has taught Neapolitans to deal with authority creatively. Many credit this aspect of Naples' past for the advent of organized crime here.

Via Pessina becomes Via Toledo, Naples' principal shopping street. In 1860, from the white marble balcony of the Neoclassical building overlooking Piazza Sette Settembre, the famous revolutionary Garibaldi declared Italy united, and Victor Emmanuel its first king. Not until 1870, when Rome fell to the unification forces, was the dream of Italian unity actually realized.

Continue straight on Via Toledo (even though the arterial jogs left). At the next left (Via Maddaloni), about three blocks below Piazza

Dante (and a block past Piazza Sette Settembre), you cross the long, straight street called **Spaccanapoli** ("Split Naples"). Look left. Look right. Since ancient times, this thin street (which changes names several times) has bisected the city. (We'll return to this street later. If you want to abbreviate this walk, turn left here and skip ahead to "Part 2," page 359.)

NAPLES

Via Toledo runs through **Piazza Carità,** with fascist architecture (from 1938, sternly straight and obedient lines) overlooking the square.

To see the best fascist architecture in town, make a brief side-trip from here. With your back to Via Toledo, leave Piazza Carità downhill on the right-hand corner, going a block to the Poste e Telegrafi building. There you'll see several government buildings with stirring reliefs singing the praises of a totalitarian society.

From Piazza Carità, wander down Via Toledo a few blocks, past more fascist architecture—the two banks on the left. Try robbing the second one (Banco di Napoli, Via Toledo 178).

From here, side-trip uphill three blocks into the **Spanish Quarter,** Naples at its rawest, poorest, and most historic. The only thing predictable about this Neapolitan tide pool is the ancient grid plan of its streets (which survives from Greek times), the friendliness of its shopkeepers, and the boldness of its mopeds. Concerned locals will tug on their lower eyelids, warning you to be wary. Pop into a grocery shop and ask the man to make you his best ham-and-mozzarella sandwich. The price should be around €4.

Return to Via Toledo (with more people than cars) and work your way down to the immense **Piazza Plebiscito,** which celebrates the historic 1861 vote when Naples chose to join Italy. From here, you'll see the Church of San Francesco di Paola with its Pantheon-inspired dome and broad, arcing colonnades. Opposite is the **Royal Palace** (Palazzo Reale), which has housed Spanish, French, and even Italian royalty. Look for eight kings in the niches, each from a different dynasty (left to right: Norman, German, French, Spanish, Spanish, Spanish, French—the brother-in-law of Napoleon—and, finally, Italian: Victor Emmanuel II, King of Savoy). The statues were done at the request of V.E. II's son, so his dad is the most dashing of the group. The huge and lavish palace welcomes the public (€4, Thu–Tue 9:00–20:00, closed Wed, shorter hours off-season, last entry one hour before closing, audioguide-€4/1 person, €5/2 people).

Next door, peek inside the Neoclassical **Teatro San Carlo,** Italy's second-most-respected opera house—after Milan's La Scala. Guided visits (€5, about 3/hr, 2-language tours last 20 min—you listen to English for 10 min, then are free to wander for 10) basically just show you the fine auditorium with its 184 boxes, each with a big mirror to reflect the candle lighting—until it burned down in 1816 (daily 9:00–18:00, tel. 081-664-545, www.teatrosancarlo.it). The huge castle on the harborfront just beyond the palace houses government bureaucrats and the Civic Museum, featuring 14th- to 16th-century art (€5, Mon–Sat 9:00–19:00, closed Sun).

Under the Victorian iron and glass of the 100-year-old **Galleria Umberto I,** enjoy a coffee break or sample a unique Neapolitan pastry called *sfogliatella* (crispy scallop shell–shaped pastry filled with sweet

ricotta cheese). Go through the tall yellow arch at the end of Via Toledo or across from the opera house. Gawk up.

Once inside, **Gambrinus Café**—taking you back to the elegance of 1860—is the classic place for a *sfogliatella* (sfohl-yah-TEHL-lah) pastry. Or you might prefer the mushroom-shaped, rum-soaked doughnuts called *babà* (huge variety). Pay double to sit, or stand at the bar (Mon–Sun 7:00–24:00).

Part 2: Spaccanapoli Back to the Station

To continue your walk, double back up Via Toledo to Piazza Carità, veering right on Via Morgantini to Via Maddaloni. You're back at the straight-as-a-Greek-arrow street, Spaccanapoli—formerly the main thoroughfare of the Greek city of Neapolis.

The rest of this walk is basically a straight line down the series of streets locals have nicknamed Spaccanapoli. Stop at **Piazza Gesù Nuovo** to visit the two bulky old churches (both free, daily 7:00–13:00 & 16:00–19:00). The square is marked by a towering monument to the Counter-Reformation (Baroque, early 18th century). With Naples' Spanish heritage, Jesuits were powerful here. But locals never attacked Protestants with the full fury of the Spanish Inquisition.

Check out the austere, fortress-like **Church of Gesù Nuovo.** The unique pyramid grill facade was from a fortress (1470), which predated the church (1600s). Step inside for a brilliant Baroque interior. The second chapel on the right features a much-kissed statue of Giuseppe Moscati, a Christian doctor famous for helping the poor. Moscati was made a saint in 1987. Continue on to the third chapel and enter the Sala Moscati for a huge room filled with *Ex Voto*—tiny red-and-silver plaques of thanksgiving for miracles attributed to St. Moscati. Each has a relief symbolic of the ailment cured. Naples' practice of *Ex Voto*, while incorporated into its Catholic rituals, goes back to its pagan Greek roots. A glass case displays possessions and photos of the great doctor. As you leave, notice the big bomb casing hanging in the corner. It fell through the church's dome in 1943, but caused almost no damage...yet another miracle.

Across the street, the simpler Gothic **Church of Santa Chiara** dates from a period of French Angevin rule (14th century). Notice the stark Gothic/Baroque contrast between this church and the Gesù Nuovo. The faded Trinity (from the school of Giotto, left of entry on back wall) is an example of the fine frescoes that once covered the walls (most removed during Baroque times). The altar is adorned with the finely carved Gothic tomb of an Angevin king. The Bourbon

NAPLES

Pizza in Naples

Naples is the birthplace of pizza, baked with just the right combination of fresh dough, mozzarella, and tomatoes in traditional wood-burning ovens.

Drop by one of the two most traditional pizzerias.

Antica Pizzeria da Michele, a few blocks from the central train station, is for purists (Mon–Sat 10:00–24:00, closed Sun, filled with locals; from the station, head to the left off Piazza Garibaldi, turn left onto Corso Umberto—juts off Piazza Garibaldi at 11 o'clock with the station to your back—then turn right on Via Pietro Colletta, look for the vertical red *Antica Pizzeria* sign, tel. 081-553-9204). It serves two kinds: *margherita* (tomato sauce and mozzarella) or *marinara* (tomato sauce, oregano, and garlic, no cheese). A pizza with beer costs €5.

Some locals prefer **Pizzeria Trianon,** across the street. Da Michele's archrival offers more choices, higher prices (€4–7), air-conditioning, and a cozier atmosphere. (If you're looking for less chaos, head upstairs.) In the entryway pizza kitchen, you can survey the evolution of a humble wad of dough into a smoldering, bubbly feast (daily 11:00–15:30 & 18:30–23:00, Via Pietro Colletta 42, tel. 081-553-9426).

chapel, stacked with Bourbon royalty, is just to the right.

Continue straight down traffic-free Via B. Croce. Since this is a university district, you'll see lots of students and bookstores. This neighborhood is also extremely superstitious. You may see incense-burning women with carts of good-luck charms for sale.

The next square is **Piazza S. Domenico Maggiore**—marked by an ornate 17th-century plague monument. The venerable **Scaturchio Pasticceria** is another good place to try Naples' *sfogliatella* pastry (€1.40 to go, costs double at a table on the square, daily 7:20–20:40).

From this square, detour left along the right side of the castle-like church, then follow yellow signs and take the first right and walk one block to **Cappella Sansevero** (€6, Mon and Wed–Sat 10:00–18:00, Sun 10:00–13:30, closed Tue, Via de Sanctis 19). No photos are allowed in the chapel (postcards available in gift shop).

This small chapel is a Baroque explosion mourning the body of Christ, who lies on a soft pillow under an incredibly realistic veil. It's also the personal chapel of Raimondo de Sangro, an eccentric Freemason. The monuments share the Freemason philosophy of freedom through enlightenment.

Study the incredible *Veiled Christ* in the center. It's all carved out of marble and is like no other statue I've seen (by Giuseppe "Howdeedoodat" Sammartino, 1753). The Christian message (Jesus died for our salvation) is accompanied by a Freemason message: The veil represents how the body and ego are an obstacle to real spiritual freedom. As you walk from Christ's feet to his head, notice how the expression of Jesus' face goes from suffering to peace.

Raimondo de Sangro lies buried at the far (altar) end. An inventor, he created the deep-green pigment used on the ceiling fresco. The inlaid M.C. Escher-esque maze on the floor around de Sangro's tomb is another Freemason reminder of how the quest for knowledge gets you out of the maze of life.

To the right of the altar, the statue of *Despair* struggles with a marble rope net (carved out of a single piece of stone), symbolic of a troubled mind. The Freemason symbolism shows how knowledge—in the guise of an angel—frees the human mind. On the opposite side of the altar from *Despair*, a veiled woman fingers a broken plaque, symbolizing...something.

Your Sansevero finale is downstairs: two mysterious skeletons. Perhaps another of the mad inventor's fancies: injecting a corpse with a fluid to fossilize the veins so that they'll survive the body's decomposition.

Return to Via B. Croce (a.k.a. Spaccanapoli), turn left, and continue your Spaccanapoli cultural scavenger hunt. At the intersection of Via Nilo, find the statue of *The Body of Naples* on your left, with the abundant cornucopia symbolizing the abundance of Naples. (I asked a Neapolitan man to describe the local women, who are famous for their beauty. He replied simply, "Abundant.") This intersection is considered the center of old Naples.

Five yards farther down (on the right) is the tiny **"Chapel of Maradona"**—a niche on the wall dedicated to Diego Maradona, a

soccer star who played for Naples in the 1980s. Locals consider soccer almost a religion...and this guy was practically worshipped. You can even see a "hair of Diego" and a teardrop from the city when he went to another team for more money. In later years he was (like Naples itself) sullied with organized crime, drugs, and police problems.

A few blocks farther, at the little square, Via San Gregorio Armeno leads left into a very colorful district (kitschy Baroque church on left with a Vesuvius lava shrine in its portico, lots of shops selling tiny components of fantastic manger scenes).

As Via B. Croce becomes Via S. Biagio dei Librai, notice the gold and silver shops. Some say stolen jewelry ends up here, is melted down immediately, and appears in a salable form as soon as it cools. The inimitable Sr. Grassi runs the Ospedale delle Bambole (doll hospital) at #81.

Cross busy Via Duomo. The street and side-street scenes along Via Vicaria intensify. This is known as a center of the Camorra (organized crime). Paint a picture with these thoughts: Naples has the most intact street plan of any ancient Roman city. Imagine this city then (retain these images as you visit Pompeii), with street-side shop-fronts that close up after dark to form private homes. Today, it's just one more page in a 2,000-year-old story of a city: all kinds of meetings, beat-ings, and cheatings; kisses, near misses, and little-boy pisses.

You name it, it occurs right on the streets today, as it has since ancient times. People ooze from crusty corners. Black-and-white death announcements add to the clutter on the walls. Widows sell cigarettes from buckets. For a peek behind the scenes in the shade of wet laundry, venture down a few side streets. Buy two carrots as a gift for the woman on the fifth floor if she'll lower her bucket to pick them up. The neighborhood action seems best at about 18:00.

At the tiny fenced-in triangular park, veer right onto Via Forcella (which leads to the busy boulevard that takes you to the central train station). But first, turn right on busy Via Pietro Colletta, walk 50 yards and step into the North Pole at the oldest *gelateria* in Naples (since 1931), **Polo Nord Gelateria** (Mon–Sat 10:00–24:00, Sun 10:00–14:00 & 17:00–24:00, sample their *bacio* or "kiss" flavor before ordering, Via Pietro Colletta 41). Via Pietro Colletta leads past Napoli's two most competitive **pizzerias** (see "Pizza in Naples" sidebar) to Corso Umberto.

Turn left on the grand boulevard Corso Umberto. From here to the central train station, it's at least a 10-minute walk (if you're tired, hop on a bus; they all go to the station). To finish the walk, continue on Corso Umberto—past a gauntlet of purse/CD/sunglasses salesmen and shady characters hawking stolen camcorders—to the vast, ugly Piazza Garibaldi. On the far side is the station. You made it.

Open-Air Fish Market

For those with a little more time, Naples' fish market squirts and stinks as it has for centuries under the Nolana Port (gate in the city wall) just four blocks from the central train station. Of the town's many boister-ous outdoor markets, this will net you the most photos and memories.

From Piazza Nolana, wander under the medieval gate and take your first left down Vico Sopramuro, enjoying this wild and entirely edible cultural scavenger hunt (Tue–Sun 8:00–14:00, closed Mon).

Two other markets with more clothing and less fish are at Piazza Capuana (several blocks northwest of the central train station and tumbling down Via Sant'Antonio Abate, Mon–Sat 8:00–18:00, Sun 9:00–13:00) and a similar cobbled shopping zone along Via Pignasecca (just off Via Toledo, west of Piazza Carità).

Pompeii

Stopped in its tracks by the eruption of Mount Vesuvius in A.D. 79, Pompeii offers the best look anywhere at what life in Rome must have been like 2,000 years ago. An entire city of well-preserved ruins is yours to explore. A thriving commercial port of 20,000, Pompeii grew from Greek and Etruscan roots to become an important Roman city. Then, around noon on August 24, A.D. 79, Vesuvius erupted, burying everything in hot volcanic ash. For archaeologists, this was a shake-and-bake windfall, teaching them volumes about daily Roman life. Pompeii was rediscovered in the 1600s; excavations began in 1748.

POMPEII

ORIENTATION

Cost and Hours: €11, or €20 combo-ticket includes Herculaneum (called Ercolano) and three lesser sites (valid 3 days), daily April–Oct 8:30–19:30, Nov–March 8:30–17:00 (last entry 90 minutes before closing).

Getting There: Pompeii is about 35 minutes from Naples on the Circumvesuviana train that goes to Sorrento (€3.20 one-way, not covered by railpasses, at least hourly). Get off at the "Pompei Scavi, Villa dei Misteri" stop. Check your bag at the train station (at the bar, €1.50, pick up by 19:00 March–Sept, by 18:00

Oct–Feb) or, better yet, at the Pompeii site for free. From the Pompei Scavi train station, turn right and walk down the road about a block to the entrance (first left turn). The TI is farther down the street, but it's not a necessary stop for your visit.

Information: A good map and information booklet are included with your admission, but you must pick them up yourself at the TI window (to the left of the WCs). Tel. 081-857-5347, www .pompeiisites.org.

The bookshop sells the small Pompeii and Herculaneum *Past and Present* book. Its helpful text and plastic overlays allow you to re-create the ruins—with the "present" actually being 1964 (€12 in bookstores; if you buy from a street vendor, pay no more than €12).

Tours: Live guides (€115 for 2 hours) cluster near the ticket booth. If you gather 10 people, the price is reasonable when you split the cost. Knowledgeable, energetic **Gaetano Manfredi** is intense, theatrical, and a joy to follow for two hours as he brings the dusty ruins to life. Avoid Gaetano impersonators. Find the real Gaetano only at the Porta Marina entrance; he'll be wearing his official badge bearing his name (mobile 338-725-5620, tel. 081-863-9816, 3387255620@tim.it).

Audioguide Tours: €6.50/1 person, €10/2 people, with basically the same info as your free booklet. They're available from a kiosk near the ticket booth at the Porta Marina entrance (ID required).

Length of This Tour: Allow three hours.

Baggage Check: A free baggage check is near the site entrance turn-stiles (retrieve bags by 19:20).

Cuisine Art: Inside the site, there's a decent-value cafeteria offering three options: basic sandwiches, a self-service cafeteria line, and a fancier restaurant in a more elegant ancient gymnasium setting. A few mediocre restaurants cluster between the entrance and the train station.

Starring: Roofless (collapsed) but otherwise intact Roman buildings, plaster casts of hapless victims, a few erotic frescoes, and the dawning realization that these ancient people were no different from us.

Background

Pompeii was a booming Roman trading city. Not rich, not poor, it was middle class, making it a perfect example of typical Roman life. Most streets would have been lined with stalls and jammed with customers from sunup to sundown. Chariots vied with shoppers for street space. Two thousand years ago, Rome controlled the entire Mediterranean—making it a kind of free-trade zone—and Pompeii was a central and bustling port.

There were no posh neighborhoods in Pompeii. Rich and poor mixed it up as elegant houses existed side by side with simple homes.

While nearby Herculaneum would have been a classier place to live (traffic-free streets, fancier houses, far better drainage), Pompeii was the place for action and shopping. It served an estimated 20,000 residents with more than 40 bakeries, 30 brothels, and 130 bars, restaurants, and hotels. With most buildings covered by brilliant, white, ground-marble stucco, Pompeii in A.D. 79 was an impressive town.

As you tour Pompeii, remember that its best art is in the Archaeological Museum in Naples (described on page 351).

SELF-GUIDED TOUR

• *Just past the ticket-taker, start your approach up to the...*

Porta Marina

This was the original town gate. Before Vesuvius blew, the sea came nearly to here. Look down to the left to see the stone rings that were used to tie ships to the dock. Also notice the two openings in the gate (ahead, up the ramp). Both were left open by day to admit major traffic. At night, they would close the larger one for better security.

• *Pass through the Porta Marina and continue up the street, pausing at the three large stepping stones in the middle.*

Pompeii's Streets

Every day, Pompeiians flooded the streets with gushing water to clean them, and the stones let pedestrians cross. These three stones

tell us that this street was a major thoroughfare. Chariots (all with standard-sized axles) could straddle the stones traveling in either direction. One stone in a road means it was a one-way-street, two stones an ordinary two-way, and three a major arterial like this.

• *Continue up the street a few steps, where it opens up into...*

Pompeii

KEY RUINS
OTHER RUINS

200 YARDS
200 METERS

1. Forum
2. Plaster Casts
3. Baths of the Forum & Cafeteria
4. "Fast-Food" Place & House of the Tragic Poet
5. House of the Faun
6. Original Lead Pipes
7. House of the Vetti
8. Bakery & Mill
9. Taberna Hedones
10. Brothel
11. Temple of Isis
12. Theater & Little Theater
13. To Amphitheater

POMPEII

❶ The Forum (Foro)

Pompeii's commercial, religious, and political center stands at the intersection of the city's two main streets. While it's the most ruined part of Pompeii, it's grand nonetheless. Picture the piazza surrounded by two-story buildings on all sides (some building ruins remain). The pedestals that line the square once held statues, now in the museum in Naples.

At this (closest to you) end of the square are the squat remains of the **city hall** *(curia)*, built with brick and mortar, but originally faced with marble. Note that while Pompeii was destroyed by the eruption of A.D. 79, it was also devastated by an earthquake in A.D. 62. It's safe to assume that any brick you see dates from between A.D. 62 and A.D. 79 —restoration work done by Pompeiians after the quake.

The forum was dominated by the **Temple of Jupiter,** at the far end. You can still see remains of the grand staircase and a few tall columns.

Facing the Temple of Jupiter, with your back to the city hall, look to the building on your left, the **basilica.** Step inside and see the layout of the column stumps. This ancient law court has the same floor plan as many Christian churches (which are also called basilicas). Two narrower aisles flank a central nave, or hallway. The columns are made of bricks in a flower-petal pattern, originally covered with a plaster made of marble dust. Along the side walls are traces of original marble.

Cross to the opposite side of the forum to look down Pompeii's **main street.** Lined with shops, bars, and restaurants, it was a lively place and a pedestrian-only zone (notice the traffic barriers that kept chariots out). Many of Pompeii's streets were off-limits to chariots during shopping hours, and were marked with street signs showing pictures of men carrying vases—pedestrians only. On this busy street, to keep rowdy late-night crowds from getting out of hand, a gate at the head of the street dropped to seal off the forum (see the remains).

Looking north beyond the Temple of Jupiter, five miles away looms the ominous back story to this site: **Mount Vesuvius.** Mentally draw a triangle up from the two remaining peaks to reconstruct the mountain before the eruption. When it blew, Pompeiians had no idea they were living under a volcano, since Vesuvius hadn't erupted for 1,200 years. (Still active, Vesuvius last blew in 1944.) Imagine the wonder—then the horror—as the column of smoke roared upward, and then began to fall like hail, rain, and snow, collapsing roofs and burying everything in a blanket of ash.

• *Walk toward the far end of the forum along the right side. At the temple of Jupiter, turn right through a door into what used to be the fish and produce market, where you'll find two glass cases containing...*

❷ Plaster Casts of Victims

Two thousand Pompeii citizens suffocated under the ash, and these

eerie casts capture them in their last moments. Archaeologists made these casts when, while excavating, they detected hollows underfoot—left by decomposed bodies. They'd pour liquid plaster into the cavities (which acted as molds), let it dry, and dig up the casts. The sheds also display many *amphorae*—the tall clay jars Romans used to transport food, wine, and olive oil. Pompeii, a seaport trading town, had thousands of these.

Just past the sheds, turn left into an **ancient public WC** that once served the forum. Notice the ditch that led to the sewer (marked by an arch in the corner). The stone supports once held wooden benches with the appropriate holes.

• *From the toilets, backtrack a while, then turn left on Via del Foro, passing a convenient 21st-century cafeteria. Just past the cafeteria, on the left-hand side at #24, is the entrance to the...*

❸ Baths of the Forum (Terme del Foro)

The leafy courtyard you enter used to be the gymnasium. After working out, clients would find four rooms: a waiting room, cold-plunge bath *(frigidarium)*, warm bath *(tepidarium)*, and hot bath *(caldarium)*.

The first room you tour is the dressing room. Adjoining that is the *frigidarium*—a circular marble basin with the spout spewing frigid water. The *tepidarium* is ringed by mini-statues or *telamones* (male caryatids, figures used as supporting pillars), which divided clients' lockers. They'd warm up here, perhaps stretching out on one of the benches near the bronze heater for a massage. Notice the ceiling: half crushed by the eruption and half surviving, with its fine blue-and-white stucco work.

Next, in the *caldarium*, you'd get hot. Notice the engineering. The double floor was heated from below—so nice with bare feet (look into the grate to see the brick support towers). The double walls with brown terra-cotta tiles held the heat. Romans soaked in the big tub, which was filled with hot water. To keep condensation from dripping annoyingly from the ceiling, the fluting (ribbing) was added to carry the drips down the walls.

Next came the cold plunge in the *frigidarium*—a circular marble

The Eruption of Vesuvius

Around noon on August 24, A.D. 79, Mount Vesuvius blew, sending a mushroom cloud of ash, dust, cinders, and rocks

12 miles into the air. It spewed for 18 hours straight, as winds blew the cloud southward. The white-grey ash settled like snow on Pompeii, collapsing roofs and floors, but leaving the walls intact. Two thousand of the town's 20,000 residents were entombed under eight feet of fine powder.

The next morning, Vesuvius' column of ejected material collapsed, picking up speed as it fell to earth, creating a cloud of ash, pumice, and gas. The red-hot avalanche (a "pyroclastic flow") sped down the side of the mountain at nearly 100 mph. Four minutes later, it engulfed the city of Herculaneum four miles away, burying it in nearly 60 feet of hot mud. The mud cooled into stone, freezing the moment in time.

basin with the spout spewing frigid water, opposite the entry.
• *As you exit the baths, directly across the street are rectangular marble counters with holes in them.*

❹ Fast Food and Barking Dogs

This shop was a **fast-food place.** The holes in the counters held the pots for the food. Most ancient Romans did not cook for themselves in their tiny apartments, and to-go places like this can be found on many of Pompeii's streets. Notice the groove in the shop's front doorstep. Shops had sliding doors (or, more precisely, folding accordion doors) that fit into these grooves. Holes out on the curb likely were for cords that

stretched awnings over the sidewalk to shield the clientele.

Just up the street a few steps (also on the right) is the **House of the Tragic Poet** (Casa de Poeta Tragico), with its famous "Beware of Dog" *(Cave Canem)* mosaic in the entryway.
• *Facing the House of the Tragic Poet, turn right and walk downhill. In the pavement, notice the oxcart-wheel grooves, dug in by centuries of use.*

There are also more stepping stones for pedestrians to cross the flooded streets. Continue downhill two blocks. On your left, at #1, you'll find the...

❺ House of the Faun (Casa del Fauno)

The small bronze statue of the *Dancing Faun* (original is in Naples' Archaeological Museum—see page 351) welcomes you to Pompeii's largest home.

With 40 rooms and 27,000 square feet, the House of the Faun covers an entire city block. Wander past the welcome mosaic (*HAVE* or "hail to you") and through its courtyards. The next floor mosaic, with an intricate diamond-like design, decorates the homeowner's office. Beyond that is the famous floor mosaic of the *Battle of Alexander* (original is in Naples' Archaeological Museum—see page 351). This reproduction was only recently placed here in its original location. The restoration team first traced a photo of the original and laid the tracing on wet clay to make an impression. Then they painstakingly filled in the outlines with 1.5 million tiny pieces of tile and rock to recreate the 18-foot-by-9-foot mosaic. The House's back courtyard leads to the exit in the far right corner. It's lined with pillars rebuilt after the A.D. 62 earthquake. Take a close look at the brick, mortar, and fake marble stucco veneer. (If this exit is closed, return to the entrance and make a U-turn left, around to the back of the house.)

• *Exit the House of the Faun at the back end and turn right. Along the right-hand side of the street are metal cages protecting...*

❻ Original Lead Pipes

These 2,000-year-old pipes (made of lead imported from Britannia) were part of the city's elaborate water system. A huge water tank—fed by an aqueduct—stood at the high end of town. Three independent pipe systems supplied water to the city from here: one for baths, one for private homes, and one for public water fountains. If there was a water shortage, democratic priorities prevailed: First the baths were cut, then the private homes. The last water to be cut was that which fed the public fountains, the place where everyone could get their water for drinking and cooking.

• *Take your first left (on Vicolo dei Vetti) and find the entrance (on the left) to the...*

POMPEII

❼ House of the Vetti (Casa dei Vetti)

If it's not closed for renovation, enter Pompeii's best-preserved home. The House of the Vetti, which has retained its mosaics and frescoes, was the bachelor pad of two wealthy merchant brothers. In the entry-way (even if it's closed), see if you can spot the erection. This is not pornography. There's a meaning here: The penis and the sack of money balance each other on the goldsmith scale above a fine bowl of fruit. The meaning: Only with a balance of fertility and money can you have abundance.

Step into the atrium, with its ceiling open to the sky to collect light and rainwater. The pool, while decorative, was a functional

water-supply tank. It's flanked by large money boxes anchored to the floor. The brothers were certainly successful merchants, and possibly moneylenders, too.

Exit on the right, passing the tight servant quarters, and go into the kitchen, with its bronze cooking pots (and a touchable lead pipe on the back wall). The passage dead-ends in the little Venus Room, with its erotic frescoes behind glass.

Return to the atrium and pass into the big colonnaded garden. It was planted according to the plan indicated by traces of roots excavated in the volcanic ash. Richly fres-coed entertainment rooms ring this courtyard. Circle counterclockwise. The dining room is finely decorated in "Pompeiian red" (from iron rust) and black. Study the detail. Notice the lead humidity seal between the wall and the floor, designed to keep the moisture-sensitive frescoes dry. (Had Leonardo da Vinci taken this clever step, his *Last Supper* in Milan might be in better shape today.) Continuing around, notice the square white stones inlaid in the floor. Imagine them reflecting like cat eyes as

the brothers and their friends wandered around by oil lamp late at night. Frescoes in the Yellow Room (near the exit) show off the ancient mastery of perspective, which was not matched elsewhere in Europe for nearly 1,500 years.

• *After visiting the House of the Vetti (or just looking in the door, if it's currently closed), get oriented from the entrance to the House.*

Facing the entrance to the House of the Vetti, turn left and walk one long block (along Vicolo dei Vetti) to a T-intersection

(Via della Fortuna), marked by a stone fountain with a bull's head for a spout. Intersections like this were busy neighborhood centers, where the rent was highest and people gathered. Turn left, then immediately right, walking along a gently curving road. On the left side of the street, at #22, find four big stone cylinders.

❽ The Bakery and Mill *(Forno e Mulini)*

The brick oven looks like a modern-day pizza oven. And the stubby stone towers are flour grinders. Grain was poured into the top, and donkeys pushed wooden bars that turned the stones. The powdered grain dropped out of the bottom as flour—flavored with tiny bits of rock.

• *Continue to the next intersection (Via degli Augustali, where there's another fast-food joint) and turn left. About 50 yards down this (obviously one-way) street, on the left at #44 you'll find the...*

❾ Taberna Hedones

This bar must have been a happy, hedonistic place. The cute welcome mosaic reads *HAVE* ("hail to you"), with the bear licking his wounds. The place still has its original floor and, deeper in, the mosaic arch of a grotto fountain.

• *Just past the tavern, turn right and walk downhill to #18, on the right.*

❿ The Brothel *(Lupanare)*

Prostitutes were nicknamed *lupe* (she-wolves). Wander into the brothel, a simple place with stone beds and pillows. The ancient graffiti includes tallies and exotic names of the women, indicating they came from all corners of the Mediterranean. The faded frescoes above the cells may have served as a kind of menu for services offered. Note the idealized portrayal of women (white, considered beautiful) and men (dark, considered horny).

• *Leaving the brothel, continue going downhill two blocks to the intersection with Pompeii's main drag, Via dell'Abbondanza. (The forum—and exit—are to the right, for those who may wish to opt out from here. The huge amphitheater—which is certainly skippable—is 10 min to your left.) But we'll go straight ahead, down Via dei Teatri, then left before the columns, downhill to the...*

⓫ Temple of Isis

This Egyptian temple served Pompeii's Egyptian community. The little shrine with the plastic roof housed holy water from the Nile.

POMPEII

Pompeii must have had a synagogue, but it has yet to be excavated.

• *Exit the temple where you entered, and take an immediate right down an alleyway to our last stop, the...*

⑫ Theater and Little Theater

Originally a Greek theater (Greeks built theirs with the help of a hillside), this marks the spot of the birthplace of the Greek port here in 470 B.C. During Roman times, the theater sat 5,000 in three price

ranges: the five marble terraces up close (filled with romantic wooden seats for two), the main section, and the cheap nosebleed section (surviving only on the right). The square stones above the cheap seats used to support a canvas rooftop. Notice the high-profile boxes, flanking the stage, for guests of honor. From this perch, you can see the gladiator barracks—the colonnaded courtyard beyond the theater. They lived in tiny rooms, trained in the courtyard, and fought in the nearby amphitheater. Just next door, the **Little Theater** (Teatro Piccolo) is a more intimate space that seated a thousand.

• *You've seen Pompeii's highlights. When you're ready to leave, backtrack to the main road and turn left, going uphill to the forum, where you'll find the main entrance/exit.*

Or consider taking a look at...

More Pompeii Sights

There's much more to see—75 percent of Pompeii's 164 acres has been excavated, and our tour has only covered about one-third of the site. After the theaters—if you still have energy to see more—go back to the main road, and take a right toward the eastern part of the site, where the crowds thin out. A 10-minute walk leads to the **amphitheater.** Climb to the upper level and—with Vesuvius looming in the background—mentally replace the tourists below with gladiators and wild animals locked in combat.

Walk along the top of the amphitheater and look down into the grassy rectangular area surrounded by columns. This is the **Palaestra,** an area once used for athletic training. Facing the other way, look for the bell tower that tops the roofline of the modern city of Pompeii, where locals go about their daily lives in the shadow of the volcano, just as their ancestors did 2,000 years ago.

• *The exit near the amphitheater deposits you in Piazza Anfiteatro. To get back to the main Pompeii entrance (and exit), take a right down Via Plinio and walk for 15 minutes.*

HAVE!

POMPEII

ROMAN HISTORY

THREE MILLENNIA IN SIX PAGES

History in a Hurry

Ancient Rome lasted a thousand years (500 B.C.–A.D. 500), half as an expanding republic, half as a dominating empire. When Rome fell to invaders, all Europe suffered a thousand years of poverty and ignorance (A.D. 500–1500), though Rome's influence could still be felt in the Catholic Church. Popes rebuilt Rome for pilgrims—in Renaissance, then Baroque and Neoclassical styles (1500–1800). As capital of a newly united Italy, Rome followed fascist Mussolini into World War II (and lost) but rebounded in Italy's postwar economic boom.

Want more?

Legendary Birth (1200–500 B.C.)

Aeneas flees burning Troy (1200 B.C.), wanders like Odysseus, and finally finds a home along the Tiber. His descendants, Romulus and

Remus—orphaned at birth, suckled by a she-wolf, and raised by shepherds—grow up to steal wives and build a wall, thus founding Rome (753 B.C.).

Closer to fact, the local agrarian tribes were dominated by more sophisticated neighbors to the north (Etruscans) and south (Greek colonists). Their convenient location on the Tiber was perfect for a future power.

Sights
- Romulus' "hut" and wall (Palatine Hill)
- *She-Wolf* statue (Capitoline Museums)
- Frescoes of Aeneas and Romulus (National Museum of Rome)
- Bernini's Aeneas statue (Borghese Gallery)
- Etruscan wing (Vatican Museum)
- Etruscan Museum (in Villa Borghese Gardens)
- Etruscan legacy (the original Circus Maximus, the drained Forum)

The Republic (509–27 B.C.)
The city expands throughout the Italian peninsula (500–300 B.C.), then defeats Hannibal's North African Carthaginians (the Punic Wars, 264–146 B.C.) and Greece (168 B.C.).

Rome is master of the Mediterranean, and booty and captured slaves pour in. Romans bicker among themselves over their slice of the pie, pitting the wealthy landowners (the ruling Senate) against the working class (plebs) and the rebellious slaves (Spartacus' revolt, 73 B.C.). In the chaos, charismatic generals like Julius Caesar, who can provide wealth and security, become dictators. Change is necessary...and coming.

Sights
- Forum's Curia, Temple of Saturn, Temple of Castor and Pollux, Rostrum, Basilica Aemilia, Temple of Julius Caesar, and Basilica Julia (all rebuilt later)
- Appian Way built, lined with tombs
- Aqueducts, which carry water to a growing city
- Portrait busts of citizens (National Museum of Rome)
- The republic's "S.P.Q.R." monogram and motto, seen today on statues, buildings, and even manhole covers: *Senatus Populusque Romanus,* or the "Senate and People of Rome." (Some northern Italians, who feel the South is dragging them down, translate S.P.Q.R. as *Sono Porci Questi Romani*—"These Romans are Pigs.")

The Empire—The "Roman Peace," or Pax Romana (A.D. 1–200)
After Julius Caesar was killed by disgruntled republicans, his adopted son Augustus took undisputed control, ended the civil wars, declared

himself emperor, and adopted a family member to succeed him, setting the pattern of rule for the next 500 years.

Rome ruled an empire of 54 million people, stretching from Scotland to Africa, from Spain to Turkey. The city, with more than a million inhabitants, was decorated with Greek-style statues and monumental structures faced with marble... it was the marvel of the known world. The empire prospered on a (false) economy of booty, slaves, and trade, surviving the often turbulent and naughty behavior of emperors such as Caligula and Nero.

Sights

- Colosseum
- Forum
- Palatine Hill palaces
- Ara Pacis ("Altar of Peace")
- Poems by Virgil, Catullus, Horace, and Ovid (from time of Augustus)
- Augustus' house (House of Livia and Augustus) on Palatine Hill
- Pantheon
- Trajan's Column and Forum
- Greek and Greek-style statues and emperors' busts (National Museum of Rome, Vatican Museum, Capitoline Museums)
- Piazza Navona (former stadium)
- Hadrian's Villa (Tivoli) and tomb (now Castel Sant'Angelo)

Rome Falls (200–476)

Corruption, disease, and the constant pressure of barbarians pecking away at the borders slowly drained the unwieldy empire. Despite Diocletian's division of the empire and Constantine's legalization of Christianity (313), the city was sacked (410), and the last emperor checked out (476). Rome fell like a huge column, kicking up dust that would plunge Europe into a thousand years of darkness.

Sights

- Arch of Constantine
- The Forum's Basilica of Constantine
- Baths of Diocletian
- Old Roman Wall (gates at Via Veneto or Piramide)

Medieval Rome (500-1500)

The once-great city of a million people dwindled to a rough village of 10,000, with a corrupt pope, forgotten ruins, and malaria-carrying mosquitoes. Cows grazed in the ruined Forum, and wolves prowled the Vatican at night. During the 1300s, even the popes left Rome to live in France. What little glory Rome retained was in the pomp, knowledge, and wealth of the Catholic Church.

Sights

- The damage done to ancient Roman monuments, caused by disuse, barbarian looting, and pillaging for pre-cut stones
- Early Christian churches built before Rome fell (Santa Maria Maggiore, San Giovanni in Laterano, and San Clemente)
- Churches of Santa Maria sopra Minerva and Santa Maria in Trastevere
- Castel Sant'Angelo

Renaissance and Baroque Rome (1500-1800)

As Europe's economy recovered, energetic popes rebuilt Rome to attract

pilgrims. The best artists decorated palaces and churches, carved statues, and built fountains. The city was not a great political force, but as the center of Catholicism during the struggle against Protestants (c. 1520–1648), it was an influential religious and cultural capital.

Renaissance Sights

- Michelangelo's Sistine Chapel (Vatican Museum), dome of St. Peter's, *Pietà* (St. Peter's), *Moses* (St. Peter-in-Chains Church), Christ statue (Santa Maria sopra Minerva), Capitol Hill Square, Santa Maria degli Angeli church (in former Baths of Diocletian)

- Raphael's *School of Athens* and *Transfiguration* (Vatican Museum)
- Paintings by Raphael, Titian, and others (Borghese Gallery)

Baroque Sights

- St. Peter's Square and interior (largely by Bernini)
- Bernini statues (at Borghese Gallery; also *St. Teresa in Ecstasy* at

Rome in World War II

By 1943, as bombs began falling just outside the walls of Rome, it was clear to all that Italy's alliance with Nazi Germany was a huge mistake, leading the country to ruin. The fascist Grand Council dismissed Mussolini, and the king ordered his arrest. The ex-dictator fled north, and fascism collapsed without violence. Rome was declared an "open city" (meaning a city with no military bases). Italy surrendered to the Allies. The king fled to Allied-occupied southern Italy, abandoning Rome to Nazi forces, which occupied it for nine terrible months. The Romans and the Vatican joined forces to save many from the Nazis.

The Gestapo demanded 110 pounds of gold from the Roman Jews, who, with great difficulty and help from non-Jews, succeeded in providing it. Regardless, more than 2,000 Jews were deported to Germany. After Italian partisans planted a bomb near the Trevi Fountain that killed 32 Germans, more than 300 people randomly chosen from Rome's prison were killed in retaliation. As the Allies marched closer, they bombed Rome and its surroundings, but avoided striking the center.

Thankfully, Hitler granted the occupying Nazi troops permission to leave the city, which he declared a "place of culture" that should not be "the scene of combat operations." Pope Pius XII agreed, declaring, "Whoever raises a hand against Rome will be guilty of matricide to the whole civilized world and in the eternal judgment of God." Finally, the Germans marched out, the Americans marched in (through the gate of San Giovanni), and the exhausted city welcomed them with joy and relief.

Santa Maria della Vittoria church) and fountains (Piazza Navona, Piazza Barberini)
- Ancient obelisks erected in squares (Piazza del Popolo, Piazza Navona)
- Trevi Fountain and Spanish Steps
- Gesù and San Ignazio churches
- Caravaggio's *Calling of St. Matthew* (San Luigi dei Francesi Church) and other paintings (Borghese Gallery and Vatican Museum)
- Baroque paintings (Borghese Gallery)
- Borromini's facade of Santa Agnese Church (Piazza Navona)

Modern Rome (1800–present)

Rome becomes the capital of a newly reunited Italy (1870), is modernized by fascist Mussolini, and survives the destruction of World War II. Italy's postwar "economic miracle" makes Rome a world-class city of cinema, banking, and tourism.

Sights

- Victor Emmanuel II Monument, which honors modern Italy's first (democratic) king
- Mussolini: the balcony he spoke from (at Palazzo Venezia, on Piazza Venezia), his planned city (E.U.R.), grand boulevards (Via dei Fori Imperiali, Via della Conciliazione), his home (Villa Torlonia), and Olympic Stadium
- Cinecittà film studios and Via Veneto nightlife, which have faint echoes of Fellini's *La Dolce Vita* Rome
- Subway system, broad boulevards, smog

Rome Today

After surviving the government-a-year turbulence and Mafia-tainted corruption of the postwar years, Rome is stabilizing. Today, the average Roman makes more money than the average Englishman. The city is less polluted and more organized. Several years ago, in celebration of the millennium, the Eternal City gave its monuments a facelift. The world turned its attention on Rome once again in 2005, as the Vatican mourned the death of a pope...and elected a new one. Today's Rome is ready for pilgrims, travelers, and you to come and make more history.

APPENDIX

CONTENTS

RESOURCES

Tourist Offices in the US

Before you go, you can contact the nearest Italian tourist office (abbreviated **TI** in this book) in the US to briefly describe your trip and request information. You'll get the general packet and, if you ask for specifics (city map, calendar of festivals, etc.), an impressive amount of help. If you have a specific problem, they're a good source of sympathy. Their website is www.italiantourism.com.

Their offices are...

In New York: Tel. 212/245-5618, brochure hotline tel. 212/245-4822, fax 212/586-9249, enitny@italiantourism.com; 630 Fifth Ave. #1565, New York, NY 10111.

In Illinois: Tel. 312/644-0996, brochure hotline tel. 312/644-0990, fax 312/644-3019, enitch@italiantourism.com; 500 N. Michigan Ave. #506, Chicago, IL 60611.

In California: Tel. 310/820-1898, brochure hotline tel. 310/820-0098, fax 310/820-6357, enitla@italiantourism.com; 12400 Wilshire Blvd. #550, Los Angeles, CA 90025.

Websites on Rome: Check out www.whatsoninrome.com (events and news), www.romaturismo.com (music, exhibitions, and events), www.wantedinrome.com (job openings and real estate, but also festivals and exhibitions), and www.vatican.va (the pope's website).

Resources from Rick Steves
Guidebooks and Online Updates
This book is updated every year—but once you pin down Italy, it wiggles. For the latest, visit www.ricksteves.com/update. Also at my web-

site, you'll find a valuable list of reports and experiences—good and bad—from fellow travelers (www.ricksteves.com /feedback).

Rome 2009 is one of more than 30 books in my series on European travel, which includes country guidebooks, city guidebooks (Florence, Venice, Paris, London, etc.), and my budget-travel skills handbook, *Rick Steves' Europe Through the Back Door.* My phrase books—for Italian, French, German, Spanish, and Portuguese—are practical and budget-oriented. My other books are *Europe 101* (a crash course on art and history, newly expanded and in full color), *European Christmas* (on traditional and modern-day celebrations), and *Postcards from Europe* (a fun memoir of my travels over 25 years). For a complete list of my books, see the inside of the last page of this book.

Public Television and Radio Shows
My TV series, *Rick Steves' Europe,* covers European destinations, with 14 episodes on Italy, including two on Rome. My weekly public radio show, *Travel with Rick Steves,* features interviews with travel experts from around the world, including several hours on Italy and Italian culture. All the TV scripts and radio shows (which are easy and free to download to an iPod or other MP3 player) are at www.ricksteves.com.

Free Audiotours for Rome
Rick Steves and Gene Openshaw (the co-authors of this book) have

produced a free series of self-guided audiotours for Rome—of the Colosseum, Roman Forum, Pantheon, St. Peter's Basilica, and Sistine Chapel—for users of iPods and other MP3 players.

The tours, based on this book, allow you to focus on what you're seeing rather than what you're reading. Additional walking tours are available for Venice, Florence, and Paris, covering

Begin Your Trip at www.ricksteves.com

At our travel website, you'll find a wealth of free information on European destinations, including fresh monthly news and helpful tips from thousands of fellow travelers.

Our **online Travel Store** offers travel bags and accessories specially designed by Rick Steves to help you travel smarter and lighter. These include Rick's popular carry-on bags (wheeled and rucksack versions), money belts, totes, toiletries kits, adapters, other accessories, and a wide selection of guidebooks, planning maps, and DVDs.

Choosing the right **railpass** for your trip—amidst hundreds of options—can drive you nutty. We'll help you choose the best pass for your needs, plus give you a bunch of free extras.

Rick Steves' Europe Through the Back Door travel company offers **tours** with more than two dozen itineraries and about 450 departures reaching the best destinations in this book...and beyond. Our Italy tours include "the best of" in 17 days, Village Italy in 14 days, South Italy in 13 days, Venice–Florence–Rome in 10 days, The heart of Italy in 9 days, Sicily in 9 days, and week-long city tours (one for Rome and one for Florence). You'll enjoy great guides, a fun bunch of travel partners (with small groups of generally around 26), and plenty of room to spread out in a big, comfy bus. You'll find European adventures to fit every vacation length. For all the details, and to get our Tour Catalog and a free Rick Steves Tour Experience DVD (filmed on location during an actual tour), visit www.ricksteves.com or call us at 425/608-4217.

the greatest sights of these magnificent cities.

These free tours are available through www.ricksteves.com and at iTunes. Simply download them onto your computer and transfer them to your iPod or other MP3 player. (Don't forget to bring a Y-jack and extra set of earbuds for your travel partner.)

Maps

The black-and-white maps in this book, designed by my well-traveled staff, are concise and simple. The maps are intended to help you locate recommended places and get to local TIs, where you can pick up a more in-depth map (usually free) of the city or region. More detailed maps are also sold at newsstands and bookstores—look before you buy to be sure the map has the level of detail you want. For drivers, I'd recommend a 1:200,000- or 1:300,000-scale map.

Other Guidebooks

For most travelers, this book is all you need. But when you consider the improvements they'll make in your $5,000 vacation, extra maps and books are $30 or $40 well spent.

The tall, green Michelin guide to Rome has solid, encyclopedic coverage of sights, customs, and culture, though very little on hotels and restaurants (also sold in English in Italy). The Access guide to Rome is well-researched, organized by neighborhood, and color-coded for sights, hotels, and restaurants. Focusing mainly on sights, the colorful Eyewitness guide to Rome is fun for its great graphics and photos, but it's relatively skimpy on content and weighs a ton. You can buy it in Rome (no more expensive than in the US) or simply borrow it for a minute from other travelers at certain sights to make sure that you're aware of that place's highlights. *Let's Go Rome* is youth-oriented, with good coverage of hostels and nightlife.

For a book of city walking tours, try *City Secrets: Rome* (Kahn) or *City of the Soul: A Walk in Rome* (Murray). For a list of bookstores in Rome, see page 22.

Recommended Books and Movies

To get the feel of Rome past and present, consider reading some of these books or seeing these films.

Non-Fiction

Written in the 18th century, Edward Gibbon's *Decline and Fall of the Roman Empire* is considered *the* classic history of ancient Rome.

Originally published as a series of *New Yorker* articles in the 1950s, *Rome and a Villa* reads as if it's Eleanor Clark's journal. Of Paul Hofmann's multiple books about Italy, *The Seasons of Rome* is the favorite among readers. Another good Americans-in-the-Eternal-City memoir is *As the Romans Do* (Epstein). Elizabeth Gilbert's *Eat, Pray,*

Love sets a third of her spiritual memoir/travelogue in Rome.

The holy center of Christendom has plenty of worthwhile books documenting its history. *Saints & Sinners* (Duffy) is a warts-and-all illustrated guide to the popes. In *When in Rome,* Robert Hutchinson writes as a lapsed (sometimes irreverent) Catholic discovering the roots of Christianity in Vatican City. *Michelangelo and the Pope's Ceiling* (King) describes the drama behind the masterpiece. *The Pope's Elephant* (Bedini), written by a historian from the Smithsonian, tells the story of Pope Leo X's favorite pet.

A Literary Companion to Rome (Varriano) also includes 10 self-guided walking tours. Kids (and adults who like cool pictures) enjoy David Macaulay's two books about Rome: *Rome Antics* and *City: A Story of Roman Planning and Construction* (both for ages nine and up).

Fiction

No modern crime drama or soap opera can top the world of ancient Roman politics. Colleen McCullough—who also wrote *The Thorn Birds*—describes the early days of the Roman Republic in her work of historical fiction, *The First Man in Rome.* Robert Graves wanders from Caesar Augustus to Caligula and beyond in *I, Claudius.*

Ancient Rome makes a great backdrop for mysteries, as shown in *Roman Blood* (Saylor) and *Silver Pigs* (Davis), both the first in a series. *Cabal,* by Michael Dibdin, takes place in modern Rome. In the blockbuster book *Angels and Demons,* written by *The Da Vinci Code* author Dan Brown, murders are linked by Rome's Bernini statues.

For a literary take on Rome, try *Open City: Seven Writers in Postwar Rome* (edited by William Weaver).

Films

Two masterpieces of Italian Neorealism—set in the bleak, post-WWII years—take place in Rome: Roberto Rossellini's *Open City* (1945) and Vittorio De Sica's touching, heartbreaking film, *Bicycle Thieves* (1949).

A feel-good love story, *Roman Holiday* (1953) made a star out of Audrey Hepburn. *Three Coins in the Fountain* (1954) is another romantic crowd-pleaser.

During the era of epics, Hollywood couldn't get enough of ancient Rome. *Quo Vadis* (1951) contains three hours of religious-historic drama. *Ben-Hur* (1959) is a campy mash-up of Christianity, Charlton Heston, and chariot races. *Spartacus* (1960) cast Kirk Douglas as a rebel fighting Rome.

La Dolce Vita (1961) is Federico Fellini's seductive masterpiece. (His 1972 film *Roma* seems tacky in comparison.)

Originally a BBC miniseries, *I, Claudius* (1976) puts Derek Jacobi and John Hurt at the center of a pulpy classic. *Gladiator* returned to ancient Rome in 2000, and won five Academy Awards for its portrayal of life in the bloody arena.

TELEPHONES, EMAIL, AND MAIL

Telephones

Smart travelers learn the phone system and use it daily to reserve or reconfirm rooms, get tourist information, reserve restaurants, confirm tour times, or phone home.

Types of Phones

You'll encounter various kinds of phones on your trip.

Card-operated phones—where you insert a locally bought phone card into a public pay phone—are common in Europe.

Coin-operated phones, the original kind of pay phone, require you to have enough change to complete your call.

Hotel room phones are sometimes cheap for local calls, and 800 numbers can be free (confirm at the front desk first), but hotel phones can be a rip-off for long-distance calls unless you use an international phone card (described below). Calling direct to the US from your hotel phone can run about $1–2/minute. But incoming calls are free, making this a cheap way for friends and family to stay in touch, provided they have a good long-distance plan for calls to Europe.

American mobile phones work in Europe if they're GSM-enabled, tri-band or quad-band, and on a calling plan that includes international calls. They're convenient, but pricey. For example, with a T-Mobile phone, you'll pay $1–2 per minute for calls, and $0.35 for text messages.

European mobile phones run about $40–75 (for the most basic models) and come without contracts. They're loaded with prepaid calling time that you can recharge as you use up the minutes. As long as you're not "roaming" outside the phone's home country, incoming calls are free. If you're traveling to multiple countries within Europe, make sure the phone is electronically "unlocked," so that you can swap out its SIM card (a fingernail-sized chip that holds the phone's information) for a new one in other countries.

Using Phone Cards

Get a phone card for your calls. Prepaid phone cards come in two types: international and insertable (both described below). Note that neither kind of card will work outside of Italy. While traveling, you can share either type of card with your companions (and, in the case of an international phone card, your buddy doesn't even need the actual card—just the numbers on it). If you have time left on a phone card when you leave the country (as you likely will), simply give it to another traveler—anyone can use it.

You'll get the best deal with an **international phone card.** It enables you to make calls to the US for as little as a nickel per minute, and also works for local calls. You can use these cards from any phone,

Important Phone Numbers

Embassies
US Embassy: 24-hour emergency line—tel. 06-46741, non-emergency—tel. 06-4674-2406 (Mon–Fri 15:00–17:00, closed Sat–Sun, Via Vittorio Veneto 119/A, www.usembassy.it)
Canadian Embassy: tel. 06-854-441 (Via Zara 30, www.canada.it)

Emergency
English-speaking police help: 113
Ambulance: 118
Road Service: 116

Assistance
Telephone Help (in English; free directory assistance): 170
Directory Assistance (for €0.50, an Italian-speaking robot gives the number twice, very clearly): 12

including the one in your hotel room (check to make sure your phone is set on tone instead of pulse, and ask the hotel about hidden fees on toll-free calls). You can buy the cards at small newsstand kiosks, *tabacchi* (tobacco) shops, Internet cafés, hostels, and hole-in-the-wall long-distance phone shops. Because there are so many brand names, simply ask for an international phone card (*carta telefonica prepagata internazionale*, KAR-tah teh-leh-FOHN-ee-kah pray-pah-GAH-tah in-ter-naht-zee-oh-NAH-lay). Tell the vendor where you'll be making most calls ("*per Stati Uniti*"—to America), and he'll select the brand with the best deal.

Buy a lower denomination in case the card is a dud. I've had good luck with the Europa card, which offers 220 minutes from Italy to the US for €5.

To use an international phone card, dial the toll-free number listed on the card; you'll reach an automated operator. When prompted, dial in a scratch-to-reveal code number. Then dial your number.

Generally you'll get more minutes—sometimes up to five times as many—if you use your international phone card from your hotel room, rather than from a pay phone.

An **insertable phone card** can only be used at a pay phone. These Telecom cards, considered "official" since they're sold by Italy's phone company, give you the best deal for calls within Italy and are reasonable for international calls.

You can buy Telecom cards (in denominations of €5 or €10) at *tabacchi* shops, post offices, and machines near phone booths (many phone booths have signs indicating where the nearest

European Calling Chart

Just smile and dial, using this key:
AC = Area Code, LN = Local Number.

European Country	Calling long distance within ...	Calling from the US or Canada to ...	Calling from a European country to ...
Austria	AC + LN	011 + 43 + AC (without the initial zero) + LN	00 + 43 + AC (without the initial zero) + LN
Belgium	LN	011 + 32 + LN (without initial zero)	00 + 32 + LN (without initial zero)
Bosnia-Herzegovina	AC + LN	011 + 387 + AC (without initial zero) + LN	00 + 387 + AC (without initial zero) + LN
Britain	AC + LN	011 + 44 + AC (without initial zero) + LN	00 + 44 + AC (without initial zero) + LN
Croatia	AC + LN	011 + 385 + AC (without initial zero) + LN	00 + 385 + AC (without initial zero) + LN
Czech Republic	LN	011 + 420 + LN	00 + 420 + LN
Denmark	LN	011 + 45 + LN	00 + 45 + LN
Estonia	LN	011 + 372 + LN	00 + 372 + LN
Finland	AC + LN	011 + 358 + AC (without initial zero) + LN	999 + 358 + AC (without initial zero) + LN
France	LN	011 + 33 + LN (without initial zero)	00 + 33 + LN (without initial zero)
Germany	AC + LN	011 + 49 + AC (without initial zero) + LN	00 + 49 + AC (without initial zero) + LN
Greece	LN	011 + 30 + LN	00 + 30 + LN
Hungary	06 + AC + LN	011 + 36 + AC + LN	00 + 36 + AC + LN
Ireland	AC + LN	011 + 353 + AC (without initial zero) + LN	00 + 353 + AC (without initial zero) + LN

European Country	Calling long distance within ...	Calling from the US or Canada to ...	Calling from a European country to ...
Italy	LN	011 + 39 + LN	00 + 39 + LN
Montenegro	AC + LN	011 + 382 + AC (without initial zero) + LN	00 + 382 + AC (without initial zero) + LN
Netherlands	AC + LN	011 + 31 + AC (without initial zero) + LN	00 + 31 + AC (without initial zero) + LN
Norway	LN	011 + 47 + LN	00 + 47 + LN
Poland	LN	011 + 48 + LN (without initial zero)	00 + 48 + LN (without initial zero)
Portugal	LN	011 + 351 + LN	00 + 351 + LN
Slovakia	AC + LN	011 + 421 + AC (without initial zero) + LN	00 + 421 + AC (without initial zero) + LN
Slovenia	AC + LN	011 + 386 + AC (without initial zero) + LN	00 + 386 + AC (without initial zero) + LN
Spain	LN	011 + 34 + LN	00 + 34 + LN
Sweden	AC + LN	011 + 46 + AC (without initial zero) + LN	00 + 46 + AC (without initial zero) + LN
Switzerland	LN	011 + 41 + LN (without initial zero)	00 + 41 + LN (without initial zero)
Turkey	AC (if no initial zero is included, add one) + LN	011 + 90 + AC (without initial zero) + LN	00 + 90 + AC (without initial zero) + LN

- The instructions above apply whether you're calling a land line or mobile phone.
- The international access codes (the first numbers you dial when making an international call) are 011 if you're calling from the US or Canada, or 00 if you're calling from virtually anywhere in Europe (except Finland, where it's 999).
- To call the US or Canada from Europe, dial 00, then 1 (the country code for the US and Canada), then the area code and number. In short, 00 + 1 + AC + LN = Hi, Mom!

phone-card sales outlet is located).

Rip off the perforated corner to "activate" the card, and then physically insert it into a slot in the pay phone. It displays how much money you have remaining on the card. Then just dial away. The price of the call is automatically deducted while you talk.

Using Hotel-Room Phones, Metered Phones, VoIP, or US Calling Cards

The phone in your **hotel room** is convenient...but expensive. While incoming calls (made by folks back home) can be the cheapest way to keep in touch, charges for *outgoing* calls can be a very unpleasant surprise. Make sure you understand all the charges and fees associated with outgoing calls before you pick up that receiver.

Dialing direct from your hotel room—without using an international phone card (described above)—is usually quite expensive for international calls. Always ask first how much you'll be charged, even for local and (supposedly) toll-free calls.

If your family has an inexpensive way to call Europe, either through a long-distance plan or prepaid calling card, have them call you in your hotel room. Give them a list of your hotels' phone numbers before you go. Then, as you travel, send them an email or make a quick pay-phone call to set up a time for them to give you a ring.

Metered phones are sometimes available in bigger post offices. You can talk all you want, then pay the bill when you leave—but be sure you know the rates before you have a lengthy conversation.

If you're traveling with a laptop, consider trying **VoIP (Voice over Internet Protocol)**. With VoIP, two computers act as the phones, allowing for a free Internet-based call. The major providers are Skype (www.skype.com) and Google Talk (www.google.com/talk).

US calling cards (such as the ones offered by AT&T, MCI, and Sprint) are the worst option. You'll nearly always save a lot of money by paying with a phone card (see above).

How to Dial

Calling from the US to Europe, or vice versa, is simple—once you break the code. The European calling chart on page 388 will walk you through it.

Dialing Within Italy

Italy has a direct-dial phone system (no area codes). To call anywhere within Italy, just dial the number. For example, the number of one of my recommended Rome hotels is 06-482-4696. That's the number you dial whether you're calling it from Rome's main train station or from Milan. Keep in mind that Italian phone numbers vary in length; a hotel can have, say, an eight-digit phone number and a nine-digit fax number.

Italy's toll-free numbers start with 800 (like US 800 numbers, though in Italy you don't dial a 1 first). In Italy, these 800 numbers—called *freephone* or *numero verde* (green number)—can be dialed free from any phone without using a phone card or coins. Note that you can't call Italy's toll-free numbers from America, nor can you count on reaching America's toll-free numbers from Italy.

Dialing Internationally
If you want to make an international call, follow these steps:

Dial the international access code (00 if you're calling from Europe, 011 from the US or Canada). If you see a phone number that begins with +, you have to replace the + with the international access code.

Then dial the country code of the country you're calling (39 for Italy, or 1 for the US or Canada).

Then dial the local number. Note that in most European countries, you have to drop the zero at the beginning of the local number—but in Italy, you dial it.

So, to call the Rome hotel from the US, dial 011 (the US international access code), 39 (Italy's country code), then 06-482-4696. To call my office in Edmonds, Washington, from Italy, I dial 00 (Europe's international access code), 1 (the US country code), 425 (Edmonds' area code), and 771-8303.

Email and Mail
Email: Many travelers set up a free email account with Yahoo, Microsoft (Hotmail), or Google (Gmail). Email use among European hoteliers is quite common. Internet cafés and little hole-in-the-wall Internet-access shops (offering a few computers, no food, and cheap prices) are popular in most cities. More and more hotels now offer Internet access in their lobbies for guests, and some have wireless connections (Wi-Fi) for travelers with laptop computers. Ask if your hotel has access. If it doesn't, your hotelier will direct you to the nearest place to get online.

Because of an anti-terrorism law in Italy, you may be asked to show your passport (carry it in your money belt) when using a public Internet terminal at an Internet café or in a hotel lobby. The proprietor will likely make a copy of your passport.

Mail: While you can arrange for mail delivery to your hotel (allow 10 days for a letter to arrive), phoning and emailing are so easy that I've dispensed with mail stops altogether.

2 0 0 9

JANUARY

S	M	T	W	T	F	S
				1	2	3
4	5	6	7	8	9	10
11	12	13	14	15	16	17
18	19	20	21	22	23	24
25	26	27	28	29	30	31

FEBRUARY

S	M	T	W	T	F	S
1	2	3	4	5	6	7
8	9	10	11	12	13	14
15	16	17	18	19	20	21
22	23	24	25	26	27	28

MARCH

S	M	T	W	T	F	S
1	2	3	4	5	6	7
8	9	10	11	12	13	14
15	16	17	18	19	20	21
22	23	24	25	26	27	28
29	30	31				

APRIL

S	M	T	W	T	F	S
			1	2	3	4
5	6	7	8	9	10	11
12	13	14	15	16	17	18
19	20	21	22	23	24	25
26	27	28	29	30		

MAY

S	M	T	W	T	F	S
					1	2
3	4	5	6	7	8	9
10	11	12	13	14	15	16
17	18	19	20	21	22	23
24/31	25	26	27	28	29	30

JUNE

S	M	T	W	T	F	S
	1	2	3	4	5	6
7	8	9	10	11	12	13
14	15	16	17	18	19	20
21	22	23	24	25	26	27
28	29	30				

JULY

S	M	T	W	T	F	S
			1	2	3	4
5	6	7	8	9	10	11
12	13	14	15	16	17	18
19	20	21	22	23	24	25
26	27	28	29	30	31	

AUGUST

S	M	T	W	T	F	S
						1
2	3	4	5	6	7	8
9	10	11	12	13	14	15
16	17	18	19	20	21	22
23/30	24/31	25	26	27	28	29

SEPTEMBER

S	M	T	W	T	F	S
		1	2	3	4	5
6	7	8	9	10	11	12
13	14	15	16	17	18	19
20	21	22	23	24	25	26
27	28	29	30			

OCTOBER

S	M	T	W	T	F	S
				1	2	3
4	5	6	7	8	9	10
11	12	13	14	15	16	17
18	19	20	21	22	23	24
25	26	27	28	29	30	31

NOVEMBER

S	M	T	W	T	F	S
1	2	3	4	5	6	7
8	9	10	11	12	13	14
15	16	17	18	19	20	21
22	23	24	25	26	27	28
29	30					

DECEMBER

S	M	T	W	T	F	S
		1	2	3	4	5
6	7	8	9	10	11	12
13	14	15	16	17	18	19
20	21	22	23	24	25	26
27	28	29	30	31		

HOLIDAYS AND FESTIVALS

Italy celebrates many holidays, which close sights and bring crowds. Each town has a local festival honoring its patron saint. Italy shuts down on these national holidays: January 1, January 6 (Epiphany), Easter Sunday and Monday (April 12 and 13 in 2009), April 25 (Liberation Day), May 1 (Labor Day), Ascension Day (May 21 in 2009), June 2 (Anniversary of the Republic), August 15 (Assumption of Mary), November 1 (All Saints' Day), December 8 (Immaculate Conception of Mary), and December 25 and 26 (Christmas).

In addition, holidays celebrated in Rome include April 21 (City Birthday), June 24 (St. John the Baptist), June 29 (Feast Day of Saints Peter and Paul), and August 10 (St. Lawrence Day). The Vatican closes for many lesser-known Catholic holidays—confirm its schedule at www.vatican.va.

Note that this isn't a complete list. Holidays strike without warning. Your best source for general information is the Rome tourist information office (see page 20). You could also check with Italy's national tourist offices (listed at the beginning of the appendix).

CONVERSIONS AND CLIMATE

Numbers and Stumblers

- Europeans write a few of their numbers differently than we do. 1 = 1 , 4 = 4 , 7 = 7 .
- In Europe, dates appear as day/month/year, so Christmas is 25/12/09.
- Commas are decimal points and decimals commas. A dollar and a half is 1,50, and there are 5.280 feet in a mile.
- When pointing, use your whole hand, palm down.
- When counting with fingers, start with your thumb. If you hold up your first finger to request one item, you'll probably get two.
- What Americans call the second floor of a building is the first floor in Europe.
- On escalators and moving sidewalks, Europeans keep the left "lane" open for passing. Keep to the right.

Roman Numerals

In the US, you'll see Roman numerals—which originated in ancient Rome—used for copyright dates, clocks, and the Super Bowl. In Italy, you're likely to observe these numbers chiseled on statues and buildings. If you want to do some numeric detective work, here's how: In Roman numerals, as in ours, the highest numbers (thousands, hundreds) come first, followed by smaller numbers. Many numbers are made by combining numerals into sets: V = 5, so VIII = 8 (5 plus 3). Roman numerals follow a subtraction principle for multiples of fours (4, 40, 400, etc.) and nines (9, 90, 900, etc.); the number four, for example, is written as IV (1 subtracted from 5), rather than IIII. The number nine is IX (1 subtracted from 10).

Rick Steves' Rome 2009—written in Roman numerals—would translate as *Rick Steves' Rome MMIX*. Big numbers such as dates can look daunting at first. The easiest way to handle them is to read the numbers in discrete chunks. For example, Michelangelo was born in MCDLXXV. Break it down: M (1,000) + CD (100 subtracted from 500, or 400) + LXX (50 + 10 + 10, or 70) + V (5) = 1475. It was a very good year.

M = 1000	XL = 40
CM = 900	X = 10
D = 500	IX = 9
CD = 400	V = 5
C = 100	IV = 4
XC = 90	I = duh
L = 50	

Metric Conversions (approximate)

1 foot = 0.3 meter	1 square yard = 0.8 square meter
1 yard = 0.9 meter	1 square mile = 2.6 square kilometers
1 mile = 1.6 kilometers	1 ounce = 28 grams
1 centimeter = 0.4 inch	1 quart = 0.95 liter
1 meter = 39.4 inches	1 kilogram = 2.2 pounds
1 kilometer = 0.62 mile	32°F = 0°C

Rome's Climate

First line—average daily high; second line—average daily low; third line—days of no rain. For more detailed statistics, check www.world climate.com.

J	F	M	A	M	J	J	A	S	O	N	D
52°	55°	59°	66°	74°	82°	87°	86°	79°	71°	61°	55°
40°	42°	45°	50°	56°	63°	67°	67°	62°	55°	49°	44°
13	19	23	24	26	26	30	29	25	23	19	21

Temperature Conversion: Fahrenheit and Celsius

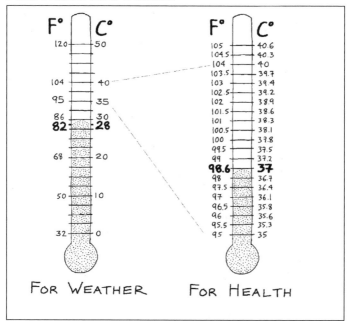

For Weather   For Health

Europe takes its temperature using the Celsius scale, while we opt for Fahrenheit. For a rough conversion from Celsius to Fahrenheit, double the number and add 30. For weather, remember that 28°C is 82°F—perfect. For health, 37°C is just right.

Essential Packing Checklist

Whether you're traveling for five days or five weeks, here's what you'll need to bring. Remember to pack light to enjoy the sweet freedom of true mobility. Happy travels!

- ❏ 5 shirts
- ❏ 1 sweater or lightweight fleece jacket
- ❏ 2 pairs pants
- ❏ 1 pair shorts
- ❏ 1 swimsuit (women only—men can use shorts)
- ❏ 5 pairs underwear and socks
- ❏ 1 pair shoes
- ❏ 1 rain-proof jacket
- ❏ Tie or scarf
- ❏ Money belt
- ❏ Money—your mix of:
  - ❏ Debit card for ATM withdrawals
  - ❏ Credit card
  - ❏ Hard cash in US dollars
- ❏ Documents (and back-up photocopies)
- ❏ Passport
- ❏ Airplane ticket
- ❏ Driver's license
- ❏ Student ID and hostel card
- ❏ Railpass/car rental voucher
- ❏ Insurance details
- ❏ Daypack
- ❏ Sealable plastic baggies
- ❏ Camera and related gear
- ❏ Empty water bottle
- ❏ Wristwatch and alarm clock
- ❏ Earplugs
- ❏ First-aid kit
- ❏ Medicine (labeled)
- ❏ Extra glasses/contacts and prescriptions
- ❏ Sunscreen and sunglasses
- ❏ Toiletries kit
- ❏ Soap
- ❏ Laundry soap (if liquid and carry-on, limit to 3 oz.)
- ❏ Clothesline
- ❏ Small towel
- ❏ Sewing kit
- ❏ Travel information
- ❏ Necessary map(s)
- ❏ Address list (email and mailing addresses)
- ❏ Postcards and photos from home
- ❏ Notepad and pen
- ❏ Journal

Italian Survival Phrases

English	Italian	Pronunciation
Good day.	Buon giorno.	bwohn JOR-noh
Do you speak English?	Parla inglese?	PAR-lah een-GLAY-zay
Yes. / No.	Sì. / No.	see / noh
I (don't) understand.	(Non) capisco.	(nohn) kah-PEES-koh
Please.	Per favore.	pehr fah-VOH-ray
Thank you.	Grazie.	GRAHT-seeay
I'm sorry.	Mi dispiace.	mee dee-speeAH-chay
Excuse me.	Mi scusi.	mee SKOO-zee
(No) problem.	(Non) c'è un problema.	(nohn) cheh oon proh-BLAY-mah
Good.	Va bene.	vah BEHN-ay
Goodbye.	Arrivederci.	ah-ree-vay-DEHR-chee
one / two	uno / due	OO-noh / DOO-ay
three / four	tre / quattro	tray / KWAH-troh
five / six	cinque / sei	CHEENG-kway / SEHee
seven / eight	sette / otto	SEHT-tay / OT-toh
nine / ten	nove / dieci	NOV-ay / deeAY-chee
How much is it?	Quanto costa?	KWAHN-toh KOS-tah
Write it?	Me lo scrive?	may loh SKREE-vay
Is it free?	È gratis?	eh GRAH-tees
Is it included?	È incluso?	eh een-KLOO-zoh
Where can I buy / find...?	Dove posso comprare / trovare...?	DOH-vay POS-soh kohm-PRAH-ray / troh-VAH-ray
I'd like / We'd like...	Vorrei / Vorremmo...	vor-REHee / vor-RAY-moh
...a room.	...una camera.	OO-nah KAH-meh-rah
...a ticket to ___.	...un biglietto per ___.	oon beel-YEHT-toh pehr
Is it possible?	È possibile?	eh poh-SEE-bee-lay
Where is...?	Dov'è...?	DOH-veh
...the train station	...la stazione	lah staht-seeOH-nay
...the bus station	...la stazione degli autobus	lah staht-seeOH-nay DAYL-yee OW-toh-boos
...tourist information	...informazioni per turisti	een-for-maht-seeOH-nee pehr too-REE-stee
...the toilet	...la toilette	lah twah-LEHT-tay
men	uomini, signori	WOH-mee-nee, seen-YOH-ree
women	donne, signore	DON-nay, seen-YOH-ray
left / right	sinistra / destra	see-NEE-strah / DEHS-trah
straight	sempre diritto	SEHM-pray dee-REE-toh
When do you open / close?	A che ora aprite / chiudete?	ah kay OH-rah ah-PREE-tay / keeoo-DAY-tay
At what time?	A che ora?	ah kay OH-rah
Just a moment.	Un momento.	oon moh-MAYN-toh
now / soon / later	adesso / presto / tardi	ah-DEHS-soh / PREHS-toh / TAR-dee
today / tomorrow	oggi / domani	OH-jee / doh-MAH-nee

In the Restaurant

I'd like...	Vorrei...	vor-REHee
We'd like...	Vorremmo...	vor-RAY-moh
...to reserve...	...prenotare...	pray-noh-TAH-ray
...a table for one / two.	...un tavolo per uno / due.	oon TAH-voh-loh pehr OO-noh / DOO-ay
Non-smoking.	Non fumare.	nohn foo-MAH-ray
Is this seat free?	È libero questo posto?	eh LEE-bay-roh KWEHS-toh POH-stoh
The menu (in English), please.	Il menù (in inglese), per favore.	eel may-NOO (een een-GLAY-zay) pehr fah-VOH-ray
service (not) included	servizio (non) incluso	sehr-VEET-seeoh (nohn) een-KLOO-zoh
cover charge	pane e coperto	PAH-nay ay koh-PEHR-toh
to go	da portar via	dah POR-tar VEE-ah
with / without	con / senza	kohn / SEHN-sah
and / or	e / o	ay / oh
menu (of the day)	menù (del giorno)	may-NOO (dayl JOR-noh)
specialty of the house	specialità della casa	spay-chah-lee-TAH DEHL-lah KAH-zah
first course (pasta, soup)	primo piatto	PREE-moh peeAH-toh
main course (meat, fish)	secondo piatto	say-KOHN-doh peeAH-toh
side dishes	contorni	kohn-TOR-nee
bread	pane	PAH-nay
cheese	formaggio	for-MAH-joh
sandwich	panino	pah-NEE-noh
soup	minestra, zuppa	mee-NEHS-trah, TSOO-pah
salad	insalata	een-sah-LAH-tah
meat	carne	KAR-nay
chicken	pollo	POH-loh
fish	pesce	PEH-shay
seafood	frutti di mare	FROO-tee dee MAH-ray
fruit / vegetables	frutta / legumi	FROO-tah / lay-GOO-mee
dessert	dolci	DOHL-chee
tap water	acqua del rubinetto	AH-kwah dayl roo-bee-NAY-toh
mineral water	acqua minerale	AH-kwah mee-nay-RAH-lay
milk	latte	LAH-tay
(orange) juice	succo (d'arancia)	SOO-koh (dah-RAHN-chah)
coffee / tea	caffè / tè	kah-FEH / teh
wine	vino	VEE-noh
red / white	rosso / bianco	ROH-soh / beeAHN-koh
glass / bottle	bicchiere / bottiglia	bee-keeAY-ray / boh-TEEL-yah
beer	birra	BEE-rah
Cheers!	Cin cin!	cheen cheen
More. / Another.	Ancora un po.' / Un altro.	ahn-KOH-rah oon poh / oon AHL-troh
The same.	Lo stesso.	loh STEHS-soh
The bill, please.	Il conto, per favore.	eel KOHN-toh pehr fah-VOH-ray
tip	mancia	MAHN-chah
Delicious!	Delizioso!	day-leet-seeOH-zoh

For hundreds more pages of survival phrases for your trip to Italy, check out *Rick Steves' Italian Phrase Book & Dictionary* or *Rick Steves' French, Italian, and German Phrase Book*.

APPENDIX

Hotel Reservation

To: _____ _____
     hotel   *email or fax*

From: _____ _____
       name   *email or fax*

Today's date: _____ /_____ /_____
               day   *month* *year*

Dear Hotel _____ ,
Please make this reservation for me:

Name: _____

Total # of people: _____ # of rooms: _____ # of nights: _____

Arriving: _____ /_____ /_____   My time of arrival (24-hr clock): _____
          day *month* *year*   (I will telephone if I will be late)

Departing: ____ /____ /_____
           day *month* *year*

Room(s): Single____ Double ____ Twin ____ Triple ____ Quad____

With: Toilet _____ Shower_____ Bath_____ Sink only____

Special needs: View____ Quiet____ Cheapest ____ Ground Floor____

Please email or fax confirmation of my reservation, along with the type of
room reserved and the price. Please also inform me of your cancellation
policy. After I hear from you, I will quickly send my credit-card information
as a deposit to hold the room. Thank you.

_____
Name

_____
Address

_____
City   *State*   *Zip Code*   *Country*

*Before hoteliers can make your reservation, they want to know the informa-
tion listed above. You can use this form as the basis for your email, or you can
photocopy this page, fill in the information, and send it as a fax (also available
online at www.ricksteves.com/reservation).*

INDEX

Rick Steves
EUROPEAN TOURS

Experience Europe the Rick Steves
way, with great guides,
small groups...and no grumps!

See 30 itineraries at ricksteves.com

▸ Plan Your Trip

Browse thousands of articles and a wealth of money-saving tips for planning your dream trip. You'll find up-to-date information on Europe's best destinations, packing smart, getting around, finding rooms, staying healthy, avoiding scams and more.

▸ Eurail Passes

Find out, step-by-step, if a rail pass makes sense for your trip—and how to avoid buying more than you need. Get a bunch of free extras!

▸ Graffiti Wall & Travelers' Helpline

Learn, ask, share—our online community of savvy travelers is a great resource for first-time travelers to Europe, as well as seasoned pros.

Rick Steves' Europe Through the Back Door, Inc.

rn your travel dreams into affordable reality

Free Audio Tours & ravel Newsletter

iet your nose out of this guide-
ook and focus on what you'll be
eeing with Rick's free audio tours
f the greatest sights in Paris,
ome, Florence and Venice.

Subscribe to our free *Travel
Jews* e-newsletter, and get monthly
rticles from Rick on what's
appening in Europe.

▶ Great Gear from Rick's Travel Store

Pack light and right—on a
budget—with Rick's custom-
designed carry-on bags, roll-
aboards, day packs, travel
accessories, guidebooks, journals,
maps and DVDs of his TV shows.

130 Fourth Avenue North, PO Box 2009 • Edmonds, WA 98020 USA
Phone: (425) 771-8303 • Fax: (425) 771-0833 • www.ricksteves.com

Rick Steves.

www.ricksteves.com

TRAVEL SKILLS
Europe Through the Back Door

EUROPE GUIDES
Best of Europe
Eastern Europe
Europe 101
European Christmas
Postcards from Europe

COUNTRY GUIDES
Croatia & Slovenia
England
France
Germany
Great Britain
Ireland
Italy
Portugal
Scandinavia
Spain
Switzerland

CITY & REGIONAL GUIDES
Amsterdam, Bruges & Brussels
Athens & The Peloponnese NEW IN 2009
Budapest NEW IN 2009
Florence & Tuscany
Istanbul
London
Paris
Prague & The Czech Republic
Provence & The French Riviera
Rome
Venice
Vienna, Salzburg & Tirol NEW IN 2009

PHRASE BOOKS & DICTIONARIES
French
French, Italian & German
German
Italian
Portuguese
Spanish

RICK STEVES' EUROPE DVDs
Austria & The Alps
Eastern Europe
England
Europe
France & Benelux
Germany & Scandinavia
Greece, Turkey, Israel & Egypt
Ireland & Scotland
Italy's Cities
Italy's Countryside
Rick Steves' European Christmas
Spain & Portugal
Travel Skills & "The Making Of"

PLANNING MAPS
Britain, Ireland & London
Europe
France & Paris
Germany, Austria & Switzerland
Italy
Spain & Portugal

JOURNALS
Rick Steves' Pocket Travel Journal
Rick Steves' Travel Journal

CREDITS

Researcher

To update this book, Rick relied on the help of...

Amanda Scotese

 Amanda freelances as a journalist and editor in Chicago. Her travels in Italy include a stint selling leather jackets in Florence's San Lorenzo Market, basking in the Sicilian sun, and, of course, helping out with Rick Steves' guidebooks and tours.